INTERNATIONAL SERIES IN
EXPERIMENTAL PSYCHOLOGY

GENERAL EDITOR: H. J. EYSENCK

VOLUME 24

THE EFFECTS OF PSYCHOLOGICAL THERAPY

Second Enlarged Edition

OTHER TITLES IN THE SERIES IN EXPERIMENTAL PSYCHOLOGY

NOTICE TO READERS

Dear Reader

If your library is not already a standing order customer or subscriber to this series, may we recommend that you place a standing or subscription order to receive immediately upon publication all new issues and volumes published in this valuable series. Should you find that these volumes no longer serve your needs your order can be cancelled at any time without notice.

The Editors and the Publisher will be glad to receive suggestions or outlines of suitable titles, reviews or symposia for consideration for rapid publication in this series.

ROBERT MAXWELL
Publisher at Pergamon Press

THE EFFECTS OF PSYCHOLOGICAL THERAPY

SECOND ENLARGED EDITION

by

S.J. RACHMAN

Professor of Abnormal Psychology,
Institute of Psychiatry, London

and

G.T. WILSON

Professor of Psychology,
Rutgers University, New Brunswick

PERGAMON PRESS

OXFORD · NEW YORK · TORONTO · SYDNEY · PARIS · FRANKFURT

U.K.	Pergamon Press Ltd., Headington Hill Hall, Oxford OX3 0BW, England
U.S.A.	Pergamon Press Inc., Maxwell House, Fairview Park, Elmsford, New York 10523, U.S.A.
CANADA	Pergamon of Canada, Suite 104, 150 Consumers Road, Willowdale, Ontario M2J 1P9, Canada
AUSTRALIA	Pergamon Press (Aust.) Pty. Ltd., P.O. Box 544, Potts Point, N.S.W. 2011, Australia
FRANCE	Pergamon Press SARL, 24 rue des Ecoles, 75240 Paris, Cedex 05, France
FEDERAL REPUBLIC OF GERMANY	Pergamon Press GmbH, 6242 Kronberg/Taunus, Hammerweg 6, Federal Republic of Germany

First edition 1971

Second edition 1980

British Library Cataloguing in Publication Data

Rachman, Stanley
The effects of psychological therapy. — 2nd enlarged ed.
— (International series in experimental psychology;
vol. 24).
1. Psychotherapy
I. Title   II. Wilson, Godfrey Terence
III. Series
616. 8'914   RC480   79—42656

ISBN 0-08-024675-3   Hardcover
ISBN 0-08-024674-5   Flexicover

Printed and bound in Great Britain by
William Clowes (Beccles) Limited, Beccles and London

CONTENTS

CHAPTER 1

CONVENTIONAL OUTCOME RESEARCH

In the 10 years that have passed since the First Edition was prepared, a number of significant findings have been reported. Some of them are surprising and one is unusually ironical. New trends and methods have emerged, some old claims have earned the right to a respectable burial, and sad to report, the accumulation of discouraging results has not ceased.

Before we describe and interpret these events, it is necessary to explain that they have prompted us to adopt substantially new views on outcome and research strategy and on evaluation criteria. These views, which will be explained in this opening chapter and then re-examined in the concluding chapter, lead us to recommend major changes in the planning and evaluation of outcome research, so that we have been obliged to refer to the prevailing approach as *conventional psychotherapeutic-outcome research*. As the bulk of the available data falls into this category of conventional research, there is no alternative but to carry out a conventional consideration of conventional outcome research, even though we feel that such research is bound to be of limited value, leaves little room for development, and is at times misleading. Adoption of an alternative strategy, preferably along the lines set out here, could lead the way to more fruitful research and the production of more accurate findings.

The main alternative proposals, while none of them novel in themselves, can be combined to produce a marked change in the design and direction of outcome research. A case will be made for setting aside medical definitions of psychological problems and replacing them with more properly psychological definitions; among many other changes that would flow from this substitution (to be elaborated presently), it would involve the dismissal of the concepts of "cure", "relapse", "prognosis", the notion of neurotic *illnesses* and so forth. Instead, the persons' problems would be assessed and described in psychological terms, and the effects of interventions designed to deal with these problems would be assessed by psychological methods rather than by methods borrowed from medical practice. The shift from a medical to a psychological perspective will also require the development of alternative care systems — people seeking assistance in overcoming their problems would go to advisory centres instead of hospitals. Allied to this shift from a medical to a psychological perspective, but not necessarily an integral part of it, we have been led to support a shift in emphasis away from the common assumption of exaggerated generality of human behaviour and towards an increasing emphasis on the specificity of behaviour and the importance of situational determinants of conduct, feelings, and so on. The next proposal is that the changes already described should be allied to the establishment of explicit goals before any modification or intervention programme is under-taken — plainly, this proviso is especially important in outcome *research*. Unless the aims of the programme are made explicit and stated in quantified degrees of success, rather than as at

1

present in terms of generalized reports of cure, relapse, or improvement, many unsatisfactory aspects of the conventional outcome research will persist.

We will also argue that the selection of measurements and the design of the outcome studies would benefit from a three-systems analysis instead of the current assumption that most psychological problems are unitary. It would require a move away from the continuing reliance on what has been called the "lump" theory of emotions (see Lang, 1970; Rachman, 1978). The adoption of a three-systems analysis would enable us to study both process and outcome questions simultaneously and, we hope, in a fruitful manner.

A proposal of a different character arises from our dissatisfaction with the undirected accumulation of disparate facts. Where possible, outcome studies should be designed to collect evidence that bears on significant theoretical questions. One should attempt to determine whether the observed effects can be accommodated by existing theory. Questions of this kind can be put in the narrow sense (e.g. does controlled drinking achieve the specified theoretical goals?), or they can be asked in a broader sense (e.g. is this method of change best conceived as a form of conditioning?).

The next proposal is concerned with the efficacy of modification or treatment programmes, seen in their social context. Even if a form of therapy is effective in the individual case it does not follow that it is an effective psychological procedure for dealing with the larger problems of incidence, suffering, etc. Some form of cost-benefit analysis will have to be carried out in order to help planners and administrators provide an effective service.

RECENT DEVELOPMENTS

Our reasons for formulating the alternatives will be gone into presently, but before doing so a résumé of some of the interesting and surprising events of the past decade is desirable. Ten years ago it was difficult to locate satisfactory evidence to support the claim that psychotherapy was effective. Indeed, it was the continuing shortage of satisfactory evidence about psycho-therapeutic effectiveness that played a large part in the development of what was the strongest form of competition—behaviour therapy. For example, one of the pioneers of behaviour therapy, Professor Wolpe, turned his energies towards the development of alternative forms of treatment partly because of his dissatisfaction with the poor effects of psychotherapy. In these circum-stances it is a matter of amusement and irony that some of the best recent evidence indicating that psychotherapy may indeed be an effective form of treatment has come from research workers who have included psychotherapy as a control treatment against which they expected to demonstrate the superior effectiveness of behaviour therapy. Whatever the motives of the research workers concerned, in a few instances comparative studies of this kind have, by virtue of the improved rigour of the experimental designs, yielded new and better evidence to support the claim that psychotherapy may be effective. As we shall see in Chapter 12, these comparative evaluation studies contain flaws that prevent one from drawing definitive conclusions. It remains true, however, that they have, sometimes inadvertently, provided considerable encouragement for psychotherapists. It is also ironical that the quality of the research carried out in these comparative evaluations, despite its shortcomings, is superior to almost all of the earlier research into the effects of psychotherapy evaluated in its own right.

Some of the surprises that have emerged during the past decade include the following two examples chosen from a wider list of possibilities. The large and ambitious comparative study carried out by Sloane *et al.* (1975) revealed that the behaviour therapists who took part in the study were rated as equal or higher in those therapist qualities that have often been said to be uniquely characteristic of psychotherapists. Another and rather more significant development of the past few years is the comparative failure of psychotherapists to deal successfully with sexual problems despite the considerable emphasis which most of the psychodynamic theories place on sexual matters (see Broadhurst, 1977; Sotile and Kilmann, 1977).

As we shall see, the promise offered by client-centred psychotherapy has not been fulfilled; unhappily, progress in providing support for the challenging theoretical and practical claims of this group of therapists has been slow and disappointing. Moreoever, some of the claims have been seriously undermined. Almost as if to replace this unfulfilled hope, the past few years has seen the growth in popularity of various forms of cognitive therapy. In recognition of this important development we have included a special chapter on the subject.

The past decade has seen the execution of a number of comparative evaluative studies, practical comparisons and reviews of the literature. The clinical studies are laborious and extremely expensive, not to speak of the considerable theoretical obstacles which have to be overcome — and in some important instances the attempt was unsuccessful. So, for example, the carefully thought-out and prepared efforts of Candy *et al.* (1972) floundered on some of these insuperable problems (see Chapter 6). It will be agreed that when comparative studies are successfully completed, useful information does emerge, but there is a case for concluding that the enormous effort which they absorb is misplaced, and that far greater gains could be achieved by the adoption of a more direct strategy in which specific methods are tested for their specific effectiveness, employing assessment procedures that are appropriate and designed for the particular purpose.

One of the major contributions of behaviour therapy has been the development of a number of different research strategies for evaluating treatment effects. Among these innovative strategies are single-case experimental designs, and dismantling and constructive designs for determining the effective components of treatment packages (see Hersen and Barlow, 1976; Kazdin and Wilson, 1978b). In most instances it is desirable to demonstrate the initial efficacy of a particular method under specific, controlled conditions using these alternative methodological strategies before taking the plunge of carrying out a complex comparative outcome study in a clinical context. Different designs will be appropriate at different points in the systematic development of an effective treatment technique (see Agras, Kazdin, and Wilson, 1979).

The early promise of the behavioural methods has been fulfilled in some respects but not in others. Behaviour therapy is no longer regarded as a radical alternative. Its scientific progress is reflected by the steep increase in publications on the subject, and the extent of its acceptance among orthodox psychiatrists in the United States (see Brady and Wiencowski, 1978). The views expressed in Brady's survey ranged from those psychiatrists who regarded behaviour therapy as a useful approach of limited scope, to a minority who hope that it will develop into the predominant method of dealing with the psychological problems. The scientific penetration of behaviour therapy is a remarkable story that can be reflected in publication trends (see Chapter 9 below). The large and steep increase in the number of scientific publications is plain — a development that is familiar, perhaps even too familiar, to people interested in this field when they are confronted by rapidly growing lists of books on behaviour therapy. It is no exaggeration to say that a major text on the subject is published each month. The status of behaviour therapy as a means of producing beneficial changes in psychological problems —

in conventional terms, its therapeutic effectiveness — is a complex subject which deserves at least the two chapters devoted to it here.

A number of encouraging findings about the effectiveness of psychotherapy have been published during the past decade, and these will be dealt with in due course. During the same period, however, the flow of dismal findings, in which the effects of psychotherapy barely exceeded or even failed to exceed the beneficial changes observed in a control group, continued. So too did the flow of unsupported and occasionally extravagant claims made on behalf of psychotherapy.

The disappointing reports include a careful prospective study of the fate of 100 alcoholic patients. Orford and Edwards (1977) were unable to find any significant contribution attributable to the (usually) informal psychotherapy that was provided for half of these patients as part of a larger treatment programme. The medium- and long-term outcome for those patients who received treatment was no different for those who were provided simply with advice. This study, which had its limitations (e.g. no double blinds), was not intended to provide a test of psychotherapy as such, but rather to evaluate a treatment programme which included psychotherapy, as deemed desirable. The therapeutic outcome for the treated group was no better than that for the untreated group, nor was there any relation between the amount of treatment accepted and the eventual outcome.

May et al. (1976b) reported a 3- to 5-year follow-up of 228 first-admission schizophrenic patients who had received one of five types of treatment. Those patients who received psychotherapy-alone did significantly worse than those who were treated by drugs-alone, drugs plus psychotherapy, or ECT (p. 483). McCord (1978) obtained equally disappointing results in her follow-up investigation of 500 men who participated in the Cambridge Somerville youth project. Roughly half of the total group had received a great deal of help over several years, including psychotherapy when required, but their eventual adjustment was no better than that of the untreated control subjects. The provision of psychotherapy, even when accompanied by other forms of social treatment, had no discernible beneficial effects. Frank et al. (1978) compared the outcome of treatment in a group of neurotic patients at the end of treatment, 5 years later, 10 years later and, again, 20 years after termination of treatment. They could find no significant differences between those patients who received psychotherapy and the control patients who received minimal contact (p. 111).

The Menninger Clinic Report describes a painstaking and laborious investigation of psychoanalysis, carried out over 14 years by a large and changing group of research workers at a cost of over a million dollars (Appelbaum, 1977), The Report was finally published in 1972. The outcome of this extraordinary effort, sometimes obscured by the mass of details and advanced statistical analyses contained in the final report, is unlikely to improve property prices in Topeka.

Before returning to one of the major themes of this Introduction, the unsatisfactory assumptions underlying conventional research, an historical comment is in order. It would appear that towards the end of the 1960s, the increasingly obvious complexities of carrying out satisfactory outcome research, plus the embarrassing shortage of evidence capable of supporting the far-reaching claims of therapists, generated a great deal of pessimism. It was said that the problems are impossible to resolve. By the middle of the decade, however, new hopes were seeded by recourse to what can be referred to as the homogeneity argument. According to this view, virtually any respectable form of psychotherapeutic assistance produces beneficial results, and there is little to choose between the methods. The well-known quotation from Alice in Wonderland, "Everybody has won and all must have prizes", was used by Luborsky *et al.* (1975) with effect. The reassurance came at a propitious moment, but there is some doubt about its accuracy and value (see Kazdin and Wilson, 1978b and Chapter 12 below). Regardless of the fate of this argument, there can be little doubt that at the time of its introduction, it was welcomed by the receptive and troubled professions of psychology and psychiatry.

It should also be mentioned that the easy and often uncritical acceptance of this argument provoked a strong reaction, particularly from proponents of behaviour therapy. This development coupled with the relative failure of comparative studies to demonstrate that behaviour therapy was in all ways superior to psychotherapy, added to the dismay of behaviour therapists. Although the failure to demonstrate that behaviour therapy is necessarily superior to psychotherapy, if taken uncritically and at face value, would provide reasonable grounds for uneasiness among behaviour therapists, the slow accumulation of evidence to support some of the claims on behalf of psychotherapy, however modest this evidence, should be welcomed. Indeed, it flows from our major argument that psychological problems often require particular (and sometimes therefore dissimilar) answers. Nevertheless, it remains true that the success of behavioural methods leads to serious difficulties for psychodynamic theories.

Before providing our analysis of the nature, causes and remedy for the apparent impasse, it is essential to draw attention to the range of non-neurotic psychological problems that can be modified by behavioural methods. In considering the well-publicized comparative studies on neurotic samples, these other and in certain respects more important applications tend to be ignored or dismissed [(e.g. "We have not, however, covered the huge literature specifically on habit disorders (e.g. addiction [sic] and bedwetting . . ."), Luborsky *et al.*, 1975, p. 1006)]. If the evaluation of behaviour therapy is, like psychotherapy, confined mainly to studies carried out on neurotic samples, and if the studies follow the conventional outcome designs, there is a risk that potentially and demonstrably effective psychological methods will be discarded foolishly and needlessly. The effects of behaviour therapy, and psychotherapy to a lesser extent, must be examined on a broad canvas which should include (in the case of behaviour therapy) those methods which have been developed for helping retarded people to learn to care for themselves, overcoming enuresis, and so on. Several of these behavioural techniques cannot be made the subject of comparative studies for the very good reason that, literally, there is no comparison.

By the same token, it is not possible to carry out a comparative evaluation of the effectiveness of psychotherapy and behaviour therapy in bringing about psychodynamic growth, or greater insight into one's unconscious mental life, and so on. Once more, there can be no comparison.

As far as the effects of behaviour therapy on neurotic problems are concerned, the need for a reappraisal of strategy is now evident. Conventional outcome studies have their merits and undoubtedly are a great improvement on the unsystematic accumulations of case reports that formerly provided the sole evidence on which to reach conclusions about therapeutic effects (e.g. Freud, 1922). The main features of these conventional outcome studies are the inclusion of control groups, random allocation to treatment, the use of more than one type of pre- and post-treatment measurement (with an emphasis on clinical ratings, and the employment of independent and blind assessors). These tactics all contributed to improving the reliability of the findings, but most of them embody unstated assumptions that need to be identified and then examined critically.

The main part of the present argument is that a revision of three of the important assumptions will allow a restructuring of outcome research and enable us to progress more satisfactorily and quickly. Although the shortcomings of conventional treatment are most evident in considerations of behaviour therapy, some of them apply equally to psychotherapy. Nevertheless this discussion deals mainly with the problems of assessing the outcome of behaviour therapy.

THE FIRST ASSUMPTION

The first of these assumptions, the implicit accommodation of psychological difficulties and deficits within a medical model (sometimes described as the disease model), has been the subject of detailed critiques during the past few years (e.g. Ullmann and Krasner, 1969, 1975; Eysenck and Rachman, 1965; Bandura, 1969; Rachman and Philips, 1975, 1978, 1979 among others) and will not be given at length. Instead we will concentrate on the relationship between this assumption and the design of conventional outcome research. Before proceeding, however, it should be noted that the critics of the medical model are by no means in full agreement about either the nature of the model or its crucial weaknesses (it should be added that the defenders of the medical model also have their disagreements, e.g. Kendell, 1975; Wing, 1978). Nevertheless, most critics would agree that *the over-extensive and undiscriminating construal of psychological deficits and difficulties as illnesses or signs and symptoms of illnesses, is mistaken.* They would also agree that the undiscriminating application of the medical model has important practical and theoretical consequences, and they probably would agree that most of these consequences are unfortunate.

Turning immediately to some of the implications for outcome research, we can illustrate the matter by choosing three examples. In the first place, if a person's psychological problems are construed as signs or symptoms of illness, this virtually precludes attempts to directly change the specific problem behaviour, or to directly retrain him, and so on. Incidentally, when the relevant predictions, such as those referring to symptom substitution, were eventually put to the test, the medical model received little support (e.g. Yates, 1975). Secondly, if psychological problems are signs of illnesses, then the person is automatically regarded as a patient, and this process of labelling turns out to be of considerable psychological significance (e.g. Rosenhan, 1973). It also follows of course that these psychological problems require medical or paramedical assistance, usually in a hospital or clinic. A third implication of regarding psychological problems as illnesses is that treatment should be an attempt to achieve a cure. Of course, the concept of *cure* in its turn has implications for outcome research (and incidentally lends itself to qualitative rather than quantitative measures of change). So we can trace a direct pathway from the conception of psychological difficulties and deficits as pathology, to the design and conduct of conventional outcome research.

If instead we act on our critical assessment of the limitations of applying the medical model to psychological problems, then new tactics become possible. As a start the person's problems (not the patient's illness) can be described in psychological terms, using psychological methodology — and in keeping with current thinking, this would mean, among other things, a greater emphasis on the specificity of behaviour. Outcome measures of a *general* character, such as percentage of cures and clinical ratings of severity of illness, would be replaced by specific behavioural descriptions, specific subjective reports, and specific psychophysiological reactions to specific stimuli. Greater emphasis would be placed on observed behaviour, performance (deficits or errors) and so on, without excluding the vital subjective elements. Each programme of retraining, or modification, or therapy (if and when that term is applicable) would be based on explicit target goals, and it follows of course that the outcome of the programme should be assessed by the degree of progress achieved in attaining these goals. Hence the assessment of outcome is inevitably quantitative and there is no place for the concept of cure. One would ask questions such as: To what extent has the behaviour increased or decreased? How widely have the changes generalized? To what degree have the changes persisted?

Among other advantages, this tactical change would make it far easier to compare the results obtained in different studies, i.e. the opportunities for sound comparison and replication studies would be enhanced.

Another consequence of using a psychological rather than a medical model is that the treatment context, the description of the participants and of the agents of change, will all be regarded in a new manner. An incidental result of these changes is that the distinction between analogue research and clinical research will largely fall away (Borkovec and Rachman, 1979). The term "analogue research" rests on a distinction between clinical samples, i.e. between patient and non-clinical samples. If, however, we restrict the terms *patient, clinical* and so on in the way proposed here, there is little reason to retain the adjective "analogue". The participants in these programmes will be described by the type, range and degree of their problems and not by their diagnostic category. Nor indeed will they be defined by their attendance at hospital or a clinic. We would be obliged to concentrate on problems rather than on diagnoses, or to put it another way, programmes would be problem-orientated rather than illness-orientated, as is presently the case. The use of so-called analogue subjects in therapy research, particularly by behaviour therapists, raises a number of important questions which will be examined presently (see page 262).

A third consequence of using a psychological model is that the people who seek assistance, no longer regarded by themselves and by others as psychiatric patients, will be expected by themselves and others to play a more active part in overcoming their difficulties. The significance of this change is conveyed, in part, by replacing the term *patient* by the term *client*.

It is evident that we will need to establish a more satisfactory vocabulary for what we are doing. At present it is difficult to avoid using words such as *patients, cures, treatments*, etc., even though in doing so we are aware that a misleading impression is inevitably conveyed. Regrettably we do not have satisfactory alternatives at present; the term *clients*, with its connotations of the legal profession, seems stiff, distant, and inappropriate. So far no acceptable alternative has been proposed. The term clinic can more easily be replaced by any of the following possibilities, depending on the particular agency concerned — couselling centre, psychological advice bureau, or a plain *guidance centre*. The term *cure* can more easily be dispensed with, particularly as the reluctance to use the term is not confined to non-medical professions.

THE SECOND ASSUMPTION

This assumption is especially important in research on the treatment of neuroses, whether by psychotherapy or behaviour therapy. It is assumed that certain key concepts such as fear and anxiety are best conceived in terms of what has been called "the lump theory" (Rachman, 1974), following Lang's (1970) fresh analysis of fear. Anxiety (and fear) usually is regarded as a unitary phenomenon, but Lang has argued persuasively for a more complex conception in which fear is viewed as a set of at least three loosely coupled components — verbal reports, behavioural avoidance, and psychophysiological changes. The application of this three-systems analysis to phobias and to obsessional—compulsive disorders (see Rachman and Hodgson, 1980) generates an expanding conception of these problems, gives rise to numerous predictions about therapeutic change and provides a basis for a new strategy on which to base outcome research. Applications to sexual behaviour have made a promising start, and Philips (1978) is using it in her research on pain.

In brief, applying a three-systems approach to outcome research would result in a new type of design, one that incorporates measures of all three components. The inter-relations between these components, and particularly their relative speeds of change (see Hodgson and Rachman, 1974), will become the focus of interest. If this proposal is carried out, we will then be in a position to study not only the effects of therapy in general, but also the effects on each of the three components. The application of the three-systems analysis may take different forms in behaviour therapy, because of the varying emphases of these two approaches. So in the case of psychotherapy, the earliest and probably the largest changes would be expected to occur in the verbal cognitive system, unlike behaviour therapy where the first and largest effects often will be observed in the behavioural component (e.g. Rachman *et al.*, 1979). The two approaches, behaviour therapy and psychotherapy, can be said to be directed at different aspects or different components of the problem.

The three-systems analysis has also led to the introduction of the concepts of concordance, discordance, synchrony, and desynchrony (e.g. Hodgson and Rachman, 1974; Rachman, 1974, 1978; Rachman and Hodgson, 1974). Outcome research which makes allowance for these concepts will also enable us to carry out experimental analyses of the processes of therapeutic change. More than sixteen predictions about the course of behavioural therapeutic changes have been made in terms of synchrony and desynchrony. Although some of these predictions were deducible from other starting-points, many of them flow directly from a three-systems analysis. Regardless of the fate of these specific predictions, there is good reason to expect a crop of new ideas and observations when outcome research designs shift from a lump theory to the expanded and expanding view encouraged by a three-systems analysis.

By contrast, the lump-theory approach to outcome research inevitably has the effect of blunting and distorting the very processes under investigation. Low correlations between subjective reports and behavioural performance are regarded as unfortunate, and no more than a reflection of the low reliability of the measures. Hence, one excludes measures that fail to produce high correlations. Instead, preference is given to measures that reduce the likelihood of producing a diversity of effects. This desire for homogeneity, reinforced by the ease and convenience of paper and pencil assessments, generally ends in the selection of broad and generalized ratings. It can also lead to the use of the same or similar scales by the patient, the therapist, and the assessor. This tactic brings reassuringly higher correlations between scores but there is some question about whether this kind of reliability is worth the effort.

By emphasizing the diversity of the person's reactions to therapy, and the temporal sequence of these changes, we are more likely to approach an understanding of the operative mechanisms. Such an emphasis will also make it easier to identify the mode of action of different types of intervention, or if you will, "treatment". In the case of behaviour therapy, one might be interested in comparing the relative effects of modelling, desensitization, and flooding — and it may turn out that these variants of fear-reduction procedures operate by different modes of action, and almost certainly at different speeds. In the case of psychotherapy it is not too difficult to predict a different sequence of changes and different speeds of altering the three major components — with a person's verbal reports and cognitions changing first — especially in, say, client-centred psychotherapy. By carrying out a component analysis of each type of intervention or treatment, we would be in a stronger position to trace the advantages and weaknesses of each method of approach.

The lump theory, with its emphasis on homogeneity and generalized outcome measures, blurs the differences between treatments. As mentioned earlier, a remarkable feature of most of the recent outcome research on neurosis has been the relative failure to uncover major differences in the effects of various forms of treatment (e.g. Sloane *et al.*, 1975; di Loreto *et al.*, 1971; Kazdin and Wilson, 1978b). In part this reflects the operation of powerful and pervasive, but as yet unspecified, influences that apparently are common in many forms of treatment. It is likely, however, that the relative failure to find difference in treatment effects can be attributed in part to the tactics dictated by a restrictive assumption about the nature of the disorders under study, i.e. the lump theory. Another reason for this failure is that, given the considerable amount of spontaneous improvement that occurs in neuroses, the room for demonstrating differential therapeutic changes over and above the spontaneous ones is limited. If we use the crude spontaneous remission rate of 66% within a 2-year period as a baseline (see Chapter 4), any behavioural or any other method of treating neuroses needs to produce improvements that exceed this large naturally occurring rate of change. Obviously it is easier to demonstrate the positive therapeutic effects of a method that addresses a problem with a low rate of spontaneous change, e.g. the speech deficiencies of retarded children.

The best way of *blurring* the potential differences between treatments is to use broad, general, qualitative outcome measures of limited range, and to confine oneself to problems with a high spontaneous remission rate. By contrast, the best way of *uncovering the differences* produced by various treatments is to use specific outcome-measures that are quantifiable and of extended range, and to select problems which have a low spontaneous remission rate.

THE THIRD ASSUMPTION

Instead of setting up their own and more appropriate measures of therapeutic change, many behaviour therapists, working outside the mainstream of operant procedures, adopted the existing soft signs of therapeutic change, such as ratings of general improvement on a 1–5 scale, measures of social adjustment on a 1–5 scale, the therapist's impression, the patient's expression of satisfaction, scores on personality tests, an increase in the number of coloured ink blots perceived, and so on. Apart from the fact that many of these signs are inappropriate indices of the effects of behaviour therapy, they are all based at least to some degree on the assumption of an exaggerated generality of behaviour, traits, and psychological difficulties. The nature and weaknesses of assumptions and undue psychological generality are lucidly discussed by Mischel (1968, 1977).

For immediate purposes we need merely note the consequences of this assumption for the design and evaluation of outcome research. Measures of outcome that assume far greater generality than exists, and most of the measures employed in conventional outcome research are of this type, are bound to yield imprecise and, therefore, misleading information.

If we translate a specific improvement in an agoraphobic patient's ability to travel independently on buses, into a rating of "general clinical improvement", expressed on a 1–5 point scale, and based on a secondhand verbal report from the most interested party to the second most interested party, then we rapidly lose accuracy and indeed validity as well. It is scarcely surprising that degraded information of this sort seldom correlates well with other information about the patient's progress. Nor is it surprising that such information provides a poor basis for predicting the patient's behaviour across situations, e.g. her ability to resume work.

In his review of outcome research, Mintz (1977) found that the therapist was the most common "instrument" of assessment, and furthermore, "almost all (88%) of the therapist ratings were global ratings . . . at the end of treatment" (p. 590). He also discovered that "the main finding is that most patients are seen as making slight to moderate gains (from 52% to 69%)".

Reliance on imprecise, degraded information that assumes a non-existent degree of generality of behaviour is bound to obscure the effects of any form of therapy — and hence, to preclude the conduct of exact evaluation research. Crude measuring instruments, based on a mistaken conception of the properties of the material to be measured, are a poor foundation for research.* In passing it is worth mentioning that the use of generalized measures in assessing the effects of therapy is more than a research problem; therapeutic decisions based on low-grade information are against the interests of the client or patient.

The specific therapeutic contributions of psychotherapy or of behaviour therapy, such as they are, are best evaluated by objective, direct, explicit measures of change. The continued use of generalized measures will simply reproduce the inconclusive results of the comparative studies mentioned earlier. Azrin (1977) has pointed out that the use of generalized and degraded outcome measures in psychological intervention work is comparable to assessing the effects of an anti-hypertensive drug by asking the patient and his doctor for clinical ratings of improvement, while failing to measure his blood pressure! "The best measure of behavior is behavior, not reports about it" (Bandura, 1978a).

It is inevitable that comparisons based on generalized, obscuring measures will always lean slightly to the right of the mid-point of any scale and will blur the differences between treatments — any treatments. If, on the other hand, one wishes to isolate the specific and differential effects of particular tactics, then it is advisable to select closely specified and replicable measurement procedures. Behavioural tests, psychophysiological assessments of reactivity to specific stresses, self-monitoring and standardized data-based interviews of the client/patient and an informed relative or friend, may replace generalized rating scales, projective tests, personality questionnaires, degrees of "constructive personality change" and percentages of cure/improvement/no change categories. For example, the success of a programme for modifying compulsive behaviour can be assessed by behavioural tests of the avoidance of contaminated material, the frequency of compulsive washing activities, self-monitoring of urges, heart rate responses to contaminating stimuli, and so forth.

The case for undertaking ambitious evaluative studies that follow the pattern of conventional outcome research is weak. Some positive alternatives follow.

---

*We offer the following recipe for research guaranteed to produce a result showing that psychotherapy is moderately effective and that all forms of therapy are equally moderate. Select educated young patients with "high ego-strength" and mild anxiety disorders of recent onset, use retrospective data, and base it on the therapists' ratings of global improvement as shown on a 5-point scale in which the interval from 3–4 says "slightly improved". Avoid behavioural tests, information provided by external informants, frequency counts and specific descriptors. The group results will show moderate improvements and/or that roughly 65% of the patients have improved.

POSITIVE PROPOSALS

By setting aside the three assumptions concerning the medical model, the lump theory, and the generality of psychological problems, we can proceed to a new attack on the question of therapeutic effectiveness. As adumbrated earlier, the definition of the person's problems and the means of assessing them would become more properly psychological and more specific. Unsuitable delivery systems would have to be changed or replaced. The selection of closely specified measurements in the design of outcome experiments based on a three-system analysis will make it possible to study both process and outcome questions simultaneously.

The move towards greater directness and specificity of measurements is, or should be, allied to the establishment of explicit treatment goals. In this way the effects of treatment could be stated in quantified degrees of success rather than in generalized reports of cure, relapse or improvement.

A proposal of a different character arises from dissatisfaction with the trend towards the undirected accumulation of disparate facts. Where possible, outcome studies should collect evidence that bears on significant theoretical questions. So, for example, one should question whether the observed effects, be they positive or negative, can be accommodated by existing theory. As argued earlier, questions of this kind can be put in the narrow sense or in the broad sense. Plainly, it is easier to put important theoretical questions to the test if the outcome study is designed with this purpose in mind. Too often the theoretical questions are posed after the completion of the research.

The next proposal concerns the effectiveness of behaviour therapy, seen in its social context. Although the therapist or the clinical research worker is in the first instance, and indeed mainly, concerned with the type of question discussed so far, people who have to plan and administer health-care services are interested in answering questions of effectiveness from a different standpoint. Even if a form of therapy is effective in the individual case, it does not follow that it is an effective psychological procedure for dealing with larger problems of incidence, suffering, etc. A method that deals successfully with a particular person's psychological problems may be inefficient from a social point of view. For example, it could be argued that even if psychoanalytic treatment were effective in the narrow sense, it would remain an inefficient procedure because of its extremely high cost. When therapeutic or intervention techniques are being developed it is desirable to assess the social as well as the personal value of the method. There is an understandable reluctance to apply cost—benefit analyses to problems of human suffering but it is difficult to see how a rational development and allocation of inevitably limited resources can be achieved unless and until competing approaches to psychological disorders are subjected to some form of social and economic examination (see Kazdin and Wilson, 1978a). The extension of behavioural methods and ideas into community work is occurring with speed and enthusiasm (see Kazdin's 1978 review).

NOTES ON THE PRESENT REVISION

The main changes in the structure and content of the original Edition are as follows. The chapter on the effects of psychotherapy carried out with children has been deleted, for two reasons. On the one hand, there appears to have been a little significant advance in the position described in the First Edition while, on the other hand, the subject of behaviour therapy with children has grown into such a large and vigorous activity during the past decade that it could not comfortably be incorporated as a chapter in a book of this kind; it demands extensive examination in its own right. The chapter on the negative effects of psychotherapy has been incorporated into the chapter on Rogerian psychotherapy, partly because that is where the debate began and also in recognition of the fact that the argument has not been advanced significantly during the past few years. The considerable expansion of work on the effects of behaviour therapy is acknowledged by the expansion of the original two chapters and, indirectly by the inclusion of a new section dealing with comparative evaluation studies. The growth of cognitive therapies is dealt with by adding an entirely new chapter. The remaining chapters have been brought up to date and, where necessary, the conclusions reached in the First Edition have been modified.

In that Edition it was argued that for a large number of people, psychotherapy is a comforting or satisfying experience, regardless of whether or not the patient's original hopes and expectations are fulfilled. Despite the embarrassing sparseness of scientifically acceptable evidence demonstrating the effectiveness of psychotherapy, considerable numbers of people express satisfaction with the experience of undergoing psychotherapy. The divergence between what might be referred to as "patient satisfaction" and scientific validity is seen most clearly in the practice of psychoanalysis (see Chapter 5). Events that have taken place during the past decade reinforce the idea that whatever else the various forms of psychotherapy can or cannot achieve, they often are a source of comfort to people who have a need for assistance of some form. Needless to add, recognition of the comfort which sometimes is provided by psychotherapy should neither cloud nor impede the scientific appraisal of its effects. If it turns out to be the case that most forms of psychotherapy successfully provide comfort, without bringing about significant changes in the person's major problems, this distinction should be made plain to people who are contemplating a course of psychotherapy.

As argued above, the most significant change in the evaluation of the effects of psychotherapy that has taken place during the past decade, is the emergence of a set of findings and ideas that make it desirable to introduce fresh strategies of evaluation. From many points of view, the older approach — labelled the conventional approach — is wanting.

We find ourselves in the difficult and slightly embarrassing position of reviewing a considerable body of evidence on the effects of therapy which rests upon and was carried out within a strategic framework that is inadequate to the task. The bulk of the evidence consists of conventional findings drawn from conventional research using conventional outcome designs. In their very nature it is extremely difficult and sometimes quite impossible to draw sharp and conclusive generalizations. Despite these shortcomings and difficulties, the task has to be completed as it would be foolish to neglect the available information, providing one remains alert to its limitations. In addition to carrying out what might be called our conventional evaluation of outcome research, we hope to convey a need to renew the search for more satisfactory methods of determining the precise effects of closely specified methods of therapy.

CHAPTER 2

THE NEED FOR EVALUATIONS

Professor Jerome Frank (1968) observed that "we should not forget that, at least in the United States, psychiatrists and psychologists combined, treat far fewer persons than chiropractors and religious healers" (p. 39). A satisfactory explanation of the persistence of these practices might take us a long way in coming to grips with the effects of placebos and the array of psychotherapeutic procedures currently offered. Although Frank (1961) has provided an absorbing account of the common ground between faith healing, persuasion, and psychotherapy, the analogy should not be stretched. Unlike faith healing, psychotherapy is recommended and practised by professionals who have undergone scientific and critical training. This is not, however, a guarantee that its use is justified on scientific grounds. The rise and fall of insulin treatment is an instructive example of misguided therapy and serves as a useful reminder.

After a period of widespread use in the treatment of schizophrenia, the popularity of insulin coma therapy began to decline in the late fifties. Writing in 1959, Sargant gave a moderately favourable account of the treatment and stated that of sixty-seven psychiatric hospitals in southern England, "every hospital except 1 private mental hospital and 2 neurosis centres in this area have been using Sakel's insulin coma treatment of schizophrenia during the last 10 years" (p. 148). A few years later Bennet (1966) reported that of 214 hospitals which had active insulin coma clinics in the 1950s, no less than ninety-three had discontinued these clinics. He also observed that insulin therapy and electro-shock had not altered hospital statistics — unlike the newer psychotropic drugs. After having endorsed insulin coma therapy in his well-known textbook, Kalinowsky (1967) wrote that "at present, insulin coma therapy is used in very few places throughout the world". He felt that there was a need for this treatment, "perhaps 1 hospital in each area would be sufficient" (p. 1286). In his textbook published 15 years earlier, however, he had stated that "acute cases of schizophrenia should have preference as it is an established fact that the chronic patient responds less well; but even in the chronic group there is a sufficient number of patients who show improvement and these should therefore not be excluded from treatment" (Kalinowsy and Hoch, 1952, p. 12). Again, "insulin shock treatment was introduced for the cure of schizophrenia . . . in manic depressive psychoses and involutional psychoses, insulin is far less effective" (p. 11). Curran and Guttmann (1949, p. 158) observed that "the treatment of schizophrenia has been revolutionized by the introduction of shock therapy" (i.e. insulin shock and convulsive treatment). They recommended it as the treatment of first choice for schizophrenia and also stated that "it may be considered that insulin treatment should always be given in cases of recent origin and should be considered even in chronic cases . . . the better quality of the remission is one of the most striking effects of insulin therapy" (p. 160). In the following edition of this book (Curran and Partridge, 1955) their

13

advice was more reserved: "Although it can hardly be considered curative, it is the most effective way of treating schizophrenia that we have and the great majority of authorities agree that it produces remissions that are of better quality, are reached more quickly and last longer, than those obtainable by any other means" (p. 373). The next edition of the book appeared in 1963 and this time the pertinent paragraph was deleted; the authors pointed out that insulin coma therapy "has been so largely replaced by the use of tranquilizers that details of the technique must be sought elsewhere" (p. 387).

These consecutive quotations illustrate the spectacular rise and fall of insulin coma treatment as seen by Curran and his colleagues. In the space of a mere 14 years — from 1949 to 1963 — it changed from being a revolutionizing treatment to one which did not merit description in a standard textbook.

Mayer-Gross *et al.* (1960) wrote in the second edition of their textbook that insulin coma treatment "is still recognized as one of the effective methods of treating early schizophrenia. If applied in the first year of the illness, it more than doubles the number of remissions that can be expected to occur" (p. 298). In the following edition, by Slater and Roth (1969), they pointed out that drugs had largely replaced insulin coma treatment, and the matter was dismissed in one sentence of an 800-page book. In the second edition, published in 1960, the authors had remarked that "the empirical character of therapies such as insulin coma treatment has been the target of much criticism and an excuse for sceptical inertia" (p. 296). The third edition of the textbook contains a witty alteration in this sentence: "The empirical character of therapies such as ECT and pharmacological treatment has been the target of much criticism and an excuse for sceptical inertia" (p. 329).

In the 1947 edition of their textbook, Henderson and Gillespie were somewhat critical and reserved. Although they gave a detailed account of the treatment, they went on to say that "the efficacy of insulin coma treatment is still therefore somewhat difficult to estimate" (p. 404). And they added that there is a "suspicion that treatment with insulin, even if it is undertaken early, does not increase the ultimate rate of recovery" (p. 404). They seem to be justified (or better placed) in stating in their 1962 edition (Henderson and Batchelor) that, "we are of the opinion that the treatment should be abandoned" (p. 347). They added that, "we have ceased to use insulin coma treatment and so have many others, some of whom were previously enthusiasts for the treatment" (p. 347). In a survey of 205 senior English psychiatrists published in 1965 (Willis and Bannister), only 6.8% regarded insulin coma as a suitable treatment for schizophrenia.

The story of insulin coma treatment is an interesting episode in the history of psychiatry and would repay close analysis. It would be reassuring if we could believe that the abandonment of this method of treatment came as a direct consequence of a detached evaluation of scientific evidence. Although it is almost certainly true that evaluation of this type did play a part in the abandonment of the treatment, the major cause for its decrease in popularity was probably the appearance of new and powerful tranquilizing drugs. We appear here to be dealing with a clear case of "treatment substitution". It has been observed that theories (and techniques) seldom succumb to abstract argument: "Theories pass from the scientific stage not because they have been disproved but because they have been superseded — pushed off and replaced by others that are new. I have searched long through the history of science without finding a single instance in which one could with any assurance say that criticism was the *coup de mort* of theory" (Dallenbach, 1955). Nevertheless, people are, of course, responsive to argument and evidence. Criticism can provoke further thoughts and a search for supporting evidence.

It can also promote a more vigorous search for satisfactory alternatives. The fact that some critics expressed their doubts and reservations about insulin coma treatment probably facilitated the transition to tranquilizing drugs. Even though psychotherapy today probably has very many more advocates than critics, it is recognized that supporting evidence is scarce. The main purpose of this book is to examine the nature and quality of the evidence, but a few remarks about the possible reasons for the uncritical and seemingly over-optimistic attitude towards psychotherapy will not be out of place.

Both patients and therapists can over-estimate the effects of treatment. For example, Feifel and Eells (1963) asked patients and therapists to assess the same psychotherapy and found large differences in their evaluations. Sixty-three patients and twenty-eight therapists gave their views on the relative frequency of change after treatment. On symptom relief, only 27% of the patients claimed benefit, whereas 57% of the therapists felt that significant symptom-relief had been obtained. On the behavioural assessment, 47% of patients claimed improvements, whereas 71% of therapists reported improvements. In both cases there was a statistically significant difference between the reports of the patients and their therapists — with the therapists claiming far more improvement than their patients. In the famous Cambridge Somerville study on the prevention of delinquency, both the clients and the therapists reported more benefit than was evident in the factual information about offences and court appearances (Powers and Witmer, 1951; Teuber and Powers, 1953; McCord, 1978). The literature on placebo reactions is replete with examples of reported improvements after the administration of inert substances (e.g. Koegler and Brill, 1967, who found that 52% of their neurotic patients claimed such benefits). In the growing literature on behaviour therapy, similar instances of "mistaken" impressions are emerging. In his experimental treatment of fear of public speaking in a college population, Paul (1966) found that a significant minority of his subjects in a control group, who received a nonsensical form of treatment (described as "attention placebo"), felt that they had benefited from the experience. In the study by Lang et al. (1966) a group of snake-phobic students who had been given a meaningless form of verbal pseudo-therapy also reported that they had benefited — despite the fact that their fears were unaltered. Gillan and Rachman (1974) found that psychotherapists overrated the effects of treatment in comparison with their patients, as did Rogers et al. (1967, pp. 77—79). This list of examples could be extended.

The major point is no longer in dispute. There are many non-specific elements in almost all forms of treatment which have apparently beneficial results. This built-in inflation, combined with the natural spontaneous remission which takes place in many psychological disorders, makes it difficult to isolate the specific contribution made by any therapeutic technique. These obstacles increase the fascination of the problem and can be moderately well tolerated as both of these processes operate in a manner which is desirable as far as the patients are concerned. It may turn out, in the long run, that psychotherapy does no more than provide the patient with a degree of comfort while the disorder runs its natural course. If this is so, then the sooner we establish such a finding the sooner we will be in a position honestly to provide effective comfort.

Although doubts about the effectiveness of psychotherapy had been expressed before the publication of their important findings, Teuber and Powers (1953) argued convincingly that the burden of proof lay with those who practise or advocate psychotherapy. In 1952 Eysenck published his now-famous evaluation of the effects of psychotherapy and concluded that the case was not proven. This important contribution is the starting-point for most critiques of psychotherapy, and with his expanded assessment published in 1960, will be described first.

The focus of interest in Eysenck's papers and in the present book is on *outcome* studies. The technical problems involved in such studies are of secondary concern, and an extensive literature on this subject is available (e.g. successive issues of the *International Journal of Psychiatry*, February and March 1969; the *Annual Reviews of Psychology* over the past 15 years, etc.). Unless otherwise specified, "psychotherapy" is intended to mean *interpretive therapy* and *not* the support, reassurance, encouragement, guidance, and sympathetic listening which still form the mainstay of psychiatric practice. Our reason for paying so much attention to interpretive types of therapy is that the most important and far-reaching claims have been made for this method. It is said to offer important benefits in excess of those provided by "superficial" types of psychotherapy and to be capable of helping patients who would otherwise remain beyond treatment.

The cautionary tale of the rise and fall of insulin coma therapy recommends a sceptical attitude to far-reaching therapeutic claims, but one hopes that scepticism will be expressed in a constructive manner whenever possible. It should help to frame searching and incisive questions, and to promote rather than discourage research. We hope that readers will have their curiosity roused by our examination of the evidence, and the accompanying or consequent problems.

CHAPTER 3

EYSENCK'S ARGUMENT

Landis (1937), Denker (1946), and Zubin (1953) – among others – questioned the claims made on behalf of psychotherapy and other forms of treatment prior to or shortly after the appearance of Eysenck's classic paper of 1952. Prompted by such views, Eysenck carried out an astringent and challenging examination of the evidence on the effects of psychotherapy, and came to the conclusion that the emperor had no clothes. The reactions of shock and disbelief have passed and now, 27 years later, we can re-examine the emperor's sartorial progress.

In this brief recapitulation we have attempted to extract the most salient points from Eysenck's argument as presented in 1952 and extended in 1960 and 1969. In his first evaluation he pointed out that an accurate assessment of psychotherapeutic effects is impeded by the methodological shortcomings of most studies. In the absence of suitable control studies he had to rely on non-controlled studies and this precluded definitive conclusions. In an attempt to provide a baseline with which to compare the results of treatment conducted without controls, he attempted to derive a "best available estimate" of remissions which occur in the absence of therapy. Recognizing the difficulty of this task, he pointed out the defects involved in an attempt of this kind. The matching of cases is difficult, the cases are inadequately described, the nature and severity of the illnesses are not given in unequivocal detail, the data on duration and type of treatment are inadequate, and follow-up information is scanty. For these reasons he cautioned that his actuarial evaluations should not be regarded as providing precise comparisons.

Using the data provided by Landis and by Denker, his first estimate of the crude spontaneous remission rate in neurotic disorders led him to propose that approximately two out of three patients can be expected to recover within 2 years – even in the absence of formal treatment. In his second evaluation, Eysenck (1960a) supplemented this baseline with data provided by Shepherd and Gruenberg (1957). They attempted to estimate the duration of neurotic illnesses by reference to the general rule that "the prevalence of an illness in a population is equal to the product of its incidence and duration". They observed that the incidence and prevalence curves for neurotic illnesses were of similar shape and ran an almost parallel course. From this they concluded that the average duration of neurotic illnesses is between 1 and 2 years:

"While it is well known that neurotic illnesses can occur at any age and exhibit extremely long courses as well as very brief courses, the available data are remarkably consistent in suggesting that neurotic illnesses are not characteristic of early adult life, that there is a rising incidence and prevalence during the twenties and thirties, a parallel rising prevalence continuing into the forties, and then a rapid decline in prevalence of recognized neuroses. From these data it is perfectly clear that, in the mass, neuroses must have a limited course even if untreated; in fact, the best available data would suggest an average duration of between 1 and 2 years."

This conclusion, published 5 years after Eysenck's original article, was even more optimistic than his estimate.

As Eysenck's initial estimate was based on the data provided by Landis and by Denker, a brief description of their work is necessary. Landis examined the amelioration rate in state mental hospitals for patients classified under the heading of "neurosis". He observed that in New York State 70% of neurotic patients were discharged annually as recovered or improved. For the United States as a whole, the figure was 68%. Because of the obvious shortcomings of an estimate of this kind (e.g. the patients must have been severely disturbed in order to require admission, some of them may well have received some psychotherapy, etc.) Landis was cautious in his conclusion: "Although this is not, strictly speaking, a basic figure for 'spontaneous' recovery, still any therapeutic method must show an appreciably greater size than this to be seriously considered."

Denker's (1946) baseline of spontaneous remission was calculated from 500 consecutive patients with disability claims due to neurosis who were treated by general practitioners. Nothing more than the most superficial type of psychotherapy was given, but sedatives, re-assurance, and suggestion played a regular part in the treatment. These patients were followed up for a minimum of 5 years and often as long as 10 years after the period of disability had begun, and reasonably strict criteria of improvement were used. Denker found that 45% of these patients recovered within a year and an additional 27% after 2 years. The combined figure of 72% recoveries within 2 years increased during the course of the next 3 years and reached an eventual total of 90% recoveries after 5 years.

While recognizing the defects of these two studies, Eysenck was struck by the extent of similarity between them despite the fact that they were dealing with very different populations.

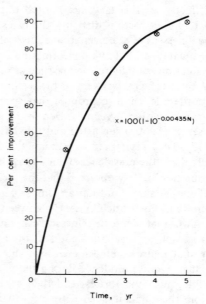

$$X = 100(1 - 10^{-0.00435N})$$

FIG. 1. Curve fitted to Denker's data on 500 untreated neurotic patients (Eysenck, 1960a). Improvement shown by 500 severe neuro-tics not receiving psychotherapy after between 1 and 5 years. In the formula X denotes the proportional improvement, while N denotes the number of weeks elapsing from the beginning of the experiment.

He fitted an exponential curve to the data to illustrate the natural course of neuroses (see Fig. 1). These necessarily gross estimates have now been supplemented by small-scale studies, including experimental investigations. Having established a rough baseline, Eysenck compared the rate of improvement reported in treated case-series with the spontaneous remission baseline.

In his first evaluation he selected twenty-four of the most informative studies, covering over 7000 cases. Five of the reports described the results of psychoanalytic treatment. The results from the various studies were analysed into four categories of improvement ranging from cured or much improved to unimproved. In view of the variations between reports, Eysenck often had to use his judgement in determining some of the classifications of improvement and diagnostic groupings (an attempt was made to exclude all non-neurotic cases). He acknowledged that a "slight degree of subjectivity inevitably enters into this procedure, but it is doubtful if it caused much distortion". The calculations based on these figures led him to conclude that, "patients treated by means of psychoanalysis improved to the extent of 44%; patients treated eclectically improved to the extent of 64%; patients treated only custodially or by general practitioners improved to the extent of 72%. There thus appears to be an inverse correlation between recovery and psychotherapy", but this last conclusion "required certain qualification". The main qualification is that, if one excludes patients who break off psychoanalytic treatment before the therapist feels that it should be concluded, then the recovery rate with this form of treatment rises to 66%. That is, if one excludes the defectors, the chances of improvement with psychoanalytic treatment are approximately equal to the chances of improvement under eclectic treatment.

Having pointed out the limitations of actuarial comparisons of the type which he had undertaken, Eysenck stated this provoking conclusion: "They fail to prove that psychotherapy, Freudian or otherwise, facilitates the recovery of neurotic patients. They show that roughly two-thirds of a group of neurotic patients will recover or improve to a marked extent within about 2 years of the onset of their illness, whether they are treated by means of psychotherapy or not."

In his re-examination of the evidence carried out 8 years later, Eysenck included a number of studies which had employed control groups, and went beyond the neuroses. He gave "pride of place" to the Cambridge Somerville study on the prevention of delinquency. Over a period of 8 years, Powers and Witmer (1951) and Teuber and Powers (1953) attempted to prevent delinquency by guidance, counselling, and therapy in a group of 650 under-privileged boys who had been designated as likely to become delinquent. Half of the boys were randomly allocated to the treatment group and the other half served as controls. The treatment consisted of individual therapy, and the majority of the therapists were either psychoanalytic or non-directive in orientation. As it was a complex study and the results are extensive, we will draw attention to the main findings. According to Teuber and Powers, the "treatment did not . . . reduce the incidence of adjudged delinquency in the treatment group"; this despite the fact that the therapists felt that more than two-thirds of their sample had "substantially benefited". Similarly, 62% of the treated clients stated that the help provided had been of value to them. Despite these feelings of success and optimism, the objective evidence was "paradoxical", for the authors found that "instead of confirming the expectation that the treatment group would be less delinquent than the matched control group, there is a slight difference in favour of the control group". Teuber and Powers placed greater weight on the "quantitative indices", and concluded that "the data yield one definite conclusion: that the burden of proof is on anyone who claims specific results for a given form of therapy".

In a remarkable piece of retrieval and persistence, McCord (1978) followed up over 500 of the men who constituted the original sample of 650. They were traced some 30 years after the termination of the project. McCord confirmed the original finding that many of the people who participated in the prevention and treatment programmes reported that they had benefited from such intervention. Despite these assertions, comparisons made between the treatment and control groups showed that the programme had no significant effect on any of the major measures of outcome. The programme failed to achieve a major aim, that is, to prevent the clients from committing crimes. McCord observed that "the objective evidence presents a disturbing picture" (p. 288), for there were some slight indications that the programme had what she calls "negative side effects" as measured by criminal behaviour, alcoholism, mental disorders, and low job satisfaction. The treated clients were found to be slightly worse off than the control clients on each of these measures.

In the next study used by Eysenck, 150 neurotic patients had been tested on the MMPI before and after therapy (Barron and Leary, 1955). If one could allow that the MMPI is a satisfactory measure of psychiatric improvement, which is doubtful, then the study completely failed to demonstrate the effectiveness of psychotherapy (in this case predominantly psycho-analytic in orientation). Barron and Leary attempted to salvage some comfort from the study by arguing that a commitment to undertake psychotherapy in the future, and the initial contact with the clinic, were themselves therapeutic events. Although this seems to be stretching the point somewhat, their claim is not wholly unreasonable. The fact remains, however, that their study failed to demonstrate that psychotherapy facilitated the improvement of these groups of patients (see p. 101).

The Rogers and Dymond (1954) study of the effects of non-directive therapy employed a double control group technique. Some of the treated patients acted as their own controls by undergoing a 60-day waiting period before commencing therapy. In addition to the twenty-nine treated cases, twenty-three "normal volunteers" acted as a further control. The authors claimed to have demonstrated a significant therapeutic effect, but Eysenck's criticisms were telling. In the first place, the use of normal subjects as a control group for patients is unsupportable: "No one has, to our knowledge, advanced the hypothesis that a group of normal people not subjected to any kind of psychotherapeutic or other manipulation should change in the direction of greater integration and better mental health" (Eysenck, 1960a, p. 707). In regard to the waiting control procedure, he pointed out that the time intervals were not comparable. The waiting period was only 60 days, and it is improbable that much spontaneous remission would have occurred during this short period. As the therapy period was of greater duration, the possibility of spontaneous changes occurring during *this* period was enhanced. Lastly, Eysenck drew attention to the absence of any behavioural criteria of outcome. He might also have added that the use of the Q-sort was perhaps unwise (see below).

The Brill and Beebe (1955) study is a statistical analysis of data collected on military patients. In a detailed analysis of substantial data they found that treatment had no apparent effect on the patient's condition after discharge, nor on the percentage who were considered fit to return to duty. Although the authors searched long and hard, they were unable to find evidence to support the claim that psychotherapy had been effective in the treatment of these patients. Despite its retrospective quality, this study is impressive in the care and effort taken to collect, sort, and interpret the evidence. As far as the argument for psychotherapy is concerned, it brought cold comfort. The study reported by Ellis (1957), which compares the effects of three types of therapy, suffers from serious defects but is not without interest (see

Chapter 5). He compared the results obtained with seventy-eight patients treated with his own brand of "rational psychotherapy", seventy-eight patients treated by psychoanalytic-orientated psychotherapy, and sixteen who received orthodox psychoanalysis. The patients were all treated by Ellis himself, who also carried out the assessments of outcome (an unwise undertaking). He found that 90% of the group who received rational therapy improved, whereas only 63% of the analytic group showed a similar degree of improvement. Of the sixteen patients who received orthodox psychoanalysis, only 50% showed the same degree of improvement. The other studies described at some length by Eysenck are discussed in Chapters 5 and 6.

This abbreviated account of Eysenck's (1960a) evidence and argument is best concluded by stating its eight major conclusions, which go a "little beyond" those of the original survey. The shift is towards increasing pessimism about psychotherapy — a move from "unproven" to "unlikely". The conclusions are:

"1. When untreated neurotic control groups are compared with experimental groups of neurotic patients treated by means of psychotherapy, both groups recover to approximately the same extent.

2. When soldiers who have suffered a neurotic breakdown and have not received psychotherapy are compared with soldiers who have received psychotherapy, the chances of the two groups returning to duty are approximately equal.

3. When neurotic soldiers are separated from the service, their chances of recovery are not affected by their receiving or not receiving psychotherapy.

4. Civilian neurotics who are treated by psychotherapy recover or improve to approximately the same extent as similar neurotics receiving no psychotherapy.

5. Children suffering from emotional disorders and treated by psychotherapy recover or improve to approximately the same extent as similar children not receiving psychotherapy.

6. Neurotic patients treated by means of psychotherapeutic procedures based on learning theory improve significantly more quickly than do patients treated by means of psychoanalysis or eclectic psychotherapy, or not treated by psychotherapy at all.

7. Neurotic patients treated by psychoanalytic psychotherapy do not improve more quickly than patients treated by means of eclectic psychotherapy, and may improve less quickly when account is taken of the large proportion of patients breaking off treatment.

8. With the single exception of psychotherapeutic methods based on learning theory, results of published research with military and civilian neurotics, and with both adults and children, suggest that the therapeutic effects of psychotherapy are small or non-existent, and do not in any demonstrable way add to the non-specific effects of routine medical treatment, or to such events as occur in patients' every-day experience."

Eysenck's arguments have not gone unchallenged. A great deal of discussion and research has been generated by these contributions, and many writers have debated these matters at some length, despite Sanford's (1953) advice: "The only wise course with respect to such a challenge is to ignore it." In the event it was Sanford's advice which was ignored.* The views expressed range from outright rejection to ready acceptance of Eysenck's assessment.

---

*The view that a statistical examination of the effects of psychoanalysis is unwise and/or unnecessary was introduced by Freud (1922), and still has supporters.

Arguing that the entire question is "scientifically meaningless", Sanford stated his view in a manner which, despite his assertion, was less than obvious. He stated that "it is obvious that some people change in some ways under the influence of some kinds of therapeutic activities while other people do not change, or change in different ways, under the same therapeutic activity, and that still other people change in ways similar to the above without any therapeutic activity" (p. 336). Not very enlightening.

Several writers drew attention to the limitations of the data on which Eysenck's evaluation was based (to be fair, most of the problems were mentioned by Eysenck in his original paper). Rosenzweig (1954), for example, mentioned the difficulties involved in comparing outcome criteria across different studies. Although Eysenck discussed this problem in a slightly different form, the conclusion drawn by Rosenzweig in his argument is different but not uncharacteristic. Having discussed the shortcomings of the data, he argued that the criticisms of psychotherapy were not crucial and that they do not prove that psychotherapy is ineffective. This point of view has been adopted by several people, but appears to miss the main issue. As Teuber and Powers (1953) remarked in their discussion of the Cambridge study, the burden of proof rests with those who recommend or practise psychotherapy and not with those who persist in reminding us that the evidence in support of the beneficial effects of psychotherapy is embarrassingly scanty.

A good deal of the discussion provoked by Eysenck's work has been constructive and provoking. Meehl (1955), for example, discussed the problem in a productive and thoughtful manner. Malan *et al.* (1968), accepting that "the case for a high rate of symptomatic remission in neurotic patients . . . is proved and that is the end of it", made an unusual and interesting attempt to study the psychodynamic changes which occur in untreated neurotic patients. Their study, based on a 2- to 8-year follow-up of forty-five untreated Tavistock Clinic patients, showed that 51% were "at least symptomatically improved", but they argued that a proportion of these changes were "psychodynamically suspect". The value of this type of investigation, attempted in part in response to Eysenck's analysis, is beyond question, but the methods adopted were not satisfactory. The main difficulty arises from their mixture of interpretation with factual evidence. Despite this drawback, their investigation is of considerable interest and will, one hopes, prompt improved studies of this kind.

Another advance in our knowledge which must be attributed indirectly to Eysenck's analysis is the recognition that future studies of remissions (both spontaneous and treated) will be more precise and valuable if they are carried out within rather than across diagnostic groupings.

One of the developments to flow from Eysenck's argument is the concept of "average therapeutic effects". This, in turn, gave impetus to those research workers engaged in the study of effective therapist variables, with particular reference to non-directive therapy (see Chapter 7). Bergin (1966) was one of the most articulate advocates of the "average therapeutic effect" argument. His attempt at an optimistic reconciliation of the predominantly disappointing evidence on the effects of psychotherapy was so astute that it deserved success. Unfortunately, it would be too successful if it were correct, and as it turns out, the facts are against it (see below). He argued that while reports and studies show little difference in the average amount of change occurring after treatment, a "significant increase in the variability of criterion scores appears at post-testing in the treatment groups". This spread of criterion scores, he argued, implies that treatment has a beneficial effect on some patients and an unfavourable effect on others. "When these contrary phenomena are lumped together in an experimental group, they cancel each other out to some extent and the overall yield in terms of improvement . . . is no greater than the change occurring in a control group."

Like Bergin, Truax and Carkhuff (1967) accepted the argument based on an average therapeutic effect and then extended their search for the variables which determine successful or unsuccessful treatment outcomes. On average, psychotherapy appears to be ineffective. If we assume that at termination treated groups show interest variability then we need to isolate those factors which improve some patients and make others worse. While allowing for the influence of other determinants, Truax and Carkhuff and their colleagues devoted most of their attention to an examination of the characteristics of successful and unsuccessful therapists. This line of argument and the associated research are examples of the fruitful effects which can emerge from a critical, if unpopular, examination of a prevailing belief.

Eysenck (1960a, 1969a) discussed many of these problems as he developed the argument and reiterated his view that the proof of psychotherapeutic effectiveness rests with those who advocate it: "Psychoanalysts and psychotherapists generally assert that their methods cure psychoneurotic disorders, and are in fact the only methods which can achieve this end. Clearly, therefore, it is on them that the onus of proof must rest" (Eysenck, 1969a). He went on to say that "they must define clearly and unambiguously what is meant by neurotic disorder and what is meant by cure; they must put forward methods of testing the effects of the treatment which are not dependent on the subjective evaluation of the therapist, and they must demonstrate that their methods give results which are clearly superior to any alternative methods, such as those of behaviour therapy or of spontaneous remission. It is indisputable, I suggest, that psychotherapists and psychoanalysts have failed to do any of these things, and until they have all been done I find it very difficult to see how any doubt can be thrown on my conclusion that published research has failed to support the claims made" (p. 100). Acknowledging the limitations of actuarial and similar types of information, he went on to urge "the necessity of properly planned and executed experimental studies into this important field", with recommendations about the manner in which some studies might be conducted.

Shortly after the publication of his 1952 review, Eysenck became interested in the possibility of developing an alternative to psychotherapy. During the past 25 years he has advocated the development of behavioural therapy, the progress of which is discussed in Chapters 9 and 10. "We are not, therefore, faced with the alternative ... of psychotherapy or nothing; we are in the position of having two contenders in the ring between whom a rational choice should not be impossible" (Eysenck, 1969a, p. 99).

This, then, is the background to the debate about psychotherapy which is the subject of this book.

CHAPTER 4

MOST REMARKABLE PROVIDENCES: THE SPONTANEOUS REMISSION OF NEUROTIC DISORDERS*

There are few historical accounts of spontaneous remissions from mental illnesses, a fact which MacAlpine and Hunter (1963) ascribe to the "unlimited trust" in the value of treatment. This unlimited trust resulted in a blindness to the occurrence of such improvements. "A disease which had withstood repeated therapeutic onslaught was considered not only incurable but irrecoverable." If, however, the patient did recover, "it was regarded as an act of grace or remarkable providence" (p. 271). MacAlpine and Hunter attribute the denial of spontaneous remission — recoveries which take place without the benefit of medical intervention — to what they call "this conceit of physicians".

MacAlpine and Hunter quote from a description of one such remarkable providence, written in 1697 by William Turner. It would appear that Mr. Francis Culham developed a serious mental disorder several days after Christmas in 1671 and "lost the use of his reason". His unfortunate condition continued for several years until, on the 12th May, when "by the miraculous power and mercy of God", his health returned. The authenticity of this remarkable providence was attested to by two prominent physicians of the time.

The earliest full account of the history and management of Bethlem Hospital, the first and for many years the only asylum for the mentally ill in England, was published by Strype in 1720. His description contains some fascinating information about the therapeutic success rate achieved at the time. The superintendent of the hospital, Dr. Tyson (remembered in the contemporary hospital by the ward which is named after him), informed Strype that, "from the year 1684 to 1703 . . . there had been in this Hospital 1,294 patients; of which number had been cured and discharged 890, which is above 2 patients in 3 . . . " (MacAlpine and Hunter, 1963, p. 308). This familiar sounding success rate was achieved despite the fact that at that time the Bethlem Hospital "stood in an obscure and close place, near unto many common sewers". It is historically fitting that a psychologist associated with the Bethlem Hospital, Professor Eysenck, should have played so prominent a part in the contemporary debate on spontaneous remission.

If we set aside the objection that Dr. Tyson was misguided or misleading, one can only conclude that the often curious methods of treatment which were employed at the time were rather successful — or that approximately two-thirds of the patients recovered regardless of any treat-

---

*We are grateful to Professor Grünbaum for reminding us of G. B. Shaw's amusing remark that, "A doctor is a man who helps pass the time while Nature performs the cure."

ment which they did or did not receive at the hospital. The simplest way of removing any disquiet about our easy confidence in progress is to dismiss the recovery figure as hopelessly inadequate. Nevertheless it may be as well to give at least momentary consideration to the possibility that the spontaneous remission rate remains relatively constant across time, and in widely varying social conditions.

The remainder of this chapter deals primarily with the accuracy and justification for Eysenck's (1960) claim that "roughly two-thirds of a group of neurotic patients will recover or improve to a marked extent within about two years of the onset of their illness". Inevitably, the discussion will range beyond the confines of the hypothesis but it forms the focus for most of this analysis. It should be pointed out that spontaneous remissions are not presumed to occur without cause; they are defined as *spontaneous* in the sense that they occur in the absence of any formal therapeutic intervention.

Recognition that the majority of neurotic disorders can be expected to remit within 2 years of onset, even in the absence of formal treatment, is the first step in what has become a long and complex process of investigation. In company with other commentators, it was recommended in the First Edition that attention should be focused on the remission rates that occur in different diagnostic categories, and there can be little argument that this is a desirable step (as the title of this chapter indicates, the present discussion is confined to neurotic disorders; remissions in psychotic disorders are considered briefly in Chapter 8). Commentators such as Bergin (1975), who have expressed reservations about the nature and extent of remissions, now accept the desirability of determining intradiagnostic rates of remission. In his earlier contribution, the rates reported for various types of disorder, neurotic and non-neurotic, were combined (Bergin, 1971).

The case for determining separate spontaneous remission rates for different types of disorder can be justified on three counts. In the first place, greater knowledge of the spontaneous remission rate for particular disorders would enable us to provide far more accurate information for patients and their relatives when we counsel them about the prognosis of the disorder. Secondly, the most important long-term justification for determining separate rates for different disorders is that the spontaneous remission rate provides an essential yardstick against which to measure the effects of any form of therapy. The more precise and more specific the spontaneous remission rate, the better the comparison and the more reliable the conclusions that can be drawn from any such comparison. Thirdly, we are more likely to approach an understanding of the mechanisms involved in spontaneous remission if our knowledge of the frequency with which such remissions occur is particular and precise.

A number of interesting problems have emerged from a recognition that spontaneous remissions occur. Every investigation reported so far has produced evidence of a group of patients whose difficulties fail to remit spontaneously. The figures for such patients range from 20% to as high as 50%, and we need to identify and describe these persisting disorders with greater accuracy. We also need to investigate why these disorders persist and why they worsen in a percentage of cases. Another important problem which requires explanation arises from the observation that *treated patients* seem rarely to show an improvement rate which greatly exceeds the spontaneous remission rate. Indeed, on some occasions, it has been reported that a proportion of the treated patients have shown an improvement rate which is lower than that of the *spontaneous remission rate* (e.g. Barron and Leary, 1955; Saenger, 1970). So, for example, on the triad of neurotic traits measured by the MMPI, "the average decrease is slightly greater for the controls than for the group of psychotherapy patients" (Barron and Leary, 1955, p.

244). Even if we allow for the possibility that therapy may make some patients worse, it is most improbable that a large discrepancy between the improvement rates of treated patients and the improvement rates that occur spontaneously can be accounted for satisfactorily in this manner. The large discrepancies which have been recorded may be attributable to the selection of unrepresentative samples of patients for inclusion in these treatment series. For example, if a treatment series includes a disproportionately large number of severely disturbed patients, then the improvement rate may well fail to reach the spontaneous remission rate of two-thirds. A second factor which may contribute to treated improvement rates which fall below the spontaneous rate figure is the duration of treatment and follow-up, where applicable. If the treatment period is relatively brief then the outcome figure may fall below those of the spontaneous improvement rate, which is usually quoted in terms of a standard period of 2 years (in keeping with Eysenck's hypothesis).

Although the implications of the argument about spontaneous remission rates extend well beyond the specific statements made by Eysenck, what we refer to as his main hypothesis, is the focus for the present discussion. It will be recalled that he asserted that approximately two-thirds of those people who develop neurotic disorders will experience a spontaneous remission "within about two years of the onset of their illness" (see page 19). A number of important implications flow from Eysenck's specification that the greatest part of spontaneous remissions will occur within a defined time. It means among other things that in order to carry out *a strict test of the hypothesis,* one should study first admissions, i.e. those patients whose neurotic disorders are of recent onset. Studies carried out on patients whose neurotic conditions have already taken a chronic course, and have lasted say more than 5 years, will inevitably produce a significantly lower rate of spontaneous remissions. It follows from this deduction that if one wishes to subject any form of therapy to a particularly rigorous test of its efficacy, it might be advisable to conduct the research on a population of patients with *chronic* neurotic conditions. So, for example, one might test out the value of say rational psychotherapy on a group of patients whose neurotic disorders exceed 5 years' duration: in this way, the untreated control group with its relatively low rate of spontaneous remissions will provide a better opportunity for demonstrating the specific value of the therapeutic intervention. On the other hand, therapeutic outcome studies carried out on neurotic populations with short duration illnesses, will be hard put to it to demonstrate that the specific contribution of their therapy exceeds the predictably high rate of spontaneous remission in the untreated group. In order to exceed the spontaneous remission rate, the therapists need to achieve an extremely high success rate.

Although it seems highly probable that patients with recent onset illnesses do have a higher spontaneous remission rate, it has to be admitted that there are no reports in which a comparison has been made between the spontaneous remission rates of recent onset neuroses versus chronic neuroses. A comparison of this kind is overdue. Moving forward from Eysenck's hypothesis, one can make specific predictions about what will happen when this comparison is made. Samples of patients with a high proportion of recent onset neuroses will have a high spontaneous remission rate; by contrast, samples of patients with chronic neuroses (i.e. those with a duration of, say, 5 years or more) will show a significantly lower rate of spontaneous remission. Without anticipating the full review of the available evidence which will follow shortly, it can be mentioned here that Saenger (1970) carried out a survey on "first admission adult patients" (p. 39), and examined their condition at the end of a 1 year period. The design of his survey comes unintentionally close to meeting the requirements of a direct test of Eysenck's hypothesis (see below). Ideally, the hypothesis should be tested on a sample of some magnitude, should be confined to cases of recent onset, exclude all patients whose diagnosis is not one of neurosis, and rest on the condition of the patient at a 2-year assessment point. Despite the fact that no studies have been conducted specifically with this hypothesis in mind, some of the available work, such as Saenger's, has provided evidence that is relevant while yet falling short of a direct test of the hypothesis.

Eysenck's statement, that the spontaneous remission rate in neurotic samples should be based on cases of recent onset, also has implications for the design of psychotherapeutic outcome investigations. If he is justified, it follows that any therapeutic trial which includes a disproportionately high number of neurotic cases of recent onset will produce a high recovery rate. In order to avoid reaching false conclusions, it is essential to include a control group which has a comparable proportion of recent onset cases. The hypothesis also serves to emphasize the importance of matching control and experimental patients for the *duration* of their neurotic disorders. If the control and experimental groups differ in the duration of the neurotic disorder, it will be extremely difficult to exclude the potentially large influence of spontaneous remission effects on the eventual outcome and interpretation of such a comparison.

The claim that spontaneous remissions of neuroses do not occur at all is a matter for demonstration rather than argument. The evidence reviewed in this chapter, despite its limitations, appears to us to demonstrate beyond doubt that it does occur. In fact there appear to be very few survivors of the view that spontaneous remissions do not occur (e.g. Subotnik, 1972). Denial of the phenomenon leads to one of two untenable positions: (a) all improvements are therapist-induced or (b) there are no improvements of any sort. The related but different question of whether or not "spontaneous remission" is an accurate or a misleading description of the phenomenon is debatable. A satisfactory definition can be agreed upon, but even if such agreement remains elusive, the varying opinions on the subject are capable of being defined in such a way as to prevent confusion. We can begin by dismissing the simple-minded view which objects to the term because inclusion of the adjective *spontaneous* is taken to mean un-caused. It has been pointed out repeatedly that it is not the mere passage of time which is presumed to be responsible for the improvement in neurotic disorders; obviously, it must be events that occur over the time period which are responsible for the improvement (Eysenck and Rachman, 1965, p. 277). The attribution of causal influences is of course difficult, but it is misleading to give the impression that there is no theory which attempts to come to grips with these questions (e.g. Eysenck, 1963a or b, 1979). It should be clear from earlier publications and the present work that the term *spontaneous remission* is used to describe improvements (in neurotic disorders) which occur in the absence of formal psychological treatment. Undergoing a psychiatric examination, even with a possible view to treatment, does not constitute treatment — although it has to be said that there are indications that a full diagnostic consultation may have surprising therapeutic value. Discussing one's problems with a relative, lawyer, priest, or neighbour does not constitute treatment. Events such as promotion, financial windfalls, and successful love affairs may all be therapeutic but are not reasonably regarded as forms of psychological treatment. There is little doubt that such acts and events are potentially therapeutic and may contribute largely to the process of spontaneous remission. The active research into those significant life events which precipitate psychological disorders encourages the hope that greater attention will be turned on to those life events which have a therapeutic value. It is difficult to see how a comprehensive explanation of spontaneous remissions can be achieved unless a great deal of information is collected on the relations between life events and such improvements.

Before our examination of the available evidence is conducted, two other aspects of the problem require clarification. In the first place, collections of therapeutic failures add nothing to our appreciation of the phenomenon of spontaneous remissions. There is nothing in the hypothesis that excludes the occurrence of therapeutic failures; they are irrelevant to the case. The occurrence of such failures has no bearing on spontaneous remission rates, which are of course defined as improvements that take place in the absence of formal treatment.

Collections of therapeutic failures add nothing to the attempts to determine the rate with which spontaneous remissions occur. There is nothing in Eysenck's hypothesis, or variations of it, that excludes therapeutic failures; their occurrence is consistent with the hypothesis. If one adopts a hard line and denies that therapeutic interventions of any kind exert a significant influence on the course of neurotic disorders, then one must expect a therapeutic failure rate that resembles the rate of unremitting neuroses, i.e. 33% of recent onset cases will continue essentially unchanged for at least 2 years, with or without therapy. If, however, we adopt a hopeful view of therapy, then it follows that at the 2-year assessment point the therapeutic failure rate for recent onset cases will be significantly smaller than the spontaneous remission rate of a comparable but untreated group of patients. Either way, whether one adopts a hard or a hopeful line towards the influence of therapy on the course of the disorder, a significant minority of neurotic patients will be found to have made little or no improvement after 2 years.

The occurrence of unremitting neuroses is an essential part of Eysenck's hypothesis. For if we postulate that two-thirds of all neuroses will show marked improvement within 2 years of onset, we are left with a remainder of one-third who will not show improvement over this period. In any reasonably representative sample of neuroses there will be a significant minority of patients whose complaints do not remit spontaneously. Drawing attention to examples of patients whose neurotic disorders have persisted for longer than 2 years is of little value beyond confirming that the spontaneous remission rate is less than 100%. The identification of persisting cases of neurosis in a satisfactorily large and representative sample of patients is, by contrast, of great interest, providing as it does an estimate of the *rate* of spontaneous remission.

The sheer occurrence of therapeutic failure, or of cases of persisting neuroses, is not in dispute. However, the first of these phenomena is irrelevant to the spontaneous remission hypothesis, and the second is relevant only when placed in the context of a representative sample of neurotics. Bergin's (1970) introduction of these two phenomena into the analysis of spontaneous remissions of neurotic disorders was regrettably misleading and led to an unnecessary confusion which was then confounded by Lambert (1976). A significant part of Bergin's argument rests on studies in which therapeutic failures were reported. This is supplemented by descriptions of patients whose suffering had lasted for considerable periods before they were given treatment. The significance of unremitting neuroses (and of the therapeutic failures, if one assumes that the therapeutic intervention was entirely useless) can be assessed only when they are considered as part of a larger sample. We need to know what proportion of a representative sample of neurotic disorders will remit within 2 years of onset — indeed, if the spontaneous remission hypothesis did not allow for a 33% failure rate of chronicity rate, then we would be in the happy Shavian position of being able to advise anyone who develops a neurotic disorder that his problems will be significantly diminished within 2 years if he has the patience to keep away from our professional facilities. In this sense, the subject of this book is about what happens to those people who do seek our professional assistance.

A "REMARKABLE PROVIDENCE" RATE OF 77%

The ambitious comparative evaluation study, carried out by Sloane and his colleagues (1975) on ninety-four patients suffering from moderately severe neuroses and personality disorders, produced some fresh and important information about spontaneous remission rates. Notwithstanding the limitations of this study, which are discussed at length in Chapter 12 below, and the admixture of personality disorders, the information obtained from the waiting-list control patients is of great interest. (The direction of influence of the personality disorders is unknown, but if we use the data from children as a guide (e.g. Robins, 1970) it probably decreased the remission rate.) After undergoing extensive assessment procedures, the patients were randomly assigned either to behaviour therapy or analytic psychotherapy, or to a waiting-list control group. At the end of 4 months, each patient was interviewed once more by his original assessor, and the full assessment battery was repeated. Sloane *et al.* summarized the overall results:

"Ninety-three per cent of the patients treated by behavior therapy were considered improved, while 77% of both psychotherapy and waiting-list patients were either improved or recovered ($p<0.05$). Two patients were felt to have deteriorated overall during the four-month period, one in psychotherapy and one in the waiting-list group. Curiously, two waiting-list patients but no behavior therapy patients were considered completely recovered" (p. 103). These results are shown in Figs. 2 and 3.

Despite the overall results, it should be noted that the patients in the waiting-list group showed a smaller degree of improvement (48%) on the assessor's ratings of target symptoms. Even this figure for 4 months is, however, not inconsistent with Eysenck's estimate of 66% *over 2 years.**

We can do no better than quote the conclusions reached by the authors of this report.

"Thus the treatment was successful. The lack of greater overall differences between the treated and untreated patients appeared due to the impressive 77% improvement of the untreated, in contrast to Bergin's reported median of 30% improvement in untreated control groups. This highlights the necessity of matching treated and untreated patients in any study of psychotherapy.... Ninety-three per cent of behavior therapy patients improved overall. This figure would have seemed not merely significant, but downright miraculous, if it were compared to Bergin's 30% figure, rather than to the 77% improvement this sample actually showed without formal treatment" (p. 103).

In the light of our earlier discussion, the Sloane study falls into the class of a rigorous test, but it is not confined to neurotic disorders.

Some interesting pointers that may facilitate controlled investigations into the nature of remissions, whether spontaneously occurring or therapeutically induced, are to be found in a monograph by Greer and Cawley (1966), who carried out a 4- to 6-year follow-up investigation of 160 neurotic patients who were admitted to the Maudsley Hospital, and many of whom received psychotherapy. The investigation was thorough and extensive, and only certain findings can be mentioned here. One of their conclusions was that, "two of the principal prognostic indicators in neurotic illness are pre-morbid personality and the nature of the illness" (p. 88). These indicators were not always related to each other. In regard to diagnostic groupings they found that patients with depressive, hysterical, or anxiety reactions had the most favourable

---

*In their revised table of results of studies of spontaneous remission, Bergin and Lambert (1978) quote this low figure of 48% as the remission rate of the Sloane study, omitting the *overall rate* of a 77% improvement in the waiting-list group. It is not clear why Bergin and Lambert ignored Sloane's own estimate.

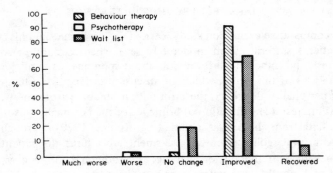

FIG. 2 shows overall adjustment at 4 months of the patients in the study by Sloane *et al.* based on assessor's ratings.

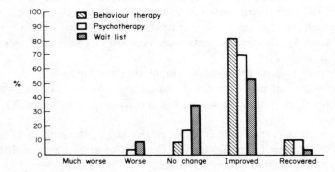

FIG. 3 shows overall improvement at the same point rated by the patients. Considerable improvements are evident in the non-treated controls at 4 months. Reproduced from *Psychotherapy Versus Behavior Therapy*, by Sloane, Staples, Cristol, Yorkston & Whipple. Harvard University Press, 1975.

outcomes, while those with obsessional—compulsive or hypochondriacal symptoms had a poor prognosis. Patients with obsessional problems were found to have the longest duration of symptoms and depressive patients to have the shortest duration. Patients with anxiety and hysterical reactions had illness durations of moderate length. These findings lead to the suggestion that obsessional and hypochondriacal patients may constitute a disproportionately large number of the hard-core patients. Prognosis was related to a number of variables describing pre-morbid personality and precipitating events.

The variables which were found to be "significantly associated with a favourable prognosis include: (a) married civil status; (b) normal pre-morbid personality; (c) satisfactory pre-morbid social adjustment with respect to work record, inter-personal relations and marital relations; (d) evidence of precipitating factors preceding the onset of illness; (e) less than 5 years' duration of symptoms; (f) presence of depressive symptoms and absence of disorders of thought content — in particular hypochondriacal preoccupations; (g) a diagnosis of depressive or hysterical reactions; (h) . . . patient lives in a domestic group the members of which show a sympathetic and tolerant attitude towards him. . . ."

It will not pass unnoticed that item (e), that patients whose disorders had endured for less that 5 years had a better prognosis, is consistent with our extrapolation from Eysenck's hypothesis. Some of the main variables found by Greer and Cawley to be associated with an *unfavourable* prognosis included disturbed pre-morbid personality, unsatisfactory interpersonal relations, unsatisfactory work record, absence of precipitating factors, duration of more than 5 years, disorders of thought content. Equally interesting are some of the variables which appeared, in this study at least, to have no significant relationships to outcome in neurotic disorders. They include: "age, sex, social class, family history, childhood environment, neurotic traits in childhood, intelligence, pre-morbid sexual adjustment, a history of previous psychiatric illness, length of stay in hospital, presence or absence of associated organic disease, material circumstances after discharge from hospital, and occurrence of stressful events since discharge" (p. 88). In light of the psychoanalytic theory of the genesis of neurosis, which traces the roots to early childhood, the negative findings on childhood environment and on neurotic traits in childhood are a touch surprising. Equally discordant is the fact that the patients' pre-morbid sexual adjustment had no relation to the outcome of his or her neurotic disorder.

If they are used with care, the findings reported in this study have value. It must be remembered, however, that the sample is in certain respects atypical. It probably contained a disproportionately large number of severe cases (these are the ones who are likely to be admitted to an in-patient unit), and the Maudsley Hospital is a major teaching institution and in this sense uncharacteristic. Despite these qualifying factors, the findings may well have some generality (e.g. Saenger, 1970).

Although our aim should continue to be the construction of spontaneous remission rates for various diagnostic groups (for reasons given above), it is still too early to make accurate estimations of this kind. However, on the basis of the Greer—Cawley study, the work of Marks (1969), Agras *et al.* (1972), and a fair amount of incidental evidence found in the studies discussed in this chapter, supplemented by clinical observations, it is possible to risk some speculations of a general character. The league table for spontaneous remissions in different disorders may look something like this (in descending order): affective neurotic disorders, anxiety states, hysterical disorders, phobias, obsessional illnesses, sexual disorders, and hypochondriacal disorders. In view of the findings of Agras *et al.*, it may be necessary to distinguish between agoraphobia and other types of phobia. They also reinforce the need to prepare separate rates for remission in adults and in children. Although there is good evidence that many phobias disappear spontaneously during childhood (Agras *et al.*, 1972; Rachman, 1978) it seems that those few circumscribed phobias which persist into adulthood tend to take an unremitting course.

Variables other than diagnostic category should also be taken into account as spontaneous remissions are neither complete nor wholly absent in any of the diagnostic groupings. Some of these contributing factors were referred to in our discussion of the Greer-Cawley study and no doubt they will be given further attention in due course. Even though Greer and Cawley found a clear relationship between long-term duration of the disorder prior to hospital admission and poor prognosis (consistent with Eysenck's hypothesis), we can anticipate some aspects that will be dealt with later in this chapter by saying that the relationship between duration and prognosis can be distorted by the use of certain kinds of treatment. Such distortions are seen clearly in the treatment of circumscribed phobias which, even though they probably have a low spontaneous remission rate among adults, respond well and promptly to desensitization or flooding or modelling procedures.

Global estimates of remission can be supplemented by a number of reports and investigations carried out on smaller samples of untreated patients. Wallace and Whyte (1959) reported on the progress made by "83 psycho-neurotic patients who had been promised psychotherapy and who failed to receive it" because of an absence of sufficient facilities. The patients were followed up 3 to 7 years later and valid information was obtained on forty-nine of them. The overall spontaneous improvement rate was 65.3% and the improvement rate for each diagnostic group was: anxiety states 68%, hysteria 50%, miscellaneous 75%. Wallace and Whyte found that those patients who had recovered tended to have more stable marriages and more satisfactory group relationships than those who failed to recover, a finding that is in keeping with the Greer—Cawley report. They also found evidence to support the idea that spontaneous improvements tend to occur within the first 3 years of the onset of the disorder — in keeping with Eysenck's hypothesis. Although the overall spontaneous remission rate accords well with the gross estimate described earlier, the report is based on too small a population for us to place excessive reliance on its findings. Nevertheless, their demonstration that patients with different diagnoses show different rates of improvement is of interest.

A similar type of study was reported by Saslow and Peters (1956). They followed up eighty-three patients who had been considered suitable for treatment but had not received it. The follow-up inquiries were conducted by post or by interview and took place from 1 to 6 years after notification. Regrettably they provide no indication of a possible relationship between the extent of improvement and the follow-up time which had elapsed. It is, of course, likely that there would be differences in the estimates provided at a year after notification and at 6 years after notification. Despite some flaws in their procedure, Saslow and Peters' study did produce useful information, and their overall spontaneous remission rate figure is lower than usual. They found that 37% of the patients were significantly improved. If we exclude from this overall rate the 16% who were diagnosed as schizophrenic and 4% who had the label "mental deficiency", then the remission figure would certainly be increased. Even so the figures are lower than usual. In addition to the reasons already proposed, it is possible that their findings can be accounted for by the inclusion of a surprisingly high proportion of patients with hysteria — 30%. Most of these patients had a poor outcome, and while this observation is consistent with that reported by Wallace and Whyte whose patients with hysteria also showed a lower spontaneous remission rate than the rest of the sample, it is not consistent with the Greer—Cawley results.

Piper et al. (1977) reported significant improvements in their group of twenty-four neurotic-type patients after a gap of only 3 months during which they were awaiting treatment. The value of these results is considerably diminished by a drug confound, as half of the patients used at least some medication during the period of study.

Schorer et al. (1968) traced 138 patients who had been placed on a waiting list for psycho-therapy, and of these fifty-five (39%) were found to have received no treatment in the follow-up period which averaged 5 years. The spontaneous remission rate for these untreated patients, comprising neurotics and people with personality disorders, was 65% "proved to be definitely improved". The improvements were widespread and included increased social effectiveness as well as significant changes in the presenting complaints. A group of forty-one patients who obtained treatment elsewhere were found to have an improvement rate of 78% which was not significantly more than those who improved without treatment. The authors comment on the similarity of their results to those reported by Wallace and Whyte (1959) but could detect "little predictability about who would improve without treatment and who would not".

Unfortunately the inclusion of personality disorders·detracts from the value of their study for our purposes.

In an exceptionally long-term follow-up averaging 24 years, of 120 neurotics who received little or no specific treatment, Ernst (1959) found that 93 (i.e. 77%) were much improved. In an actuarial study covering twenty-four New York clinics where the main method of treatment is psychotherapy, Saenger (1970) reported a spontaneous remission rate of 55% in 1 year. The sample consisted of 882 cases who entered clinic treatment and 305 who did not enter treatment either in the clinics or elsewhere. As mentioned earlier, this study is of particular interest because it was confined to first-admission adult patients and hence has a more direct bearing on Eysenck's hypothesis than most of the studies reported so far. It also has the advantage of being based on detailed interviews which were carried out in the patients' homes by social workers and clinical psychologists. While the fifty-eight untreated neurotic patients showed a 62% improvement rate at the end of one year, the comparable groups of 298 neurotic patients who did receive treatment showed an improvement rate of only 51%. He also reached the somewhat surprising conclusion that "among those with a good prognosis . . . the untreated tended to improve more often than treated patients" (p. 37), but this quotation refers to the total sample population which included psychotic as well as neurotic patients.

An original and interesting study of patients attending the psychoanalytic Tavistock Clinic was described by Malan et al. (1968). Starting with the view that the case for a high rate of symptomatic remission in neurotic patients is proven, they attempted to discover the psychodynamic changes which occur in untreated patients. Their case material is absorbing but unfortunately the conclusions which they reach tend to be blurred by the mixture of facts and interpretation. The case reports are open to other and simpler explanations which require no psychodynamic assumptions and which would, of course, lead to different conclusions. Nevertheless the bald findings from this novel 2- to 8-year follow-up study of forty-five untreated patients were that 51% were found to be "symptomatically improved", but a minority of these were felt to be "psychodynamically suspect". However, if a similar examination were made of treated cases, there seems little doubt that a proportion of them would also be regarded as suspect. An extension of this work along two lines would appear to be worthwhile. Assessors could be asked to rate the treated and untreated cases in ignorance of the therapeutic actions recommended or instituted. In addition, non-psychoanalytic assessors could carry out blind analyses of the same case material.

Kedward (1969) found that the spontaneous remission rate showed little change in the period between 1-year and 3-year follow-up amongst 346 patients diagnosed by their general practitioner as having a psychiatric illness. These data, which introduced the suggestion that the greatest part of the spontaneous remission rate can be accounted for by changes which occur within the first year of onset, are based on 82% of an original sample of 422 patients, some of whom had only mild illnesses. At the 3-year follow-up assessment, 73% of all new cases "were regarded as free from psychiatric symptoms" (p. 3), a similar proportion to those said to be recovered in one year. In addition to suggesting that the maximum remission occurs within the first year of onset, the study confirms that there is a minority of patients whose illnesses run "a refractory course which continues longer than three years" (p. 3).

In their 5-year follow-up of 100 neurotic patients, Giel et al. (1964) found that 71% of the patients were recovered or much improved. In 90% of these improved cases, the recovery had taken place within 2 years of their first attending an outpatient clinic. This finding is consistent with the Eysenckian hypothesis. Although the rate of recovery observed in this group is consistent with an estimation of a gross spontaneous remission rate of 66%, it cannot be quoted without reservation as a half of the patients had received "at least a modicum of out-patient care and 20 patients were temporarily admitted to hospital". According to the authors, however, the untreated half of their sample did not show a different pattern of outcome to that observed in the treated group. "No difference was found between the outcome of these patients (i.e. the treated ones) and the remainder of the group. Evidence was not available to show that their treatment had shortened their period of disability or relieved their subjective distress. This study therefore confirmed that any new treatment for the neuroses must show better than 70% improvement before it can claim to represent a significant therapeutic advance" (p. 162). They were unable to find evidence of a relationship between outcome and a variety of variables including diagnostic category, degree of disturbance, sudden onset, and so on. However, twenty-two of the twenty-four cases with a history of less than 3 months' illness had a good outcome. In those fifty-eight instances where they were able to date the patient's improvement, it was found to have occurred within the first year of the initial contact in 79% of the sample. Although it appears to support the view that spontaneous remissions occur within 2 years of onset, this study is somewhat unusual in failing to reveal a relationship between outcome and diagnostic category.

In a later study employing similar methods, Giel *et al.* (1978) found that twenty-nine neurotic patients who had been identified during a survey of a Dutch village in 1969 showed a large significant improvement when reassessed 5 years later. According to the authors, "approximately two-thirds were found to have recovered" (p. 235). They found that the persistence of psychiatric problems was related to adverse life experiences, and at the same time obtained information to support the idea that favourable life events exert a "therapeutic" influence on neurotic problems. Although the numbers of patients in each category were too small to permit an analysis of the relationship between diagnostic category and outcome (a pity in view of Giel's earlier findings), it was possible to calculate the improvement rates for different types of symptomatology. Anxiety *symptoms* showed the greatest propensity to diminish, followed by obsessional and depressive symptoms, while schizophrenic and paranoid *symptoms* showed relatively little change. While this pattern is consistent with other information, particularly the lower tendency for psychotic symptoms to remit spontaneously, unfortunately it does little to advance our construction of separate spontaneous remission rates for different types of problem or diagnostic category.

As in his earlier study, Giel paid particular attention to the type and amount of treatment which the recovered patients had received in the 5 years that elapsed between original identification and reassessment. Most of the recovered patients had received some assistance from their general practitioner, but as far as Giel *et al.* were able to ascertain, none of the recovered patients had received formal psychiatric care beyond a few brief visits at long intervals.

Although their attempts to obtain information about the prognostic variables that play a part in spontaneous remissions were unsuccessful, the small study reported by Endicott and Endicott (1963) is of some interest. They carried out a 6-month follow-up of forty untreated psychiatric patients, and although the groups were too small to allow statistical analyses to be carried out, it was found that 52% of the patients with neuroses or psychophysiological reactions improved. On the other hand, a mere 9% of the schizophrenic or "borderline" patients showed similar improvement. The authors drew attention to the main limitations of their study. "From one point of view the most serious deficiency of the study was the brief duration of the waiting period" (p. 581). They add that a second limitation was the small size of the patient sample, particularly when it is borne in mind that the sample had to be divided into improved and unimproved groups. After the second evaluation of these patients had been carried out, those who still wanted treatment were provided with psychotherapy, but "it is of interest that after the passage of six months, only 12 of the 33 remaining non-hospitalized patients still desired psychotherapy" (p. 537). This may well be an indirect indication of the improvements that had taken place spontaneously, thereby reducing the need or the desire for psychotherapeutic help.

On similar lines, Cartwright and Vogel (1960) examined the characteristics of improvers and non-improvers, both before and during treatment. The study is difficult to evaluate as very little information about the patients is provided, other than stating that "30 subjects who applied to the University of Chicago counseling centre for therapy, were asked to participate in a research study" (p. 121). The status of the patients prior to therapy and their changes with and without therapy were assessed on a Q adjustment scale and on the TAT. Unfortunately, eight of the thirty subjects were lost before they had completed the six interviews, and these attrition cases were excluded from the analysis. The remaining twenty-two subjects showed, on the whole, improvements during the pre-therapy period, and these improvements apparently were associated with longer waiting periods. Despite their poorly chosen outcome measures, the results obtained by the authors are worth mentioning. Even in the very short waiting period of 1 to 2 months, five out of the ten subjects obtained positive changes on the TAT. Those twelve subjects who waited from 2 to 6 months before entering therapy showed evidence of even greater change, in that 6 of them reported positive changes on the Q-sort and almost all of them (9 out of 12) showed positive changes on the TAT. An evaluation of the effects of therapy is precluded by the fact that the results on the two measures, the TAT and the Q-sort, conflicted. Incidentally, the claim by Cartwright and Vogel that self-report on the Q-sort "reflected their deep improvement on the conscious level in an improved self-description" is an odd remark. Presumably, advocates of the TAT regard *their findings* as reflecting equally deep improvements.

Jurjevich (1968) preferred to examine the spontaneous remission of particular symptoms rather than work within diagnostic categories. Two groups of fifty and of sixty-two psychiatric out-patients were retested on a symptom check list after about 10 days or after 6 months. "Significant reduction of symptoms occurs after longer intervals (i.e. 6 months) on the raw and weighted full scales of anxiety and psychosomatic complaints and weighted scales of anxiety, immaturity and compulsiveness" (p. 199). Analysing the results in a slightly different way, the author found that 60% of the patients were improved within 6 months. He drew attention to the fact that "about one-third of the subjects do not seem to possess self-restorative mechanisms, tending to remain stable in their maladjustment or even to become worse. This finding gives support to the psychiatric rule of thumb that about two-thirds of patients recover with or without treatment, and one-third remain unchanged in spite of treatment of various types if sufficient time is given for the operation of (spontaneous) homeostatic psychological processes" (p. 196). His analysis shows that of the 40% of patients who were not improved within 6 months, 13% were unimproved and 27% had deteriorated. Detailed analysis of the symptom changes showed that the most changeable symptoms over the 6-month period included cardiac acceleration, bad dreams, twitching, and irritation. Although the overall findings are not inconsistent with the estimate of the gross spontaneous remission rate, the smallness of the sample and the relatively short period of observation place limitations on the generality of these data. Siegel *et al*. (1977) also used a symptom checklist in their study of analytic therapy. The two-thirds of their control sample of eighty-three patients who filled in the checklist after 9 months showed negligible improvements. This unusual result has to be kept in mind but their sole reliance on an unknown, undescribed checklist is a major drawback.

Cremerius (1969) has argued that there is a very small spontaneous remission rate in "organneurotischen Bechwerdn". He selected from a polyclinic of 21,500 patients those who had what can be described as "organ functional syndromes". This initial screening process produced no fewer than 7400 patients, that is one-third of the total sample. An astonishingly high figure of this order, with its implication that every third patient attending the clinic had important neurotic features in his illness, raises serious doubts about the nature of the diagnosis. An examination of the six groups of syndromes described by Cremerius increases these doubts. The groups are: functional stomach syndromes, functional cardiovascular syndromes, functional syndromes of the lower digestive tract, functional respiratory syndrome, functional headache syndrome, functional ailments of a heterogeneous and changing nature (whatever that refers to). In the functional respiratory group, for example, patients with chronic bronchitis are included. It is possible that in evaluating this work one cannot overcome the linguistic problems that arise from translating the German terms into English. In German the terms *Neurosen* and *Psychoneurosen* are distinguished, but in English usage they tend to be regarded as synonymous. For example, Psychrembel (1964) in his clinical dictionary, *Klinisches Worterbuch,* contrasts psychoneuroses which are psychic disorders that include behavioural disturbances and abnormal experiences, with neuroses which are manifested in physical symptoms. It is extremely unlikely that Cremerius's large group of patients would be diagnosed as "neurotic" in a British or American polyclinic or general hospital.

From the 7400 patients with organ neuroses, Cremerius selected 2330 (excluding those whose illnesses had lasted for less than 2 years) and sent them a letter requesting them to reattend the clinic 11 to 30 years after their initial admission. In other words, two-thirds of the sample were excluded and these exclusions ensured that patients with short-lived illnesses were not assessed. (From the point of view of our evaluation of Eysenck's hypothesis, Cremerius unfortunately excluded precisely those patients in whom we are interested – those with an illness onset of less than 2 years.) The remaining one-third of the sample who were studied by Cremerius showed a very poor response. Only 15% (371 cases) reattended as requested. Put in another way, only 1 out of every 200 patients was reassessed. As noted above, patients with short-lived illnesses were specifically excluded – i.e. any patient whose neurotic problems might have remitted spontaneously. In addition, as will be shown presently, a comparable study carried out by Friess and Nelson (1942) indicated that patients who fail to respond to this type of request for reattendance show a disproportionately large number of recoveries. If you no longer suffer from the problem, it seems that you are unlikely to respond to a request to return to the clinic some years later. Moreover, it seems extremely unlikely that patients with distressing illnesses would fail to seek other treatment for as long as 11 to 30 years after a diagnosis has been reached. Indeed, there is evidence in Cremerius's paper indicating that at least some of them were treated during the interim period.

In view of these limitations, and particularly the exclusion of patients whose illnesses lasted for less than 2 years, the Cremerius study adds little to our understanding of the spontaneous remission rate of neurotic disorders. For the record it is worth mentioning that the spontaneous remission rate, such as it was, was extremely low (8%) and the majority of patients either showed a persistence of the original difficulty, or the original organ neurosis had changed to "psychic symptoms" (24%), or to physical syndromes (26%).

One of the few studies in which a minor or insignificant spontaneous remission rate was detected is that described by Subotnik (1976). He collected a sample of fifty-nine respondents by drawing from a general practice those patients who had a score of 30 or more on the Cornell Medical Index. These fifty-nine respondents constituted slightly more than half of the patients in this practice who had scores above his cut-off point; only 46% of the 147 patients returned the follow-up questionnaire (which formed the basis for concluding whether they had improved or not). Three-quarters of the patients were women and the mean age was 51. Subotnik divided the patients into five sub-groups according to the amount of time which had elapsed between the administration of the original Cornell Index and the follow-up. The groups did not differ significantly on any demographic feature, and he found no differences among the five groups, and no differences between the first and second testing. The greatest improvement, although it was slight, appeared in the group with the shortest time interval between the original administration of the CMI and follow-up. Curiously, the group who were reassessed between 1 and 2 years after the initial administration of the test appeared to deteriorate slightly. From these results Subotnik concluded that if spontaneous remission occurs, it takes place entirely during the first year of onset. However, his scepticism goes deeper than this and he argued that the failure to produce evidence of an increasing amount of improvement with time, contradicted Eysenck's original hypothesis. As this result is so out of tune with almost all of the other evidence — and particularly with the prospective study carried out by Sloane *et al.* (1975), in which 77% spontaneous remission rate was recorded, it bears close examination. In the first place, Subotnik was not studying the scores of a neurotic sample; his assumption that scores of more than 30 on the Cornell Medical Index are equivalent to a diagnosis of a neurotic disorder is unfounded (see below). Secondly, more than half of the selected sample failed to respond to the questionnaire, therefore producing a potentially biased estimate of change. Thirdly, the assessment of improvement was based entirely on a postal questionnaire, which is not a satisfactory method for determining the psychiatric status of a group of patients, or as in the present case, patients without diagnosed neurotic conditions.

The most serious shortcoming of this study is that it is based entirely on the scores returned by general practice patients on the Cornell Medical Index. As the main developers of this test were careful to point out, the data from the CMI provide correct diagnoses in not more than 44% of cases (Brodman *et al.*, 1959). It was not intended as a replacement for clinical examinations. Similarly, in their review of the evidence on the validity of the CMI, Abramson *et al.* (1965) showed that it has a 34% error rate in psychiatric samples. Even worse, 41% of non-psychiatric female patients obtained a score of 30 or more on the CMI; following the practice adopted by Subotnik in his study on spontaneous remission, an extraordinarily high proportion of non-psychiatric patients would be mis-classified. Abramson *et al.* found that in a random sample of 449 families, the correlation between the general practitioners' rating of his patients' emotional health and their CMI scores was 0.38.

Doubts about the wisdom of using the CMI as an index of neurotic disturbances are multiplied by the findings reported by the group of workers who developed the instrument. In a study of emotional disturbance among patients in a general hospital, the CMI results indicated the presence of "clinically significant psychological disturbances" in 70% of one sample of patients even though the physicians in charge of these same people failed to diagnose psychiatric disorder in a single case (Brodman *et al.*, 1952b, p. 290). In the same study, physicians in charge of patients in another department made a psychiatric diagnosis in 30% of their cases, whereas the results from the CMI indicated that 73% of the patients had significant disturbances. Obviously, the CMI used in isolation, produces grossly exaggerated frequences of psychological disturbance. As Brodman *et al.* (1972a) point out, the CMI "does not make automatic diagnoses" (p. 123).

How then can we reconcile Subotnik's negative result with the 77% spontaneous remission rate reported by Sloane *et al.*? There seems little doubt which of the two studies is the more reliable. Sloane *et al.* had a properly randomized sample of subjects whom they studied by clinical interview, psychometric assessment, and information provided by an informant who knew the patient well. As opposed to this, Subotnik lost half of his sample who failed to return the questionnaires, based his conclusions about their clinical condition and changes solely on a postal questionnaire, and used a rough and probably misleading medical questionnaire for determining the presence or absence of emotional disorder.

Agras and his colleagues (1972) identified thirty phobics in an epidemiological study carried out in Burlington in 1965. The information was gathered by interview and supplemented by psychometric fear survey questionnaires. When the patients were reassessed after 5 years it was found that the phobias of the adults had shown a 43% improvement rate (with 20% unchanged and 33% worse) while the childrens' phobias showed a 100% improvement rate. Each probable phobic subject was interviewed by at least two psychiatrists who reached their conclusions independently. None of the thirty patients had received psychiatric treatment for their phobic condition during the 5-year period. They concluded from this unusually careful study that "many phobics improve without treatment . . . (and this) confirms the clinical observation that children improve more rapidly than the adult variant" (p. 316). As they point out, their findings disagree with Eysenck's estimate that the adult remission rate is of the order of 66% within 2 years of onset. "Either phobia has a worse prognosis than other neuroses, or the studies examined by Eysenck are inadequate" (p. 317). There is a third, more plausible, explanation. The remission rate is roughly 66% for cases of recent onset (within 2 years of onset), but lower than that figure for cases of remote onset (were these prominent in Agras' group?).

In 1955, Barron and Leary reported the results of a study in which 150 neurotic patients were tested on the MMPI, before and after an interval of time during which some of them received psychotherapy and some of them did not. All of them had applied for psychotherapy at a psychiatric clinic and had been accepted for treatment. However, twenty-three patients had to be placed on a waiting list for 6 months before treatment could be provided. The remaining 127 patients received individual or group psychotherapy without delay. Although it should be said at the outset that the MMPI is not the best instrument for assessing *changes* in neurotic disorders, the results are nevertheless worth a mention. While the waiting-list patients had fewer complaints at the second testing, carried out approximately 7 months after the initial test, most of their scale scores did not change significantly. However, on those MMPI scales which assess the so-called neurotic triad, the improvement in the untreated group averaged 61%, "which is slightly but not significantly less than in the psychotherapy groups" (p. 244). On the neurotic triad the average decrease was, however, slightly *greater* for the untreated patients than for those who had group therapy. In brief the untreated patients showed the same amount of significant improvements as did the treated patients, i.e. a small amount of significant improvement on some of the key symptom scales.

SPONTANEOUS REMISSION RATES IN CHILDHOOD

It is probable that the neurotic disturbances observed among children have a higher spontaneous remission rate than those of adults. Levitt (1963) calculated that the overall improvement rate for children who did not have psychotherapy, even though it had been prescribed, was 72.5%. The comparison group which he used was particularly apt and consisted of "defectors" from treatment, i.e. those children for whom therapy had been recommended but not accepted or not completed. This comparison group provides an interesting estimate of the spontaneous remission rate and was compiled from two reports in which disturbed children who defected from treatment were reassessed one year later in the first study, and 8 to 13 years later in the other study. Levitt provided three independent types of evidence to demonstrate that the defector cases were equally as disturbed as those children who finally received treatment (Levitt, 1957, 1963). In his first study Levitt showed that "the defector cases and those who have had some treatment do not differ on 61 factors, including two clinical estimates of severity of symptoms and 8 other factors relating to symptoms". In his second study the treated and untreated children were compared on a 5-point severity scale by experienced workers. The mean severity rate of the treated group was 2.98 and that of the defector group was 3.02. Although other investigators have identified some differences between treated and defector groups, Levitt's (1963) reservations about the significance of these studies are well taken. In any event, his own findings cannot be ignored.

Independent support for his conclusions has been provided by other workers, and one of the highest spontaneous remission rates ever recorded was described by Clein (1959) in a study carried out at the Maudsley Hospital. Thirty-eight defectors were traced 3 to 5 years after applying for treatment. None of these children had received psychological treatment in the intervening period, but 86.9% of them were found to be improved or much improved at follow-up. However, the composition of this group of non-attenders was slightly atypical. Another very high spontaneous remission rate was reported by Agras et al. (1972) in the study referred to earlier. All of the children with significant phobias showed a spontaneous improvement.

A high spontaneous remission rate was also detected by Shepherd et al. (1966) when they carried out a comparison between a group of fifty children attending child-guidance clinics and a group of non-attenders who were matched by age, sex, and behaviour. "The matched group were taken from a representative 1 in 10 sample of supposedly healthy children attending Local Authority schools in the county of Buckinghamshire. The results indicate that referral to a child guidance clinic is related as much to parental reaction as morbidity and that approximately two-thirds of both groups had improved over a two-year period" (p. 48). They comment that "the transient nature of these reactions is demonstrated by the tendency to spontaneous improvement in the untreated children".

Additional information about spontaneous improvements is provided by MacFarlane et al. (1954) in their survey of behaviour disorders in normal children. They found that the frequency of most disorders declined with increasing age. Further information on the spontaneous remission of children's fears is provided by Holmes (1938). O'Neal and Robins (1958) conducted a long-term follow-up of 150 children who had attended a child-guidance clinic but had not received treatment. These former (untreated) patients did not display more neurotic disturbances in adulthood than did the treated patients. In general, neurotic disturbances of childhood appear to be short-lived (Robins, 1970). However, as some of the data described here do not refer solely to neurotic disturbances, new prospective studies, in which rates are determined separately for various neurotic and conduct disorders, would be welcome.

What can be concluded from all this information? Firstly, there is a good deal of evidence to show that a high proportion of neurotic disorders improve spontaneously. Secondly, it is probable that most of this spontaneous improvement takes place within one year of onset. It follows by implication that the chances of a neurotic disorder remitting spontaneously say five or more years after onset, are considerably diminished. The evidence on the remaining aspects of spontaneous remission is less satisfactory, either because it is of poor quality and/ or because it is indirect. Even so, it is safe to assert that the different types of neurotic disorder remit at differing speeds and to varying degrees, but the information is too scanty to set down firm figures. Our information on prognostic indicators is similarly scanty but it is likely that factors such as pre-morbid personality, occupational skills and satisfactions, etc., do have predicitve significance.

Returning to Eysenck's hypothesis — that roughly two-thirds of neurotic patients will show marked improvement within 2 years of the onset of their illness — the best that one can say at present is that it probably is correct in general, but needs refinement. The terms in which it was originally stated now appear to be too broad; greater specificity will make it more easily testable. In particular, an attempt to specify spontaneous remission rates for different types of neuroses would be a helpful development of the hypothesis. Until the estimates are refined it might be preferable to refer to Eysenck's hypothesis as a gross rate for the spontaneous remission of neuroses, within 2 years of onset.

Objections: Before turning to a consideration of the objections which have been raised in opposition to claims of a substantial spontaneous remission rate, it is worth remarking that the occurrence of spontaneous remissions is a basis for hope rather than despair.

The views on spontaneous remission proposed by Eysenck, and developed over the course of the 16 years by a number of writers, have been challenged. Objections have been raised by behaviour therapists, psychoanalysts, Rogerian therapists, and non-clinical research workers. It has been argued that neuroses do not remit spontaneously or, if they do, it is not a spontaneous process (e.g. Goldstein, 1960; Kiesler, 1966; Rosenzweig, 1954; Subotnik, 1972, 1975). These claims are discounted by the evidence set out above. Another point of view is presented by Bergin (1971) and supported by Lambert (1976), who agree that neuroses can remit spontaneously but argue that Eysenck's estimate is grossly inflated. Bergin (1971) proposed that a spontaneous remission rate of 30% is a much closer approximation to the truth that Eysenck's estimation of a rate of 66%.

More recently, Bergin and Lambert (1978) have suggested that the spontaneous remission rate for patients who receive minimal treatment, or who remain untreated, are 50% and 43% respectively, on average. They stress that *"It can be noted that a two-thirds estimate is not only unrepresentative but is actually a most unrealistic figure for describing the spontaneous remission rate or even rates for minimal treatment outcomes"* (p. 147, original emphasis). In the face of such a large discrepancy it is essential to study the figures and arguments in detail. If in the course of this examination, we appear to have fallen among book-keepers, it is regrettably unavoidable.

Bergin opened his 1971 review with the statement that "there has actually been a substantial amount of evidence lying around for years on this question" (p. 240), and concluded from this rediscovered evidence that "generally, rates are lower than the Landis—Denker figures, thus justifying those critics who have emphasized the inadequacy or irrelevance of these baselines". Bergin compiled a table containing fourteen studies, and provided percentage improvement rates for each. The rates vary from 0 to 56% and "the median rate appears to be in the vicinity of 30%!" Although his figures "have their weaknesses", Bergin nevertheless felt that "they are the best available to date" and rest "upon a much more solid base than the Landis–Denker data". Before commencing the close examination of what Bergin presents as the best available data, two points should be borne in mind. In the first place it seems to be a curious procedure in which one rediscovers data and then calculates a median rate of improvement, while ignoring the data on which the original argument was based. The new data (actually some of them are chronologically older than those of Landis–Denker) should have been considered in conjunction with, or at least in the light of, the existing information. The second point is that although Bergin considered some new evidence, he missed a number of more satisfactory, and indeed more recent, studies which are more pertinent to the question of spontaneous recovery rates. His estimate of a 30% spontaneous recovery rate is based on the fourteen studies which are incorporated in table 8 of his work. It will be noticed that the list omits some of the studies discussed earlier in this chapter, which antedate Bergin's review.

The fourteen studies are listed, with the percentage improvement rates quoted by Bergin. Friess and Nelson (1942), 29%, 35%; Shore and Massimo (1966), 30%; Orgel (1958), 0%; Masterson (1967), 38%; Vorster (1966), 34%; Hastings (1958), 46%; Graham (1960), 37%; O'Connor et al. (1964), 0%; Cappon (1964), 0%; Endicott and Endicott (1963), 52%; Koegler and Brill (1967), 0%; Paul (1966), 18%; Kringlen (1965), 25%.

Bergin gives a spontaneous remission rate of 0% for Cappon (1964), but the first surprise is its title — "Results of psychotherapy". Cappon reports on a population consisting of 201 consecutive private patients "who underwent therapy between 1955 and 1960". Their diagnoses were: psychoneurosis 56%, psychopathic personality 25%, psychosomatic reactions 8%, and others 3%. As 163 had ended their therapy in 1960, "this was the operative sample". Cappon describes his treatment as being "applied Jungian". The results of the treatment were "admittedly modest", and the follow-up was conducted by mail. Unfortunately, only 53% of the patients returned their forms, and the follow-up period varied from 4 to 68 months. In addition, the follow-up sample "was biased in that these patients did twice as well at the end of therapy, as rated by the therapist, as those who did not return the forms". It was also noted that "the operative patient sample (n = 158) was still different (sicker) from a controlled normal sample, at the time of the follow-up. Patients showed more than 4 times the symptoms of normals. This ensured the fact that the sample was indeed composed of patients."

Cappon states that "the intention of this work was not so much to prove that results were actually due to psychotherapy as to show some of the relationships results. Consequently, there was no obsessive preoccupation with 'controls' as the *sine qua non* dictate of science." We seem in the midst of all this to have strayed from the subject of spontaneous remissions. In fact, Cappon did make some brief comments on the subject. He argued that "if worsening rather than improvement were rated, 4 to 15 times as many patients changed (got worse) in the follow-up (control) period combined with the therapeutic (experimental) period, depending on the index used". As the follow-up period averaged some 20 months and the therapeutic period some 6½ months, "this fact alone casts great doubt on Eysenck's data on spontaneous remission which led him to the false conclusion that patients did better without treatment than with treatment". Leaving aside the fact that Cappon unfortunately lost approximately half of his sample between termination of treatment and follow-up, we can perhaps leave uncontested his conclusion that many of the patients got worse after treatment. Cappon's report adds slender support to the belief that some patients get worse after psychotherapy. It tells us nothing at all about spontaneous remission rates, and far from giving a spontaneous remission rate of 0%, Cappon does not provide *any figures* on which to calculate a rate of spontaneous remission.

Bergin's figure of a 0% spontaneous remission rate appears to be drawn from Cappon's introductory description of his patients, in which he says that they "had their presenting or main problem or dysfunction for an *average of 15 years* before the treatment" (original italics). Clearly, one cannot use this single-sentence description in attempting to trace the course of neurotic disorders or to determine their spontaneous remission rate. Nearly half of Cappon's patients apparently had disorders other than neurotic; we are not aware that they had been untreated prior to attending Cappon; we cannot assume that their diagnosis at the beginning of treatment would correspond with their condition in the years prior to treatment; we do not know whether the 201 patients constitute 90% of the relevant population or even 0.00001% of that population. Without labouring the point, this incidental sentence cannot be taken as evidence for or against the occurrence of spontaneous remissions. Bergin's use of the information is unjustified. His introduction of Cappon's report, coming from someone who complains of the "irrelevance" and "inadequacy" of the studies by Landis, Shepherd, and others, is baffling. In any event, the occurrence of therapeutic failures, and of a large minority (33%?) or unremitting neuroses, are consistent with the Eysenckian argument. A special collection of therapeutic failures no more demonstrates a spontaneous remission of 0% than a similar collection of patients who have recovered without treatment (easy to compile) would demonstrate a spontaneous remission rate of 100%. The matter rests on the proportion of neurotic patients who show marked improvements within 2 years of the onset of their disorder — or if one prefers a longer or shorter period of study, then a modified hypothesis can be put forward.

Bergin also gives a 0% spontaneous remission rate for the paper by O'Connor *et al*. (1964). Once again, the title — "The effects of psychotherapy on the course of ulcerative colitis" — is surprising as the subject under discussion is the spontaneous remission rate in neurotic disorders. Ulcerative colitis is defined by O'Connor and his co-authors as "a chronic non-specific disease characterized by inflammation and ulceration of the colon and accompanied by systemic manifestations" (p. 738). According to them, "its course is marked by remissions and exacerbations, its aetiology is considered multifactorial, and it has been variously attributed to infections, genetic, vascular, allergic and psychological phenomena" (p. 738). It will not pass unnoticed that "psychological phenomena" are only one in a list of five types of attribution, nor indeed, that the course of the disease is "marked by remissions". The observation that patients who have ulcerative colitis can show remissions is of interest to gastroenterologists. The study compares the progress made by fifty-seven patients with colitis who received psychotherapy and fifty-seven patients who received no such treatment. The patients in both groups continued to receive medical and even surgical treatment, and those who had psychotherapy are said to have progressed better. In the treated group, "19 patients were diagnosed as schizophrenic, 3 were psychoneurotic, 34 were diagnosed as having personality disorders, and 1 received no diagnosis". In the control group, however, "3 of the patients were diagnosed as schizophrenic, 3 as psychoneurotic, and 14 as having personality disorders. The remaining 37 control patients were not diagnosed because of the lack of overt psychiatric symptoms." As only three of the control group subjects were diagnosed as psychoneurotic, the spontaneous remission rate over the 15-year period would have to be expressed as the number of spontaneous remissions for a group with an n of 3. Bergin's use of the data in this report also raises a methodological point. He quotes the spontaneous remission rate for colitis patients as 0% over 15 years. In fact no percentage rate can be obtained from the report as all the results are given as group means — it is possible, and indeed likely, that numbers of patients experienced remissions even though the *group* mean showed little change. The study leaves us in no position to determine the spontaneous remission rate in three neurotic patients with ulcerative colitis.

Orgel's (1958) report on fifteen *treated* cases of peptic ulcer is quoted as showing a 0% remission rate. Bergin appears to argue that because the patients had suffered from stomach ulcers for 4 to 15 years prior to entering treatment, this indicates a remission rate of 0. Factually, Bergin is incorrect in stating that the peptic ulcers "had persisted from 4 to 15 years without change". Several of the patients had experienced remissions prior to entering psychoanalytic treatment. Furthermore, some of them experienced remissions and recurrences *during* the treatment. Far more serious, however, is Bergin's assumption that these fifteen ulcer cases are representative of the relevant population — it is possible that 1500 cases not seen by the psychoanalyst experienced a different course in their illness. Moreover, the introduction of material on the "natural history" of patients with peptic ulcer into a discussion on spontaneous remissions in neurotic disorders is not justified.

In his table, Bergin quotes a 37% spontaneous improvement rate for a study by Graham (1960). In the text he stated that, "Hastings (1958) found a 46% (spontaneous remission) rate for neurotics and Graham (1960) observed a range from 34 to 40% for sexual problems". What Graham reported in his brief paper was a comparison of the sexual behaviour of sixty-five married men and women before beginning psychoanalytic treatment, with that of 142 married men and women who had been in treatment for from several weeks to 49 months. He found that for most, but not all of the comparisons, the patients in treatment expressed greater satisfaction in and greater frequency of sexual activity than did the patients awaiting treatment. Of course, this tells us nothing about the spontaneous remission of neurotic disorders. It is simply a comparison of the sexual activity of two groups of people at a particular point in time. We are given no details about the patients in either group — not their diagnosis, nor even their ages. We are told that before treatment the men in this sample ($n = 25$) reported a mean level of satisfaction of 2.81, but this figure is nowhere explained. We do not know what the range is, nor are we told how the figure is derived. At very best a study of this type might tell us about the spontaneous remission rate in sexual disorders, but as we do not know what complaint these patients had or how they progressed, this study tells us nothing about the spontaneous remission rate in sexual (or neurotic) disorders.

From a study of the sexual life of potential patients, Bergin turned to a study which reported the fate of ten juvenile delinquents (Shore and Massimo, 1966). As the patients comprising the untreated group of ten were not suffering from neurotic disorders, their inclusion in an estimation of spontaneous remission in neuroses is difficult to justify. Although Bergin's discussion of this report adds nothing to our understanding of remission in neuroses, his handling of the data requires some comment. According to him, three of the ten untreated delinquents remitted spontaneously (actually, on a basis of "known offences", the figure should be four out of ten). A major point, however, is that Bergin used this figure of three out of ten remitting, to obtain a remission rate of 30%. This figure was then included in his table and added to other studies with much larger samples to yield a median rate of remission — surely a dubious way of proceeding. The point is emphasized by referring back to some of the studies which provided the material for a gross spontaneous remission rate. It will be recalled that the studies of Landis, Denker, and Shepherd and Gruenberg with hundreds and even thousands of cases. Readers interested in the "natural history" of delinquency will find superior information on several hundred youngsters in the thorough and extensive investigation carried out by Powers and Witmer (1951), and brought up to date by McCord (1978).

We turn next to the Masterson (1967) study for which Bergin quotes a spontaneous recovery rate of "only 38%". Masterson reports the clinical status of seventy-two patients (from an original group of 101) who received treatment in an out-patient clinic during their adolescence. It is immediately apparent that we are dealing not with an investigation of spontaneous remission but with a follow-up study of the effects of treatment provided during adolescence. We then learn that "during the 5-year follow-up period, 38 patients received out-patient treatment, 11 received in-patient treatment, and 31 received no treatment" (p. 1340). In other words, nearly 60% of the sample received further treatment during the follow-up period — hardly then, a measure of spontaneous remission. The matter is complicated by the fact that Masterson used two methods for evaluating the psychiatric status of the patients. In the first place he used the psychiatrist's "clinical judgement to rate the level of impairment of functioning". Later we read that, "we re-defined impairment not in terms of functioning but in terms of underlying conflict with regard to dependency needs and sexual and aggressive impulses" (p. 1339). The level of impairment observed in seventy-two adolescents at follow-up is summarized by Masterson in a table on page 1340. A simple combination of the patients showing minimal or mild impairment at this stage, yields a total of twenty-seven out of seventy-two — the source apparently of Bergin's conclusion that the sample showed a 38% spontaneous remission rate. It turns out, however, that relatively few of the seventy-two patients had a diagnosis of neurosis. In Masterson's own words, "breaking this down by diagnosis, we note that those with character neurosis did well, all having only minimal or mild impairment functioning, whereas those with schizophrenia and personality disorder did poorly, 75% having moderate or severe impairment of functioning. When the personality disorder group is further subdivided by type we find that 100% of the sociopaths, 63% of those with a passive—aggressive disorder, 75% of the miscellaneous, and 8% of epileptics continued to have severe or moderate impairment of functioning" (p. 1340). If we now exclude the patients with schizophrenia and the psychopaths from our consideration, an interesting sum emerges. The remission rate, with schizophrenics and psychopaths omitted, is exactly 50%, but we hasten to add that this is *not* a spontaneous remission rate as an unspecified number of this remaining group received treatment during the period under consideration and also because some of the diagnostic labels (e.g. "passive—aggressive") are ambiguous. It can thus be seen that Bergin's statement that "Masterson found only 38% spontaneous recovery or adolescent disorders" is misleading.

Kringlen's study is described by Bergin as follows: "Kringlen (1965) followed the course of a sample of neurotics for 13 to 20 years and found that spontaneous changes varied with diagnosis. The overall spontaneous improvement rate was 25%." In fact the rate was neither spontaneous, nor was it 25%. Kringlen carried out a carefully conducted long-term follow-up study of ninety-one obsessional patients who were seen 13 to 20 years after admission to hospital. On admission, "most of the patients got some form of somatic therapy, either ECT or drugs" (p. 714). Of these, 44% were improved on discharge. During the follow-up period "most of the patients received some form of treatment; 32 by drugs, 9 by ECT, 7 psychotherapy, 3 leucotomy, and 7 a mixture of several forms of therapy" (p. 716). Thirty-three of the ninety-one patients received in-patient psychiatric treatment.

The outcome figures for Kringlen's patients, irrespective of type of treatment, were not encouraging. Combining the cured, much improved, and slightly improved groups, we find that only twenty-eight (30%) had changed favourably at the 3-month follow-up period, forty-six (50%) at the 5-year follow-up, and forty-four (48%) at the 10-year follow-up period. We can conclude that slightly under half of these obsessional patients were improved during a course of in-patient treatment and that the figure for the group as a whole increases only slightly after 5 or even 10 years — despite further treatment. A high rate of treatment failures.

Bergin quotes Paul's (1966) experiment as yielding a spontaneous remission rate of 18%. He says that "after 2 years speech-anxious neurotic students spontaneously improved on speech anxiety at the rate of 22% and on more general anxiety at 18%". Bergin is justified in praising the thoroughness of this study, but unfortunately it tells us nothing about the spontaneous remission rate in neuroses and nor indeed, was it designed to do so. It was concerned with the treatment of fear of public speaking. Contrary to Bergin's description, the students were not *neurotic*, but were drawn from a normal undergraduate population of "710 students enrolled in public speaking" (Paul, 1966). Paul states that "students who, prior to contact, had entered treatment elsewhere or dropped the speech course were also excluded" (p. 25). He also points out that in the final screening of the subjects, "those students who have received previous psychological treatment ... were to have been dropped" (p. 25); in the event, however, "no subject needed to be excluded for these reasons". In other words, any student who had received psychological treatment, or was currently receiving such treatment, was automatically excluded. Moreover, each subject was subjected to extensive psychological investigation before and after treatment — no fewer than five types of psychological test were administered. The means obtained by the students on these tests did not fall into a neurotic classification on any of the tests. A comparison between the mean scores obtained by Paul's "no-treatment" control subjects and those reported in an earlier study by Endler (1962) on a group of subjects drawn from the same university (Illinois), shows the essential "normality" of the experimental subjects. The pre-treatment means for the control subjects are given first and are followed by the means recorded for the Illinois University undergraduates in 1962, which are given in parentheses. On the SR Inventory of Anxiousness sub-test entitled "contest", the mean was 33.4 (32.9); the "interview" item mean was 34.1 (31.62 with a standard deviation of 9.9); the "examination" item mean was 38.9 (37.6 and standard deviation of 10.9). On a measure of general anxiety, Cattell's IPAT, the mean was 35.6 with a standard deviation of 11.7 (34.5 and standard deviation of 7.4). For the Pittsburgh scales of extraversion and of emotionality, the normative data were reported by Bendig in 1962 on a sample of 200 students. Paul's subjects obtained a pretreatment mean of 16.3 and Bendig's group had a mean of 17.6. On the emotionality scale, Paul's subjects had a mean of 17.8 with a standard deviation of 6.1 and Bendig's a mean of 14.6 with a standard deviation of 7.

The students used by Paul as experimental subjects cannot justifiably be included in an attempt to determine the spontaneous remission rate of neurotic disorders — any more than the large number of subjects who have been used in the numerous similar studies.

Although the report by Hastings (1958) is not, strictly speaking, a paper on spontaneous remission rates, Bergin's inclusion of it is at least defensible. The spontaneous remission rate of 46% quoted by Bergin, while correct, needs some elaboration in order to be appreciated. Hastings followed up 1638 patients who were consecutive admissions to a psychiatric ward between 1938 and 1944. As the treatment available was limited, he regards the clinical outcome of these patients as a measure of spontaneous remission, and also argues that it is most unlikely that these patients received further treatment during the follow-up period as they resided in a rural community. The follow-ups, which ranged from 6 to 12 years, were almost all conducted by interview (two-thirds of the original sample were interviewed). Among the neurotics, Hastings concluded that "taken as a group (371 cases), the outlook for satisfactory adjustment without specialized therapy appears fairly good" (p. 1065). Of this group, 46% were classified into the "excellent" or "good" outcome groups. However, it is probable that the outcome figures are deflated by the exceedingly poor outcome (25%) observed in the surprisingly large group who were diagnosed as suffering from "hypochondriasis" — no fewer than 95 out of the total of 371 cases. The fourteen anxiety neurotics had a good outcome (65%), the twenty-three obsessionals moderate to poor (44%), and the seventy-three hysterics had a moderate outcome (56%). Although the figures obtained by Hastings do not reflect a true spontaneous remission rate — "minimal treatment rate" would be a better description — the findings are of some interest because of the personal assessments which were carried out and also because of the length of the follow-up period. As far as they go, they reinforce the need for intradiagnostic estimates of remission.

The study by Endicott and Endicott (1963), in which a 52% spontaneous remission rate was obtained over a period of 6 months, is justifiably included in Bergin's table and has been discussed above.

Bergin's use of Vorster's (1966) paper is puzzling. He states that: "Vorster (1966) reported that only 34% of the neurotic sample had improved after more than 3 years." Apart from some asides in the introduction, Vorster does not mention spontaneous remissions. In fact he reports an 80% improvement rate in sixty-five treated neurotic patients, fifty-five of whom received private treatment. The age range of the sample was from 9 to 52 years and he provides meagre follow-up information. Only twenty-four of the sixty-five cases were followed up, for either months or years. The results of the treatment were assessed by the therapist (i.e. Vorster himself). The treatment consisted of psychotherapy which varied from eclectic to "psycho-analysis bordering on the orthodox", narcoanalysis (beneficial in seven out of eight cases), some drugs, "temporary hospitalization", and "behaviour therapy" principles. An evaluation of Vorster's therapeutic claims is not our concern, but we are unable to trace the origin of the 34% spontaneous remission rate quoted by Bergin and willingly admit defeat.

Bergin's use of the report by Friess and Nelson (1942) is uncritical. He quotes two spontaneous remission figures: "Twenty of the no-therapy group of 70 had improved, or 35%." He then concludes that "thus, after 5 years and upon careful examination by skilled clinicians, these cases showed recovery rates less than half the rates reported among Landis and Denker's admittedly inadequate samples". The report by Friess and Nelson is a 5-year follow-up of patients who attended a general medical clinic in the period September 1932 to December 1933. The authors selected from the clinic records 498 patients for whom a *retrospective* diagnosis of psychoneurosis was determined. These 498 patients constituted 14% of the total clinic sample and 269 were traced in the follow-up study — i.e. just over half of the selected sample. Of the 269 patients who were traced, 177 were interviewed, 69 were visited by a social worker, and/or supplied the information by post. The remaining patients were traced but little infor-mation was available as they were either in state psychiatric institutions or had died during the 5-year period.

The diagnoses seem somewhat atypical, and a substantial number of the patients can at most be regarded as suffering from psychosomatic disorders. For example, 111 (41%) had a diagnosis "referred to the gastrointestinal tract. In the order of their frequency the symptoms were abdominal pain, belching or flatulence, nausea, constipation, vomiting, halitosis, sore tongue, anorexia, difficulty in swallowing, and rectal pain" (p. 545). Fifty-seven of the patients had skeletal symptoms, mainly aches and pains in muscles or joints. Of the 269 patients only 7 had "phobias" (from the brief description supplied they were probably obsessional) and 4 of them had tics. As can be seen, this was scarcely a representative sample of neurotic disorders. No matter. The data on the *entire* sample of 269 patients shows that 115 had no psychiatric care whatever. This figure excludes the 15 patients for whom an incorrect diagnosis had been made and the 11 patients who had died during the 5-year period. We find that 50 of these untreated patients (i.e. 44%) were found to be either cured or improved. Sixty-five were found to be unchanged or worse (i.e. 55%). Of the total, 14 were categorized as "worse" and 1 was in a psychiatric hospital. Bergin's figure of 29% is an under-estimation of the spontaneous remission rate, but in this instance it can be explained. Before doing so, however, it is instructive to compare the spontaneous remission figures with the remissions found in the group of patients who had received "much psychiatric care". Of the 36 treated patients, none were cured and 10 got worse (including 4 in state psychiatric hospitals). Only 12 out of 36 showed any improvement. These figures can be compared with those reported for the patients who received no psychiatric care. Of the 116 untreated patients, 23 were cured, 27 were improved, and 15 were worse (including 1 in a state psychiatric hospital). Stated in a slightly different way, none of the *treated* patients were cured but one-fifth of the *untreated* patients were cured. Friess and Nelson sum up: "There was no noteworthy difference between the psychiatrically and non-psychiatrically treated groups" (p. 577). Reading these catalogues of therapeutic failures (including the examples offered by Cappon, Kringlen, and Masterson), sceptics might be forgiven for feeling that the term "remarkable providence" should be reserved for *successfully* treated cases.

Bergin's figure of a 29% spontaneous remission rate is obtained by relying exclusively on the patients who were interviewed at the end of the 5-year period, despite the fact that Friess and Nelson specifically drew attention to the higher remission rate obtained from those patients who did not reattend the clinic when invited. They even mention three of the most prominent reasons given by the patients who declined the invitation. They were: there was no need to return to the clinic as they had improved; it was difficult or inconvenient for them to reattend; they were dissatisfied with the treatment they had received. The essential point is, however, that the people who accepted the clinic invitation to reattend were demonstrably unrepresentative. A significantly larger proportion of the refusers were well. Of the forty-eight untreated patients who refused the invitation to reattend (but were later visited by the social worker and/or supplied information by post), no fewer than thirty were cured or improved. This yields a spontaneous remission index of 62% (ten patients were unchanged, six were worse, and two had been incorrectly diagnosed). If this finding were repeated in the 229 patients who were neither traced nor contacted (and this is a reasonable expectation), then the spontaneous remission rate would approximate the usual figure — despite the fact that it is doubtful whether the sample from this clinic is neurotic. If, however, we were unwise and decided to ignore the demonstrated distortion of the sample, and if we were also to suppress our doubts about the nature of the disorders under consideration, we would settle on the spontaneous remission rate of 44% mentioned above. Fortunately, the shortage of adequate studies is not so desperate that it demands the inclusion of such doubtful information.

The study of Koegler and Brill (1967) does not provide figures on spontaneous remission rate, and is discussed in the section of psychotherapy. In all, Bergin's substitution of a 30% spontaneous remission rate overall, appears to be ill-founded, and it is regrettable that Lambert (1976) reintroduced so many items from this tawdry collection of therapeutic failures, gastro-intestinal illnesses, and juvenile delinquencies.

In a recently published revision of his original contribution, Bergin acknowledges that his arguments and evidence have been subjected to numerous criticisms (Bergin and Lambert,

1978). In an impressive display of indifference, no attempt is made to reply to these criticisms. The discredited data are reprinted, a few more studies are added and then Bergin and Lambert reassert the original argument with increasing conviction.

The few additions to their list suffer from the same defects and do not advance the case. For example, they include Beiser's (1971) report in their table of spontaneous remissions, even though his sample of patients included cases of drug or alcohol abuse, "brain syndrome", and even mental deficiency! In the Bergin/Lambert table these patients are classed under "neurotic/personality disorder". The spontaneous remission rate was low, at one-third, but Bieser suggested that this figure may have been depressed by the inclusion of the severe, non-neurotic cases in his heterogeneous sample. The report by Noyes and Clancy (1976) describes the condition of *neurotic* patients, 3–8 years after diagnosis, and is quoted by Bergin and Lambert as yielding a spontaneous remission rate of 67%. Interestingly, they also reported that the median duration of the neuroses experienced by these fifty-seven patients was 1.5 years. Unfortunately, the original authors provided no information on the *treatment* received by the patients, even though it is strongly suggested that some or many did not go untreated. Also, the "outcome" data do not give evidence of change, as the four assessment measures were used at follow-up but not at initial assessment. In the absence of any pre-tests, it is impossible to estimate the degree of improvement.

For reasons that are not explicit, neither Bergin nor Lambert (separately or jointly) appear to be willing to confine their analyses to the question in hand, i.e. the rate of spontaneous remission in neuroses. They repeatedly introduce irrelevant information – on the effects of treatment, on recovery rates in surgical patients, on remissions in schizophrenia, on the fate of delinquents, and so on. Lambert (1976, p. 116) took this inexplicable process one step further and objected to analyses that are confined to untreated neurotic disorders. Contrary to the drift of his argument, the inclusion of studies should not be dictated by caprice, but rather should be an exercise in applying firm standards of selection. It is, after all, simple – if you wish to determine the rate of remission in neurotic disorders, then study data on neurotic disorders.

CONCLUSION

It is curious and regrettable that we still are not in a position to revise and improve on Eysenck's (1952) original estimate of a spontaneous remission rate of roughly two-thirds, within 2 years of onset. Nevertheless, some valuable progress has been made. We are now in a position to state the desirable goals and how to achieve them. Two broad goals, one narrow and the other wide, can be stated: (i) to determine the spontaneous remission rate, within 2 years of onset, of the main types of neuroses (a narrow aim based on Eysenck's hypothesis) and (ii) to determine the time course of spontaneous remissions among the main types of neuroses (a broad aim that goes well beyond Eysenck's formulation). As the narrow aim has been considered at length, here we need merely justify the second aim. For sundry purposes, the needs of practical counselling of patients and design of outcome studies among them, it is necessary to settle estimates of the likelihood of particular disorders remitting, say, within 6 months of onset, and more importantly, the chances of a 5-year-long neurosis remitting spontaneously. Closely allied to this broad aim, but relevant also to the narrow aim, is the need to gather data on which to formulate a correction for age. Of course there is bound to be a correlation between age and chronicity, but it is probable that over and above this relationship, the age of the person affected may have a direct bearing on the chances of remission.

Above all else, however, the evidence gathered since the original estimate was attempted, emphasizes the need for more refined studies and more accurate statistics. In particular, one can now postulate that the gross spontaneous remission rate is not constant across different types of neurotic disorder. For example, obsessional disorders probably have a lower rate of spontaneous remission than anxiety conditions. Future investigators would be well advised to analyse the spontaneous remission rates of the various neuroses within, rather than across, diagnostic groupings. If we proceed in this manner it will be possible to make more accurate estimates of the likelihood of spontaneous remission occurring in a particular type of disorder and, indeed, for a particular group of patients.

Although the gross spontaneous remission rate has thus far been based on a 2-year period of observation (and this serves well for many purposes), attempts to understand the nature of the process will be facilitated by an extension of the periods of observation. The collection of reliable observations on the *course* of spontaneous remissions will, among other things, greatly assist in making prognoses.

The determination of a reliable rate of spontaneous remission is only the first stage in a process of exploration. Both for its own sake and for practical reasons, we need to approach an understanding of the causes of spontaneous remission. Eysenck (1963) adumbrated a theory to account for remissions and relapses which drew attention to the role of differences in personality, but it remains to be tested. In addition, numerous bits of incidental information pertinent to the subject are contained in clinical reports, follow-up studies, and the like (e.g. Stevenson, 1961). Respondents who have recovered from neurotic disorders often attribute their improvements to the occurrence of fortunate *events*. Some of the more commonly mentioned are financial gains, improvements in occupation, successful marriages and personal relationships, the amelioration of pressing difficulties, and so on (e.g. Friess and Nelson, 1942; Imber *et al.*, 1968). The identification of these restorative events, and study of the manner in which they affect the process of remission, would be of considerable value (see Giel *et al.* 1978).

Unfortunately, the encouragement which can be derived from the occurrence of spontaneous remissions in neuroses must be tempered by recognition of the fact that a sizeable minority of problems do not remit spontaneously. Approximately one-third of all neurotic patients do not improve spontaneously within the time specified earlier, and it could be that in future it is this group of people — those with resistant neuroses — who will absorb the attention of clinicians and research workers. The size of the problem can be estimated from the current rates of rejection, defection, and failure by therapists.

Recognition of the occurrence of spontaneous remissions in neurotic disorders leads us to consider the possibility, and the utility, of determining an index of spontaneous deterioration. Although some types of neurotic behaviour (e.g. specific phobias) are relatively stable, others are unstable, and it follows that the changes which occur can move in a positive or negative direction. Fortunately, the majority of the changes are towards improvement. It seems highly probable that a proportion of the remaining third who do not improve get *worse* over time. At present it is not possible to say much that is useful on this topic, but it is to be hoped that future studies of the course of neurotic-behaviour patterns will also explore the occurrence of deteriorations and the factors which contribute to this process. In time it should be possible to determine the spontaneous remission index *and* the spontaneous deterioration index for various types of neurotic disorder.

CHAPTER 5

THE EFFECTS OF PSYCHOANALYTIC TREATMENT

In the 80-year history of psychoanalytic practice surprisingly little has been learnt about its therapeutic value. Excluding single case-reports, retrospective surveys and non-controlled clinical reports, there are only four studies in which any form of research control was introduced. As will be seen, the conclusions that can be drawn from these few sources are limited or unsatisfactory or both.

This lack of interest in outcome research, so evident in contemporary psychoanalytic publications, can be traced to Freud:

"Friends of analysis have advised us to counter-balance a collection of failures by drawing up a statistical enumeration of our successes. I have not taken up this suggestion either. I brought forward the argument that statistics would be valueless if the units collated were not alike and the cases which had been treated were in fact not equivalent in many respects. Further, the period of time that could be reviewed was short for one to be able to judge of the permanence of the cures; and of many cases it would be impossible to give any account. They were persons who had kept both their illness and their treatment secret, and whose recovery in consequence had similarly to be kept secret. The strongest reason against it, however, lay in the recognition of the fact that in matters of therapy, humanity is in the highest degree irrational, so that there is no prospect of influencing it by reasonable arguments." (*Introductory Lectures on Psychoanalysis*, 1922, pp. 386–387.)

Over a randomly selected period of 5 years, two prominent psychoanalytic journals between them published only one article containing data on therapeutic outcome. Most of the journal articles are speculations about psychological mechanisms and phenomena, controversies about such speculations, and case-reports selected to illustrate and defend the speculations. In addition, there is a trickle of oddities such as papers on Houdini, Watergate, and the Xerox machine.

Writing in the *Psychoanalytic Quarterly* in 1976, Boesky introduced the appearance of "a new symbol" — the Xerox machine. "Because of its copying function it serves as a vehicle for the symbolization of phallic-reproductive functions" (p. 290). After reminding us that in 1915 Freud "described complicated machinery as a phallic symbol", and that Eder "reported the camera and X-ray apparatus as phallic symbols" in 1925, Boesky claims that, "to my knowledge the present paper is the first report of the Xerox machine as a phallic symbol" (p. 290). Presumably he based his argument on functional rather than visual similarity. However, he may have overlooked one important difference: the Xerox cannot carry out its functions unless it is connected to the electric mains supply.

Over the 5-year period from 1972 to 1976 inclusive, 122 papers were published in the *Psychoanalytic Quarterly,* but none of them reported on the effects of analytic treatment. Over the 5-year period from 1972 to 1976 inclusive, the *International Journal of Psychoanalysis* published over 200 papers, but only one of them dealt with therapeutic outcome — using the statistical method introduced by Knight in 1941, Sashin *et al.* (1975) carried out a retrospective study of 183 patients treated at the Boston Psychoanalytic Institute from 1959 to 1966. In the absence of any form of control, or random allocation to treatment, or independent assessments of treatment outcome, this study does not advance our understanding significantly. Overall the results appear to be highly favourable but the authors were unable to identify any predictive variables of therapeutic success. They also presented some figures to support the idea that "those who ended analysis by mutually agreed upon termination showed improvements, while those who had to be prematurely stopped did worse on the whole than the others" (p. 350).

Returning to Freud's six arguments against gathering outcome data, the last three were perhaps not intended to be taken seriously (people will talk, some cases are beyond description, and humanity is irrational regarding therapy). His fourth objection, that the follow-up periods could not be sufficiently lengthy, is a practical matter than can be overcome to a large extent with adequate facilities and staff. The remaining two obstacles are more serious.

Freud argued that the statistics would be "valueless" if the units (of change?) were not alike, and if the cases were heterogeneous. It should not be thought that our translation of these problems into contemporary terms (e.g. outcome criteria, comparability of samples, etc.) means that satisfactory solutions have been found. As much of the present text makes plain, major problems remain and those of assessing the effects of therapy in a valid manner are among the most taxing.

At the outset, it should be acknowledged that acceptance of Freud's pessimism cannot be confined to psychoanalytic treatment. If his resignation was justified, then there is little hope of evaluating *any* form of psychological treatment — or for that matter, *the effects of drugs* on psychological disorders. For those who agree with Freud, it would be more consistent, and more candid, to describe psychoanalysis as a treatment of unproven value (indeed of *unprovable* value), rather than offer it in the form of therapy for many complicated disorders, and even to insist that sometimes it is the only treatment that is suitable (see Grünbaum, 1977, for a critical examination of this claim).

The counter-view implied in this book, and indeed in all studies on the effects of psychological therapy, from dynamic interpretive forms to rational therapy, non-directive therapy, and behaviour therapy, is that adequate units can be employed, and that relatively homogenous samples can be collected. Few writers would care to assert that present methods are entirely satisfactory, and we probably are more critical than most. As argued here, especially in Chapters 1 and 13, outcome measures should be target-related, quantitative, precisely specified, specific, and make as few assumptions about the morbid nature of the target problems as possible. Bearing in mind the available data on the estimates of spontaneous (and treated) remission rates among different types of neurotic disorder, care should be taken to test therapy on matched groups of patients. There is very little argument about this. It is also agreed that for most purposes, the patients in the comparison groups should be matched on type of disorder, severity, duration, age, sex, marital status, presence or absence of related psychological or neurological problems, and so on. The process of selection can be tiresome but it is not, in principle, intellectually taxing. As Grünbaum (1976) pointed out, if patients are as significantly different from each other as Freud implies, then no generalizations about treatment can ever be drawn. If, however, we agree that the effects observed on one patient may tell us something of value that can be applied in the treatment of another patient, we implicitly accept that generalizations can be made. Notwithstanding the acknowledged existence of individual differences, there are sufficient similarities to permit one to generalize from patient to patient. To deny that there is a sufficient basis for judicious generalization is to signal defeat. The nature of and the basis for judicious generalization are of course complex subjects that lie at the heart of the literature on outcome research. The extensity of the literature is itself an affirmation that the effects of psychotherapy can be assessed rationally.

In the course of considering the philosophical basis of psychoanalysis, Grünbaum (1977, 1979) carried out an incisive examination of the nature and status of analytic treatment and presented many fresh comments on this well-worked subject. Although the major thrust of his argument is to oppose Popper's (1963) conclusion that psychoanalytic theory is non-falsifiable, all of his formidable arguments repay careful study. The parts that are most pertinent to the present discussion are Grünbaum's assertions that (i) the effectiveness of psychoanalytic therapy is of importance to theory as a whole — contrary to the common view on this topic — and that (ii) the claims for therapeutic effectiveness are testable.

He argues that the evaluation of psychoanalytic therapy should not be relegated "to the pragmatic limbo of theoretical unimportance" (1977, p. 220), and asserts "that one must reject the suggestion ... that the appraisal of therapeutic success be dismissed as essentially irrelevant to the scientific scrutiny of the corpus of psychoanalytic hypotheses" (p. 220). He argues further that psychoanalytic treatment "is conceived as being *predicated* on the correctness of Freud's developmental and psychodynamic theory" (original emphasis, p. 240), and points out that Freud aimed to impart self-knowledge to his patients. "Unless and until the bold psychoanalytic theory of personality on which this acquisition of self-understanding is predicated does have good epistemic credentials, this avowed objective is pretentious to the point of being a snare and a delusion for the unwary" (pp. 240–241).

Disregarding the philosophical objections, psychoanalysts continue to act as if the psycho-analytic theory itself has, and should have, an existence that is independent of its therapeutic effectiveness — witness the publication patterns referred to earlier. Whether by design or in the face of opposition (probably the latter), there seems to be some evidence of a declining appetite for psychoanalytic treatment. For example, Lazar (1973) attempted to analyse the "drastic reduction in the number of patients applying for treatment at the Columbia University Psychoanalytic Clinic" (1973, p. 579). In 1964 there were 803 applications, in 1967 there were 500, and finally, in 1971, there were only 162 applications.

Two of the major conclusions reached by Eysenck in 1960 were: "When untreated neurotic control groups are compared with experimental groups of neurotic patients treated by means of psychotherapy, both groups recover to approximately the same extent", and "neurotic patients treated by psychoanalytic psychotherapy do not improve more quickly than patients treated by means of eclectic psychotherapy, and may improve less quickly when account is taken of the large proportion of patients breaking off treatment." These controversial con-clusions have not been resolved to the satisfaction of everyone concerned, but there appears to be fairly wide agreement that the case for psychotherapy is a weak one. There is also agreement on the need for controlled studies of the effects of psychotherapy and a recognition that reports of uncontrolled studies are of little value. With the exception of psychoanalytic treatment, and one or two non-analytic reports, this book deals exclusively with studies that have employed controls. The special exemption for psychoanalysis can be justified.

It was felt that psychoanalysis requires a good deal of attention, even in the absence of controlled studies. Most forms of interpretive psychotherapy owe their genesis, directly or indirectly, to psychoanalysis. Secondly, the evaluation of psychoanalytic results presents serious difficulties which are particular to it. Furthermore, even when a measure of agreement has been reached about the status of other forms of psychotherapy, disputes about psychoanalysis continue. For example, Bergin (1971) was critical of many of the Eysenckian arguments and conclusions but found himself in agreement about the effects of psychotherapy, other than psychoanalysis. "It is striking that we should agree so closely on the results of eclectic psychotherapy and differ so sharply on our evaluations of psychoanalysis" (Bergin, 1971, p. 226). For these three reasons it was felt desirable to include a discussion of psychoanalytic treatment despite the many obstacles.

An evaluation of psychoanalysis presents numerous difficulties and one of the most serious of these is how to deal with the bias that operates in the selection of patients, and the related problem of premature terminations of treatment. There is evidence of serious selection bias and an astonishingly high rate of premature terminations, so that even if one were to conclude that psychoanalysis is an extraordinarily effective treatment, it would be necessary to add the qualification that it has a remarkably narrow range of applicability. A second qualification would be that there is a strong risk of patients leaving before treatment is completed. Again, even if one put the best possible face on the effects of psychoanalytic treatment, the very high rate of premature terminations of treatment demonstrates a serious deficiency in the criteria and techniques used by psychoanalysts in selecting patients for treatment.

One of the implications that flows from the estimates of the gross spontaneous remission rate in neurotic disorders is that any form of treatment for these disorders must attain a success rate that is as good as or better than the gross rate. However, it is unlikely that crude comparisons between treated and untreated groups of heterogeneous patients will advance our knowledge and understanding at more than a snail's pace. The more economic and sensible course is to attempt comparisons between treated and untreated groups of neurotic patients with similar types of disorders of comparable severity (and hence, with similar prognoses). The inclusion of untreated control groups is, strictly speaking, a prerequisite for the evaluation of treatment techniques. The undesirability of withholding treatment from sufficiently large numbers of patients to satisfy experimental needs is too obvious to require elaboration. There are, however, several alternatives, such as the use of "own-controls", limited waiting periods, placebo trials, and the rest (see Kazdin and Wilson, 1978; O'Leary and Borkovec, 1978; Gurman and Razin, 1977; Strupp and Bergin, 1969).

In any therapeutic evaluation study there are numerous difficulties that have to be dealt with: diagnostic uncertainties and unreliability, the provision of adequate and pertinent outcome criteria, fixing the duration of treatment, selecting and matching an appropriate pair of patient groups, incorporating blind assessments, and so on. Each of these problems becomes more prominent in attempting to assess the effects of psychoanalysis than is the case with other forms of treatment. Psychoanalytic theory implies its own and quite distinctive diagnostic concepts, criteria of success, definition of the nature of a failure, and perhaps central to all these, the *purpose* of treatment. For example, Grünbaum (1977) quotes the claims of Erich Fromm: "Many patients have experienced a new sense of vitality and capacity for joy, and no other method than psychoanalysis could have produced these changes." Most often, it is claimed that the purpose of psychoanalysis is to improve the person's self-knowledge and/or improve the total functioning of his personality. Unfortunately the claims often are as extravagant as they are nebulous. Nevertheless, it is possible to reach some agreed definitions (e.g. Knight, 1941). Few people would dispute that evaluations of psychoanalysis are difficult to contemplate unless and until agreement is reached on the purpose of the treatment. Are we trying to help the patient overcome his difficulties and reduce his complaints, or are we hoping to change his "character structure"?

Most of the information on the effectiveness of psychoanalysis consists of single case-reports, which we can largely discount in assessing the effectiveness of the method, and series of patients treated by a single analyst or by several analysts at a single clinic, which are inevitably inconclusive. We have, in addition, access to a few studies in which psychoanalysis has been compared with other types of treatment. Although some seemingly extravagant claims are made on behalf of psychoanalysis (e.g. "psychoanalysis has emerged not only as the most effective method known for the study of the human psyche, but as the most effective method known for the treatment of emotional disorders" (Brody, 1962, p. 732), it is significant that the authors of the reports to be dealt with rarely make specific claims for the therapeutic value of psychoanalysis. Indeed, in some instances specific disclaimers are recorded (e.g. Dudek, 1970; Kernberg, 1972; Hamburg, 1967).

KNIGHT'S MOVE AND OTHER SURVEYS

The most suitable starting-point for an examination of the results of psychoanalytic therapy is the commendable survey attempted by Knight in 1941. He set out to remedy the fact that "to the knowledge of the writer there is not a single report in the literature on the therapeutic results of an analyst in private practice or of any such group of analysts" (p. 434). After listing the difficulties involved in his task, Knight proposed five criteria on which to assess the outcome of treatment, and then analysed the "brochure reports" of the Berlin Institute (1920–1930), the London Clinic (1926–1936), the Chicago Institute (1932–1937), the Menninger Clinic (1932–1941), and the work of Kessel and Hyman (1933). He analysed the reports separately and jointly in order to produce a composite picture of the results. A total of 952 cases were listed by diagnosis and therapeutic results, surrounded by the appropriate words of caution about the accuracy of both the diagnosis and outcome. A specific point of importance is that the analyses of results from the Berlin, London, and Chicago clinics include *only those patients who had completed at least six months of analysis*. Moreover, "in order to promote uniformity this same selection was used in the study of Menninger Clinic cases and of course in the composite . . . however, the writer is well aware that the excluded cases, i.e. those treated for less than six months, represent an important group of 'failures' . . . it is emphasized here again that this group deserves special study, statistical analysis, and evaluation of the failure factors" (p. 438).

By its very nature the information compiled by Knight cannot provide an answer to the question of whether or not psychoanalysis is effective. It is retrospectively gathered information, selection biases were operating, the success of therapy was judged by the therapist, no independent assessments were included, there was no provision for controlling the non-specific contributions to outcome, no controls were incorporated, and so on. Nevertheless, the interclinic and interdiagnostic comparisons are of some interest to connoisseurs, and provide a general if blurred picture of analytic practice. Knight's overall conclusion, given in his composite table, is that the percentage cured and the much improved rate for psychoanalytic treatment is 55.9%. Additional information can be obtained by analysing sub-categories separately or in different combinations. For example, one can exclude the psychotic cases (who tended to do worse than the neurotics) and produce a useful increase in the improvement-rate. On the other hand, inclusion of the 292 patients who terminated treatment before completing 6 months of their analysis causes the overall improvement-rate to drop sharply. If we adopt both of these procedures (i.e. exclude the psychotics and include the premature terminators) we arrive at an overall recovery rate of 30%. The interesting aspects of this information should not cloud the main issue. These brochure reports do not demonstrate the effects, positive or negative, of psychoanalytic treatment.

Bergin and others have taken the view that premature terminations of psychoanalytic treatment should be excluded when attempting to evaluate the efficacy of the method. As the majority of patients who break off the treatment appear to do so after having received what would be regarded by any other psychotherapist as a great deal of treatment, we feel that the terminators should be included as failures unless there is demonstrable evidence to the contrary. Moreover, as mentioned earlier, Sashin et al. (1975) produced evidence from the Boston Psychoanalytic Institute showing that the terminators did significantly less well than those patients who completed treatment. Even though it would appear to be obvious that people who are dissatisfied with the progress they are making in treatment are more likely to terminate prematurely than those who perceive some positive changes, one should not place too much weight on the evidence put forward by Sashin and his colleagues. Retrospective and contaminated evidence of this type can be misleading.

Aronson and Weintraub (1969) were unable to confirm that early terminators had a worse outcome. Like Hamburg et al. (1967) they found very high rates of defection, and like Kernberg (1972) they found the same predictors of therapeutic success as those reported in the Menninger report (e.g. high ego-strength predicts good outcome). Furthermore, Aronson and Weintraub (1968) confirmed that patients undergoing classical psychoanalysis are grossly unrepresentative of the population at large (see below).

There is, however, a more serious methodological problem lying beneath the surface. As will be seen presently, some accounts of the effects of psychoanalytical treatment report astonishingly high rates of recovery. For example, Bergin (1971) computed a recovery rate of 91% from his examination of the published reports. It is probable that these figures are an artefact of the psychoanalytic procedure in that the analyst does not regard the patient as having completed the treatment unless and until he/she has recovered. To take an extreme example, if a patient has failed to recover after 7 years of treatment and consequently decides to discontinue attending, then he/she would be regarded as a premature terminator rather than as a failed case. If one adopts the view, as most analysts appear to do, that psychoanalytic treatment is *a complete treatment,* it follows that failures can only occur as a result of an incomplete analysis. It is only by coming to grips with this viewpoint that one can understand why the premature termination rates are so high. It brings to mind Galen's famous observation: "All who drink this remedy recover in a short time except those whom it does not help, who all die and have no relief from any other medicine. Therefore it is obvious that it fails only in incurable cases."*

*See, for example, Brody's (1962) comments on the report of the American Psychoanalytic Association. He says that, "One might draw the conclusion that of the patients who undertook analysis for neurotic reactions and completed treatment, 97% were cured or improved". Then later on the same page (p. 732) he points out that of "the patients who undertook analysis for neurotic reactions but did not complete their treatment, 50% discontinued because they were improved. The other half discontinued treatment because of external reasons." The awkward fact is that we have no agreement on, or even definition of, a psychoanalytic *failure.* Unless we know what constitutes a failure, a comprehensive success rate is unattainable.

It is also worth noting that the average duration of psychoanalytic treatment is 3 to 4 years. As argued above, the spontaneous remission rate in neurotic disorders is roughly 66% within 2 years of onset. Consequently one would expect a group of newly diagnosed patients undergoing psychoanalysis to show an overall recovery rate in excess of 66%. The predicted spontaneous rate should, of course, be adjusted to take into account not only the 3-year duration of treatment, but also the duration of the disorder.

The questionnaire investigation of patients receiving psychoanalytic treatment, carried out by Bieber *et al.* (1962), was procedurally similar to that conducted by the American Psychoanalytic Association (see below) but more successful. Seventy of the 100 members of the Society of Medical Psychoanalysts responded to a request that they complete research questionnaires on homosexual male patients in their care. Each analyst was asked to complete three questionnaires, but if they were treating fewer than three homosexuals they were asked to complete questionnaires on heterosexual male patients instead. These heterosexual patients formed the comparison group. The analysts were given "unrestricted choice" in the selection of comparison patients, few of whom had been in therapy for less than 100 hours. These initial questionnaires were supplemented later, and the sample of therapists was extended. Varying amounts of information were finally obtained on the 106 male homosexual patients and 100 heterosexual male comparison cases. As the authors point out, the samples were by no means random. In addition to the selection carried out by the responding analysts (were the 30% who failed to respond more, or less, successful therapists?), the patient sample was unrepresentative of the general population, indeed as unrepresentative as all of the patients described in psychoanalytic reports and surveys carried out in the United States. The patients were predominantly from higher-than-average socioeconomic classes, highly educated (two-thirds having completed university education), and two-thirds were in professional occupations. Obviously the selection bias and unrepresentative character of the samples preclude any generalizations about homosexual patients, or of their similarities and differences with other types of patients. The authors drew attention to these limitations and mentioned, among other studies, the dissimilar composition and nature of the British sample of homosexuals described by Westwood (1960). The generality of Bieber's findings is further limited by the psychoanalytic bias incorporated in the questionnaires, and then again in the interpretations which were placed on the data collected. Despite all of these shortcomings, some fresh suggestions emerged from their extensive survey.

Of course their comparison group is in no sense a control group and is irrelevant to a consideration of the effects of treatment. Their results cannot be used to prove or to disprove the putative benefits of psychoanalysis, but they are not without interest. Of the 106 homosexuals treated, 27% became exclusively heterosexual, and 15 of the 30 patients who began treatment as bisexuals eventually became heterosexual. Only 19% (14 out of 72) of those who began treatment as exclusively homosexual eventually became heterosexual. Seven per cent of those patients who had fewer than 150 hours of treatment became heterosexual, whereas 47% of those who had 350 or more hours of analysis became heterosexual. The "favourable prognostic indicators" included bisexuality, motivation to become heterosexual, heterosexual genital contact at some time prior to treatment, below 35 years of age.

THE APA SURVEY

In 1952 the American Psychoanalytic Association commendably set up a Central Fact-gathering Committee (Hamburg, 1967) in order to compile what they described as an "experience survey". All members of the Association were sent questionnaires to be completed on up to twenty-five patients per analyst. The Committee received approximately 10,000 completed questionnaires from roughly 800 participants, i.e. approximately 80% of the analysis complied with the first request. The second questionnaire, entitled Final, yielded a far less satisfactory response, and they were able to obtain information on only 3000 patients — as opposed to the original 10,000. The initial questionnaire requested information on the statistics of patients and their presenting symptoms, while the final questionnaire requested information about the outcome of treatment. The loss of information on more than two-thirds of the patients who survived the first round (remembering that 20% of the analysts did not respond to the first questionnaire) is extremely serious. The members of the Committee were understandably puzzled by this sharp fall in the number of participating analysts and point out that their sample was biased because of this lost material, and "any conclusions based on this set of data must be qualified by our doubts about the representativeness of the sample" (p. 847). One need not take too seriously Brody's suggestion that the participating analysts declined to return the majority of the questionnaires on their patients because of "resistance" (Brody, 1962, p. 731). The important fact to bear in mind is that only 300 of the 1000 analysts submitted final reports, i.e. outcomes on at least one neurotic patient whom they had analysed and selected as suitable for reporting to the Committee. The range of patients reported by each therapist was from one patient to twenty-four with the mode being one patient-report and the median about six.

The Committee found that of the 595 neurotic patients who had undertaken analysis (and on whom information had survived the losses at each stage of the survey), only 306 were reported as having being completely analysed. That is to say that slightly over 50% completed the course and the average duration of the analysis was 3 to 4 years. The Committee then sent follow-up questionnaires to the participants who had reported on the 306 completed patients. They received only 210 replies, that is 70%. On these 210 supplementary questionnaires, eighty patients were listed as cured. In thirty-five of these, it was reported that all of the symptoms had been cured and in forty-five patients some residual symptoms were said to remain. In the remaining 130 questionnaires the improvement rates were high and the Committee concluded that "one might draw the conclusion that about 97% of the patients who undertake analysis for neurotic reactions and 'complete' it are 'cured' or 'improved'. Of the 50% who did not complete their psychoanalysis, about half discontinued apparently because they were improved. The other half discontinued because of 'external' reasons, or because they did not improve, or because they were considered to be untreatable, or because they were transferred to other analysts, or required hospitalization." The most frequent reason given for discontinuing, aside from being improved, was "external reasons". It will not pass unnoticed that the findings on patients who had completed analysis are based on only *210 cases out of the original 10,000* who were described in the initial questionnaires.

In the light of the striking improvement rate, some of the other findings of the Committee are a little surprising. For example, 650 of the analysts were asked about their expectations of treatment outcome, given a young person whom they could analyse for 4 years or more, with all conditions favourable. The analysts were asked to estimate the expected results for patients with neuroses, character disorders, and so on. The replies were candid. Forty-five per cent of those analysts who replied "expected no cure in any of the conditions".

Analysing the admittedly unrepresentative data, the Committee found that "96.6% of the patients reported that they felt benefited by their treatment". Similarly, 97.3% of the patients were "judged by their therapist to be improved in total functioning". Once again, "virtually all patients reported to their therapists that they felt benefited by completed treatment". Equally impressive results were reported for the effect of treatment on the "character structure" of the patients. However, one of the findings is sufficient to upset this encouraging portrayal of the results. The "overall incidence of symptom cure is only 27%". Whatever the temptation, the findings do not allow one to draw the provocative conclusion that psychoanalysis is capable of achieving everything except a removal of the patient's symptoms.

As already noted, the sub-group on which the data analysis was carried out is "significantly different from the parent group of 10,000 in the distribution of patients between psycho-analysis and psychotherapy, and in this respect, at the very least, is not a random sample" (p. 854). To this one must add the unknown effects produced by the *literal* loss of a great deal of the data between the inception of the study in 1952 and the appearance of the report some 15 years later. Moreover, an astonishingly large number of patients did not complete treatment. "Of the 2,938 reports examined, 43% were in psychoanalysis, 47% in psychotherapy, and 10% in both at different times. Of those in psychoanalysis, 57% completed treatment and 43% did not. In psychotherapy these figures were 37% (completed) and 63% (who did not); in both, 47% completed and 53% did not complete". The Committee added that "there is no information in the study as to whether termination was initiated by therapist or patient" (p. 584). The salient feature to emerge from all this is that *more patients terminated therapy prematurely than completed it.* The raw figures are as follows: 1589 did not complete and 1393 did complete it. The Committee report contains little information about the patients who terminated their analysis before completion. It would appear from their inadequate figures that slightly under half of the premature terminators were "improved". Regrettably there are no data provided on the effect of an incomplete analysis on character structure, total functioning, or symptoms.

One of the more interesting aspects of this report, and one for which the Committee can be commended, is the information provided on the vital statistics of the patient sample. The Committee points out that the patient sample is highly selected and that they are grossly unrepresentative of the population. For example, 60% of all the patients were *at least* college graduates, compared with 6% in the general population. The income and professional status of the group were well above the United States average. In 94% of cases, treatment was carried out privately. Sixty-one per cent of the patients in analysis attended their therapist four or five times per week. Approximately one-sixth of all the patients had undergone previous analyses. Nearly 7% of the sample were themselves psychiatrists (presumably undergoing a training analysis).

The Committee expressed the view that figures cannot "be used to prove analytic therapy to be effective or ineffective", and apart from providing some interesting peripheral infor-mation, it is to be hoped that the survey might prompt others to carry out scientific inquiries into the effectiveness of psychoanalytic treatment.

SELECTION PROBLEMS

In 1961 Professor Barendregt of Amsterdam University published an interesting follow-up study of three groups of patients. These were drawn from a pool of patients who were tested psychologically when they applied for psychotherapy at the Institute for Psychoanalysis in

Amsterdam, and then retested approximately 2½ years later. Of these patients, the forty-seven in Group A had received psychoanalysis, the seventy-nine patients in Group B had received psychotherapy (not at the Institute), and the seventy-four patients in Group C had no therapeutic assistance during the relevant period. The follow-up study deals with a comparison of the changes that occurred, and it is of central importance to know why patients were assigned to one or other group. It will be seen that this is not a controlled study in the ordinary sense but rather a comparison which, in its important respects, was largely retrospective. The "patients were classified to Group B for various reasons. The decision in favour of psychotherapy for a number of patients was made for practical reasons (mainly financial), when psychoanalysis would actually have been more desirable . . . for some of the patients in Group C psychoanalysis or psychotherapy was advised but impractical. Moreover, patients for whom psychoanalysis had been indicated and were put on a waiting list were included in the control group if by the time of the second psychological examination they were still awaiting treatment." Barendregt considered the possibility that selection bias may have vitiated comparisons between the groups. Unfortunately the criteria of change were not chosen with the care that might have been given, and included two projective tests of doubtful validity. A third reservation derives from the fact that the psychoanalytic treatment was carried out predominantly by inexperienced analysts.

The results of the study failed to yield evidence in favour of the therapeutic usefulness of either psychoanalysis or of psychotherapy. The few positive results dealt with incidental effects, e.g. it is not the patient's sense of well-being or his neuroticism which is affected, but rather his score on the Lie Scale, the meaning of which is difficult to ascertain. The author concluded that "all the same the study is felt to have been useful. For one thing, patients' opinion of feeling better after some time of psychotherapy has proved to be of little meaning in favour of psychotherapy.* For another, the present study has shown two ways which may possibly lead to compelling evidence of the usefulness of psychotherapy. However, such evidence has not been arrived at by this investigation."

In their statistical appraisal of the putative effects of psychoanalytic therapy, Duhrssen and Jorswieck (1969) compared the number of occasions on which three types of patients were admitted to hospital for any complaint in a 5-year pre-treatment period and a 5-year post-treatment period. The sheer number of hospital admissions was obtained from insurance cards, and the nature and cause of the admission was not specified. None the less they compared 125 patients who completed psychoanalysis during 1958 with another 100 patients who were on a psychiatric waiting list and with yet another 100 subjects who were normal. They found that there was no significant difference between the treated and untreated patients before psychoanalysis, but both groups of patients had more admissions to hospital prior to treatment than did the normals. After psychoanalysis the treated group had fewer hospital admissions than the untreated group; the members of this group showed no change in the number of days spent in hospital.

The author's idea of using numbers of hospital admissions as an index of response to treatment is interesting but peripheral. In the absence of direct evidence of the psychological state of the treated and untreated patients, little can be deduced about the effects of psychoanalytic treatment. The study also suffers from other defects such as a failure to explain why the treated patients *were* treated, while the waiting-list controls failed to receive treatment. One

*See also Koegler and Brill (1967, p. 55) for another example of this discrepancy.

wonders why the untreated subjects were expected to, or required to, wait for 5 years before receiving treatment. Unless of course they did receive treatment during the 5-year follow-up period. This point is not made clear in the paper. Certainly one needs to know what type of patients they were and what sort of disorders they had, that enabled them to wait patiently for 5 years while expecting to be given treatment. Evidently they were not suffering from impulsiveness.

Another serious limitation of this study is the absence of psychological information about the patients and the curious but striking absence of any psychological assessment either before or after the treatment period.

Although Klein's (1960) paper is concerned mainly with changes that take place during analytic treatment, some of the information is relevant to the present discussion. She carried out a retrospective analysis of thirty patients who had completed a minimum of 200 analytic sessions, given four to five times weekly. They had all been out of treatment for more than a year and had had an original diagnosis of neurosis. The "arbitrary length of treatment" chosen in this study "automatically rules out those patients whose psychoanalytic treatment at the clinic is discontinued early" (p. 156). Klein admits that "this procedure may appear to favour a trend of excluding treatment failures ... but we were interested primarily in finding a method for studying therapeutic changes" (p. 156). The degree of selection involved in assembling these thirty patients is indicated by the fact that they were chosen from an original group of 288. The characteristics of the thirty patients are comparable to those described by the Fact-finding Committee of the American Psychoanalytic Association (see above). Klein's description of the criteria for selecting patients for psychoanalytic treatment at the clinic (the Columbia University Psychoanalytic Clinic) is of interest. The patient "must possess sufficient motivation to improve his current functioning". The assessing psychoanalyst then attempts to determine the patient's degree of rigidity and ego strength. Both of these have to be favourable before the patient can be considered suitable for treatment. In addition, the patients whose "prognosis is most favourable and who are, therefore, regarded as most suitable for psychoanalytic treatment are those who present structured symptomatology of a relatively short duration" (p. 155).* Furthermore, the selected patients "are expected to be capable of a degree of effective functioning, either currently or in the recent past". Again, "these patients must be capable of significant pleasure response". To complete the list, the patients must "have the ability to form affective relationships with others and a history of having been capable of such relationships with others in the past". It is reassuring to learn that "these basic criteria of psychoanalysability are used flexibly" (p. 155).

The selection of patients for this retrospective study was based on the diagnosis made at the end of the third month of treatment, and at this stage patients with "schizotypal disorders" were excluded, as it is the policy of the clinic not to undertake treatment of these patients by standard psychoanalytic methods. In view of the formidable list of excluding criteria and the intensiveness of the selection procedures, it is surprising to learn that at the time of the follow-up study, seven of the patients who were "originally diagnosed as psychoneurosis, were (now) diagnosed schizotypal disorder by the five interviewers" (p. 170). The remaining twenty-three patients apparently retained the original diagnosis. If one were to take this information on the shift of diagnosis at its face value, a course which we do not recommend, at least two explanations are possible. Either the selection and screening procedures were so faulty as to

---

*Reminiscent of the main factor in predicting spontaneous remissions.

allow seven major errors in thirty cases, or the diagnoses were correct at both stages and the change of diagnosis resulted from the psychoanalytic treatment.

Be that as it may, it was found that 76% of this group of thirty patients rated themselves as considerably improved at the follow-up period. This outcome was consistent with the conclusion reached by the psychoanalytic raters who examined the case-notes of each patient. It is, however, necessary to qualify the favourable impression given by the overall results. The ratings made by the psychoanalytic judges were not blind, and nor were they uncontaminated. The raters were aware that the patients had completed analytic treatment, and they also "had the knowledge of the patients' functioning at all three periods when rating any one period". Secondly, about one-half of the patients had received therapy previously. It is probable that the sample was far from representative, and the absence of a control group is an obvious shortcoming. Finally, it is noted that after the follow-up, "more than one-fourth of the group had returned to treatment with an analyst, usually on a one to two times per week basis" (p. 165).

The serious problem of selection bias is underlined by some incidental information which emerges from the work by Knapp and others (1960), who attempted to setttle criteria for judging the success of analytic treatment. Like Klein and the Fact-gathering Committee, these workers found that analytic patients had a disproportionately large number of highly educated patients. For example, in their sample of 100 cases, no fewer than 64 had received *post-graduate* education. Seventy-two per cent were in professional and academic work, and approximately half of all the cases were "engaged in work related to psychiatry and psychoanalysis" (p. 463). They also found that "interviewers accepted approximately one-third of all applicants". The unrepresentative nature of the patients who receive psychoanalysis, at least in the United States but probably elsewhere as well, is confirmed by the work of Hollingshead and Redlich (1958), Hamburg (1967), and Weber, Elinson, and Moss (1967), among others.

The marked bias operating in the selection of patients chosen for psychoanalysis would make any attempts at generalization about the effectiveness of the treatment exceedingly risky. As mentioned earlier, the very high rejection rate is compounded by the unacceptably large number of patients (roughly one-half) who terminate treatment prematurely. Rightly or wrongly, psychoanalysts appear to believe that their method is suitable for only a tiny fraction of the cases of psychological disorder. Moreover, in considerations of social utility one has to bear in mind that psychoanalysis is extremely time-consuming. Given that the average course of analytic treatment lasts 3 to 4 years,* and that an analyst using classical analysis is unlikely to carry more than eight patients at any time, it can be estimated that a practising psychoanalyst will complete treatment on roughly two or three patients *per year*. Carrying these calculations a little further, we find that a psychiatric clinic or hospital which aims to complete treatment on 1000 cases each year would require in the region of 300–500 full-time psychoanalysts. With this perspective in mind, it seems reasonable that if psychoanalytic treatment is to be offered, then we have grounds for expecting it to do more than provide relief for a highly selected, tiny group of people. For example, it could be argued that the treatment process helps to increase our understanding of psychological processes or mechanisms. The point remains that if it is judged on grounds of social utility, psychoanalytic treatment has little justification. Naturally, its scientific value needs to be judged by other criteria (e.g. Eysenck, 1963 a or b; Eysenck and Wilson, 1973; Grünbaum, 1977, 1979; Rachman, 1963 Wolpe and Rachman, 1960). The scientific, medical and social aspirations were severely dealt with in the examination conducted by a doyen of British psychiatry (Slater, 1970).

*United States Committee's figures. At the London Psychoanalytic Clinic, the average duration of treatment is given as 41 months (report of the British Psychoanalytic Society, 1967).

TABLE 1

The Effects of Different Types of Therapy (Eysenck's 1969 account of
the Cremerius study of 1962)

Therapy	Position at end of treatment			Position at follow-up		
	Abolition of symptom (%)	Symptom improve- ment (%)	Treatment terminated (%)	Abolition of symptom (%)	Symptom improve- ment (%)	Symptom substitution or worsening (%)
Analytic psycho- therapy	41	29	30	21	31	18
Verbal discussion	48	33	19	12	13	37
Hypnosis	54	31	15	7	10	47
Autogenic training	38	32	30	12	17	28
Combined methods	32	26	42	7	14	39
Total	47	31	22	11	14	37

The comparative study reported by Cremerius (1962) is defective in the same respect as the Barendregt study because the selection of patients for analytic treatment was not random. In both studies there was a careful selection of patients; those thought most likely to benefit from analysis were given prime choice and constituted a small minority of the total patient pool. As we have seen, patients who are selected for psychoanalysis are unrepresentative and comprise a disproportionately large number of highly educated and persistent middle-class people. The Cremerius report deals with the fate of 605 neurotic outpatients who were treated by some form of psychotherapy during the period from 1948 to 1951. A further 175 patients were excluded because they were not considered to be suitable for psychotherapy, either because they refused treatment, were of an inappropriate age, or were suspected of having a psychotic disorder, etc. The majority of patients were between 30 and 50 years of age, and the sexes were equally distributed. About one-third of the patients expressed a desire for psychotherapy and about one-half had no idea of the nature of psychotherapy and had no desire for such treatment. Their ideas and views played a considerable part in the selection of therapy. Nine per cent (56 cases) were treated by psychoanalytic therapy, 160 cases (27%) by verbal discussion and psychotherapy, 194 (32%) received hypnotic treatment, 40 cases (7%) had narcohypnotic treatment, 105 (17%) received autogenic training, and 50 cases (8%) received a combination of treatments. A majority of the patients who were psychoanalysed had psycho-somatic symptoms, whereas very few of those who received hypnosis or narcohypnosis had such a diagnosis. The treatment allocation correlated highly with social class, in the expected direction.

The figures for the outcome of therapy in 573 cases are shown in Table 1. The criteria for outcome of treatment were the same for all groups but it will be noticed that the outcome categories exclude patients who were unchanged or worse at the end of treatment. For the total sample the overall improvement rate was 78%. The figures at termination of treatment

TABLE 2

The Effects of Therapy on Different Diagnostic Groups (Eysenck's
account of the Cremerius study of 1962)

	Condition at follow-up				
	Symptom abolition (%)	Symptom improvement (%)	Symptom unchanged (%)	Symptom worse (%)	Symptom substitution (%)
Hysteria	9	11	24	3	53
Anxiety state	9	12	31	3	45
Obsessive–compulsive	5	10	67	9	9
Hypochondria	6	13	52	21	8
Neurasthenia	8	16	29	5	42
Neurotic depression	12	15	19	14	40

are most favourable for hypnosis and least favourable for the combined treatment methods. Psychoanalysis was inferior to hypnosis and superior to the combined method. The success rate was roughly comparable to the rate for autogenic training. The proportion of patients who abandoned therapy (presumably this figure includes unchanged or deteriorated cases as well) was largest for psychoanalysis and autogenic training. This failure (?) rate occurred in spite of the rigorous selection which isolated those patients deemed most likely to succeed with psycho-analytic treatment. Within diagnostic categories, hysteria and anxiety neuroses showed the best results with the remarkable figures of 97% and 94% of "cures and improvements". Depression, hypochondria, and obsessional disorders responded rather less well and there were fewer instances in which the symptoms disappeared. However, 92% of all patients were at work at the end of treatment, compared with only 63% prior to treatment.

The follow-ups were carried out between 8 and 10 years after termination of treatment and the excellent figure of 86% were traced. These figures are shown in Table 1 but the cases in which the symptom remained unchanged (38%) have been omitted. The most notable feature of the follow-up figures is the sharp reduction in the overall percentage of improvement, which fell from 78% to a mere 25%. The most striking change is the large deterioration in the group of patients who received hypnotic treatment. The patients who received psychoanalysis showed a much smaller deterioration rate and at follow-up, the difference between these two types of treatment was statistically significant. In addition to this difference between treatment types, the figures also suggest some differences in outcome according to *diagnostic* category. These figures are shown in Table 2. They indicate a marked degree of so-called symptom substitution, which is particularly noticeable in hysterics but appears also in anxiety conditions and depression. The hypochondriacal group shows a large number of patients who got worse, and among the obsessionals an extremely high percentage of patients whose symptoms remained unaltered. Two-thirds of the patients with obsessional disorders showed little variation in their condition over the 8- to 10-year period.

As mentioned earlier, the most striking feature of these figures is the exceedingly poor recovery rate over the long-term, averaging only 25% compared with the figure of 78% improved at the termination of therapy. The suggestion that patients who had psychoanalytic therapy did slightly better over the longer terms, despite the absence of any superiority at the time of treatment termination, is interesting and might be worth investigating in a control study where the selection of patients is randomized. The psychoanalysed patients received far more treatment than patients in the other groups — in the region of 300 hours of treatment as opposed to the 12 hours or less received by patients in some of the other groups. Another point worth noticing is that the alternative treatments, hypnotic methods and autogenic training, are less commonly used in Britain or the United States. A comparison with types of treatment used more frequently in these two countries would be of interest.

STUDIES AND SERIES

Ellis (1957) reported a comparative study in which he compared the efficacy of orthodox psychoanalysis with an analytic type of psychotherapy and what he then described as "rational psychotherapy". A group of 16 patients received orthodox psychoanalysis over an average of 93 sessions. Two other groups of patients, matched as to diagnosis, age, sex and education, were constituted. Each consisted of 78 patients, and the first group received rational therapy over an average of 26 sessions. The remaining group of 78 patients received psychoanalytic-oriented therapy over an average of 35 sessions.

Ellis (1957) found that the "therapeutic results appear to be best for patients treated with rational analysis and poorest for those treated with orthodox (psycho) analysis . . . significantly more clients treated with rational analysis showed considerable improvement and significantly fewer showed little or no improvement than clients treated with the other two techniques". The proportions of cases showing distinct or considerable improvement were 90% for rational therapy, 63% for psychotherapy, and 50% orthodox psychoanalysis. Orthodox psychoanalysis continued for three times as many sessions as rational psychotherapy.

These results are uninterpretable in view of such methodological shortcomings as the fact that Ellis administered all treatments and then conducted the assessment of outcome himself. Differences among the treatments are open to alternative interpretations because of the potential sources of bias and contaminating influences. The interesting fate of Ellis's form of rational psychotherapy, which had a lengthy gestation, is taken up in Chapter 11.

Orgel's (1958) report on the successful psychoanalytic treatment of ten out of twelve patients with peptic ulcers is regarded by some writers as one of the major successes of psychoanalysis. Of those twelve patients who had more than seventy analytic sessions, ten were said to have made a complete recovey — "I believe these 10 peptic ulcer patients to be cured" (Orgel, p. 122). If this claim were confirmed by independent research it would indeed be a cause for celebration. However, the validity of the claim is uncertain because of the absence of independent verification of the analyst's claims. He is the sole reporter of the outcome of treatment; there were no independent assessments, no information on the physical status of the cured patients, and no comparisons with a matched group of ulcer patients of comparable severity. As Orgel acknowledges, "My study is not a large one and I have no controls since all these patients were treated privately" (p. 123). Even though 20 years have passed without any attempt at independent replication having been reported, it is not too late to seek confirmation of Orgel's ambitious claims.

Weinstock (1961) reported the effects of psychoanalytic psychotherapy on forty selected cases of ulcerative colitis seen at the Mount Sinai Hospital. Although 70 cases were treated during the 12-year period under consideration, follow-up data were available on only 40, and the conclusions drawn from this investigation are based on 57% of the total sample. Of these 40 patients, the "discharge note in 26 indicated improvement", while in 14 "the final note" indicated no change or unimproved. Unfortunately their status at follow-up was distinctly worse. Weinstock states that, "of 40 cases only 4 were completely or nearly free of symptoms . . . an analysis of these 4 nearly or completely well cases" showed that 3 were rather mild and the fourth case was not definitely diagnosed as having colitis. This dispiriting result was summed up by the author: "In the severe form of chronic recurrent ulcerative colitis requiring hospitalization, intensive short-time psychotherapy failed to prevent further recurrences in the group followed-up, which finally reached the same percentage of (surgical operations) as a comparable group without psychotherapy, i.e. 50%. There is no evidence that the course of the colitis in the remaining cases was favourably altered by psychotherapy" (p. 512).

There are grounds for concluding that this pessimistic outcome is not necessarily the final word on the subject. The patients had illnesses that were sufficiently severe to warrant admission to hospital, the psychoanalytic therapy provided by residents in their first few years of training, and only 50 hours of therapy were provided, on average.

A favourable outcome was claimed by Schjelderup (1955) who attempted to follow-up as many of his chronic neurotic patients as possible. He managed to obtain information on twenty-eight patients whom he had analysed over a 17-year period. Patients who responded to the initial postal inquiry were asked to complete a questionnaire describing their condition before analysis (sometimes as long as 10 or 15 years earlier), on termination of treatment, and in the subsequent period. On most of the measures, the claimed success rate was extremely high, usually well above 70%. Unfortunately, few conclusions can be drawn from solo efforts of this kind, in which a single therapist with a vested interest in the success of his efforts, is the judge of the outcome of therapy. Fisher and Greenberg (1977), whose favourable attitude to Freud's theory and therapy is undisguised, remarked that studies of this sort are "questionable as tests of the efficacy of psychoanalysis, since they are each based on the cases of one therapist . . . the results obtained in these investigations could be as easily attributed to specific therapist characteristics . . . there is no way of determining the comparability of the treatments . . . or of knowing how control groups of non-treated patients will have progressed in the same time period" (p. 321).

MALAN'S CONTRIBUTION

The integrity of Malan's (1963, 1976a, 1976b) work and his exceptional readiness to ask hard and even painful questions have earned special attention. An authoritative, practising psychoanalyst, Malan is one of the few writers willing to grasp the nettle of evaluating the effects of psychoanalytic therapy. Not many practising psychotherapists would be willing to concede that outcome studies "have almost entirely failed to provide evidence favourable to psychotherapy" (Malan, 1963, p. 151). He is also one of the few writers to devote thoughtful consideration to the consequences for analytic theory of recognizing the occurrence of spontaneous remissions. A firm advocate of high scientific standards, he has carried out, in association with various colleagues, two investigations into the efficacy of psychoanalytic psychotherapy.

In 1963 he published a report on the effects of brief psychotherapy conducted with twenty-one patients. The second study was intended as a replication of the first, "with longer follow-up and more rigorous scientific safeguards" (Malan, 1976a, p. 7). Following Malan's style of reporting, the results obtained in the first study are referred to as the First Series and the results obtained in the second study are referred to as the Second Series.

In the First Series he challenged the view that the value of brief psychotherapy is limited to mild cases of recent onset. A detailed examination was made of the twenty-one patients, all of whom had been treated for a relatively short period by experienced analysts. For each patient a plausible set of psychodynamic criteria of outcome was built up. Malan took the interesting step of basing his psychodynamic hypotheses on the manifest evidence of disturbances in social relationships, and assumed that each symptom was an expression of a compromise between id and superego forces. The success or failure of the therapy was classified according to the success with which this conflict was resolved. If a substantial improvement in social relationships took place, without symptom improvement or with a limited improvement in both social relations and symptoms, the outcome was classified as a partial resolution of the conflict. If, however, the symptom was diminished at the cost of the patient withdrawing from social relationships, the outcome was registered as a false resolution. Malan elaborated these themes and provided detailed clinical material to illustrate their operation.

Leaving aside for the moment the validity of his method of assessing the outcome of psychodynamic therapy, it must be said that the effects of the treatment were discouraging. Out of the eighteen patients on whom a conclusion was reached, no less than ten of them scored zero, which indicates no change of significance. Only five of the twenty-one patients obtained a score of 3, which indicates a substantial resolution of the main problem.

Although it can be argued that this first study cleared the ground for a more determined second attack on the problems, it made no substantive contribution to the debate about whether or not analytic psychotherapy produces beneficial effects. The deficiencies of the study preclude any such conclusion about the effectiveness of the therapy. No controlled comparisons were carried out. Secondly, the assessments of outcome were made retrospectively. Thirdly, they were based on interpretations of the written case material and were not subject to external validation. Fourthly, all of the ratings were carried out by Malan himself rather than an independent assessor who, ideally, should have been blind to the nature of the treatment being evaluated. This methodological shortcoming is especially important because of the subjective nature of the treatment outcome ratings. Qualitative, subjective measures of psychological change are particularly susceptible to distortion caused by the assessor's bias, albeit unintentional. Furthermore, some of the patients on whom the effects of the therapy were assessed had been treated by Malan himself. Then there is the weakness of the outcome summary. After going to considerable lengths to provide a sophisticated, new perspective on criteria of outcome, Malan rested his conclusion for each patient on a single-digit score. Finally, as Malan pointed out, "this series of patients still form a *very highly selected population*" (Malan, 1963, p. 179, original emphasis).

His bold attempt to resolve the difficulty of bringing psychoanalysis treatment under scrutiny revived a thorny problem. Malan's strategy operates entirely within the confines of psychoanalytic theory, and the problem is this: can one construct an outcome strategy that does *not* require a prior commitment to the theory? Or to put the problem more positively, is it possible to develop means of assessing the effectiveness of psychoanalytic therapy that are independent of the theory? The absence of such an independent judgement, one that is not embedded in acceptance of psychoanalytic theory, seriously weakens any attempt at evaluation.

In the Second Series, Malan tried to improve and extend the methods and findings of the first study. An attempt was made to relate the patient's condition at outcome to a set of psychodynamic hypotheses that were arrived at after the first therapeutic sessions. These hypotheses were agreed by two raters working on the original interview material, supplemented by the results of a projective test and the outcome of the first session of therapy. The hypotheses were intended to serve several important, related functions. In each case the raters tried to define the kinds of stress to which the patient was vulnerable, the main criterion of recovery, "which must obviously consist of his ability to overcome his central difficulty, or to face his specific stress and to cope with it in a new way without developing symptoms" (p. 14). The third function served by the hypothesis construction was to define whether or not the patients were avoiding their difficulties instead of overcoming them. These hypotheses were then transformed into criteria of improvement which were tailored to suit each patient.

There can be no denying that this was a worthy and ambitious plan, and one that must have demanded a great deal from the raters who were obliged to assimilate the information, impose a structure on it, formulate it into a set of related hypotheses, and then translate it into improvement criteria. Moreover, the two raters had to reach agreement. The complexities of the task and the difficulties encountered are well described by Malan.

However, the next step comes as a disappointment. After devoting so much careful thought to the strategy, and going to such trouble to collect and evaluate all this information, the hypotheses and the extent to which the criteria of improvement were achieved, were reduced to a single number on an 8-point rating scale, which ranged from zero to 4.

The entire undertaking, involving a great deal of effort and thought, is reduced to a single, crude measure of outcome in which zero to 0.5 indicates that the patient was essentially unchanged, 0.625 to 1.87 indicates that he was slightly to moderately improved, 2.0 to 2.75 indicates that he was improved, and so on up to 4.0 which denotes full recovery. Even if all other aspects of this outcome study were flawless, the condensation of large amounts of subtle clinical information into a single digit would be a serious if not fatal weakness. Aside from other considerations, it is a great pity that Malan and his co-workers did not give themselves the opportunity to uncover any of the potentially significant relationships between patients, treatment, and outcome variables.

Can the effects of psychotherapy sessions, which ranged in number from 3 to as many as 400, be encapsulated in a single point on an 8-point scale? How can the work of psychotherapy, which sometimes extended over more than 2 years, be summarized in this manner? It should be remembered that the raters were required to estimate the extent to which the following treatment goals were achieved: the patient's ability to overcome his central difficulty, to face specific stresses and to overcome them, to decrease his vulnerability, and to face and overcome rather than avoid difficulties or stresses. The answer to this set of complex questions cannot be condensed into a single-digit outcome.

Turning to another aspect of the study, it has often been observed that blind assessors tend to be more conservative in judging therapeutic improvements than assessors who are informed of the nature and purpose of the treatment administered. Malan argues that the contaminated raters in his study did not differ in their judgements from those of the blind raters (who were in any event not properly blind). An examination of the results presented in the text shows, however, that the two raters in Team 1 scored more favourable outcomes in 9 out of 13 cases, whereas the "blind" raters gave more favourable scores on only 3 occasions out of 13. Despite all this, and the fact that the patients were carefully chosen for this study rather than being randomly selected, the overall success rate was again discouraging. Using the admittedly unsatisfactorily outcome figures arrived at by the two teams, 11 out of the 30 patients would have to be classified as failures. Only 5 out of 30 patients had a score of more than 3 (out of a possible 4). Of these 5 successes, 2 were regarded by Malan as having occurred spontaneously.

As mentioned above, two raters in Team 1 were not blind; Malan correctly refers to them as the "contaminated team". It has to be added that all four raters were either trained or trainee psychoanalysts and they all knew that the patients whom they were assessing had received psychodynamic treatment.

There is also the surprising fact that the ratings of outcome were made not at the termination of treatment, but at follow-up. Generally these follow-ups were carried out some years after the termination of treatment, and in some instances as long as 7 years elapsed before they were completed. Hence the outcome data refer *not* to the immediate effects of treatment, but rather to a combination of these effects plus the effects of life events experienced by the person for some years afterwards. As is evident from the detailed case material, much of it rich in interest, a number of patients experienced significant changes during the follow-up period, ranging from marked improvements to marked deterioration. The omission of information about the patient's condition at the termination of treatment detracts from the value of the findings. It makes it impossible to draw conclusions about the specific contribution of the therapy.

This objection can be illustrated by reference to Malan's First Series of patients. Here nine of the seventeen scores arrived at when treatment was terminated were subsequently found to require change when the patients were seen again at follow-up. To quote Malan (1976, p. 149): "Of the 18 patients used in the original correlation studies, further follow-up has been obtained on all but one, and it has been necessary to change the score for outcome in 9.."

Given the understandable importance which Malan attaches to the temporal relations between treatment and outcome, it is puzzling that he should report the status of the patients only some years after termination of treatment, rather than at the completion of the treatment. He writes that "there is a very important type of clinical evidence about the validity of psychotherapy . . . and which needs to be examined in the present Series. This comes from the coincidence in time between improvement in disturbances of long duration on the one hand, and therapy of brief duration on the other . . . since the argument that spontaneous remission just happened to occur at this point begins to look more implausible" (p. 143).

The argument is persuasive. Hence, his reliance, in the Second Series, on outcome data collected years after the termination of treatment, is disappointing.

On the statistical side, Malan reports that he carried out hundreds of correlational computations. A very small proportion of results reported in the book (1976a) were significant and it is probable that this proportion does not approach the number of significant correlations that would be expected to occur on a random basis. To his credit, Malan discussed this problem but might perhaps have attached greater importance to it than he appears to have done.

In his concluding chapters, Malan claims that his second study cross-validates the findings of Series 1, but the claim cannot be sustained. In the first place, the first Series is of limited value because of the serious shortcomings and weaknesses referred to earlier. Even if one had the desire to replicate a deficient study, the problems involved can be insuperable. In so far as Series 1 and 2 are similar, and there appear to be more differences than similarities, it is possible that they reflect the occurrence of repeated errors. One possibility is that the estimates of success were exaggerated by the use of contaminated ratings — provided by committed assessors who in some cases were the actual therapists involved in the treatment. Furthermore, the form and duration of treatment in the two Series differed (brief versus unlimited time therapy). More important than this objection, however, is the fact that the scoring system was changed. "I had to change the method of scoring (between the two Studies) instead of counting longer therapy as failures of brief psychotherapy scoring zero, I had either to omit them or take the score for the final improvement, whatever the length of therapy" (p. 241).

Much of Malan's argument in favour of his claim for validating psychoanalytic therapy as a whole rests on the significant correlation between therapeutic outcome and the occurrence of interpretations linking transference with parent or sibling (p. 233). However, this was the only one of the fifteen indices tested that showed a significant positive correlation. Indeed, some of the indices produced negative correlations (e.g. for some inexplicable reason, undirected interpretations were negatively but not significantly, correlated with outcome). In pursuing his argument about the significance of the relationship between parent transference interpretations and outcome, he states that it is "yet another piece of circumstantial evidence supporting the validity of psychotherapy" (p. 237). Malan goes on to say that this is an entirely expected result for "it is not surprising that those therapies concerned more with interpretations about human relationships should be the more successful" (p. 237). (See Sloane *et al.* (1975) for a contrary result.) However, the index, which refers to interpretations dealing with people other than one's parents or siblings, produced negative correlations with outcome on five out of the eight tests!

Even if it were possible to replicate the finding that there is indeed a relationship between interpretations of transference and parents, with outcome (which is doubtful), the explanation offered is partly contradicted by other aspects of the evidence. In view of the statistical objection mentioned earlier, one has to consider whether the positive correlation between outcome and interpretations of the transference in regard to parents might not be a chance result.

The deficiencies of both studies (absence of controls, contaminated ratings, statistical objections, etc.) preclude any conclusions about the effectiveness of the therapy which was provided. It is difficult to see how these studies can be interpreted as supporting the view that analytic psychotherapy produces beneficial effects; it is doubly difficult to accept the view that the studies validate the *theory* of psychotherapy.

In a retrospective study of the effects of group psychoanalytic treatment on fifty-five patients, Malan, Balfour, Hood, and Shooter (1976) found little evidence of improvements — powerful effects were "rare". These discouraging results are inconclusive because the research methods which Malan *et al.* used suffer from the acknowledged limitations of his other outcome studies (e.g. inadequate measures of outcome, contamination, absence of controls, non-random selection, etc.). The authors' main conclusions were summarized:

"Our intensive study of these 55 patients, treated by strictly psychoanalytic group therapy as used during the past years at the Tavistock Clinic, leads to the following generalizations:

1. The method can have powerful therapeutic effects, but in our sample these have occurred largely in patients who have an exceptional aptitude for psychotherapy, who are rare, and most of whom have already been prepared by previous individual psychotherapy.

2. Patients who received previous individual psychotherapy have tended to do well, either through delayed action effect, or through interactions among individual therapy, group therapy, and life experience.

3. In the ordinary run of patients referred to the Tavistock Clinic, the evidence for the therapeutic effectiveness of this form of group treatment, though present, had been weak, and the results have not been impressive.

4. The great majority of patients have felt their group treatment to be a depriving and frustrating experience, which has left them with resentment toward the clinic" (Malan *et al.*, 1976, p. 1314).

As will be evident from our critical examination of Malan's work, there are serious obstacles to establishing satisfactory criteria for determining the effects of psychodynamic, or related forms of therapy. The problems include the following. Our needs to reach agreement on the aims of therapy — an exceedingly difficult task. Are we hoping to promote insight (however that can be defined in an attempt to achieve agreement), or increased resistance to stress, or symptom removal, or constructive personality growth, or freedom of emotional expression, or changes in character structure? Although we are unlikely to obtain agreement on each of these aims, and how they are to be defined, most people will agree that therapy has more than a single goal. It follows that some combination of these goals, plus some additions perhaps, will be needed in order to assess the effects of dynamic therapy. Assuming that agreement can be reached on the number and types of goals, one then has to weight them. And this presents its own difficult problems. However, given agreement on the goals of therapy, the next problem is how to translate these goals into a set of testable statements. If this seems to be a straight-forward task, consider the exercise involved in translating the "promotion of insight" into a testable statement, or the even more complex and difficult job of translating "constructive personality growth" into a useable form.

Given that goals are agreed and satisfactorily translated, it then becomes necessary to construct appropriate measures of change. Here the literature is replete with efforts to establish valid measures of outcome, and as many of the enduring problems involved in this exercise are considered in different parts of this book, they will not be laboured here. Given then that one has appropriate measures of outcome, the arduous process of establishing the reliability and validity of these indices has to be undertaken. When this journey is completed, one needs to ensure that in each outcome experiment, the several results are an adequate and fitting test of the agreed aims of the therapy. Satisfactorily navigating each of these stages is a difficult, laborious, and demanding task. It helps to explain why there has been so little research devoted to validating the claims made by proponents of psychoanalytic therapy. Scientific problems aside, this type of research requires institutional and financial resources that are rarely available. One institution which has the personnel and facilities to undertake such a task is the Menninger Clinic.

THE MENNINGER CLINIC REPORT

With this background in mind, it is readily understandable why the publication of the Final Report of the Menninger Clinic Project, published in 1972 after 18 years of work, was awaited with great interest.

The aim of the project was to "explore changes brought about in patients by psycho-analytically oriented psychotherapies and psychoanalysis" (Kernberg, p. 3). The project sample consisted of forty-two adult patients "who had been diagnosed as suffering from neurotic conditions, borderline conditions, latent psychosis or characterological disturbances". Patients with brain injury, mental retardation or "overt psychosis" were excluded. All forty-two patients had treatment of a psychoanalytic type. Patients in psychoanalytic therapy received an average of 835 hours of treatment, and those in psychoanalytically orientated psychotherapy an average of 289 hours. A strong point in favour of this Report is that the treatment was carried out by experienced practitioners, a fact which distinguishes it from other efforts at evaluation. It is a matter for great regret that so much of the research on evaluating psychotherapy rests on the therapeutic efforts of trainee psychologists or psychiatrists.

The research workers concentrated on four main variables: the patients, the therapists, the form of treatment, and the patients' current situation. Information was obtained and collated on these variables prior to the initiation of treatment, shortly after the termination of treatment, and again at a follow-up point between 2 and 3 years after termination. Unfortunately, "the sources of data differed somewhat at these three points in time" (p. 4). The information about the patient's status and characteristics prior to treatment were obtained solely from case summaries written by the psychiatrist responsible for treating the person. This information was supplemented at termination and follow-up by special interviews and by the application of psychometric tests (although the results of these tests receive surprisingly little mention in this extensive Report). All of this information — obtained mostly from the therapists' records of the patient and his response to treatment — was condensed, collated, and then transferred on to specially constructed assessment forms (see Report Appendix). The raw material on which the entire Project and its interpretation were based "was organised . . . according to the basic assumptions of psychoanalytic theory . . . (p. 5). Hence, the collators and assessors (judges) were asked to assess, among other things, the patient's "unconscious guilt", "capacity for sublimation", etc. (p. 199). The assessment of treatment variables required them to estimate for later quantification, "the extent to which a full-fledged transference neurosis developed", the "structural changes in the ego", the "crucial insights", and so on (see Appelbaum, 1977).

These few examples serve to illustrate that the raw data used in the study were interpreted at source, in accordance with psychoanalytic theory. To complicate matters, the information was open to major errors of contamination and confounding. The contamination occurred in at least two stages of the data analysis. The collators who prepared and organized the data for transfer to the rating forms had access to the clinical record of each patient. They knew what was wrong with the patient and how he was treated, as well as how he had responded to the treatment. The second occasion for contamination occurred when the judges were required to rank the various patient and treatment variables. In carrying out their assessments, the judges had access to knowledge about the type of treatment provided. In the analysis and interpretation of the data, considerable attention was paid to those differences in therapeutic outcome which were thought to be attributable to variations of treatment, and with this in mind care should have been taken to ensure that the judges and collators were blind as to the type of treatment used. Further, in assessing the treatment variables (and this includes the response to treatment), "we had only one team of judges who completed all the comparisons, a psychiatrist and a psychologist (Drs. Kernberg and Burstein), both highly invested in the Project" (p. 13).

The most serious contamination arises from the fact that the collators and assessors had information not only about the characteristics of the patient and the type of treatment which he had received, but also the outcome of treatment. So, at the two most important points in the process of collecting the evidence (collation and assessment), the data were contaminated instead of being independent observations and scores.

Considerable effort was expended in attempting to ensure that the statistical properties of the variables were acceptable. For example, intra- and interjudge reliabilities were calculated, and in the main these were reassuringly high. However, a minority of the reliability correlations fell below accepted statistical levels. Despite this demonstrated inadequacy of some of the variables, it was decided to use all the variables that, "notwithstanding their weakness", could be scaled, even though it was acknowledged that the weaknesses of these variables "would limit to some extent the inferences we might make" (p. 15). Whatever one might feel about the wisdom of this decision, it undermines the value of the work that was put into determining the reliabilities in the first place. There seems little point in calculating reliabilities if they are not used in guiding further analysis and interpretation. More seriously, one might question whether there is any value in determining reliability coefficients for raw data which were confounded and contaminated at source.

This brings us to a general feature of the Report. Both of the major analyses of the data, one statistical and the other mathematical, were complicated, and the mathematical approach is novel and advanced. On the other hand, however, the raw data (and indeed the processed data as well) were open to serious distortion. Complex, advanced, and massive analyses of the kind used in the Project are misplaced on data of this poor quality. Incidentally the presentation of the statistical moves and their interpretation is often difficult to follow, and not merely because some of it breaks new ground. The system of paired-comparison matching, for example, appears to have been complicated in practice and borders on being muddled in description. Worse, some of the results arrived at by the statistical method are contradicted by results produced by the mathematical method (Wallerstein, 1972, p. x). One senses that having invited the help of mathematicians, the therapists were left disarmed by a mathematical orgy that obscured their therapeutic purpose.

The healthy self-criticism evident in the Report is welcome and it is important to remember that when the Project was initiated in 1954, few people were aware of the pitfalls involved in psychotherapy research. The writers point out that "all the concepts used in the quantitative study had their origin in the assumptions of psychoanalytic theory about personality and its pathology and about the technique which brings about changes . . ." (p. 62). Whether one regards this as desirable or not depends of course on one's attitude towards psychoanalytic theory. However, the limitation which it imposes on the research project is that students who are not adherents of analytic theory are scarcely likely to be satisfied with a methodology that is embedded in psychoanalysis. And as we have seen, the assessment of outcome was based on concepts that enjoy a dubious status (e.g. "structural change in the ego").

The entire Project is noteworthy for the absence of any form of control. In this study, as in most others on the subject, this omission precludes a conclusion about the therapeutic value of any or all of the analytic methods used. The writers of the Final Report point out that, "this absence did not particularly harass us . . ." (p. 60). They reason that, the "problem of control in psychotherapy research could not be solved by establishing groups of normal and non-treated cases" (p. 61). After briefly considering one or two alternatives, they concluded that the failure to construct an appropriate control group could be excused on the grounds that, "we did not set out to validate psychoanalytically oriented treatments, but to study the process and outcome of such treatments" (p. 61). Naturally, it was not incumbent on them to examine the validity of analytic treatment, but it is a pity that the opportunity was missed — bearing in mind the resources available to the Menninger Clinic. In any event, it is difficult to understand how a "study of the process and outcome" of treatment could fail to have some bearing on the validity of psychoanalysis (see Grünbaum, 1977 and 1979).

The authors also drew attention to the fact that the size of their sample was small for the needs of the project. Moreover, when the sample of forty-two was divided into smaller groups for purposes of carrying out sub-analyses, "in some instances hypotheses dealt with sub-samples . . . the number of cases per sub-group varied from 3 to 16" (p. 72). They added that their "analyses of variance may also be subject to criticism because the patients were not randomly assigned to the various groups" (p. 73). Furthermore, "another limitation to reduce the size and number of relationships was the existence of poor variables (that is variables with low reliability, restricted range or poor discrimination) and variables for which one expects curvilinear relationships" (p. 73).

In the opinion of Kernberg and his colleagues, the most severe limitation of their study was its "lack of formal experimental design" (p. 76). They point out that it was not possible to:

"(i) to list the variables needed to test the theory; (ii) to have methods of quantification for the variables, preferably existing scales which would have adequate reliability and validity; (iii) to be able to choose and provide control conditions which could rule out alternative explanations for the results . . . (iv) to state the hypotheses to be tested; or finally (v) to conduct this research according to the design" (p. 75).

This astonishing conclusion can have few equals. If we then add to their list of frank self-criticism, some of the faults already mentioned (e.g. contamination, non-random allocation, etc.) one is left with a study that is so flawed as to preclude any conclusions whatsoever. Whilst the honesty of their self-appraisal is highly commendable, one cannot help wondering how the authors succeeded in persuading large and reputable foundations to provide them with financial support extending over many years. How does one persuade a foundation to support research which, in the words of the authors themselves, lacks a formal experimental design — or methods of quantification, or hypotheses? And which cannot be conducted "according to the design"? Can it be that the foundations provided their support precisely because they were assured by the authors that "it was not possible . . . to conduct this research according to the design"?

It would be sad to conclude that the considerable expenditure of thought, time and effort which went into the conduct of this extensive project was a total waste. (According to Appelbaum, 1977, over a million dollars was spent on the project). Fortunately there is something which can be learnt from it all. Some tentative findings do emerge, albeit in tattered form. Two of the conclusions are at least consistent with findings from research carried out in recent years: patients with high ego-strength show greater changes than those with low ego strength (see also Fisher and Greenberg, 1977, for examples), and highly skilled therapists were more successful than less skilled therapists, irrespective of the patient treated or the variation of treatment that was used.

Methodologically inadequate assessment procedures undermine even this finding — the ratings of therapists' skill were not independent of knowledge about treatment outcome. Although the authors of the project drew appropriate attention to these findings, they also displayed a tendency to go beyond them in ways that were not justifiable (especially in pp. 181—195). They even contradict themselves on certain points. For example, on p. 190 it is stated that, "the analysis did not reveal any evidence to support the hypothesis that skill of the therapist influenced the outcome of treatment for patients with low ego-strength treated with psycho-analysis, supportive-expressive or supportive psychotherapy". On the other hand, it is said that from a clinical point of view, patients with low ego-strength, poor object relationships and primitive defences "require a therapist who is secure and aware of the influences of his personality, his technique and his countertransference on the therapeutic relationship" (p. 189). The conflicting results of the statistical and mathematical analyses have already been mentioned.

There are also some oddities to report. For example, the correlation matrices of patient variables drawn from the pre-, post-, and follow-up assessments show practically no change — the whole network appears to have been untouched by the treatment intervention. There are also some surprisingly low correlations. In Table 27, for example, the correlation between the therapist's skill "in this case" and the completion of the treatment goals was precisely zero. The correlation between the therapist's skill and the resolution of the transferences was a mere 0.18. There was an insignificant correlation between insight and level of psychosexual development at the termination of treatment (Table 25), but at the 2–3 year follow-up the correlation had become significant at the 0.001 level.

Information provided in Tables 24 and 25 suggests that the patients of "sound personality" prospered under all conditions and all treatments — a finding encountered in other psychotherapy projects. To his credit, the director of the project, Dr. Kernberg, had the courage to face this possibility: "This overall finding supported by both quantitative studies raises the question to what extent psychoanalysis may be considered the ideal treatment for patients who need it least, that is, for those with high initial ego-strength" (p. 182).

Students of psychotherapy will be puzzled by the following quotation from Malan's most recent book (1976a, p. 21): "When I met Dr. Kernberg at the meeting of the Society for Psychotherapy Research in Philadelphia in 1973, he said that he regarded the problem of measuring outcome on psychodynamic criteria as essentially solved, and I could only agree with him."

Before considering the foundations of this optimism, we are bound to remark that the accord reached by Malan and Kernberg has its puzzling aspects. For one thing, they appear to have reached quite different solutions to the multiple problems of evaluating outcome. To take but one, crucial, difference. Where Malan condenses all the outcome information into a single digit, Kernberg and his colleagues provide no less than ten separate measures of outcome, ranging from change in level of anxiety, through change in ego-strength to absolute change, global change, and so on. They also have as one of their ten indices of outcome, a change in health-sickness ratings, a scale which is itself based on no less than seven separate criteria (see Appelbaum, 1977, for details). Furthermore, the ten multiple criteria were reapplied in assessing *the direction of change.* So that, in all, we have well over thirty criteria of outcome. Moreover, the content of the outcome criteria which Malan used before condensing them into the single outcome figure differed from those used in the Menninger Study.

Returning to the substance of the claim that the problems have been solved, it is not the case that we are in possession of satisfactory methods and instruments for measuring therapeutically induced changes. We are not even in sight of an agreed goal for psychotherapy, let alone how to define such a goal or how to assess the extent of our success in achieving it. Lastly, as was made evident in a study in which Malan participated, comparative evaluation studies are not always feasible (see Candy *et al.*, 1972). In this ambitious but vain attempt, the selection criteria could not be operated effectively. Of the ninety potential patients, only eight were finally selected! Of these eight, three left in the very early stages despite having passed the rigorous (multiple) selection hurdles.

Earlier in this chapter we noted that Bergin (1971) concurred with Eysenck (1961) in his evaluation of eclectic psychotherapy, but differed with him on his appraisal of psychoanalysis. In suggesting reasons for the difference in their views, Bergin discounted the possibility that "our biases differ regarding psychoanalysis and that they differentially influenced our reading of essentially ambiguous stimuli . . . since neither of us can be considered friendly to psychoanalysis" (p. 226). In their recent evaluation of therapeutic outcomes, Bergin and Lambert (1978) arrived at a number of major and far-reaching conclusions about the comparative effects of psychotherapy, including: "Psychoanalytic/insight therapies . . . rest on a reasonable empirical base. They do achieve results that are superior to no-treatment and to various placebo treatment procedures" (p. 170).

They rest their argument on the findings of the Menninger group, the Sloane study, Malan's 1976 report, and the Vanderbilt study. Our evaluation of the first three reports leads to a totally different conclusion (the final report on the fourth study, carried out at Vanderbilt, is not yet published*). Neither the Menninger Report nor Malan's two series provide a satisfactory basis for reaching any conclusions, positive or negative, about the effects of psychoanalysis. The Sloane study is far more satisfactory but not free of serious problems (see Chapter 12).

Ninety patients with neurotic or personality disorders were randomly assigned to one of three groups; behaviour therapy, psychoanalytically oriented psychotherapy, or a waiting list control. Therapy lasted for 4 months and was carried out by experienced therapists who were all acknowledged experts in their own approach, i.e. behaviour therapy or psychoanalytically oriented psychotherapy. Systematic assessment of patient's functioning was made at pre- and post-treatment, and at an 8-month follow-up.

Evaluation of outcome at the end of the 4 months of therapy showed that both behaviour therapy and psychoanalytically oriented psychotherapy were followed by significantly greater improvements on the assessor's ratings of target symptoms than the waiting list control condition. Specifically, 80% of patients in both treatment groups were rated as "improved" as compared to 48% of the waiting-list control group. However, the improvement rates on the independent assessor's ratings of overall adjustment at post-treatment showed a different pattern. On this measure of outcome, 93% of the patients treated by behaviour therapy were rated as improved compared to 77% of both the analytic psychotherapy and the waiting-list control patients. Although Bergin and Lambert omit to mention the fact, this difference was statistically significant ($p<0.05$) (Sloane et al., p. 101). A third major finding was that neither the behaviour therapy nor the psychoanalytically oriented psychotherapy groups showed significantly greater improvement than the waiting-list control group on measures of general functioning such as "social isolation" and "work inadequacy". The psychoanalytically oriented psychotherapy group showed only marginal improvement in social functioning and no change at all in the work inadequacy from pre- to post-treatment assessment. All three groups tended to maintain their improvement at an 8-month follow-up, although interpretation of the follow-up data is complicated by intervening therapeutic contacts.

It is doubtful whether the results provide a "reasonable empirical base" for psychoanalytic treatment. To summarize, *on two of the three major dependent measures* (overall adjustment, and work and social functioning), the independent assessor rated the patients who had been treated by psychoanalytically oriented psychotherapy as no more improved than the waiting-list control patients. Furthermore, the superiority of psychotherapy on the measure of target symptoms does not conclusively demonstrate that this form of treatment is more effective than a placebo. Bergin and Lambert (1978) argue that the waiting-list control group can be considered to be a minimal treatment group, but as Kazdin and Wilson (1978) have pointed

---

*The report by Strupp & Hadley, published in September 1979 *(Arch. Gen. Psychiatry)*, states that the "relative amount of change for treatment and control groups disclosed no statistically significant differences" (p. 1132).

out, the adequacy of this control group for establishing a causal relationship between specific treatment effects and outcome can be questioned. It is desirable to document that control groups in outcome research are equated for variables such as hope and expectation of successful therapeutic outcome, and not simply to assume that this is so. One needs to confirm that the control group successfully "controls". In the Sloane *et al.* study, it is not implausible to suggest that a more stringent control group, equated for the amount of therapist-contact, might have produced even greater improvements on the target symptom measure. Be that as it may, the Sloane study provides a measure of support for therapeutic claims made on behalf of this type of "brief" analytic type of psychotherapy. It is nowhere near sufficient in extent or quality to support the grand structure of psychoanalytic theory and therapy. Indeed, the study was not intended as a test of the value of psychoanalysis.

Our view that the empirical basis for psychoanalytic treatment is unsatisfactory appears to be shared by Luborsky and Spence (1978) in their evaluation of the quantitative research on psychoanalytic therapy. Having reviewed the research on the outcome of psychoanalytic treatment, these authors, both of whom are associated with the psychoanalytic approach, concluded that "We must still *assume* that psychoanalysis is especially beneficial in achieving its stated aim of characterological change, in addition to a lessening of symptoms" (p. 338, original emphasis). And later in the same review, Luborsky and Spence emphasize that, *"Quantitative research on psychoanalytic therapy presents itself, so far, as an unreliable support to clinical practice.* Far more is known now *through clinical wisdom than is known through quantitative, objective studies"* (p. 358, original emphasis). The affirmation of accumulated clinical wisdom is no substitute for scientific validation (see Grünbaum's 1979, discussion).

To conclude this lengthy examination of the status of psychoanalytic therapy, we retain the view that appropriate and satisfactory methods can be developed for evaluating its effects — but the difficulties cannot be overestimated.

The conclusion reached at the end of the comparable chapter in the First Edition of this book stands. There still is no acceptable evidence to support the view that psychoanalysis is an effective treatment.

CHAPTER 6

THE EFFECTS OF
PSYCHOTHERAPY

In the First Edition it was concluded that there is modest evidence to support the view that psychotherapy produces beneficial effects. It was also noted that even though there is little incontestable evidence on which to ground this conclusion, there are many signs that a large number of people gain some *comfort* from attending psychotherapy. It has been objected, however, that many other types of treatment, and indeed many varying types of "non-therapeutic" experience, may produce the same result. We do not dispute this claim. The question of central importance is whether psychotherapy provides more than comfort. If it is not shown to do more than provide comfort, the time may have arrived at which to alter many beliefs about the power of psychotherapy.

In recent years some slight progress has been made and we have seen the addition of new pieces of evidence some of which are consistent with the modest claims described in the earlier Edition. It has to be admitted that the scarcity of convincing findings remains a continuing embarrassment, and the profession can regard itself as fortunate that the more strident advocates of accountability have not yet scrutinized the evidence. If challenged by external critics, which pieces of evidence can we bring forward? Reassuring reviews of the effects of psychotherapy, which customarily open with the confident assertion that Eysenck's claim of "not proven" can be ignored, continue to appear at regular intervals. These efforts bring comfort to the profession and especially to practitioners, but are unlikely to satisfy any but the most timid of external critics. The few clear successes to which we can point, are out-numbered by the failures, and both are drowned by the unsatisfactory reports and studies from which no safe conclusions can be salvaged. The introduction of anecdotes of the following type merely invites the risk of ridicule. In his review, Bergin (1975) claimed a victory for psychotherapy because a behaviour therapist was said to have remarked that, "My own therapist is a beautiful human being and that means more to me than his theoretical orientation" (p. 512).

In a landscape littered with studies that were unfeasible (e.g. Candy *et al.*, 1972), or major failures (e.g. Rogers *et al.*, 1967; Mitchell, 1973; McCord, 1978), or merely underwent a slow expiration over many years (e.g. Kernberg *et al.*, 1972), the only point on which advocates and critics of psychotherapy appear to agree is that the quality of the evidence is poor. Writers covering such diverse topics as criminal behaviour (e.g. Feldman, 1977; Logan, 1972), psychotic disorders (e.g. May, 1975), obsessional disorders (e.g. Cawley, 1974), and alcoholism (e.g. Orford and Edwards, 1977) express similar views. The most frequently cited defects of research include a scarcity of controlled trials, the confounding of methods (especially by drug treatments), the use of gross and inappropriate outcome measures of unknown validity, the absence

77

of independent assessments, or of behavioural observations, a failure to match patients correctly, a failure to assign them randomly to comparison groups, the use of inexperienced or even unqualified therapists, the failure to assure and confirm that the participating therapists use the assigned method, inadequate follow-ups, and so on. The number and complexity of technical problems preclude the design of a single foolproof evaluation, so that it becomes necessary to balance the pieces of reliable evidence drawn from more than a single study. This exercise of judgement gives rise to some disagreement, but its influence can be seen at the very first stage of the proceedings, i.e. the selection of studies for serious consideration. Writers who prefer strict standards end up with a small number of studies, while those who prefer to use a wider tolerance-limit end up with a considerably longer list of studies. The two extremes of these approaches are illustrated on the one side by the views of Paul (1969), with his emphasis on specificity and the appropriateness of the match between treatment and problem, and on the other side by the meta-analysis recently proposed by Smith and Glass (1977), who attempted to integrate outcome research by a statistical analysis of the analysis of individual studies. Paul recommends specificity: "What treatment, by whom, is most effective for this individual with that specific problem, under what set of circumstances, and does it come about?" (Paul, 1969, a, p. 44). Meta-analysis typifies the search for broad, statistical comparisons. Smith and Glass mixed no fewer than ten types of therapy, a wide range of patients and problems, and several other major variables in order to carry out their meta-analyses. The strengths and weaknesses of these approaches are examined in Chapter 12.

With few exceptions, psychologists appear to have accepted the need for satisfactory evidence to support the claim that psychotherapy is beneficial. Most writers also appear to accept the view that in the absence of suitable control groups, investigations cannot provide a conclusive result. Working within these terms of reference, several writers (e.g. Cross, 1964; Dittmann, 1966; Kellner, 1967; Bergin, 1970, 1975) have concerned themselves primarily with the evidence emerging from studies incorporating control groups. Although there is a continuing theme in these discussions, the writers concerned are by no means in agreement. Discussing the earlier reviews, Bergin (1970) said,

> "Cross (1964), for example, reviewed 9 control studies and determined that 6 were favourable to therapy, whereas our own review of the same reports yielded only 1 that approximated adequacy and even that one is subject to criticism (Rogers and Dymond, 1954). Dittmann (1966) added 5 more studies to Cross's group , considered 4 of them to be positive evidence, and concluded that 10 out of 14 controlled outcome studies were favourable to psychotherapy. Actually, only 2 of the studies indicate that psychotherapy had any effect and neither of them would be generally acceptable as evidence. Thus, these authors claim strong support for the average cross-section of therapy, whereas I would argue for a more modest conclusion."

While we agree with Bergin's assessment of these reviews, it should in fairness be pointed out that both Cross and Dittmann were more tentative and cautious than Bergin allows. For example, Cross mentions that some important "cautions must be kept in mind". The work referred to in his review consisted of "quite brief or superficial" treatment, the measurement techniques were "of questionable or unproven validity", and for some of the studies "the method of control itself is questionable". For these reasons, he urged caution: "Even though the reviewed studies are the most careful which have been done, various limitations proscribe any strong conclusions" (p. 416). It should also be remembered that four of the largest and best-designed studies produced negative results — Teuber and Powers (1953);

Barron and Leary (1955); Fairweather and Simon (1963); Imber *et al*. (1957). Cross placed a more optimistic interpretation on the Imber data than did the authors themselves. As will be shown below, the authors made no claims for psychotherapy, and their findings were sometime contradictory, often fluctuating, and finally, inconclusive. Cross himself points out that Rogers and Dymond used a questionable method of control and this investigation is discussed below.

Bergin's rejection of the conclusion reached by Dittmann is understandable. Dittmann had reservations: "My impression is that studies of the outcome of psychotherapy have finally allowed us to draw conclusions on other bases than intuition, but the conclusions, themselves, are modest, and are, moreover, diluted by confusion." All the same, he felt that 1966 was "a year of bumper crop in outcome studies". Dittmann argued that four out of the five control studies described by him supported the position that psychotherapy is effective.

Two of these studies can be discounted. The study by O'Connor *et al*. (1964), referred to earlier (p. 42), describes the psychotherapeutic treatment of fifty-seven patients suffering from ulcerative colitis. Their progress was compared with that achieved by fifty-seven control patients who received little or no psychotherapy. The authors concluded that psychotherapy had a favourable effect on the course of the disease, in that the psychotherapy patients had a superior outcome to the controls. They were able to find little evidence of a relationship between the amount or intensiveness of the psychotherapy which was provided, and the extent of the physiological improvements recorded. Furthermore, and this finding undermines their main conclusions, "there was no direct relationship between the degree of physical and degree of psychological improvement" (p. 600). The analysis of their results was carried out in two parts, with the physiological changes indexed by "proctoscopic change", and the patients' complaint behaviour indicative of "symptomatic change".

Taken at face value their results, presented figuratively (O'Connor *et al*., 1964, p. 595), appear to demonstrate that the patients who received psychotherapy began to make a significant physiological recovery between the third and fourth year of their treatment, and by the eighth year of observation they were significantly better off than the control patients. The symptomatic changes were roughly parallel to the physiological changes, but the differences between the two groups were less clearcut on this measure.

Regrettably, this study has so many serious flaws that the results have to be discounted. In the first place, allocation to the psychotherapy or to control group was selective. The two groups were significantly different prior to treatment (see p. 42 above). The assessment of improvement was carried out by informed raters — despite the inclusion of a physiological measure, the possibility of bias cannot be excluded, as the proctoscopic ratings of change "yield variable results with different observers" (p. 590). The psychological criteria of improvement were directly contaminated, and the changes in symptomatic manifestations of the disorder were open to bias throughout the study. Next we have to take into account the fact that most of the patients were receiving conventional medical treatment which included steroids or other drugs, dietary treatment and, in a significant minority of cases, surgery as well. No less than 25% of the patients who had psychotherapy underwent surgery at some time during the 8-year observation period. In the control group, 30% of the patients had surgery. (The mortality rate of 16% was the same for the control and the psychotherapy group of patients.)

Interpretation of the findings is marred by the discrepancy between the results given in the figures and in the tables. For example, the figures given in their table 11, which contains the most important data on the proctoscopic and symptomatic changes, do not agree with the pictorial display of what should be the same results shown in their figure 2. To take one instance, the table shows that in the eighth and last year of observation, the patients receiving psychotherapy showed large improvements, but the figure shows a slight deterioration during this period. The table also shows that there was no change in the untreated group of patients during this final year, but the figure shows a large deterioration. The presence of several discrepancies undermines one's confidence in the results.

In two further papers on the effects of psychotherapy in the management of colitis, O'Connor and his colleagues provided further information about the fate of thirty such patients, but it is not clear whether this sample was drawn from the original fifty-seven or whether it constitutes an entirely new group. It seems likely that the later papers were in fact based on a sub-sample of the original group. In any event, the flaws evident in the first report were repeated in the next two reports (Karush *et al.*, 1968; Karush *et al.*, 1969). The ratings of psychological change were contaminated, the physiological indices are of questionable validity, the patients were simultaneously receiving drug or other medical treatments. Furthermore, and somewhat inexplicably, "formal statistical analysis of the data was not used because of the large number of variables that were encountered" (Karush *et al.*, 1969, p. 203). Finally, the last two reports contain no more than a fleeting mention of the control patients.

In view of the large and unequivocal claims made on behalf of these studies, and because it should be possible to obtain more accurate and valid physiological indices of improvement, a controlled evaluation of the effects of psychotherapy on the course of colitis would be welcome. It is not implausible that supplementary psychological help may facilitate recovery from this disorder, but the evidence is inadequate and cannot support unequivocal claims of success.

In a second study quoted by Dittmann, the criterion for improvement after psychotherapy was (most unusual) a measurement of "time perspective", as interpreted on the basis of TAT stories (Ricks *et al.*, 1964). The study by Seeman and Edwards (1954) involved very small numbers of children, and in any event, on one of the major outcome criteria (teacher ratings), no differences emerged. The report by May and Tuma (1965) showed that patients given drugs improved more than those who did not receive drugs; it produced no evidence that psychotherapy was effective. The study by Ashcraft and Fitts (1964) cannot be assessed satisfactorily because they used an unpublished test as their criterion of outcome. As Dittmann allows, their "results are complicated because of the many subscores of the test and the methods of analysis, but clearly favour the treatment group".

As measurements of the self-concept feature prominently in many outcome studies, and the notion of changes in self-concept is a central feature of non-directive therapy, it seems desirable to examine the idea and its measurement in detail. Such an examination may also be instructive in so far as the assessment of assessment is concerned.

Self-Concepts

Wylie (1961) neatly summarized the predictions which flow from theories of self-concept psychotherapy. It is to be expected that successful therapy will produce various changes in self-concept, such as the following: "increased agreement between self-estimates and objective estimates of the self . . . increased congruence between self and ideal-self, if this congruence is very low at the outset of therapy . . . slightly decreased self-ideal congruence if this congruence is unwarrantedly high at the outset of therapy . . . increased consistency among various aspects of the self-concept" (p. 161).

Wylie mentions, among other difficulties, many of the problems involved in attempts to relate change in self-concept to psychotherapy. Two of the major problems are the possibility of mutual contamination between measures of improvement and measure of self-concept (p. 165) and the serious problems of scaling. (For example, one cannot say that "equal numerical changes involving different scale ranges are psychologically comparable" (p. 166).) Like Wylie, Crowne and Stephens (1961) drew attention to the large variety of tests which have been developed to measure self-regard, self-acceptance, and the like. They commented unfavourably on the assumption that these tests are equivalent "despite their independent derivation and despite the relative lack of empirical demonstration that there is a high degree of common variance among them" (p. 107). They pointed out that there is a serious absence of information on both the reliability and validity of these tests. For example, "criterion validation of self-acceptance tests is, of course, logically impossible . . . face validity, however, has apparently been assumed without question (and this) implies adherence to a further assumption . . . that of the validity of self-reports. In terms of these assumptions, a self-acceptance test is valid if it looks like a self-acceptance test and is similar to other tests and what a person says about himself self-evaluatively is accepted as a valid indication of how he 'really' feels about himself" (p. 106). Another major difficulty with these tests is the often dubious assumption that the items chosen represent a fair sample of the possible parameters. They argue that it is "of importance to draw one's sample of test items in such a way as represent their occurrence in the population". Although they are not consistent on this subject, writers generally assume that the self-reports given by subjects are valid. Crowne and Stephens drew attention to reports of extremely high correlations between self-concept rating scales and social desirability scales. In one study, for example, the correlations between Q-sort and a social desirability score were found to be 0.82, 0.81, and 0.66. Social desirability correlated 0.82 with the ideal-self rating scale score and 0.59 with the ideal-self Q-sort. In a study conducted on students, correlations of 0.84 and 0.87 were found between items on a Q-sort and a social desirability scale. In a psychiatric sample the correlation was found to be 0.67. Another study quoted by them produced what is probably a record correlation of 0.96 (between social desirability and an ideal-self score). They concluded that "failure to control for social desirability in the self-acceptance assessment operations would make the results, no matter what the outcome, uninterpretable in terms of self-acceptance" (p. 116). They even went so far as to suggest that in the absence of suitable controls, the tests in question "may better be interpreted as a measure of social desirability than of self-acceptance".

In all, Crowne and Stephens were unimpressed. "The failures of self-acceptance research can be traced, at least in a large part, to neglect of several crucial psychometric and methodological principles: the unsupported assumption of equivalence of assessment procedures, the absence of any clear construct level definition of the variable, failure to construct tests in accord with principles of representative sampling, and questions concerning the social desirability factor in self-report tests" (p. 119). Although not as harsh in their judgements, Lowe (1961) and Wittenborn (1961) were also critical of self-concept procedures.

Moving from a consideration of the general status of self-concept research, we can now examine its application to the assessment of abnormal behaviour and the effects of psychotherapy. We strike an immediate difficulty in attempting to define the relationship between the self-concept and adjustment. Although there is fairly good agreement that low self-regard is related to maladjustment, high self-regard may indicate one of three things. It may be a sign of good adjustment, or of a denial of problems or, yet again, of "unsophisticated conventionality" (Wylie, 1961). For example, Crowne and Stephens mention a study by Bills in which subjects with high self-acceptance scores were found to be more maladjusted than low scorers. Summarizing a good deal of the literature, Wylie concluded that "there is much overlap between groups" (i.e. neurotics, non-psychiatric patients, normals). Comparisons between psychotics and normals have been contradictory, with at least "3 investigators reporting no significant difference between psychotic and normal controls" (p. 216). Considering the range from normal through various types of abnormality, she concluded that "a clear linear downward trend in self-regard is not found" (p. 216). In four studies a curvilinear relationship between self-regard and severity of maladjustment was observed. An important aspect of this research was the finding that subjects who were judged to be the best adjusted in various studies had·high self-regard, "but their self-regard was not necessarily significantly better than that of the most poorly adjusted subjects". Wylie concluded that "we can see that the level of self-regard is far from being a valid indicator degree of pathology" (p. 217).

Although therapeutic claims on behalf of psychotherapy have sometimes been made on the basis of changes in self-concept scores, the omission of control groups is a crucial deficiency. In addition to the general inadequacies of the self-concept notion and its measurement (some of which have been enumerated above), it is necessary to draw attention to one further limitation. Dymond (1955) observed that a group of six subjects who showed spontaneous remission and decided not to undertake therapy after being on a waiting list, "appeared to have improved in adjustment, as measured from their self-description, about as much as those who went through therapy successfully" (p. 106). Their Q scores increased from 33 to 47.3 (significant at the 2% level). A comparison group of six apparently successfully treated patients (although there are some confounding variables here) showed changes from 34.8 to 48.3. The two groups were "not initially differentiable in terms of adjustment status at the beginning of the study". Instead of drawing what would appear to be the obvious conclusion, however, Dymond states that "no deep reorganisation appears to take place" (in the untreated patients). "The 'improvement' appears to be characterised by a strengthening of neurotic defences and a denial of the need for help" (p. 106). If Dymond's explanation is correct, then presumably one would be entitled to conclude that a similar process occurs when the self-concept changes after psychotherapy. Is psychotherapy also to be "characterised by a strengthening of neurotic defences"?

This is a suitable point at which to draw attention to the continuing temptation to "explain away" results which contradict one's beliefs. Here spontaneous remissions are said to reflect denial, and in the Ends and Page (1959) study they were discounted as evidence of an undesirable "flight into health".

Further evidence that significant changes in self-concept occur without psychotherapy was provided by Taylor (1955). He found that subjects who were required to do self and self-ideal reports repeatedly showed the changes usually attributed to psychotherapy. The subjects showed an increase in the correlation between the descriptions of self and self-ideal, increased consistency of self-concept, and an increase in positive attitudes towards the self. Although these improvements are said by Taylor to be smaller in magnitude than those reported for cases of psychotherapy, this is doubtful. The comparisons which he made were between his experimental group of fifteen subjects and three single case reports of disturbed patients. Either way, his conclusion is consistent with Dymond's and interesting in itself: "Significant increases in positiveness of self-concept, and in positive relationship between the self and self-ideal, may be valid indexes of improvement wrought by therapy, but increased consistency of self-concept is achieved so readily by self-description without counselling that it would seem a dubious criterion, especially when self-inventories or Q-sorts are used in conjunction with therapy."

Writers on the subject have expressed the following views. "When such tests are used in further research as if they had been carefully and adequately constructed, little can ensue but error and confusion. And such seems to be the case in self-acceptance research. Perhaps it is true that these tests are not yet used commonly in clinical setting where their inadequacies could lead to disservice to the client . . ." (Crowne and Stephens, 1961). Lowe (1961) cautiously concluded that, "there is, in short, no complete assurance that the cognitive self-acceptance as measured by the Q-sort is related to the deeper level of self-integration that client-centred therapy seeks to achieve" (p. 331). Concluding her analysis of twenty-nine research studies, Wylie (1961) said: "Of course nothing can be concluded from these studies concerning the role of therapy in causing the reported changes" (p. 182).

Kellner (1967) argued that the case for the effectiveness of psychotherapy is a sound one, and supported his conclusion by a detailed consideration of several studies. Many other studies are mentioned in passing and will not be taken up here, particularly as numbers of them are discussed elsewhere in this book. Here we will confine ourselves to those studies (other than with children or by counselling) on which Kellner bases the main force of his argument, but will not take up his discussion of those studies in which psychotherapy failed to produce results more satisfactory than the improvements observed in controls. It should be mentioned, however, that Kellner's assessments are not always satisfactory. In his discussion of the Barron—Leary study, for example, he suggests that the untreated patients were probably less disturbed that their treated counterparts — despite evidence to the contrary contained in the study itself. On the other hand, his reservations about the use of various outcome criteria appear to be well grounded. He notes, for example, that MMPI scores are generally inappropriate and that "self-acceptance, if used as the only measure, is at present an inadequate criterion of improvement" (p. 345). He also notes a number of studies in which this type of assessment has failed to pick up therapeutic changes.

Kellner attached particular significance to the two studies reported by Ends and Page (1957, 1959) in which they assessed the effects of various types of psychotherapy on hospitalized male alcoholics. As we feel that these studies fail to support the notion that psychotherapy is effective, it is necessary to consider them with care. Kellner described the first of these studies in some detail and noted that only sixty-three patients (out of an original group of ninety-six) completed the programme: each of four therapists had fifteen sessions with four different groups of patients. The methods of therapy were client-centred, psychoanalytic derivation, learning theory (an inappropriate designation), and lastly, a discussion group which served as control. In addition to the specific therapy, all patients participated in other presumably therapeutic activities during their stay in hospital. These included AA meetings, lectures, physical treatments, and so on. The outcome of therapy was evaluated by changes occurring in the self-ideal correlation. As Kellner points out, the MMPI which was used initially was discontinued, and the evaluation of therapy depended almost entirely on Q-sort analyses. Eighteen months after discharge from hospital, the degree of improvement was judged by independent raters and these ratings "showed a significant improvement in the 2 groups which had shown changes in the Q-sort". On the Q-sort analysis itself, there were greater "reductions in the discrepancy between self and ideal in the client-centred group and in the psychoanalytic group". The second study (Ends and Page, 1959) is referred to briefly, and Kellner points out that although the self-ideal correlation again "discriminated significantly between treated patients and untreated controls", only the paranoia scale of the MMPI discriminated significantly. As Kellner regards MMPI scores as an unsatisfactory measure of outcome (and in any event these scores failed to show therapeutic changes), we will confine ourselves largely to a consideration of the other two measures, i.e. Q-sort analyses and follow-up ratings.

The Q-sort analyses are fairly complex and will be discussed at some length below. The follow-up data which appeared to have influenced Kellner's judgement of these studies are scanty and can be discussed briefly, Ends and Page claim that the follow-up data show significant success for the psychotherapy groups but point out that the "results are by no means unequivocal" (p. 275). We might add that they are by no means clearly described. Although it is implied that follow-ups were carried out on three occasions, the results are all presented in a single table so that it is impossible to sort out the patient's progress at various stages. To make matters worse, it is not at all clear how the follow-ups were conducted or the data analysed. They say: "Follow-up data from county welfare officers, from the hospital's own follow-up clinic, and from hospital admission records were analysed. The initial follow-up was made 6 months after discharge by county welfare officers using a standard interview form. The 1-year and 1½-year follow-ups were made through the hospital follow-up clinic and hospital admission records" (p. 275). The results are presented in five categories but unfortunately the categories deal with different types of data and different time periods. For example, a rating of "greatly improved" was given when there was no evidence of further alcoholic episodes during the 1½-year period. The rating of "possibly improved" was given when there was evidence of one or two brief episodes within the first 3 months following discharge, and "as far as could be determined no evidence of a reversion to the former pattern during the follow-up period". They define recidivism as "readmission to *the same* hospital for alcoholism" (our emphasis). It is not made clear whether the patients were interviewed; from the description given it seems unlikely, but one cannot be sure. Secondly, it would appear that the follow-ups at the 1-year and 1½-year periods were carried out by examining such information as happened to be present in the hospital's clinic and records. On the basis of their criterion for recidivism, it is possible that their 1-year and 1½-year follow-ups did not include the full sample — but only those patients who made contact with the hospital after discharge. If this is the case, the most that one can conclude is that patients who had undergone psychotherapy did not return to the same hospital, and *not* that they were necessarily improved or abstinent. In view of their description of the composition of the category "possibly improved", there appears to be no certainty that the patients did not resume drinking after 3 months. As Kellner puts it, "fewer patients from the client-centred group had been readmitted to the hospital". His description of the follow-up procedure may, however, be slightly misleading. We cannot be sure that "the degree of improvement was judged by independent raters" at 1½ years "after discharge from hospital".

In dealing with the first study, Kellner might have drawn attention to the extremely high defection rate — no fewer than thirty-three of the original ninety-six patients failed to complete the programme, i.e. a 30% loss rate. It is not stated whether the defections were more common in one or other of the groups, nor whether the defectors were comparable in initial status to the patients who completed the programme. Kellner did not comment on the fact that although Ends and Page excluded the MMPI data from their *first* study because "preliminary analysis revealed that physical and psychological treatment effects were confounded in the MMPI profiles", scores from the same test *were included* in the *second* study. The authors' inclusion of the MMPI data in the later study is doubly puzzling in view of their stated reason for excluding it, i.e. physical and psychological treatment effects were confounded. It is nowhere explained how they reached this conclusion or how they were able to decide that the Q-sort analysis "held such confounding to a minimum". In any event, they appear to have changed their minds in the second study.

Their Q-sort analyses are atypical and sometimes difficult to follow. Certainly their justification for using some of the analyses is doubtful. They carried out a large number of comparisons between different variations of the self and ideal-self correlations and found a number of "movement indexes". The client-centred group showed two significant changes, the analytic group three significant changes, the learning theory group two significant changes and two negatives, and the controls one negative. A conclusion drawn from the comparisons is that the patients who received psychotherapy showed significant improvements, the control subjects showed little change and the "learning therapy" patients deteriorated slightly.

This conclusion appeared to be supported in their second study when they compared twenty-eight patients who received twice as much client-centred therapy (i.e. thirty sessions) and twenty-eight control patients who were simply assessed at the termination of the 6-week therapy period. In this comparison, however, the control patients were found to show some degree of improvement although not as large as the treated patients. One curious factor to notice here is that this second control group showed statistically significant improvements on five of the eight comparisons, whereas the control group in the earlier study showed only one positive change and one negative change. The improvements observed in this second control group are, however, explained by Ends and Page as having been "gained minimally in self-acceptance only by a defensive manoeuvre that appears to be unstable at the outset" (p. 12). The matter is made even more intriguing by comparing the control patients in the second study with the treated patients of the first study. The treated patients showed significant improvement on only four of the indexes.

The major surprises, however, occur when the authors compare the patients who had thirty sessions of therapy with an additional control group of twenty-eight patients who were simply retested after a 2-week wait period. "In general, figure 6 reveals that the control group made greater gains on 5 of the indexes than did the therapy group" (p. 23). Apparently these improvements represent "a defensive reaction", otherwise known as "flight into health". This interpretation, we are told, is supported by "a wealth of clinical observation", and a "flight into health" is distinguished from "truly integrated therapeutic change", The difference in improvement scores between the treated and untreated groups is explained by the claim that group therapy, "retards the flight into health" (p. 27). The flight into health apparently occurs "as a defence against self-examination and criticism" and on average occurs between the tenth and fifteenth therapy sessions. However, "this phenomenon seems to occur with or without therapy" (p. 24). We might note, incidentally, that if it occurs between the tenth and fifteenth therapy sessions the successful results obtained in the first study (in which fifteen treatment sessions were given) appear to be fortunate.

On the MMPI results (considered in the first study to be confounding) the treated and untreated patients were found to produce significantly different results on only two of the thirteen comparisons. The treated group showed significantly greater decreases in the paranoia scale, and the untreated patients showed significantly greater decreases in the Hy scale. We are also informed in the second study that the patients who received fifteen treatment sessions, i.e. those in the first study, "demonstrated no significant change from pre- to post- on any of the MMPI scales" (p. 14). Moreover, only one significant difference on the MMPI scales was observed between those patients who received fifteen and those who received thirty treatment sessions. This is explained by Ends and Page on the grounds that pre-treatment scores "suggest that the (first treated) group were somewhat healthier to start with as far as scale elevation is concerned. One would, therefore, expect less change on the MMPI scale simply because this group needed to move less, and, indeed, had less room in which to move since they began closer to the normal means for the scale" (p. 14). However, the same comment could be made about the untreated patients as they also show consistently lower MMPI scores than the patients who received thirty treatment sessions. We may even extend the argument to the analysis of the Q-sort data, as the control group had a z-score of 0.406 prior to treatment while the treated group had a score of 0.303.

The conclusions reached by Ends and Page are doubtful. Conclusion number 6 is particularly misleading. They state that "the flight into health phenomenon occurs in those not participating in group psychotherapy: Following the inevitable collapse, those not receiving group therapy show no indications of reintegration in a therapeutic sense but instead recover by re-erecting a structure only superficially different from the initial one" (p. 29). As the so-called flight into health phenomenon (i.e. improved self-acceptance) was most clearly observed in the group which was retested after 2 weeks, it is hard to see how they can speak of an "inevitable collapse". This control group was not retested after the second week. It is not possible to say whether or not they "collapsed" or whether they "re-erected superficial structures" or showed indication of "reintegration". On the contrary, when last tested they were showing considerable improvement.

It can be seen, then, that the studies by Ends and Page have serious shortcomings. The defection rate is extremely high and contains possible biasing factors. The selection of outcome measure, Q-sorts, and MMPI scores, is unfortunate. The follow-up data are scanty and confounded. The Q-sort and MMPI scores suggest quite different conclusions. One of the untreated control groups shows considerable improvement after a 2-week wait period — greater than that seen in treated patients. Their exclusion of MMPI data from the first study is inconsistent. Their explanation of improvement in the untreated controls is unconvincing, and, even if accepted, could be applied with equal force to the improvements observed in some of the treated patients. As a great deal of time and effort was put into these studies it is a pity that the authors did not pay more attention to the collection of "hard" information such as status at follow-up determined by direct interview and by external informants. The absence of follow-up data in the second study is particularly unfortunate. Overall, this research is devalued by implausible special pleading.

The study by Shlien *et al.* (1962) is frequently quoted as evidence in support of the effectiveness of psychotherapy. They compared the effects of unlimited client-centred therapy with time-limited client-centred therapy and time-limited Adlerian therapy. They included, in addition, two control groups. One control group consisted of normal people and can be dismissed as irrelevant. The other control group consisted of patients who requested therapy but did not receive it. These untreated controls were retested after 3 months. The sole criterion of therapeutic effectiveness was a self-ideal Q-sort.

The authors claimed to have demonstrated the effectiveness of psychotherapy and drew attention to the effectiveness of time-limited therapy. Apart from weaknesses in the experimental design, the authors reported their results in brief form, and regrettably, omitted vital details. For example, all of their results are presented as averages (mean or median?) and these are shown in the form of a graph. No figures are provided. It is nowhere stated what sort of patients they were dealing with. They do not indicate why the untreated group remained untreated. Nor do they state whether the allocation of patients to the treatment or no-treatment conditions was random — in the context of the report, it seems highly unlikely.

In regard to the experimental design used, one of the control groups is irrelevant. The other control group comprised untreated patients who may or may not have been retested at the follow-up period 12 months later. In any event they appear to have carried out the Q-sort on only two occasions as compared with four occasions for each of the treated groups. The sole criterion on which the effects of therapy were based is the Q-sort — generally agreed to be inadequate (e.g. Kellner, 1967). We are provided with no information about the psychiatric status of the patients either before or after treatment, nor are we told anything about their behaviour. In regard to the results themselves, the treatment groups appear to have shown substantial increases in self-ideal correlations. The untreated control group, on the other hand, followed a surprisingly unchanging course. Prior to treatment, the self-ideal correlation for this group was precisely zero. At the end of the 3-month waiting period, it was still precisely zero. In the graph containing the results of the study they appear to be precisely zero at the 12-month follow-up period as well — but this may be misleading because it is by no means certain that they were retested at the follow-up occasion. In any event, this remarkable stability is some-what unusual. Ends and Page, for example, found that their 2-week waiting control patients showed an increase in self-ideal correlation of 0.25, i.e. they improved from 0.35 to 0.60 on retest after 2 weeks. As mentioned earlier, other workers have found similar "spontaneous" changes in this type of correlation. In sum, the Shlien study will do as an exploratory investi-gation, but as evidence in support of the effectiveness of psychotherapy it is unconvincing.

Although Kellner's appraisal of the evidence appears to be over-optimistic, some of his comments on the problems of research into psychotherapy are well taken. In particular, he argues the case for increased specificity in a persuasive manner. Certainly, the treatment of a mixed bag of patients by a mixed bag of techniques is unlikely to further our understanding of the nature and possible effects of psychotherapy.

PHIPPS CLINIC STUDY

The by now well-known study of the effects of psychotherapy on psychiatric out-patients carried out at the Phipps Clinic has celebrated its twentieth birthday (Frank *et al.*, 1978), and the status of thirty-four of the original group of patients at the 10-year follow-up period was described by Imber *et al.* (1968). The patients were originally assigned at random to one of three forms of treatment: "Individual psychotherapy, in which a patient was seen privately for one hour once a week; group therapy, in which groups of 5–7 patients were seen for 1½ hours once a week; and minimal contact therapy, in which the patient was seen individually for not more than one half hour once every 2 weeks" (p. 71). The treatment was carried out by second-year psychiatric residents who took no part in the evaluations of their patients. These evaluations took place at the end of 6 months of treatment and again 1, 2, 3, 5, 10, and 20 years from the time of the initial treatment contact. A number of assessments were made and the two main outcome criteria were personal discomfort and social effectiveness. Significant improvements were observed in all three groups but some fluctuations occurred during the 10-year period, particularly among those patients who had minimal treatment. The main changes occurred within the first 2 years after treatment, and with some exceptions, tended to hold up at the 10-year follow-up period. As the authors remarked. "It does seem somewhat improbable that differences consequent to a brief therapeutic experience a decade earlier should persist in such a striking fashion." Their doubts are increased by a number of points, the most prominent of which is that some of the differences between treatments were absent at the 5-year follow-up period and then reappeared at the 10-year follow-up period. An overall evaluation of this admirably persistent investigation is complicated by fluctuations in the results and by an unfortunate lack of correspondence between the two major criteria. The omission of an untreated control group is understandable but unfortunate as it precludes any conclusions about the effect of psychotherapy *per se*. In view of the earlier discussion of possible events contributing to the spontaneous remission of neurotic disorders, the authors' findings on their patients' explanation of their improvements are interesting.

"Although improved patients tended to associate their better current condition to a change in their socio-economic situation or to their adaptation to general life circum-stances, including symptoms, it cannot be determined whether psychotherapy fostered these changes or whether they occurred quite independently of the treatment experienced. In any event, it is clear that, in retrospect, patients conceive of improvement as a function of adjustment to their lot in life or to a change in external socio-economic circumstances" (p. 80).

It is tempting to conclude from this study that psychotherapy was effective and that more psychotherapy was more effective (even when administered by inexperienced therapists). However, in view of the limitations of the study and the unclear outcome, we share the authors' caution. Although the results are inconclusive, they do encourage the possibility that psycho-therapy may be beneficial — even if it is provided in a brief and limited form by inexperienced therapists.

Their latest effort wins all the prizes for persistence, for Jerome Frank and his colleagues (1978) have now reported the condition of their three original groups 20 years after the termination of treatment. There were no differences whatsoever. Commenting on their results, Liberman (Chapter 4) sensibly reiterated the need to distinguish between short-term and long-term changes, between those events that initiate desirable changes and those that maintain them. The fact that very few investigators have reported long-term differences between therapy groups should not be misinterpreted as meaning that no therapeutic changes took place at any stage.

UCLA STUDY

Despite some unfortunate inadequacies in the analysis and reporting of their data, the study by Brill *et al*. (1964) contains interesting information. They carried out a long-term double-blind study of the use of placebos, prochlorperazine, meprobamate, and phenobarbital, "in conjunction with brief visits", in the treatment of 299 predominantly neurotic out-patients. The selection of patients was carried out in a systematic fashion, and on acceptance for the trial they were randomly allocated to one of the three drug treatments or to psychotherapy (given weekly for 1 hour's duration), or to a placebo control or to a no-treatment waiting list control. The authors concluded that the "patients in all 5 groups showed a tendency to improve, in contrast to a lack of improvement in the patients who were kept on a waiting list and received no treatment" (p. 594). They added that "the lack of any marked differences would suggest that neither a specific drug nor the length of the psychotherapeutic sessions was the crucial factor in producing improvement in this sample of patients" (p. 594). We may add that the patients receiving placebos did as well as the treated groups.

One of the most interesting findings was the resistance encountered by the investigators when the study was introduced and carried out. They commented on the "prejudice in favour of psychotherapy among patients and therapists" and observed that the "extent of the bias in favour of psychotherapy, even in beginning residents who had had very little experience with it, was quite startling" (p. 591). This was particularly surprising as "all of this took place at a time when, in fact, no one knew how effective or ineffective drug treatment was".

The effects of the treatment were assessed by a variety of procedures. The therapists rated the improvements on a symptom check list and a sixteen-item evaluation form. The patient was required to complete a similar item-evaluation and one relative or close friend did likewise. In addition a social worker carried out an evaluation of each patient — unfortunately the value of this information is limited by the fact that the valuation was carried out *after* the social workers had read the reports on each patient. Lastly, the patients were required to complete MMPI tests. The before and after profiles for each patient were drawn on the same profile sheet, and two independent psychologists sorted the profiles into degrees of improvement or lack of improvement. Although their evaluations agreed well ($r = 0.85$), their conclusions differed on one of the most crucial comparisons, i.e. whether the treated groups were improved to a significantly greater extent that the untreated controls.

It will be realized that this study required a great deal of effort and careful planning. It is particularly unfortunate, therefore, that the handling of the resulting information was inadequate. It is extremely difficult to evaluate the information provided because they rarely give the actual figures obtained and rely almost exclusively on graphic presentations. The absence of basic information such as the means and standard deviations of the various measures before and after treatment is particularly serious. Matters are further confounded by their failure to give adequate descriptions of many of the assessment procedures employed. For these reasons and because they were almost exclusively concerned with intergroup comparisons, we are not able to say with certainty whether any of the groups was significantly improved. In order to reach a conclusion on this point one would need to have the means and standard deviations of the pre- and post-treatment assessment (subject, of course, to the usual tests of significance). The study is also limited by the unfortunately high rate of drop-outs — 43.5% of the selected subjects either dropped out of the treatment or were not reassessed — or both. Despite some reassuring remarks made by the authors, there are indications that the drop-outs were somewhat different from the treated subjects. In their own words, "the drop-out group may be characterised as less intelligent, less passive, and more inclined to act out their problems" (p. 584). As the data for the groups are not provided, the matter remains in a degree of doubt except for the IQ scores, which are presented graphically. This shows the completed subjects to have a mean IQ of approximately 125. They were a group of superior intelligence and the drop-outs were of high average intelligence (approximately 115).

One of the drawbacks to this study is the doubt which surrounds the degree of improvement, if any, shown by the treated and placebo groups. In some of the graphical presentations (e.g. fig. 5) they appear to have made "doubtful" to "slight" improvement. In other representations the changes seem to be slightly larger. Bearing in mind all these shortcomings, one can probably agree with the general conclusion reached by Brill and his colleagues to the effect that the treated (and placebo) groups showed slight improvement over a period of 1 year. They could detect no differences between the improvements registered by the three drug-treated groups, the placebo group, and the psychotherapy group. All of these groups, however, appeared to do better than the untreated waiting-list controls. Taken at face value, the main conclusion regarding the effects of psychotherapy would appear to be that it may have produced a slight improvement overall and this degree of improvement was neither smaller nor greater than that observed in patients who received placebos. The conclusion that psychotherapy is no more effective than an inert tablet can be avoided, however, by drawing attention the the short-comings enumerated above. And one may also add that the psychotherapy was given for only 5 months and that much of it was conducted by trainee psychotherapists. As an attempt to evaluate psychotherapy, the study must be regarded as inconclusive.

The information discussed so far is based on the condition of the patients at the termination of their treatment (mean duration 5.5 months). Koegler and Brill (1967) later reported their condition after a 2-year follow-up period. The findings were striking: "The most marked improvement is in the rated status of the waiting-list (i.e. untreated) patients" (p. 77). At follow-up there were no significant differences between any of the groups. This suggests that at very best, treatment (by drugs, psychotherapy, or placebo) achieves improvement more quickly. The authors quote Jerome Frank's notion that ". . . the function of psychotherapy may be to accelerate a process that would occur in any case".

In regard to the question of spontaneous remissions, it will be recalled that Bergin was quoted as giving a zero rate for this study. In fact it is impossible to work out the rate of spontaneous remissions from the information given. The results are reported for the no-treatment waiting-list control patients as a group, and while it is true that at termination they had shown relatively little change as a group, there is no way of determining whether any of the twenty remaining patients (fourteen of the original thirty-four were lost), remitted spon-taneously. Nevertheless, they caught up within 2 years and these untreated patients were then no different from the other groups of patients.

In the study by Greer and Cawley (1966), mentioned earlier, the relationship between treatment and outcome was also examined. It will be recalled that all of the patients were sufficiently ill to require in-patient care and they had the following types of treatment. Sixty-three received supportive treatment, ten underwent leucotomy, twenty-eight had psychotherapy, and nineteen had psychotherapy combined with physical treatment. Thirteen patients received no treatment "as they remained in hospital less than 2 weeks and in most cases discharged themselves against medical advice". At discharge, the group of patients who had received psychotherapy "had significantly more favourable outcome that the remainder". The mean outcome score for the twenty patients concerned was 1.96; the mean score for the nineteen patients who had psychotherapy and physical treatment was slightly larger at 2.11 and the mean outcome for the thirteen patients who received no treatment, was 2.15. The worst out-come was recorded by the patients who underwent leucotomy, and they had a mean score of 2.60. Although this trend was seen to continue at "final outcome" (i.e. the follow-up), the difference between the patients who had psychotherapy and those who had no treatment, was no longer significant. The significant advantage for the psychotherapy patients in relation to those who had received supportive treatment or physical treatment was maintained. The patients who had undergone leucotomy had the worst outcome of all, but their numbers were small. The slightly more favourable outcome for psychotherapy patients when discharged from hospital may be misleading. Although no direct information is provided on the selection pro-cedures in operation at the time of the patients' stay in hospital, there are indications that the patients who received psychotherapy were unrepresentative of the total patient sample. Greer and Cawley examined the significance of the factor of patient selection by carrying out some comparisons between the patients who received psychotherapy and the remainder. It was found that the psychotherapy patients "differed from the other group in several important respects". All of the patients receiving psychotherapy had a history of precipitating factors, and none of the sixteen patients whose symptoms were regarded as being of life-long duration had received psychotherapy. In addition, a significantly higher proportion of psychotherapy patients were married and significantly fewer of them had an unfavourable pre-morbid personality. All of these features had previously been demonstrated by the authors to relate significantly to outcome, "so patients who had received psychotherapy would be expected to have had a more favourable prognosis, irrespective of treatment". They concluded that it would not be justifiable to ascribe the difference in outcome between the psychotherapy group and the rest of the sample to the effect of the particular treatment. Having noted that the patients selected for psychotherapy had a favourable prognosis irrespective of the particular treatment given, they went on to say that "this argument does not necessarily demonstrate that psychotherapy was ineffective in these patients. From the findings of the present study we are not entitled to draw any conclusions regarding the efficacy of psychotherapy" (p. 83). As we have already seen, however, the Greer–Cawley study contains useful information on the course of neurotic illnesses. In regard to improvement rates and eventual outcome, they unearthed a disconcerting finding. The correlation between immediate outcome (i.e. condition at discharge) and final outcome is very low, $r = 0.19$.

Modest pieces of positive evidence were collected in two studies of interpretive psychotherapy. Siegel *et al.* (1977) randomly assigned patients to immediate psychotherapy or a waiting list control, and assessed the effects of treatment by administering a symptom checklist after an interval of 9 months. The patients who received psychotherapy showed a significant decline in the average intensity of their symptoms, while the waiting list patients showed no change. However, the amount of improvement shown by the treated group was extremely small. Furthermore, the waiting-list control patients showed a slight decline in the number of symptoms reported, while the treated patients showed a slight *increase* in the number of symptoms reported. Unfortunately the weaknesses of this study recommend a cautious interpretation. The loss rate was extremely high in both the treated and control groups, with 39% being lost in the first and 25% of the group being lost in the second condition. Secondly, the information about therapeutic change rests solely on a symptom checklist which was administered before and after treatment, but whose properties are not described. Reliance on an unpublished checklist of unknown properties is a serious drawback. Lastly, caution is recommended because the treatment was carried out by trainee therapists.

The study carried out by Piper *et al.* (1977) suffers from the same weakness (the therapists were inexperienced), but scores over the Siegel study by the use of a wider and more intensive range of assessment procedures. Forty-eight neurotic out-patients were divided into two matching groups and then provided with treatment immediately or after a delay (control condition). The results showed an improvement for both the treated and control patients over the 3-month study period. On one of five criteria, the treated patients did significantly better than the control subjects. However, on the target symptoms there were no differences between the groups. On almost all of the measures, the control patients always showed superior scores, and at the end of treatment the controls were still better off than the treated patients on most measures. Another drawback to this otherwise useful study was the introduction of a drug confound. More than half of the patients reported having taken some medication during the period of study.

The patients who received psychotherapy apparently improved during the 3-month study, but these changes did not exceed those observed in the non-treated control patients except on one out of the five measures used. This slight evidence of the superior effect of psychotherapy might have been damped by the fact that inexperienced therapists were used; on the other hand, the psychotherapeutic results might have been inflated by the simultaneous use of psychotropic drugs.

Klerman *et al*. (1974) evaluated the effects of drugs or individual psychotherapy or a combination of the two, in providing long-term assistance to 150 depressed female out-patients. By excluding from the study those patients who failed to show clinical improvements when given the drug during the preliminary treatment phase, they biased their results in favour of the drugs. Nevertheless, the information which they gathered about the *maintenance* of improvement (which was, after all, their main aim) is unaffected. The most effective management was drug maintenance therapy, and the combination of drugs and psychotherapy did not offer more than either treatment alone, in preventing relapse. From our point of view, the point of immediate interest is that "psychotherapy did not offer any additional therapeutic benefit over maintenance drug therapy in the prevention of relapse" (Klerman *et al*., 1974, p. 188), despite the claims made for its longer term value. In defence of psychotherapy, it could, however, be pointed out that the psychotherapy was provided by a social worker. The authors are careful to point out that she was experienced and qualified, but it can be reasonably objected that this did not provide the right conditions for assessing the effects of psychotherapy. Even if the objection to using a social worker in an evaluation of the effects of psychotherapy is dismissed, another criticism remains. It could be argued that the study merely shows that this particular therapist was not successful. There is also one discrepant feature in their major findings. The patients who received psychotherapy plus a placebo had a high relapse rate, and it was not distinguishable from the rate recorded in that group of patients receiving little or no psychotherapy, plus a placebo, or no pill at all. Somewhat surprisingly those patients who had psychotherapy unaccompanied by any form of tablet had a low relapse rate, equivalent to the level achieved by the patients on drugs.

The same workers followed up to 150 patients 1 year after the completion of the maintenance treatment period, and found no evidence of a beneficial effect having been achieved by psychotherapy or drugs. As a group, the patients fared poorly. At the end of the 1-year follow-up period, 71% of them continued to have at least moderate and sometimes more serious symptoms. The authors expressed some surprise at their own results for, "the expectations for psychotherapy are slightly different . . . in psychotherapy the patient is expected to develop understanding about situations that may have contributed to the depression or developed as a consequence. There are several possibilities for the absence of a sustained effect" (Weissman *et al*., 1976, p. 759). These include the fact that 8 months might not have been a sufficient length of time for therapy, that it was mainly of a supportive nature, that it was given by a social worker, etc.

In an unusual study that was designed to assess psychotherapy and to show that intensive experimental investigation of psychotherapeutic changes is feasible, D. Shapiro (1971) successfully explored the value of some novel approaches derived from the work of his father, M. B. Shapiro. The immediate and longer term effects of psychotherapeutic sessions on fifteen patients were studied in depth.

The prediction that seven in-patients who received 12 weeks of individual psychotherapy would show improvement over the treatment sessions, was disconfirmed (p. 38). There was a suggestion that after a further 5½ months of treatment, some improvement may have taken place, but the author pointed out that the comparison on which this possibility is based may be an unreliable procedure (p. 45). The results are summarized as follows:

"Seven patients with long-standing personality disorders showed no evidence of within-session 'improvement' during individual psychotherapy sessions, either for the 'target symptoms' of tension and depression, or for the PQ data as a whole. Indeed, there was some suggestion of 'worsening' during interviews. There was some evidence of more variability during interviews than during comparison periods. There was no evidence of general 'improvement' over the twelve-week period intensively studied, although there was possibly some 'improvement' over the subsequent 5½ months of further, similar treatment" (Shapiro, 1971, p. 47).

In a related study of seven *out-patients*, treated over 10 months, the results were again disappointing. "Over the course of treatment, one patient seemed to 'improve', another two to get 'worse' and the remaining four to show no overall direction of change . . . there were no clear patterns relating within-sessions to longer-term change in this group of patients" (p. 269). The predicted improvements were not confirmed (p. 265).

The use of Truax measures of therapist conditions was unsuccessful, as "the raters failed to discriminate very much between the different sessions of this group" (p. 269), and the reliabilities were very poor.

Unfortunately, most of the treatment was provided by trainee psychiatrists and the effects of psychotherapy were confounded by the simultaneous use of other treatment procedures in the in-patient study. Even though the research failed to produce support for the claim that psychotherapy produces beneficial changes, it contains stimulating methodological features.

The succinct review by Feldman (1977), which incorporates an earlier review by Logan (1972), covers nine studies of the treatment of convicted offenders and four studies of the effects of treatment on potential offenders (including the famous Cambridge—Somerville study, mentioned earlier). On the question of preventive treatment of potential offenders, there is little room for argument about the fact that the results had been uniformly disappointing (e.g. McCord, 1978). On the other hand, a few therapeutic claims have been made for the value of treating convicted offenders. The most encouraging of these studies was reported by Persons (1967). Forty-one adolescents in a correctional institution received twenty individual sessions of psychotherapy over a 5-month period. The youngsters who received psychotherapy behaved better in the institution, committed fewer crimes on release, and had better job records. In the remaining eight projects reviewed by Feldman the outcome was totally disappointing or, at best, offered little comfort. As he points out, "the apparent success of psychotherapy in this study (by Persons) stands in sharp contrast to the lack of success in studies cited earlier" (p. 240). It should be pointed out, however, that there are doubts about the quality and duration of the psychotherapy provided in these other studies. Once again, the failures outnumber successes.

To conclude, there is modest evidence to support the claim that psychotherapy can produce beneficial changes. The negative results still outnumber the positives, and both are exceeded by the number of uninterpretable results. The strength and breadth of the persisting, unqualified faith in the value of psychotherapy rests on an insubstantial foundation.

CHAPTER 7

ROGERIAN PSYCHOTHERAPY

The growth of Rogerian psychotherapy was one of the more important modern developments in the field of psychotherapy. The necessary and sufficient conditions for therapeutic change were stated by Rogers (1957) with admirable clarity and lack of equivocation, and he boldly attempted to specify "a single set of pre-conditions" which he felt were necessary to produce therapeutic change. These pre-conditions were, he argued, operative in *all* effective types of psychotherapy. The necessary and sufficient conditions which have received the greatest amount of attention all relate to the therapist's attitude, set and/or behaviour. It is argued that constructive personality change is facilitated when the therapist is warm, empathic, and genuine. Rogers claimed that "if one or more of these conditions is not present, constructive personality change will not occur".* He added that when these conditions are present in large measure, then the resulting personality change is more striking. One of the most radical aspects of Roger's position was the argument that the treatment *technique* is not "an essential condition of the therapy".

He stated that "the techniques of the various therapies are relatively unimportant except to the extent that they serve as channels for fulfilling one of the conditions". Roger's theory is consistent − even to the extent of conceding that his own form of therapy is convenient but not essential. "In terms of the theory here being presented, this technique (client-centred) is by no means an essential condition of therapy."

He also adopted a radical view on the question of training. A successful therapist is a person who can provide high levels of the three therapist conditions, and "intellectual training and the acquiring of information" do not necessarily produce a successful therapist. With all these virtues − boldness, clarity, freshness − it is a matter for great regret that the development of Rogerian therapy turned into a story of unfulfilled promise.

In the first major outcome study reported by Rogers and his colleagues, a successful result was claimed (Rogers and Dymond, 1954), but the absence of a suitable control group, and a "waiting control" that was not matched on the most crucial variable, the outcome of this study

---

*The three "necessary and sufficient conditions" of effective therapy postulated by Rogers in 1957 are neither necessary nor sufficient. Their insufficiency is indicated by the addition of a fourth ingredient of self-exploration, and a fifth ingredient of "persuasive potency" (Truax, 1968), and by the therapeutic failure of the Wisconsin project. The evidence presented by Truax and Carkhuff (1967) shows that in numerous studies, therapeutic changes were observed even though one of the three conditions was low. For example, "The Hopkins data, then suggests that *when one of the three conditions is negatively related to the other two* (original italics) in any sample of therapists, then patient outcome is best predicted by whichever two conditions are most closely related to each other" (Truax and Carkhuff, p. 91). The three conditions may be facilitative but they are not necessary.

was inconclusive. In 1967 Rogers and his colleagues produced a massive report on a treatment trial carried out on twenty-eight schizophrenic patients, sixteen of whom were treated. Although this study served the useful function of clarifying and refining the methodological procedures involved in a task of this magnitude, the *therapeutic* results were disappointing. Despite the intensive measurement and data analysis undertaken by the group, they were not able to confirm either of the two crucial predictions. The treated patients did not do better than the untreated controls. The patients who experienced high levels of the three crucial therapist-conditions did not necessarily do better than those patients who experienced low levels of these conditions. The ratings of empathy can be used as an example: Hospital release was associated with *low* levels (p. 86), even if reductions on the Sc scale of the MMPI were associated with *high* levels of empathy (p. 85).

Considerable progress was made in the development of the assessment techniques, but some disconcerting findings also emerged. It was found, for example, that the scales for measuring one of the three conditions had a reliability which was so low that it precluded any useful result. It was also found that the therapists' assessments of their own behaviour differed significantly from that perceived by the patient or by an independent assessor. The therapist variables thought to be important for neurotic patients did not apply to the schizophrenic group.

This work by Rogers and his colleagues made a methodological contribution and is pertinent not only to Rogerian therapy but to all evaluations of psychotherapy. None the less, the failure to obtain clear-cut evidence of positive therapeutic effects in this intensive and carefully planned and executed study was a setback for Rogerian theory and therapy. Roger's initial theory notwithstanding, the disappointing outcome of this study may well be attributable to what seems to have been an unwise selection of patients. For implicit and explicit reasons, schizophrenic patients seem to be less promising material for this type of treatment than other types of patient (e.g personality disorders).

Apropos the earlier discussion on the putative increases in variance observed after "average therapy", the Wisconsin study provided scant support for this position. It is also worth noticing that in other studies reported by this group, treated patients did not always show increased variance. For example, in a study on the effectiveness of lay therapists Carkhuff and Truax (1965) showed that after treatment only one out of the seventy-four patients showed a deterioration. On the other hand, twelve out of the seventy non-treated control patients showed a deterioration. If anything, the effect of treatment was to *reduce* the variance.

Truax and Carkhuff (1967) provided a coherent and important treatise in which they described in considerable detail the methodology involved in measuring the therapist conditions, and assessed the relations between the measures and across measures and therapeutic effect. In addition they proposed a "fourth major ingredient of effective therapeutic encounters", namely the patient's depth of self-exploration. As the present work is concerned with the outcome of therapy, we will not examine their accounts of how the therapeutic encounter can be assessed and quantified, nor their analysis and recommendations for the training of therapists.

They discussed and described a substantial number of experiments concerned with the reliability of therapist-condition ratings and the relationship between these measures and therapeutic outcome. Unfortunately, most of these studies lacked adequate control groups. The control studies were few in number but did encourage the view that satisfactory therapeutic conditions facilitate therapeutic improvement. In view of the setback in the Wisconsin study mentioned above and for other reasons which will be gone into presently, affirmation of the effectiveness of this type of therapy is not possible.

In the control studies, differences in the therapeutic conditions obtaining in various groups were sometimes extremely small. In the Dickenson and Truax (1966) study with college under-achievers, although they found significant differences between the groups receiving high and low conditions, inspection of the ratings for the three groups shows that the differences were very slight. The mean ratings for the three groups were 13.2, 13.4, and 12.6 (presumably out of a possible total of 21). The differences were slight despite the fact that group 3 received con-ditions that were (statistically) significantly lower than the other two groups. In spite of this very small difference in therapist conditions, the outcome measures between the groups were surprisingly substantial. The study by Truax *et al.* (1966) on delinquent girls, although success-ful in the main, produced real differences that were comparatively slight (i.e. in the actual amounts of time out of institutions). Many of the difficulties which arise in evaluating the early Rogerian work were admirably discussed by Shapiro (1969), whose review was in general, favourable. Among the many important points discussed in his paper, only a few will be mentioned here. Shapiro pointed out that the three scales contain ambiguities in termi-nology; the reliabilities of the scales are occasionally dangerously low; there is little evidence on the validity of the scales; the functional independence of the three therapeutic conditions is doubtful (see also the work by Muehlberg *et al.*, 1969; Collingwood *et al.*, 1970; Chinsky and Rappaport, 1970). Discussing the outcome studies, Shapiro noted the presence of some con-tradictory and inconclusive results and suggested "that the outcome leaves much to be accounted for". He also drew attention to the inadequacies of the measures of change which are used in many of these studies — the shortcomings of some of the more popularly used ones such as the MMPI and the Q-sort have already been discussed.

Cartwright (1968) was not convinced by Truax and Carkhuff and pointed out, for example, that in the Truax and Wargo study on delinquent girls, even though there were differences in time out of institutions, the groups did *not* differ on four out of five other measures. There were no differences on anxiety, social relations, emotional stability, or self-ideal. She also questioned their assumption that the therapists were operating at high levels of warmth and empathy. According to Truax, "this was already established in previous research" but Cartwright doubted whether "we are equally understanding and warm with all patients". She wrote, "I would be very much surprised", and support for her scepticism has been reported by Moos and Clemes (1967), who found clear evidence of a patient—therapist interaction effect. There are also serious doubts about the constancy of the therapist conditions (e.g. Mitchell *et al.*, 1977).

DOUBTS ACCUMULATE

The growing disillusionment with Rogerian psychotherapy is evident from four recently published reviews, two of them comprehensive, and all of them written by commentators who had previously expressed optimism about the promise of this form of therapy. Mitchell *et al.* (1977) made a brave attempt to salvage some comfort from this growing accumulation of negative findings: "The recent evidence, although equivocal, does seem to suggest that empathy, warmth, and genuineness are related in some way to client change but that their potency and generalizability are not as great as once thought" (p. 483). Gomez-Schwartz, Hadley, and Strupp (1978) concluded that "earlier assertions of strong empirical support for the relationship between therapists' facilitative conditions and therapy outcome have been challenged by recent findings" (p. 440), and their reservations will be referred to presently.

Bergin (1975), formerly an advocate of this approach, agreed that "in recent years a number of studies have induced scepticism concerning the potency of these variables except in highly specific, client-centred type conditions" (p. 515). Wielding a more severely critical pen, Lambert, de Julio, and Stein (1978) gave only the slightest grounds for persisting hope:

"The best conclusions that can be drawn based on the existing data are as follows: (a) despite more than twenty years of research and some improvements in methodology, only a modest relationship between the so-called facilitative conditions and therapy outcome has been found. Contrary to frequent claims for the potency of these therapist-offered relationship variables, experimental evidence suggests that neither a clear test nor unequivocal support for the Rogerian hypothesis has appeared" (p. 486).

The ready availability of these reviews, including the comprehensive ones by Lambert *et al.* and by Mitchell *et al.*, preclude the necessity for another recital of the recent findings. Instead, we will concentrate on the substantive findings that have given cause for the growing pessimism — it being remembered throughout, that in the midst of the abundantly disappointing findings, some support has of course been mustered as well. The encouraging results can be found in the reviews mentioned earlier, plus those of Truax (1971) and Truax and Mitchell (1971).

What then has gone wrong? The most serious problem is the embarrassing frequency which the studies have failed to produce support for the claimed relationships between therapist conditions and outcome. In their review Lambert *et al.* (1978) pointed out that in 14 important studies reported since 1971, less than 1 in 3 of the predicted relationships have been confirmed. To take one example only, they claim that in 109 tests of the relationship between empathy and outcome, only 24 were significantly positive. One of the most disappointing results was obtained by Mitchell, Truax, Bozarth, and Krauft in 1973 (see Mitchell, Bozarth, and Krauft, 1977). In their ambitious study of the work of 75 therapists with 120 clients, only 52 of the 1600 hypotheses tested produced a significant result! On the influence of accurate empathy, only 2 out of 562 analyses were positive.

Even though this study is far from flawless (for example, only a small minority of the invited therapists agreed to participate), the major conclusions were little short of disastrous for the Rogerian arguments (see Mitchell *et al.*, 1977, p. 485). The supposedly facilitative therapist skills were not related to therapeutic outcome. Therapists who displayed high interpersonal skills did not produce better results than those who displayed low skills. The overall effects of psychotherapy were, at best, moderately effective, with an improvement rate between 43 and 70% on global measures. "The psychotherapy was not for better or for worse. Overall, only approximately 2% of the clients showed any signs of deterioration" (p. 485).

In the more satisfactory prospective controlled trial carried out by Sloane *et al.* (1975) the supposedly effective therapist variables were found to be unrelated to therapy outcome, and it is amusing to observe that the behaviour therapists were found to offer more favourable therapist conditions on three out of the four scales than did the psychotherapists (see Sloane *et al.*, p. 167).

In addition to the disconcerting incidence of experimental failures, a number of new problems have emerged, and some of the older ones have taken a turn for the worse. As Gomez-Schwartz *et al.* (1978) point out, recent findings have confirmed earlier doubts about the independence of the client-centred measures of warmth, empathy, and genuineness. Equally serious is the failure to demonstrate a high degree of relationship between different measures of empathy. So, for example, Kurtz and Grummon (1978) found little or no correlation between six different measures of empathy. In addition, there appears to be "little relationship among measures drawn from therapists, clients, and judges in regard to the level of facilitative conditions offered during psychotherapy" (Lambert *et al.*, p. 479). The validity of the measurement scales, a question of central importance, remains unresolved (see Mitchell *et al.*, p. 499, and Chinsky and Rappaport, 1970).

Previously expressed doubts about the constancy with which therapists offer the appropriate conditions have now become a serious problem. Lambert *et al.* reported that there was little evidence to support the contention that therapist conditions are kept relatively constant. Whiteley *et al.* (1975) share the view that therapists vary considerably in the way in which they function not only across sessions, but within sessions. Mitchell *et al.* provide the fullest review of this subject and their conclusions are discouraging. There are other difficulties, both methodological and evidential. In all, the past 8 years have introduced a chill.

In their summing-up, Mitchell *et al.* attempted to offer some reassurance. "We want to emphasize the commonality that psychotherapy has with other aspects of life", and they concluded that they "want to emphasize the therapist as a viable human being engaged in a terribly human endeavour" (Mitchell *et al.*, 1977, p. 498). This conclusion is so devoid of meaning as to comfort some and offend none.

Perhaps the most important limitation in all this work is the tendency to over-emphasize the importance of therapist conditions, and the consequent lack of importance attached to treatment *technique* variables, the *nature* of the patient's psychological difficulties, and, of course, the combination and interaction of these two determinants. The evidence on varying rates of spontaneous remission in different diagnostic categories and the differences in the natural history of various neurotic and other disorders have been discussed above. Neglect of this information limits the value of the Rogerian approach. The importance of selecting an effective technique is demonstrated in the research on behaviour therapy (see below). And in this connection it is worth noticing that the successful results obtained with automated desensitization are a source of embarrassment to the Rogerian position (as are the effective physical treatments, drugs, etc.). (Incidentally, Esse and Wilkins (1978) found no relationship between empathy and outcome of desensitization). Leaving aside the therapist conditions, it seems entirely reasonable to suggest that the chances of a course of therapy proving effective are determined mainly by the selection of the appropriate treatment technique for the particular disorder. Starting from this position it is far easier to then include the contribution made by the therapist, or more accurately, the therapist conditions. It is entirely reasonable to expect (even in the absence of the work by Truax and Carkhuff) that therapists will differ in skill and effectiveness. The Rogerian work has served the important function of preparing the ground for an improved understanding of the way in which a therapist can facilitate the treatment process, but continued neglect of the treatment *technique* and the psychological *problem* presented is likely to retard rather than facilitate our understanding of the contribution made by the conditions which the therapist offers. If, on the other hand, attempts were made to investigate these conditions in the context of the correct technique for the appropriate problem, we might look forward to some valuable findings.

The Negative Effects of Psychotherapy

In a curious turn of events, advocates of psychotherapy found it convenient, if not always necessary, to claim that psychotherapy is capable of producing deteriorations, as well as improvements. There appear to have been two main reasons for advancing this claim: firstly, it forms part of the average effect argument proposed by Bergin (1967), and the second reason is the more general one of demonstrating the power of psychotherapy — for good or ill. For example, Bergin has argued that, "if a deterioration effect does exist, then an 'improvement effect' is equally real. This is a serious omission because the phenomenon demonstrates that psychotherapy is powerful and, like any discovery in nature, it can have beneficial or harmful effects" (Bergin, 1970, p. 301). Of course, the demonstration of a deterioration effect would not enable one to conclude that the improvement effect is either real or equally real. And need one add that not all discoveries "in nature" can have beneficial or harmful effects?

Most people can produce a sad story describing the mismanagement of a patient, and it is easy to construct a list of negative effects that might be attributable to unsuccessful psychotherapeutic experiences: the promotion of self-distrust in patients, the encouragement of a false account of one's own and other peoples' behaviour and motives, the postponement of necessary actions, an increase in distress, the arousal of anxiety, the provocation of depression, the disparagement of alternative forms of therapy, confusion, the construction of false hopes, and so on. As it turns out, securing convincing evidence to support the claim that psychotherapy might be responsible for some of the items in this catalogue of misfortunes is almost as difficult as demonstrating that therapy has beneficial effects. Some of the obstacles are common to both endeavours. However, as it is such a serious matter, it is essential to accumulate unequivocal evidence before concluding that psychotherapy can be harmful. It should be remembered also that the putative negative effects might be short term or long term.

How can one assess the occurrence of negative changes? Once established, how can we eliminate the possibility that the changes might have resulted from events other than psychotherapy? As in the discussion on the positive effects of psychotherapy, it gradually became clear that the provision of suitable control groups and the establishment of a "spontaneous change rate" were essential prerequisites.

It is self-evident that *spontaneous* deteriorations, that is adverse changes which take place in the absence of formal therapeutic efforts, do occur. If spontaneous deterioration did not take place, mental health workers would join the ranks of the unemployed — unless one makes the insupportable assumption that people are born with neurotic disorders. Given that adverse psychological changes occur even in the absence of psychotherapy, it becomes necessary to determine the extent and frequency of such changes. That is, one has to determine a spontaneous deterioration index.

Before considering the evidence on this question, some examples of spontaneous deterioration are worth mentioning. In a recently completed clinical trial involving the treatment of severe and chronic obsessional patients, two of the patients who had been selected for treatment experienced marked deteriorations before entering the trial. One of the patients became severely depressed 2 weeks before the starting date, and another had a psychotic episode shortly before she was due to enter the trial. Obviously, if the timing of their entry into the trial had been different, it may have appeared that their deterioration had been provoked by the intervention of the therapists. In their large scale comparative study, Sloane *et al*. (1975) had two patients who "deteriorated overall during the four-month period, one in psychotherapy and one in the wait-list group. Curiously, two wait-list patients but no behaviour therapy patients were considered completely recovered" (p. 101).

As the recent review by Lambert, Bergin, and Collins (1977) confirms, there is no baseline on which to estimate the occurrence of spontaneous deteriorations. "As with spontaneous remission these figures are so variable as to be a somewhat untrustworthy baseline. Unfortunately, firm evidence for specific baselines of deterioration in treated and untreated groups is not available" (p. 463). The magnitude of the difficulty involved can be illustrated by reference to their summary table (p. 460), in which it appears that the spontaneous deterioration rates in untreated groups range from 1% to as high as 37%. Unless and until a satisfactory baseline of spontaneous deterioration, derived for separate diagnostic groups and stated within circumscribed time limits, is established, the question of spontaneous deterioration cannot be resolved.

The fact that some patients experience deteriorations during or after their participation in a course of psychotherapy cannot be taken to signify that the psychotherapy has caused the deterioration — any more than one can rashly presume that positive changes observed during and after psychotherapy are necessarily the result of that treatment. In both cases it is necessary to demonstrate that the positive or negative changes are greater than those which might be expected to have occurred in the absence of psychotherapy. The evidence put forward to support the occurrence of a deterioration effect in psychotherapy, reviewed by Bergin (1970), Bergin and Suinn (1975), by Lambert *et al*. (1977), and Bergin and Lambert (1978) is insufficient and unsatisfactory.

Over and above the clinical necessity for obtaining information about the possible deteriorative effects of psychotherapy, the occurrence of negative effects is a central feature of the important argument about the so-called "average therapeutic effect" (Bergin, 1967).

"While some research studies reveal little difference in the average amount of change occurring in experimental and control groups, a significant increase in the variability of criterion scores appears at post-testing in the treatment groups. This conclusion was drawn from 7 (well-designed) psychotherapy outcome studies and was startling in that it directly implied that some treatment cases were improving while other were deteriorating, thus causing a spreading of criterion scores at the conclusion of the therapy period which did not occur among the control subjects. Evidently there is something unique about psychotherapy which has the power to cause improvement beyond that occurring among controls, but equally evident is a contrary deteriorating impact that makes some cases worse than they were to begin with: when these contrary phenomena are lumped together in an experimental group, they cancel each other out to some extent, and the overall yield in terms of improvement (in these particular studies) is no greater than the change occurring in a control group via 'spontaneous remission factors' " (Bergin, 1967a, p. 184).

Bergin has now revised his position slightly: "current renderings . . . show that increased variance in post-test criterion scores of treated groups is not a necessary consequence of deterioration even though it occurs often. Therapy effects, including negative ones, can be distributed so as to show no change or even a restriction in variance" (Bergin and Lambert, 1978, p. 154). He has also dropped his earlier claim that there is a 10% deterioration for treated groups versus 5% for untreated control groups.

Turning now to the evidence presented by Bergin and Lambert (1978) and Bergin *et al*. (1977) in support of the case for the deterioration effect, we must begin by noting that they are uncritical in their use of the data. In particular, they seem satisfied with the results obtained from a variety of tests and other measures which are inappropriate or not known to be reliable or valid. A lengthy analysis of each of the studies cited by Bergin *et al*. (1977) in support of their case is beyond the scope of the present volume. Suffice it here to note some of the problems with the nine "well-designed outcome studies" that Bergin relies upon heavily (see table 5—4 in

Bergin and Lambert, 1978, p. 155). Consider the study by Cartwright and Vogel (1960). Bergin quotes from this study as follows:

"Thus, as measured by the Q-score, adjustment changes, regardless of direction, were significantly greater during a therapy period than during the no-therapy period" (p. 122). Unfortunately, Bergin does not quote the very next sentence in the Cartwright paper. It reads as follows: "This was not true for the adjustment changes as measured by the TAT." Moreover, inspection of Table 1 in the paper by Cartwright and Vogel shows that on both measures used in this study (Q-scores and TAT scores) the twenty-two experimental subjects show greater variance in the pre-therapy period than during the therapy period itself. Although no figures are given, it is not likely that these differences are statistically significant. In any event, the study referred to by Bergin cannot be said to support the general case that therapy increases variance.

The next study to be considered is that of Barron and Leary (1955). It will be recalled that they carried out a reasonably well-controlled study of psychotherapy and found that it produced changes no greater than those observed in a non-treated group. In 1956, Cartwright reanalysed some of their data and concluded that although there was no difference between the two groups on average, "it seems that some therapy patients deteriorated to a greater extent than did the waiting list controls, while some therapy patients did improve significantly more than the controls". However, this effect "occurred only for individual and not for group therapy" (Bergin, 1966, p. 236). Even if this evidence were acceptable, it still leaves unresolved the mystery of why the patients treated by group therapy, although showing the average effect, did not show an increased variance. On the face of it, the "average effect" observed in patients treated by group therapy cannot be accounted for by Bergin's hypothesis. This exception (and there are others) means that even if Bergin's hypothesis has merit, it cannot be a complete explanation of the so-called average effect of psychotherapy. There is a further complication. Barron and Leary in their first table (p. 242) presented the pre-treatment means and standard deviations of MMPI scores for the three groups. On three of the sub-scales quoted by Bergin in support of his argument (F, K, Sc), the standard deviations in the group of patients who eventually received individual psychotherapy are greater than those observed in the no-treatment control group. Lastly, one may point out that the MMPI is far from being a satisfactory measure of putative psychotherapeutic changes.

A third piece of evidence offered by Bergin is taken from the study by Rogers and Dymond (1954). In support of the claim that "client-deterioration" occurs, Bergin wrote that "a careful reading of the report indicates that of 25 therapy subjects, 6, or 24%, declined in self-ideal correlation between pre-therapy and follow-up testing" (p. 236). Unfortunately, seven of the control group subjects also showed a decline in self-ideal correlations (see Rogers and Dymond, table 2, p. 66). Moreover, if we examine the self-ideal correlations in the treated group, we find that at the end of treatment only two of them have "deteriorated", and of these one subject moved from −0.12 to −0.17. The figures quoted by Bergin refer to the differences between pre-therapy correlations and follow-up testing. This is, of course, permissible, but it is not consistent with Bergin's statement of the position — see above, where he states that "a significant increase in the variability of criterion scores appears at *post-testing* in the treatment groups" (our italics). If we place any reliance on these scores obtained from a self-acceptance Q-sort, it leads to the conclusion that the increased variance occurs some time after the termination of treatment, i.e. in the follow-up period. The number of patients who showed such "deterioration" in the follow-up period is similar to the number in the untreated control group.

Bergin also made use of the study reported by Fairweather *et al*. (1960), which he says "yielded similar results". Bergin then quoted two sections from the report by Fairweather *et al*., and these are indeed representative of their views, but nevertheless somewhat misleading. As Fairweather says, the "control group *usually* had the smallest variance and 3 psychotherapy groups the largest" (out italics). However, the detailed results in this report are more complex than this quotation suggests. One of the major determinants of the variance observed was the diagnostic category of the patients concerned and, furthermore, the mean variances for the control group subjects were often larger than those obtaining in the treated group. Regarding the question of diagnostic category, on all five of the major comparisons, the non-psychotic patients had smaller mean variances than the two other groups of patients (short-term psychotics and long-term psychotics). In regard to treatment groups, on every one of the numerous comparisons made, the control group (i.e. untreated) patients showed a larger mean variance than at least one of the treated groups. In some of the comparisons, the non-psychotic control patients showed larger mean variances than all of the treated groups (e.g. self-report change scores shown in table 17, change scores for five ideal-sort scales in table 20). The results of this study are detailed and complex and repay inspection. They cannot be discussed at length here but it should be remembered that, in any event, the post-treatment ratings and psychometric scores were shown to have little relation to the clinical condition of the patients at the 6-month follow-up period.

Of the other studies discussed by Bergin, one deals with a brief (three-session) counselling study, another is the Cambridge Somerville report by Powers and Witmer (1951), and the last is the Wisconsin project by Rogers and his colleagues which will be discussed below. The Powers and Witmer report provides some support for Bergin's position. Studies which run contrary to his argument include those of Gallagher (1953a, b), Cowen and Coombs (1950), and Baehr (1954). In all four of these, the improvements were within the average range and more than one therapist was involved. In all of these studies, the variance on most or all of the outcome measures was reduced after treatment.

May (1971) subjected the average effect argument to severe criticism, concluding that it rested on unacceptably flimsy evidence. Later, he produced fresh evidence that contradicted the argument. May, Tuma, and Dixon (1977) reanalysed the outcome data from their schizophrenia project (see chapter 8) and showed that treatment *reduced* "outcome variance in proportion to its efficacy" (p. 231).

Mays and Franks (in press) have reviewed all of the studies cited by Bergin and his colleagues in support of the deterioration hypothesis. They concluded that ". . . few of the studies allow for meaningful comparisons between experimental and control groups. In studies permitting such comparisons, there is no significant evidence of greater deterioration among the experimental groups." Indeed, they cite evidence that contradicts Bergin's position. In a reply to Mays and Franks, Bergin (in press) argues that they distorted the evidence by adopting overly strict methodological standards and by selective reporting of studies. While admitting that the relevant studies have many methodological flaws and acknowledging that the data contain ambiguities, Bergin none the less asserts that the research literature supports his view. However, Franks and Mays (in press) offer a compelling rejoinder to Bergin's comments, reiterating their original point that ". . . if therapy *causes* deterioration, one would expect to find one adequate psychotherapy outcome study in which a higher rate of decline occurs among the treated patients. This study has yet to be found." Bergin's reply does little to force a revision of this verdict, despite the strength of his conviction. The latter can be gauged by his insistence on the reality of therapy-induced deterioration effects because "I have observed it in at least two of my own cases. . . . Neither methodological finesse nor statistical precision is necessary to prove something you can see with your own eyes. I have directly observed negative effects." This statement is not unlike the time-worn endorsements of the efficacy of psychotherapy that have been based on personal experience and belief, but is, of course, irrelevant to the scientific appraisal of treatment outcome. So too is Bergin's (inaccurate) claim that "seventy experts surveyed by Strupp unanimously agreed on the existence of the phenonemon" (of deterioration effects, not necessarily therapy-induced negative effects).

We might also note that Strupp, Hadley, and Gomez-Schwartz (1977), while endorsing the occurrence and importance of negative effects of psychotherapy, are careful to point out that "After reviewing the psychotherapy outcome studies . . . we have concluded that nearly all of the studies are marred by multiple flaws" (p. 28).

In his response to Mays and Franks (in press), Bergin cites as evidence for his position "a growing substantive literature in the field of marital and family therapy which shows therapy-induced deterioration effects". Gurman and Kniskern (1978b) have analysed this literature as part of their exhaustive review of the marital and family therapy research. Although they review numerous studies, they are careful to point out that "only five studies . . . offer sufficient experimental controls to assert that worsening was not due to chance but was *caused* by treatment" (p. 6). One of these studies, by Most (1964), evaluated the effects of marital counselling on maritally distressed women. Leaving aside the inadequacy of measurement in this study, we note that the control group consisted of women who were visiting a Fertility Service clinic. As a group they were not experiencing marital problems and hence were an inappropriate control group. Four of the twenty women in the experimental group obtained post-treatment scores that at first sight suggests that they had become worse. However, as Most herself observes, obtaining a lower score on the questionnaire measure of marital satisfaction that was used in this study did not necessarily represent "deterioration". Rather, a lower score could have been interpreted to mean greater awareness and honesty in coping with troublesome situations "and thus represent positive movement in an area" (p. 69). The nature of the control group was such that therapy-induced deterioration could not be assessed. However, it is worth noting that of the seven women in the control group whose pre-treatment scores on marital satisfaction fell within the range of those in the experimental group, "minimal shifts were found . . . some positive and some negative in direction" (p. 71). Clearly these data cannot be adduced as support for the deterioration hypothesis.

A second study by Stover and Guerney (1967) compared the effects of training mothers of emotionally disturbed children to use filial therapy, namely to assume a more reflective and empathic role in interacting with their children. Measures of the children's behaviour showed that, compared to a control group, children of mothers in the experimental condition displayed significantly greater non-verbal aggressive behaviour following several sessions of play therapy. Gurman and Kniskern (1978b) interpreted this as evidence of deterioration. However, according to Stover and Guerney, the explicit hypotheses of this investigation were that the children of mothers in the experimental group would show an increase in aggressive acts and an increase in percentage of negative feeling statements: "Any positive results at all, with respect to *children's* behaviour in this early stage of parent training would be regarded as highly encouraging" (p. 111). In short, in terms of the goals and nature of filial therapy, the increase in aggressive behaviour by the children in the experimental condition was said to represent therapeutic success. One can debate the merit of this view, but these findings certainly do not allow a simple interpretation of the study as one that supports the deterioration hypothesis. On the contrary, it contradicts such a notion given the theoretical premises of the study.

A third study by Alexander and Parsons (1973) is also seen as providing support for the deterioration hypothesis by Gurman and Kniskern. In this study, a short-term behaviourally oriented family therapy programme was compared to a client-centred condition, an eclectic psychodynamic family condition, and a no-treatment control group in the treatment of delinquent teenagers. At the end of treatment, measures of family interaction showed that the behavioural treatment had produced significantly greater improvement than either the client-centred or the no-treatment groups. There was no evidence of deterioration in the control group on these process measures of family interaction. In terms of recidivism 6 to 18 months after the end of therapy, the behavioural treatment showed the most favourable outcome, with a recidivism rate of 26% as compared to a 50% rate in the no-treatment condition. The eclectic psychodynamic family treatment resulted in a recidivism rate of 73%. Gurman and Kniskern apparently compared this figure to that of the no-treatment control group in arriving at their conclusion that this study shows evidence of the deterioration effect. Aside from the fact that it is unclear from the original report whether or not the difference between the eclectic psychodynamic family treatment and the no-treatment control condition was statistically significant, this study serves to illustrate the problems in interpreting an investigation with multiple comparisons that are often divergent in outcome, in an all-or-nothing fashion. Any interpretation of this study as indicating possible deterioration effects would have to account for the significant superiority of the behavioural treatment over both the no-treatment and psychodynamic treatment and the fact that the client-centred treatment was no worse than the no-treatment control.

The fourth study cited by Gurman and Kniskern, by Alkire and Brunse (1974), does indicate some support for Gurman and Kniskern's conclusion about deterioration effects in marital therapy. However, it must be noted that a comprehensive review by Hung and Rosenthal (1978) of the effects of videotaped playback, the specific therapeutic intervention used by Alkire and Brunse, fails to provide much corroborative evidence of any other negative, therapy-induced consequences. The fifth study referred to by Gurman and Kniskern, by Knight, is an unpublished doctoral dissertation.

In sum, then, the evidence in support of the deterioration hypothesis is scanty. At best, the "deterioration phenomenon" may provide a partial explanation for some of the so-called average psychotherapeutic outcome figures but it fails to provide a complete explanation. Untreated patients do show deterioration, and such deterioration almost certainly varies among different diagnostic groupings. The initial Rogerian hypothesis that this deterioration is a function of therapist variables such as insufficient empathy cannot be supported.

To reiterate, investigation of negative effects of therapy should proceed by designing specific research studies to answer the question of what effects (positive or negative) a particular technique has on what problem in which person on what measure and for how long. Until now, discussions of the "deterioration phenomenon" have been too global in nature and failed to reflect the level of specificity that is required if significant progress is to be made. Not surprisingly, most of the literature on the "deterioration phenomenon" can be faulted for the same reasons that greatly undermine the value of what we have called the conventional psychotherapy outcome research literature (see Chapter 12 below).

To conclude, the fact that Bergin's explanation of negative effects in psychotherapy is, at best, incomplete, is reassuring. Acceptance of this view would imply one of the two following combinations mentioned above: psychotherapy is harmful as often as it is helpful and/or psychotherapy is conducted by therapists who are harmful about as often as they are helpful. Although this "helpful—harmful" hypothesis has been given a prominent place in the arguments of the Rogerian school of psychotherapy, it is not an essential feature. The major tenets of the Rogerian position were elaborated some years prior to the appearance of this argument.

CHAPTER 8

PSYCHOTHERAPY WITH PSYCHOTIC PATIENTS

Hopes that psychotherapy might benefit patients who have psychotic disorders are sharpened by the seriousness of these disorders and the meagre contributions so far made by practitioners of psychological methods. The suitability of such treatment has been debated for nearly 50 years, but nowadays relatively few psychotic patients receive interpretive psychotherapy. A considerable amount has been written on the subject and a great deal of advice has been offered. In their substantial text on schizophrenia, Bellak and Loeb (1969) described over twenty recommended forms of treatment. There are wide differences between the various schools of thought which include Freudian, Kleinian, Jungian, Sullivanian, direct analysis, and existential analysis. Surveys of thinking on the subject were given by Boyer and Giovacchini (1967), Auerbach (1961), Bellak and Loeb (1969), and Luborsky *et al.* (1971). Depending on one's optimism or scepticism, the profusion of ideas on the subject can be regarded as reflecting a healthy state of affairs or deplorable chaos. Rosenthal (1962) represents the sceptical point of view and listed some of the methods which have been recommended for the treatment of psychotic patients.

> "To name a few: plan emotional contact on a conceptual basis; interpret dependence rather than hostility; use the patient's own language; give direct support, talk about the weather, read children's stories to the patient, offer him cigarettes, make no demands, ask no questions, and expect no responses; explain to the patient that he is ill and tell him the meaning of his symptoms without arguing; provide symbolically all the wish-fulfilments demanded by the patient's unconscious; establish a mother—child relationship with him without its possessive, narcissistic elements; address one's self to the patient as an adult rather than as a child; make deep, surprising, and shocking interpretations; assert an authoritarian, restraining role; facilitate a narcissistic object relationship and provide gratification of the patient's instinctual drives; foster repression; make external reality simple and attractive; reach out to the patient; work through the problem of hospitalization; use non-verbal techniques; focus on the person rather that the illness; encourage non-conformity."

Notwithstanding all this advice, the sample of English psychiatrists who gave their opinions in a survey conducted by Willis and Bannister (1965) did not favour the treatment of psychotic patients by intensive psychotherapy. Only 6.8% of them considered Freudian psychotherapy to be a suitable treatment for schizophrenia, that is, exactly the same percentage who still felt that insulin-coma treatment was appropriate. However, 56.6% recommended supportive individual psychotherapy, by which they meant reassurance, advice, and sympathetic listening.

A similar survey of Scottish psychiatrists revealed that only 25% of them felt individual psychotherapy to be suitable for psychotic patients (Mowbray and Timbury, 1966).

In assessing the effectiveness of any form of psychotherapy, one has, of course, to bear in mind the spontaneous remission rate for the disorder under consideration. There have been many accounts given of the natural course of psychotic illnesses, but during the past few decades it has been understandably impossible to obtain information about patients who have received no care whatever. Current opinion has it that the spontaneous remission rate in schizophrenia varies between 20 and 40% (e.g. Lindelius, 1970), with notable differences between those illnesses which have an acute or insidious onset. In 1966 Wing reported a 5-year outcome study of early schizophrenia and found that "about one-quarter of schizophrenic patients were still severely ill 5 years after first admission and another one-quarter were handicapped by less severe symptoms". On the other hand, "half of first-admitted patients have an excellent 5-year follow-up prognosis and require little attention from psychiatric after-care or rehabilitation services." Half of the patients in this sample were discharged from hospital within 13 weeks, and although no psychotherapy was apparently provided, the majority were given drugs. The sample consisted of 111 patients admitted for the first time in 1956. Kind (1969) estimated that the spontaneous remission rate for schizophrenia varies between 20 and 40%, with differences occurring between acute and slow onset illnesses. The bad prognostic factors include slow onset and poor pre-morbid personality. Slater and Roth (1969) provide similar estimates and note that "most spontaneous remissions (occur) during the first two years of illness; after 5 years, they become negligible" (p. 311). Approximately 45% remit within 2 years, but after that the remission rate declines sharply.

In considering these spontaneous remission rates, and therefore the effects of treatment as well, one has to bear in mind that there are substantial differences in classification across different countries. For example, Cooper (1969) has shown that the diagnosis of schizophrenia is applied far more widely in the United States than it is in Britain. Many patients who in Britain would be considered to have a personality disorder would, in the United States, be diagnosed as schizophrenic. Another important difference was found in the diagnosis of "manic-depressive". Although quite commonly used in Britain, this diagnosis is seldom made in the United States. These differences in diagnostic practices are, to put it mildly, inconvenient. A consequence of these national practices is that one has to exercise a great deal of care in drawing conclusions about research conducted in different countries. As virtually all of the outcome studies on the treatment of psychotics by psychotherapy have been carried out in the United States, the problem does not arise in a serious form in this chapter. None the less, any evaluation of treatment effects must take these diagnostic differences into account. Another factor which is of some importance in assessing the value of treatment in psychoses is the fact that severely ill patients tend to show some responses to almost any increase in stimulation – whether it comes in the form of a specific therapeutic intervention or whether it consists of non-specific changes in their general care (e.g. the total push programmes described by Myerson, 1939). The value of "social treatments" of patients with chronic illnesses was summarized by Wing (1968), who also reported an investigation of the response of chronic schizophrenic patients to social stimulation in which it was shown that increased stimulation produces favourable therapeutic changes (Wing and Freudenberg, 1961). Patients who receive minimal stimulation tend to deteriorate: "Controlled trials specifically testing these measures (particularly group psychotherapy) have been carried out very infrequently, and those which have been published have not yielded very positive results. One very common finding, however, has been that deterioration occurs in the control group which has not received treatment, even when no improvement has occurred in the experimental group" (p. 311). Their findings and observations underline the necessity for including an appropriate control group whenever a treatment for psychotic conditions is investigated, and it should be ensured that the control group receives the same amount of stimulation as the experimental group.

Freud (1932, 1940) was pessimistic about the possibility of treating psychotic disorders by psychoanalysis. He felt that the patient's inability to develop a transference precluded the development of a beneficial therapeutic relationship, and he also felt that even if the analysis was successful in removing the patient's presumed defences, the overall result might be undesirable. According to Brill (1944), Freud became a little more optimistic in his later years and felt that "in time he would develop a psychoanalytic therapy for the psychoses". In view of the poor results reported by no fewer than five psychoanalytic institutes, Freud's early misgivings appear to have been well judged. Furthermore, his pessimism about the value of psychoanalytic treatment appears to be shared by the majority of psychiatrists (see also the review by Fisher and Greenberg, 1976).

In his 1941 review of the effects of psychoanalytic treatment, Knight found that in all the institutions covered by his survey, psychotic patients came off least well — "psychoses (come) last with 25% success" (p. 439). At the Berlin Psychoanalytic Institute, 61 psychotics were accepted for treatment, 32 broke off treatment, and only 7 were considered to be much improved or cured. At the London Psychoanalytic Clinic they recorded only 1 success out of 15 cases. At the Chicago Institute, 2 successes out of 6 cases. At the Menninger Clinic they claimed 14 successes out of 31 cases, and Hyman and Kessel reported 7 failures out of 7 attempts. Knight's composite improvement rate over all institutes showed only 22 successes out of 120 cases — probably as many as might be expected to improve without treatment. Heilbrunn (1966), reporting on the results of psychoanalytic treatment with 173 patients, confirmed the poor results with psychotic patients. "The results were uniformly negative for the patients with psychotic reactions and personality pattern disturbances" after considerable psychoanalytic treatment.

Despite the dismal statistics and the pessimistic views of the majority, a small number of therapists have shown persistence in attempting to treat psychotic patients by means of psychotherapy.

Before considering the studies which employed control groups, the results of Saenger's (1970) actuarial study should be mentioned. Among fifty-six patients with psychotic symptoms 42% showed untreated improvements within 1 year. The 197 patients who did receive treatment of various kinds, including psychotherapy, did slightly better, with an improvement rate of 58%.

May and Tuma (1965) carried out a study of 100 first-admission schizophrenics. Four types of treatment were compared with a control procedure consisting of basic hospital care: one group received drugs only, the second group received psychotherapy, the third group a combination of drugs and psychotherapy, and the fourth group received ECT. The patients who received psychotherapy had a minimum of 6 months' treatment consisting of not less than 2 hours per week, and the treatment was supervised by a psychoanalyst experienced in treating schizophrenics. Four outcome measures were employed, and a 3-year follow-up was carried out. It was found that the patients who had drugs did significantly better than the control patients, but there was no difference between those who received psychotherapy or control treatment (basic hospital care). They did not differ on any of the four outcome measures, including length of time in hospital, nor did they differ at the 3-year follow-up. Indeed, the control and psychotherapy patients had spent equivalent amounts of time in hospital: controls 374 days and psychotherapy patients 395 days.

In an extension of this investigation, May *et al.* (1976a, 1976b) compared the effects of the five different treatment methods on 228 first-admission schizophrenic patients. Those patients who received psychotherapy without drugs, or milieu treatment without drugs, spent significantly longer periods in hospital than the patients who had drugs alone, psychotherapy plus drugs, or ECT. Furthermore, the initial superiority of the drug treatment persisted for at least 3 years. "Patients who had been treated initially with ECT or with drug therapy showed a trend towards spending less time in hospital after their release, a delayed post-hospital advantage above and beyond the initial advantages of higher release rate, speedier release, lessened cost of treatment, and better global condition at the time of release" (p. 486). As May and his colleagues were careful to point out, the follow-up data at the 3- and 5-year points should be interpreted with caution because they no longer reflect the effects of the initial treatment. The disappointing results achieved with psychotherapy in this large controlled study are discouraging, even though one can turn to the fact that the therapists were trainees, for some comfort.

In the Wisconsin project carried out by Rogers *et al.* (1967), discussed in Chapter 7, it will be recalled that psychotherapy did not produce significantly better results than were obtained in control patients. In a comparison trial in which the experimental and control patients were well matched, Powdermaker and Frank (1953) were unable to find support for the hypothesis that psychotherapy was beneficial. A large number of statistical comparisons were made between the control and experimental group patients, including discharge rates, trial absences, etc., but they found very few differences between the groups, and those which did emerge could not be and were not interpreted as providing evidence of the effectiveness of psychotherapy. Another failure was reported by Satz and Baraff (1962). Two groups of non-paranoid non-chronic schizophrenic patients (n = 8 in each group) received 13 hours of intensive occupational therapy. In addition, the psychotherapy group received 2 hours of group psychotherapy for 10 weeks. The effects of psychotherapy, as measured by self-ideal correlations, "were negligible". In fact, the controls showed a large but non-significant superiority. It can, of course, be argued that this experiment was not a fair test of the effects of therapy as the amount of treatment given, 20 hours, was small. In addition, their use of the Butler–Haig Q-sort was ill-advised as it provides a doubtful measure of therapeutic change. Walker and Kelly (1963) described the results of limited psychotherapy on forty-four newly hospitalized schizophrenic patients, and compared the outcome for these patients with those of thirty-eight comparable patients who had not received psychotherapy. "Similar proportions of favourable outcome were found for the treated and untreated groups both with respect to overall length of community stay and in regard to readmission rates over the three-year follow-up period . . . similarly, with respect to measures of symptomatic improvement and ratings of interpersonal relationships in the community, the treated and control groups were essentially the same" (p. 351). A comparable failure was reported by Roback (1972).

Cowden *et al.* (1956) compared the effects of psychotherapy and drug treatments, alone and in combination, with routine hospital care as a control baseline. Thirty-two chronic schizophrenic patients were randomly assigned to one of the four groups, and the treatment experiment continued for 6 months, with group psychotherapy given for three sessions of 1 hour per week. The majority of outcome measures showed no difference for the treated or untreated groups, but there was one measure on which the patients who received psychotherapy and drugs were superior to the other treatment groups. This was a measure of specific types of behaviour (e.g. fighting), but the groups were grossly different prior to treatment. The measures on which no differences were found between groups included two rating scales and four psychological tests. Kraus (1959) tested the effects of twice-weekly group psychotherapy in chronic schizophrenic patients. The effects of the treatment, which were carried out for 3 months, were assessed by comparison with patients in a matched control group who received routine hospital care. The main outcome measure was the MMPI, and it failed to discriminate between the treated and untreated groups. In addition, blind ratings by a psychiatrist failed to reveal any differences between the treated and untreated patients although the ward physician — who was aware of the identity of the treated patients — rated the experimental patients as being substantially better than the control patients. Once again, it can plausibly be objected that the amount of treatment provided was not sufficient.

In their study of psychotherapeutic effectiveness, Fairweather *et al.* (1960) advisedly took into account differences in diagnostic categories. The main aim of their study was to determine the effects of individual or group psychotherapy on neurotic, short-term psychotic and long-term psychotic patients. No fewer than seven major outcome measures were used on the total of ninety-six patients involved (this includes a non-treated control group). Their findings are dominated by the effect of the major variable, i.e. diagnostic category, which accounted for most of the differences obtained. In the main, it was found that neurotic and short-term psychotic patients did best while the long-term psychotics had an unfavourable outcome, and there is even a suggestion that they did better *without* treatment. "It is evident that the major contributor to the significant interaction is the differential response of the diagnostic groups to all three psychotherapy treatments compared with the control" (Fairweather *et al.*, 1960, p. 14). Their failure to demonstrate significant treatment effects on the MMPI, Q-sort, or TAT is partly compensated for by a suggestion that the treated groups were doing slightly better at the 6-month follow-up. One of the most interesting findings in this study was the absence of any association between test-score indicators of treatment outcome and adjustment at follow-up. Closer inspection of the follow-up data, however, is somewhat deflating as the significantly better employment status of the treated patients is the only difference found in the eight criteria employed, and even this had disappeared a year later (Fairweather and Simon, 1963). No differences were found on any of these criteria: rehospitalization, friendships, interpersonal communication, general adjustment, problem behaviour, degree of illness, alcoholism, or legal violations. At the 18-month follow-up there were no differences whatever between the groups (Fairweather and Simon, 1963). Overall, this study demonstrated the prognostic importance of *diagnosis* in that the short-term psychotic patients tended to do best on most measures. As an attempt to obtain evidence demonstrating the effectiveness of psychotherapy, the study was unsuccessful.

Anker and Walsh (1961) compared the effects of a programme of special activity (drama) with group psychotherapy in two matched groups of twenty-eight chronic schizophrenics. Psychotherapy was given in groups of seven, twice a week for 1½ hours per session. The experimental period lasted for a year and the effects of treatment were assessed on a rating scale administered by the nursing staff, who were kept unaware of the group assignments of the patients. The activity programme, devoted largely to drama, produced encouraging results. According to the authors, "the activity variable was responsible for most of the change in behavioural adjustment that occurred", and "it did so with compelling strength and consistency" (p. 480). On the other hand, group psychotherapy produced non-significant results for all sub-scores, bar one, and for the total adjustment score. In terms of trial visits and discharge rates, no differences between groups were obtained. Although their study encourages the hope that special activity may be of some benefit in the rehabilitation of schizophrenic patients, the inclusion of a routine control group would have strengthened the conclusions reached by Anker and Walsh. While there can be no question about the amount of psychotherapy provided in this study, it can be argued that the psychotherapist who carried out all of the treatment was perhaps ineffective. Be that as it may, Anker and Walsh did not succeed in providing evidence of the beneficial effects of psychotherapy.

There can be little doubt about the skills of the therapists in the Grinspoon *et al.* (1968) study. They assessed the effects of psychotherapy on twenty chronic schizophrenic patients, all of whom were given psychotherapy twice weekly for 2 years. In half of the cases the therapy was supplemented by thioridazine. The remaining ten patients had their psychotherapy supplemented by placebos. It was found that patients receiving psychotherapy and thioridazine showed some improvement, but there was little sign of change when psychotherapy was combined with placebos. They concluded that "psychotherapy alone (even with experienced psychotherapists) does little or nothing for chronic schizophrenic patients in 2 years; psychotherapy for a much longer period is rarely feasible . . . and its effectiveness therefore becomes a largely academic question" (p. 1651). This useful study would have benefited from an increase in the sample size and the inclusion of a group of patients treated with thioridazine only. On the other hand, one should bear in mind the scale of the effort which the report represents — approximately 200 therapy hours for each of twenty schizophrenic patients. One of the most valuable features of this work is that the treatment was conducted by senior, experienced therapists who were mainly psychoanalytic in orientation. (It is regrettable that a good deal of our knowledge about the effects of therapy is derived from the efforts of inexperienced therapists.)

Turning next to those few studies which have claimed therapeutic successes, Semon and Goldstein (1957) provided group treatment for thirty-two chronic schizophrenic patients. The effects of four slightly varying types of treatment were compared with the changes observed in seven non-treated control patients. Although they found no differences between the four variants of treatment, the authors claimed that all were superior to the no-treatment condition. In fact, there were no differences between the treated and untreated patients on total improvement scores, or on two of the sub-scales which contributed to the total score. There was a slight superiority on the interpersonal sub-scale, however. None the less, the clinical significance of this finding is doubtful as there was a 7-point difference between the treatment and no-treatment groups before psychotherapy commenced. After the completion of psychotherapy, the treated patients were only 5 points better off than the control patients, who had undergone a 2-point decline. The minimal clinical significance of this change is amply shown by the *range* of pre-treatment scores on this particular sub-scale — 11 to 91. The failure of the treatment to produce superior results on three of the four outcome measures raises doubts about the validity of their claim, and matters are complicated by their apparent failure to avoid contamination as the ratings were not carried out "blind". Sacks and Berger (1954) studied the effects of psychotherapy on twenty-eight chronic schizophrenic patients, who were compared with twenty-eight similar patients admitted at the same time but, for some unspecified reason, not treated. No pre-therapy matching on clinical status or diagnosis was ensured. At termination, the treated patients were showing better behaviour on the ward, but there were no differences in discharge rates and no differences in referral to wards for more disturbed patients. In fact, 21% of the patients receiving psychotherapy were sent to disturbed wards. Their poorly constituted control group and their failure to provide comparable stimulation for both groups casts doubt on the claims made by Sacks and Berger. Ignoring these defects, the most that can be said for this study is that psychotherapy may have improved ward behaviour, but there is no evidence that it altered the prognosis for these patients. Feifel and Schwartz (1953) claimed to have obtained success in a group of acutely disturbed psychotic patients who received psychotherapy. Unfortunately, their control group was inappropriately selected. Moreover, both the control and experimental group patients were simultaneously receiving other treatments, including physical techniques such as shock therapy, drugs, and even individual psychotherapy. The outcome data are poor, and their follow-up information of little value.

The report by Zirkle (1961), used by Smith and Glass (1977) in their meta-analysis, claims that 15 minute sessions of psychotherapy were more beneficial than 25-minute sessions or no-treatment, in assisting chronic schizophrenics. The (contaminated) ratings on which the claim was based, were unusually crude and dubious, but failed to produce a significant result (p. 546).

These outcome studies present a bleak picture and appear to confirm only too well the early pessimism expressed by Freud. The better-executed studies yielded negative outcomes, while the favourable claims are based on studies which are manifestly poor, and even then the claims are modest. In spite of all this unfavourable evidence or, perhaps because of it, the literature on this subject is teeming with extravagant assertions, contradictory recommendations, and conflicting conclusions.

In his extensive review of the treatment of schizophrenia, covering a wide range of methods including psychotherapy, May (1975) used firm, even severe, standards of evaluation while remaining rather uncritical of psychometric evidence. His long list of criticisms include repeated instances of confounding (especially by drug treatments), non-random allocation to treatment, absence of controlled conditions, absence of follow-up, exclusive reliance on ratings provided by the therapist, and the usual sorry list of inadequacies. Using his severe standards, May was able to find only five acceptable controlled studies of individual psychotherapy. Of these only one was not confounded by drug therapy and it failed to produce a significant psychotherapeutic effect. The only unconfounded study of group psychotherapy which he could discover produced no differences between the controls and the treated patients.

He is particularly severe on the report by Karon and Vandebos (1972) which is sometimes quoted in support of the case for psychotherapy. May concluded that "fundamental inadequacies in design, analysis and interpretation . . . make it difficult to accept the investigators conclusions as anything more than tentative speculations" (p. 967). He lays particular emphasis on the non-random assignment to therapists, the puzzling discrepancies in their data, and the simultaneous use of other forms of treatment.

Karon and Vandenbos argue that their results show that "psychotherapy produces significantly greater patient change than medication, and is particularly effective in changing the thought disorder. Moreover, it is a good thing for the therapist to be experienced, benign, and to believe in the treatment he practices" (p. 118). Thirty-six schizophrenic patients "were randomly assigned to three treatment groups" (p. 11). The first group of patients received analytic therapy without medication, the second had the same treatment supplemented by medication, and the third group, who were treated in a different hospital, received mainly drugs and were therefore regarded as a control. Some of the patients were treated by trainee therapists and seven by the experienced therapists. (If the patients in the control group failed to respond to medication after a few weeks, they were transferred to a State hospital.) On the face of it, May wrongly criticized them for using an inappropriate method of assignment to groups, but the confusion has arisen from the fact that he criticized the non-random assignment to therapists, not to groups.

Each patient was examined before treatment and again after 6, 12 and 20 months. The assessments consisted of a blind clinical rating, intellectual tests, projective tests, and a visual—verbal test which was said to provide a measure of thought disorder.

The authors claimed to show that the patients who had psychotherapy, with or without medication, did significantly better than the control patients on a range of different measures. The information on time spent in hospital is difficult to interpret because of the wide range of scores. For example, the eight patients who were treated by drugs and trainee psychotherapists spent an average of 8.1 days in hospital (corrected score), whereas the patients who were treated under the same conditions but by an experienced therapist, spent 122 days in hospital. The six patients who had psychotherapy, without drugs, from trainee therapists spent 139 days in hospital. The blind clinical ratings show slight differences between the groups, but the control patients did at least as well as one of the groups receiving psychotherapy and drugs. Moreover, as we have already seen, the control patients were transferred to a State hospital if they failed to respond within a few weeks. Hence the correct comparison to use in determining the effects of psychotherapy as such would be group A versus group B, i.e. a comparison between those patients who received psychotherapy with or without drugs, while remaining in the same hospital. The authors attached considerable importance to the results obtained on the visual—verbal test, which they regard as a measure of schizophrenic thought disorder. "The measure designed specifically to reflect the schizophrenic thought disorder, the VVT, yields the most striking differences among the five groups" (p. 116). Unfortunately this key measure is of doubtful validity. Although it was introduced in 1951, very few investigators have seen fit to use it as a test of thought disorder, or for any other purpose. It receives no mention in the extensive review on the outcome of psychotherapy compiled by Luborsky et al. (1971). In a 1970 review of the test, Payne (1970) complained that the deficiencies of the test rendered it of limited value. There is a total absence of information about the age, the level of intelligence, socioeconomic level, sex, length of hospitalization, major symptomatology, and other details "which are needed if the norms are to be applied to other populations . . . unfortunately none of these data are given . . . even the mean ages of the groups are not reported" (p. 1209). Peterson (1970) points out that there is no information about the reliability of the test, and draws attention to the fact that the original sample "was composed of 37 volunteers whose cooperation was solicited while they were sitting around in a bus terminal" (p. 1210). Furthermore, the mean for chronic schizophrenic patients closely resembles that for mental defectives and is similar to scores for patients with known brain damage. "The construct validity and predicted utility of the tests are essentially unestablished" (p. 1211). In the circumstances, the neglect of this test is understandable, and attempts to evaluate the effects of psychotherapy with schizophrenic patients that rest on VVT scores cannot be taken seriously unless and until the test is properly validated.

The claim by Karon and Vandenbos that their results demonstrate the superiority of experienced therapists is not borne out by their findings. May's complaints about the inconsistencies in their data are well taken. Finally, the scientific detachment of Karon and Vandenbos is brought into question by their use of inverted commas in this statement about their control group treatment — they say, "this is 'treatment' as currently practised at 'good' public institutions" (p. 112). A replication of their study, using established methods of assessment and more conventional statistical analyses, would be most welcome.

Rosenthal (1962) has observed that one repeatedly encounters debates and discussions about the desirability of establishing transference relationships, or even if it is possible to establish such relationships. Other points of debate are whether patients should be encouraged or discouraged to regress, whether interpretations should be offered or withheld, and so on. The methods of treatment range from attempts at orthodox psychoanalytic treatment to the deliberate encouragement of infantile behaviour. The more orthodox techniques are sufficiently well known not to require any description, but some of the extraordinary variations are worth mentioning. Although it should be remembered that *these techniques are not widely practised,* they feature in many discussions on the use of psychotherapy in psychotic conditions. They are accorded serious consideration and sometimes, praise. Rosenthal (1962) described rather well the curiously uncritical attitude adopted by therapists and writers on the subject. He observed that "therapists seem to have an unwritten agreement to respect and admire each other's artistry, despite glaring differences and contradictions in points of view, and at the same time to resist concepts and formulations forged in the laboratory, as though the latter were somehow debasing". Two radical variants of psychotherapy will suffice to illustrate the range of practices.

Azima and Wittkower (1956) argued that the frustrated oral and anal needs of "schizophrenic organism can be gratified by allowing a deep but transitory regression to occur" (p. 122). They described the treatment of six patients over a period of 6 months consisting of 1 hour of treatment 5 days a week. The main feature of their treatment was "offering the patients primitive media", as it was their purpose to "provide a symbolic miniature infantile situation, in which appropriate feelings could be expressed". The treatment was divided into three phases with the first consisting of an emphasis on anal needs. "The media offered were mud, brown clay, cocoa powder, cocoa mud, plasticine, and finger paint. In addition, aggressive activities such as tearing paper and throwing darts were introduced. Patients were encouraged to smear and soil, and to cut and throw objects" (p. 122). During the second phase they concentrated on oral gratifications, and additional aggressive activities were introduced. "Patients were offered a baby bottle filled with milk with large holes in the nipple; at first they were also fed with liquids 15 minutes before the end of each session" (p. 123). In the third phase, more structured activities were introduced: "Jumping ropes, playing with dolls, listening to music and dancing, working with clay and making pots, drawing on the blackboard and cleaning it, playing games such as badminton and ping-pong, and colouring children's books" (p. 123).

Rosen (1953) developed a variation on psychoanalysis, "direct analysis", for which he claimed considerable therapeutic value. He reported cures following a course of treatment which may last from 3 days to 11 months, with the average period of treatment lasting from 2 to 3 months. In attempting to achieve his goal of a complete analysis of the transference, "as we aim to do in ordinary analytic procedures", he adopted some extremely radical procedures. According to Rosen (p. 8), "the governing principle of direct analysis is that the therapist must be a loving, omnipotent protector and provider for the patient. Expressed another way, he must be the idealized mother who now has the responsibility of bringing the patient up all over again ... since direct analysis holds that this catastrophic collapse is the consequence of unconscious malevolent mothering" (p. 9). The purpose of the direct interpretations is to indicate to the patient "that somewhere in his environment there now exists understanding, that is, magical, omnipotent understanding, the earliest understanding of him exhibited by an adult in his neonatal environment" (p. 12). In the first place the therapist has to provide for the "conscious, tangible needs of the patient which anyone can recognize, such as food, warmth, and protection". He then employs a variety of techniques designed to provide the patient with insight into his unconscious, and thereby, a resolution of the psychosis. Having achieved this goal, it is desirable to complete treatment with a course of orthodox psychoanalysis.

The techniques which Rosen employs are described in his own book, and rather more systematically by Scheflen (1961), who spent 2 years observing and recording Rosen's treatment of several psychotic patients at the Temple University Medical Center. Scheflen lists sixteen techniques: promising and rewarding, threatening and punishing, suggesting and instructing, coercing, rendering service, group pressure, ridiculing and discrediting, interrupting and diverting, appealing and challenging, offering alternatives, misrepresenting, imitating, role-playing, acting out, reassuring, and confrontation and interpretation. According to Scheflen, whose account is detached and occasionally favourable, the "principle (*sic*) techniques of direct analysis" are discrediting, arousal of shame, and ridiculing. In order to achieve certain therapeutic aims, Rosen attempts to weaken the patients' relationships with other people. For example, a female patient was isolated from her relatives because she "resisted relating" to the therapist. "A woman patient persistently refused to recognize any relatedness to Rosen, insisting on talking about her husband or one of the assistants. Rosen took various measures to break her attachment to the husband. He finally told her that her husband had divorced her and remarried. Multiple 'proofs' of this were conjured, and it was weeks before the patient was told that this was not so" (p. 125). In another case, Rosen was attempting to improve the patient's sexual adjustment. The description given by Scheflen is as follows:

"With this patient, months were spent on this matter. Rosen insisted that the patient have intercourse with him. He interpreted her flight from this idea as a fear of incest and he intermittently reassured her that there would never be a sexual relationship between them. At first these reassurances were nearly always followed by a temporary remission of many of the patient's psychotic symptoms. Later Rosen omitted the reassurances. . . . In the sequence to be related, Rosen spent about 20 minutes forcing the patient by coercion and threats to state that now she sexually preferred Rosen to her husband but would later prefer her husband. She resisted in all manners but finally said what she was told" (p. 159).

In one session the patient asked Rosen if she should take her skirt down. He replied affirmatively. "She appeared exhausted, docile. She asked Rosen to help her pull her skirt down. He reached over and pulled them down for her. She put her head on his shoulder and made no further strong defiance. Rosen sent for a blanket, covered her up and began urging her to go to sleep. As the patient complied, acting sleepy, passive and child-like, Rosen reversed his field and twice provoked a repetition of the cycle" (p. 173). Other examples of the therapist's behaviour can be conveyed in a selection of Scheflen's quotations from Rosen. "Your mother killed your sister" (a reference to a sibling who was scalded to death by falling into a tub while the mother was washing) (p. 128). "I am God and will not permit you to be harmed" (p. 95). "The milk is warm and good. Not the poison that your mother fed you" (Rosen, 1953, p. 21).

Presumably this type of conduct is defensible. It cannot be said however, that an explanation springs to mind. It will not come as a surprise that the therapeutic value of this technique has never been demonstrated, despite Rosen's claims. Scheflen (1961) adopted a reserved position on the patients he had seen treated, but Horwitz *et al.* (1958) followed up nineteen of Rosen's original thirty-seven cases and concluded, "whatever the merits of direct analytic therapy for schizophrenia, the claim that it results in a high degree of recovery remains unproven" (p. 783). An inadequately designed prospective control study by Bookhammer *et al.* (1966) produced a similar conclusion.

Perhaps the last word on this dismal scene should rest with Rosenthal. Recalling the satirical statement that psychotherapy is "an undefined technique applied to unspecified problems with unpredictable outcomes. For this technique we recommend rigorous training", he recorded his astonishment at finding the following statement in a book on the use of psychotherapy with schizophrenic patients. He assures us that the statement is intended to be taken seriously: "There is no general agreement as to what constitutes necessary, specific personal or professional attributes for the successful therapist with schizophrenic patients, except that to be a successful therapist with schizophrenic patients demands extensive training and desirable personal qualities."

CHAPTER 9

BEHAVIOUR THERAPY—I

As noted in the Introduction, the development and rapid growth of behaviour therapy has been remarkable. In the United States, it has had a major impact on clinical training programmes in clinical psychology and is also represented in psychiatric training (Brady, 1978). In addition to its wide use in Britain and the United States, behaviour therapy is practised in major centres of research and practice in Canada, Australia, and New Zealand, and in countries throughout Europe and Latin America. Behaviour therapy is now.being applied to a broadening range of diverse clinical, medical, and educational problems, outstripping the range of traditional psycho-therapy. Perhaps most dramatic of all has been the explosion of literature on behaviour therapy.

Not surprisingly, behaviour therapy has undergone important changes over the course of this accelerated growth. Nowadays it is marked by the development of new treatment techniques and the modification of existing methods, by increasing methodological sophistication and versatility, by its expanding range of applications, and by lively debates about its theoretical foundations and efficacy. These encouraging developments are in keeping with the prediction

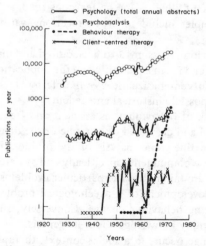

FIG. 4. The rise in publications on behaviour therapy that took place from 1950 to 1972, shown in this Figure, continues but less steeply. Client-centred therapy publications are being overtaken by work on cognitive therapy. Figure reprinted from P. Hoon and O. Lindsley (1974) *American Psychologist*, vol. 24, p. 694, by permission of the A.P.A.

made in the First Edition of this book that behaviour therapy will prove to be a successful step in the development of a scientifically based approach to psychological treatment (see Agras, Kazdin, and Wilson, 1979).

Behaviour therapy encompasses a range of heterogeneous procedures with various rationales. This is not the place to attempt a systematic analysis of the theoretical foundations or conceptual bases of behaviour therapy (see Bandura, 1978; Feldman and Broadhurst, 1976, among other works). Suffice it to point out, following Agras *et al.* (1979) and Wilson and Franks (in press), that broadly conceived of, the different approaches in contemporary behaviour therapy include applied behaviour analysis (e.g. Baer, Wolf, and Risley, 1968; Brigham and Catania, 1979); a neo-behaviouristic mediational model (e.g. Eysenck, 1976; Wilson and O'Leary, 1980), and cognitive behaviour modification (e.g Mahoney and Arnkoff, 1978; Meichenbaum, 1977).

It is important to emphasize that although these approaches involve conceptual differences, there is a common core of assumptions that behaviour therapists hold. Behaviour therapy is distinguished by two basic characteristics: (1) a psychological model of human behaviour (and especially of abnormal behaviour) that differs fundamentally from the traditional intrapsychic, psychodynamic, or quasi-disease models of mental illness; and (2) a commitment to scientific method, measurement, and evaluation. Each of these characteristics has implications for assessment, modification, and evaluation.

The emphasis on the psychological as opposed to quasi-disease model of abnormal behaviour has the following consequences:

(a) Abnormal behaviour that is not a function of specific brain dysfunction or biochemical disturbance is assumed to be governed by the same principles that regulate normal behaviour.

(b) Many types of abnormal behaviour formerly regarded as illnesses in themselves, or as signs and symptoms of illness, are better construed as non-pathological "problems of living" (key examples include neurotic reactions, various forms of sexual deviance, and conduct disorders).

(c) Most abnormal behaviour is assumed to be acquired and maintained in the same manner as normal behaviour; and it can be modified by the application of behavioural procedures.

(d) Behavioural assessments emphasize the *current* determinants of behaviour rather than the *post hoc* analysis of possible historical antecedents.

Specificity is the hallmark of behavioural assessment and treatment, and it is assumed that the person is best understood and described by what he or she does in particular situations.

(e) Treatment requires a fine-grain analysis of the problem into components or sub-parts and is targeted at these components specifically and systematically.

(f) Treatment strategies are tailored to the particular problems of the person concerned.

(g) Understanding the development of a psychological problem may be helpful, but is not essential for producing behaviour change. Conversely, success in changing a problem behaviour does not imply knowledge about its genesis.

(h) Since behaviour change occurs in a social context, therapeutic interventions may result in "side effects", i.e. changes in behaviour that were not the focus of treatment. These are not necessarily deleterious effects, nor a product of "symptom substitution". More often than not these broader treatment effects are positive.

(i) Behaviour therapy involves a commitment to an applied science approach. This includes the following characteristics:

an explicit, testable conceptual framework;

treatment that is either derived from or at least consistent with the content and
method of experimental–clinical psychology;

therapeutic techniques that can be described with sufficient precision to be measured
objectively and replicated;

the experimental evaluation of treatment methods and concepts;

the emphasis on innovative research strategies that allow rigorous evaluation of
specific methods applied to particular problems, instead of global assessments of
ill-defined procedures applied to heterogeneous problems.

THE OUTCOME OF BEHAVIOUR THERAPY

Significantly, it is an impossible task to provide a detailed analysis of the outcome evidence
on behaviour therapy even if we were to devote this entire volume to the subject. Such is the
burgeoning nature of research on behavioural methods and so extensive are their applications to
diverse clinical, medical, education, and social problems of children and adults, that a review of
the relevant outcome literature is beyond the scope of this or any other single volume.
Fortunately, several detailed evaluations of this substantial and rapidly increasing literature are
readily available (cf. Brigham and Catania, 1979; Doyle and Gentry, 1977; Franks and Wilson;
1973–1979; Kazdin, 1978 a and b; Kazdin & Wilson, 1978; Leitenberg, 1976; Marks, 1978;
O'Leary, 1977, in press; Rachman, 1977–1979; Ross, 1978). In the present volume we have
chosen to focus primarily on adult disorders, concentrating on particular techniques that
are employed with commonly encountered clinical problems. Specifically, we propose to
highlight some of the more important accomplishments of behaviour therapy and to indicate
significant problems in evaluation that require continued experimental attention. Perhaps most
importantly, we wish to emphasize the significant advances that have been made in methodology
and measurement as behaviour therapy has developed, and to indicate how these methodological
contributions are relevant not only to behaviour therapy but to the scientific evaluation of all
psychological treatment methods.

The therapeutic efficacy of a particular treatment approach has generally been evaluated by
comparative outcome research. In studies of this nature, the relative efficacy of behaviour
therapy has been compared with that of an alternative treatment method(s) derived from
different conceptual bases. Recent reviewers of this comparative outcome literature have
reached the common conclusion that there are no significant differences among equally effective
alternative treatments, including behaviour therapy. Bergin and Lambert's (1978) conclusion
that psychoanalytic therapy, humanistic or client-centred psychotherapy, and behaviour therapy
"rest on a reasonable empirical base", "achieve results superior to no-treatment and various placebo treatment procedures", and "have been found to be about equally effective with the broad
spectrum of outpatients" (p. 170), is typical. In previous chapters we have called into question
the claim that there is adequate evidence to support the value of psychoanalytic or client-
centred therapy and have challenged the increasingly prevalent view that all therapies are
equally effective. In this and the following chapters we shall sample the empirical status of the
effects of behaviour therapy.

Although they accept Luborsky et al.'s (1975) "Dodo bird verdict", Bergin and Lambert
qualify their overall conclusion about the comparative effects of different psychotherapies with

the following statement: "Although generally true [that the Dodo bird verdict], it seems clear that with circumscribed disorders, such as certain phobias, some sexual dysfunctions, and compulsions, certain technical operations can reliably bring about success" (p. 170). These "technical operations" are behavioural methods.

Luborsky *et al*. compared behaviour therapy to psychotherapy and reported that in six of the nineteen comparisons, behaviour therapy was significantly superior. They dismissed these six studies on the grounds that they were poorly controlled. Luborsky *et al*. limited their analysis to neurotic problems that would be considered to have the most favourable prognosis, and excluded a wide range of common childhood and adult disorders, remarking that behaviour therapy *might* be the preferred treatment for problems like enuresis and habit disorders. Smith and Glass (1977) compared some behavioural methods to other treatment approaches and found that systematic desensitization was most effective. Subsequent statistical recombinations of methods systematically reduced the apparent superiority of behavioural methods. More recently, Kazdin and Wilson (1978b) subjected the conclusions arrived at in the Luborsky *et al*. (1975) and Smith and Glass (1977) reviews to critical scrutiny in the context of a comprehensive analysis of seventy-five comparative clinical outcome studies. All studies were reviewed in which behavioural treatment was compared either to a specific alternative treatment or to what is typically described as routine hospital treatment. Luborsky *et al*. excluded "the huge literature specifically on habit disorders (e.g., addiction and bed-wetting)" and studies that used "student volunteers" as opposed to "bona fide patients" in "bona fide treatment". In contrast, Kazdin and Wilson's evaluative review encompassed comparative studies across the range of behaviour disorders including neurotic and psychotic disorders, sexual dysfunction and deviance, addictive behaviour, delinquency, and childhood disorders. Unlike Smith and Glass, Kazdin and Wilson evaluated only published studies. Despite their claim to being uniquely comprehensive, Smith and Glass included only 35% of the studies reviewed by Kazdin and Wilson. Rather than totally disregarding the methodological adequacy and comparability of individual studies, Kazdin and Wilson provided a critical analysis of the soundness of each study.

The overall finding of the Kazdin and Wilson evaluation was that there were few studies sufficiently well-controlled to permit unambiguous interpretation of results. Fundamental problems in experimental design and measurement of treatment outcome diminished the value of the vast majority of studies they reviewed. Many were so seriously flawed as to provide no useful information at all. Despite the many inadequacies in the uneven and heterogeneous collection of studies they reviewed, Kazdin and Wilson were able to extract the following conclusions:

1. *Not a single comparison showed behaviour therapy to be inferior to psychotherapy.* On the contrary, most studies showed behaviour therapy was either marginally or significantly more effective than the alternative treatment.

2. *No evidence of symptom substitution following behaviour therapy was obtained,* even in studies explicitly designed to uncover negative side effects. Typical of the findings in this respect is Sloane *et al*.'s (1975) comment:

> ". . . not a single patient whose original problems had substantially improved reported new symptoms cropping up. On the contrary, assessors had the informal impression that when a patient's primary symptoms improved, he often spontaneously reported improvement of other minor difficulties" (p. 100).

3. *Behaviour therapy is more broadly applicable to the full range of psychological disorders than traditional psychotherapy.* In the Sloane *et al*. (1975) study, for example, behaviour

therapy appeared to be more effective than psychotherapy particularly with the more complex problems in the more severely disturbed patients. This led Sloane *et al.* (1975) to emphasize that "Behaviour therapy is clearly a *generally* useful treatment" (p. 226). This finding of greater applicability and relevance of behaviour therapy stands in contrast to the dated view that its usefulness is limited to the treatment of monosymptomatic fears and simple habits.

4. *Behavioural therapy is capable of producing broadly based treatment effects on specific target behaviour and related measures of general psychological functioning.* A frequently voiced speculation is that behaviour therapy might have greater effects on symptom-outcome measures than on more important or fundamental processes related to general adjustment. This suggestion reflects the view that behaviour therapy is best regarded as a limited and relatively superficial form of treatment useful as an adjunct to conventional psychotherapy. The data do not support this notion.

In short, Kazdin and Wilson found that behaviour therapy was frequently more effective than alternative psychotherapeutic methods. Behaviour therapy had not been shown to be inferior to any alternative form of psychotherapy. Furthermore, behavioural methods were found to be applicable to a much broader range of human problems than verbal psychotherapy, and there was clear evidence of broad-gauged treatment effects across specific target behaviour as well as more general measures of personal, social, and vocational adjustment.

A recent study by McLean and Hakstian (1979) deserves mention in connection with a discussion of the comparative effects of behaviour therapy versus alternative treatment methods. One hundred and ninety-six depressed patients were randomly assigned to either a behavioural therapy, a psychotherapy, a pharmacotherapy, or an attention placebo condition (relaxation training treatment group). The patients were drawn from a typical out-patient clinical population and met the following requirements: between 20 and 60 years old; had been depressed for at least the last 2 months; were functionally impaired as a result of their depression (e.g. unable to work); were not involved in any other form of therapy; were diagnosed as presenting with primary depression on the basis of a clinical interview; met the diagnostic criteria for psychiatric research in clinical depression suggested by Feighner, Robins, Guze, Woodruff, Winokur, and Munoz (1972); scored within or beyond the moderate range on well-established tests of depression such as the Beck Depression Inventory (>23, Beck, 1967) and the MMPI (D Scale, > 25 for men and > 29.5 for women). In all, 72% of the sample were women, with an average age of 39 years, over half of whom were married and employed. On average, they had been depressed for close to 11 years; 25% reported at least one serious suicide attempt and 54% reported frequent suicidal thinking.

Fourteen therapists (seven males and seven females) participated in the study. All therapists were licensed physicians, psychiatrists, or psychologists who "were selected . . . on the strength of their reputations in the particular treatment they offered" with the exception of the attention-placebo or relaxation treatment. Level of therapist experience was systematically examined in this study. Junior therapists had 2 to 4 years of experience conducting therapy, the senior therapists more than 5 years. Treatment consisted of eight to twelve weekly out-patient sessions on an individual or conjoint basis. Patients were encouraged to invite their spouses or common-law partners to participate in therapy sessions. The proportion of spouses or partners who attended one or more treatment sessions was 38.1% for behaviour therapy; 38.6% for psychotherapy; 14.3% for pharmacotherapy; and 27.9% for relaxation training.

Behaviour therapy in this investigation consisted of the multifaceted approach described by McLean (1976). To summarize, patients were told that depression is the result of ineffective coping techniques used to remedy stressful life problems. An individual hierarchy of treatment goals was constructed for each patient, and specific behavioural techniques such as graduated *in vivo* practice and modelling were used to develop adequate coping skills in seven areas of functioning: communication, behavioural productivity, social interaction, assertiveness, decision-making, problem-solving, and cognitive self-control. Structured homework assignments were employed and patients equipped with well-rehearsed plans for coping with the experience of future depressive episodes.

The short-term psychotherapy in this study is described by McLean and Hakstian as modelled on the work of Marmor (1975) and Wolberg (1967). Specifically,

"the goals of psychotherapy were to relieve symptomatic complaints and to restore the client's pre-episode level of functioning, through the development of insight into the psychodynamic forces which initiated the current depression and through the recognition of personality problems as they relate to past experiences and the current depression. The methods of psychotherapy included the establishment of a good therapist–client relationship, tension release through emotional catharsis, offering insight, reality testing, the provision of emotional support, and the provision of suggestions and advice in the area of self-perception and environmental adjustment. Therapists used these fundamental principles as guides in a relatively unstructured approach to treatment" (McLean and Hakstian, 1979).

Patients in the pharmacotherapy treatment were given a biochemical rationale for their depression and received amitriptyline for a total of 11 weeks. Starting at 75 mg, patients graduated to the fixed treatment dosage of 150 mg/day over a 10-day period and, upon completion of the trial, were weaned at the rate of 25 mg/day. This medication was taken as a single daily dose at bedtime. In order to have data available on blood serum levels and compliance with this self-medication schedule, unannounced blood samples were drawn on two random visits over the 11-week treatment period for qualitative laboratory analysis (serum analysis by gas–liquid chromatography with electron-capture detection). Clients attended for weekly visits during which therapists completed a physiological review (i.e. blood pressure, weight, pulse rate and rhythm, etc.) and reviewed with clients their daily recordings on a 30-item side-effects questionnaire.

The relaxation training or attention-placebo treatment involved patients learning to relax in the therapist's office and practising this skill at home. The relationship between depression and muscle tension was emphasized and the occurrence of depressive symptoms attributed to the presence of tension.

Assessment of treatment outcome was based on multiple measures of functioning including the Beck Depression Inventory and measures of cognitive activity, coping, personal activity, social functioning, somatic indicators, mood, and overall satisfaction. An analysis of patients who terminated treatment prematurely shows that the dropout rate for behaviour therapy (5%) was significantly lower than that for either the psychotherapy group (30%) or the pharmacotherapy group (36%). The dropout rate in the relaxation training group was 26%. Dropouts were not included in the data analyses and were replaced by additional patients in order to reduce the effects of a differential attrition rate.

The results at post-treatment showed that behaviour therapy was significantly superior to psychotherapy on six of the ten main outcome measures (scores on the BDI, subjective complaints, rating of goal attainment, social functioning, general satisfaction, and mood) and significantly superior to all other treatments on three measures (complaints, goals, and mood).

Patients were also split into three categories at the end of treatment in terms of their BDI scores, a score of less than 7 representing the normal range, a score of less than 23 but more than 7 the mildly depressed range, and a score of greater than 23 as the moderate to severe range of depression. Of the behaviour therapy patients, 50% were in the normal range as compared to 25% in the psychotherapy and pharmacotherapy groups, respectively, a marginally significant finding ($p < 0.10$). There was no effect for therapist experience. A 3-month follow-up indicated fewer statistically significant differences. Behaviour therapy was more effective than all groups in terms of social functioning and superior to psychotherapy on the mood measure. Similarly, pharmacotherapy produced greater improvement on the mood measure. Overall, behaviour therapy registered the greatest improvement on seven of the ten measures, psychotherapy the weakest effects on seven of the ten outcome variables. The broad-gauged treatment effects of behaviour therapy are consistent with Kazdin and Wilson's conclusions.

Several commendable features distinguish this study, including the investigation of a large number of clinically depressed patients, random assignment to groups, the use of qualified therapists, examination of therapist experience as a source of treatment outcome, and a 3-month follow-up. Other strengths include the independent documentation that patients in the pharmacotherapy group were complying with the drug regimen and tape-recordings of all therapy sessions that showed that treatments used by the therapists were discriminably different from each other. Kazdin and Wilson (1978b) have emphasized the importance of independent evaluations of the discriminability of treatments as actually practised in comparative therapy outcome research. Measurement of treatment outcome was comprehensive but it should be noted that all outcome variables were derived from a depression questionnaire that patients returned by mail at each assessment period. The BDI is an established measure of depression, with proven reliability and validity. The extensive depression questionnaire employed by McLean and Hakstian is an unknown quantity that requires validation.

A criticism that McLean and Hakstian anticipate concerns the adequacy of their psychotherapy treatment. Critics will correctly point out that 10 weeks is insufficient time for most commonly practised forms of psychotherapy to have an optimal effect. In a related fashion one must be careful to avoid the therapy uniformity myth, and recognize that the results of this study apply only to the particular form of psychotherapy employed. It is impossible to generalize these findings to psychotherapy in general. Indeed, McLean and Hakstian's findings are best viewed as impressive support for the value of behaviour therapy rather than evidence that psychotherapy is relatively ineffective. The greater efficacy of behaviour therapy compared to pharmacotherapy at post-treatment is especially encouraging given the fact that drugs are usually the preferred treatment for depressive reactions. These results are consistent with the findings of the Rush, Beck, Kovacs, and Hollon (1977) study showing the superiority of cognitive behaviour therapy over imipramine (see Chapter 11 below). Similarly, the fact that behaviour therapy resulted in a significantly lower attrition rate than pharmacotherapy is consistent with the Rush *et al.* findings. However, this favourable showing of cognitive-behavioural methods should be viewed cautiously in the light of McLean and Hakstian's follow-up data indicating only one significant difference between behaviour therapy and pharmacotherapy.

A second source of evidence bearing on the efficacy of behaviour therapy comes from well-controlled studies in which a specific behavioural technique is compared to an attention-placebo or no-treatment control group. In some instances, operationally precise behavioural techniques are compared with each other or a particular technique with its component parts as in the case of the dismantling research strategy with systematic desensitization (Lang, 1969). This dismantling research strategy is only one among several innovative and flexible treatment outcome strategies that have been developed by behaviour therapists. Aside from versatile between-groups designs, the development of different single-case experimental designs that make possible the controlled evaluation of specific techniques in the treatment of individual patients is a signal methodological contribution that has greatly expanded the scope of experimental inquiry in therapy outcome research (Hersen and Barlow, 1976). The development of these different research strategies, the full range of which are discussed more fully elsewhere (see Kazdin and Wilson, 1978b), enables investigators to tackle seriously the important outcome question of what technique is most effective with what sort of problem in what patient on which measures and at what cost. The bulk of the extensive literature on the outcome of behaviour therapy is in this experimental tradition. Significant progress in therapy outcome evaluation will follow from research along these lines rather that global comparisons ill-defined therapeutic approaches (e.g. "psychotherapy" versus "behaviour therapy") applied to heterogeneous clinical disorders (e.g. neurotic and personality disorders) with inadequate measures of outcome (e.g. clinical ratings) that inevitably obscure potential differences between techniques.

In reviewing outcome evidence on behaviour therapy one has to organize the evaluation in terms of the problem treated or of the specific treatment techniques used. In the remainder of this chapter we selectively discuss the data on well-known anxiety-reduction techniques commonly applied to the treatment of anxiety phobic, and obsessional—compulsive disorders. Our focus here is on the effects of specific methods with particular problems. It must be recognized that in general clinical practice the behaviour therapist will usually employ a combination of different behavioural techniques (either concurrently or sequentially) in order to treat complex disorders. McLean and Hakstian's (1979) multifaceted treatment programme for depressives is an example of such an approach. It would be fair to say, therefore, that the results reviewed here from the application of specific methods in a controlled research context usually represent a conservative estimate of the clinical success of behaviour therapy.

Progressive Relaxation Training

In developing the technique of systematic desensitization, Wolpe (1958) adapted from Jacobson (1938) the procedure called progressive relaxation training as a means of producing a response that is physiologically incompatible with anxiety. Much of the research on progressive relaxation training has centred on its role in the desensitization process. In general, studies designed to identify the necessary and sufficient components of therapeutic efficacy in systematic desensitization have shown that relaxation training is not necessary for treatment success although it may contribute to successful outcomes in an indirect manner by facilitating non-reinforced exposure to the feared stimuli (cf. Gillan and Rachman, 1974; Waters, McDonald, and Koresko, 1972; Wilkins, 1971; Wilson and Davison, 1971). More recently, however, progressive relaxation training has been used increasingly as a therapeutic technique in its own right as originally proposed by Jacobson. With the marked trend in behaviour therapy towards client self-control as opposed to therapist-controlled procedures, relaxation training is viewed as an active, coping self-control skill that clients are taught to employ across diverse anxiety-eliciting situations (Goldfried, 1979). Another factor in the emphasis on progressive relaxation training is the more general interest in the therapeutic properties of what has been referred to as the "relaxation response" (Benson, 1975). A major stimulus for this work came from the interest in transcendental meditation (TM) and workers have started to explore the commonalities between different types of relaxation training, their therapeutic mechanisms, the specific problems they are best suited for, and their comparative efficacy (Borkovec, and Hennings, 1978; Davidson and Schwartz, 1976; Marlatt and Marques, 1977). Although some therapists have advocated the use of TM as a treatment method, progressive relaxation has been more intensively investigated.

CONTROLLED-TREATMENT OUTCOME STUDIES

The clinical utility of progressive relaxation training is well established in the treatment of hypertension. In a comprehensive review of the application and outcome of relaxation therapies in the treatment of hypertension, Jacob, Kraemer, and Agras (1977) concluded that progressive relaxation produces clinically significant reductions in blood pressure that cannot be accounted for by placebo influences alone. In a study by Taylor, Farquhar, Nelson, and Agras (1977), progressive relaxation training was shown to produce significantly greater decreases in blood pressure than medical treatment only or a non-specific attention-placebo control group, at the end of 5 weeks of therapy. Attention–placebo control groups have not always been adequate in controlling for the non-specific variables that might confound the treatment effects of the specific behavioural technique under investigation (cf. Jacobson and Baucom, 1977; Kazdin and Wilcoxon, 1976). However, the non-specific control treatment devised by Taylor et al. (1977) appears to rule out extraneous placebo influences in attributing decreases in blood pressure to progressive relaxation training. Five of the non-specific control treatment patients spontaneously reported that they "knew" their blood pressure had been reduced and they expressed unsolicited gratitude for treatment. Four patients requested that therapy continue at the termination of the formally scheduled treatment sessions. Although anecdotal, these observations indicate that the treatment condition was perceived as a genuine and effective therapeutic experience. Also, it was the case that these patients had been receiving medical treatment before the study and continued to do so during the study.

The significant differences obtained by Taylor et al. (1977) at post-treatment were no longer evident at 6 months follow-up due to the continued improvement of the medical treatment and non-specific treatment control groups, and a slight (but non-significant) deterioration in the progressive relaxation training group. In a replication and extension of these findings, Brauer, Horlick, Nelson, Farquhar, and Agras (1979) compared therapist-administered progressive relaxation training with self-administered progressive relaxation training using audio-cassettes and a non-specific control treatment. The therapist-administered progressive relaxation treatment resulted in significantly greater reductions in blood pressure both at post-treatment and at the 6 months follow-up evaluation.

In addition to providing confirmation of the usefulness of progressive relaxation training in the management of hypertensive patients, Brauer et al.'s (1979) findings suggest that there is no substitute for relaxation administered by a skilled therapist. For example, one of the three therapists obtained inferior results. Significantly, this therapist had little clinical experience — he was a second-year medical student with no experience in the use of progresssive relaxation training. The practice of providing patients with audio-tapes of progressive relaxation training instructions for self-administration is widespread. These and other findings (Beiman, Israel, and

Johnson, 1978; Borkovec and Sides, 1979) suggest that the greater efficiency and economy of such self-administered relaxation training may be achieved at the cost of reduced efficacy.

Tension headache has also been treated with a degree of success. Cox, Freundlich, and Meyer (1975) assigned twenty-seven adults with chronic tension headaches to either an EMG biofeedback group, a progressive relaxation group, or a placebo group. The multiple measures of the effects of 4 weeks of treatment, included headache frequency, intensity, and duration; frontalis EMG recordings; medication intake; and reports of any other psychosomatic problems. The EMG biofeedback and progressive relaxation groups were equally superior to the placebo group on all measures both at post-treatment and at a 4-month follow-up. It should be noted that progressive relaxation training in this study involved cue-controlled breathing and the active use of relaxation as a self-control coping skill. The pattern of Cox *et al.*'s (1975) results was duplicated by Haynes, Griffin, Mooney, and Parise (1975). Both EMG feedback and progressive relaxation were superior to a no-treatment control group in decreasing tension headaches, but did not differ from each other. Treatment gains appear to have persisted at a 5—7 month follow-up.*

Relaxation training has been used widely in the treatment of insomnia. The clear-cut conclusion from a number of well-controlled studies is that relaxation produces significant although relatively modest therapeutic effects in mild to severe cases of insomnia (Bootzin and Nicassio, 1977; Borkovec, 1979). Of particular importance is that the therapeutic effects of this method have been demonstrated to be independent of placebo influences. For example, Borkovec and Steinmark (1974) compared progressive relaxation training to placebo and no-treatment control conditions groups under counter-demand and normal treatment or positive demand instructions. In the counter-demand condition (sessions 1—3) treated subjects were informed that improvement would not occur until after the fourth treatment session (positive demand period). Steinmark and Borkovec (1974) found that relaxation training produced significantly greater improvement according to subjects' self-reports of improvement in latency of sleep onset than the placebo or no-treatment control groups during the counter-demand period. The relaxation and placebo groups were equally superior to the no-treatment group during positive demand instructions. Nor is this therapeutic effect confined to individuals' subjective estimates of sleep disturbance. Using the counter-demand methodology described above, Borkovec and Weerts (1976) found that compared to a pseudo-desensitization placebo group treatment and a waiting-list no-treatment condition, only the progressive relaxation treatment produced significant improvement on an EEG measure of sleep disturbance. Although not statistically significant at post-treatment, relaxation training was significantly superior to the placebo treatment as gauged by subjects' self-reports of the time they took to fall asleep. In a replication and extension of these results, Borkovec, Grayson, O'Brien, and Weerts (1970) showed that progressive relaxation training produced significant improvement in both pseudo and idiopathic insomniacs. The former report difficulties in falling asleep although EEG records indicate that their sleep latency is within normal limits; the latter show marked EEG disturbances in addition to subjective reports of sleep disorder. Progressive relaxation training produced significant improvement on subjective measures of sleep disturbance in the pseudo-insomniacs and on both subjective and objective (EEG) measures in the idiopathic insomniacs. Subjective improvement was maintained at a 1-year follow-up.

In addition to establishing the therapeutic efficacy of progressive relaxation in the treatment

*Recent findings emphasize the power of relaxation and bring into question the distinctive contribution of biofeedback (see Rachman & Philips, 1980).

of insomnia, research by Borkovec and his colleagues has also identified the critical procedural ingredients in the treatment method. It now seems apparent that the muscle tension-release component of progressive relaxation is crucial in producing positive results (Borkovec and Hennings, 1978). The role of focused attention on some neutral or pleasant repetitive stimulus, the other major procedural component of progressive relaxation as it is customarily practised, appears to reduce the negative effects of disturbing cognitive intrusions, but the tension-release process is of overriding importance in producing therapeutic improvement. The findings from this programme of research by Borkovec and his colleagues undermine the artificial dichotomy drawn between outcome and process studies in investigations of psychotherapy.

The use of the counter-demand methodology enabled Borkovec, Grayson, and Cooper (1978) to demonstrate the critical role of progressive relaxation training in significantly reducing reports of daily tension in comparison to a no-treatment control group. These effects were maintained at a 5-month follow-up. Progressive relaxation training has also been used to treat asthma. In an optimistic review of the literature, Knapp and Wells (1978) concluded that relaxation training has "consistently produced statistically significant improvement in subject's respiratory function measures . . . when compared to those subjects receiving no treatment" (p. 108). On the basis of better controlled research, however, Alexander, Cropp and Chai (1979) concluded that "the status of relaxation as a symptomatic therapy in asthma is that the effect may be very small indeed, if in fact it is reliable at all, even when present at full strength; and that, in any case, it is of little or no clinical significance even if real. This conclusion is consistent with existing data concerning the general lack of direct effect of psychologic variables on pulmonary function in asthma" (pp. 33–34). These authors note that the positive effects of relaxation training have been limited to its value in reducing fear responses to asthma rather than influencing pulmonary function itself.

As we have emphasized throughout this volume, therapy outcome should be evaluated in terms of what specific treatment method is effective with what well-defined problem on which specific measures. In contrast to the documented efficacy of progressive relaxation training with anxiety-related disorders such as hypertension, insomnia, and general tension states, relaxation training has been shown to be ineffective with problems such as obsessional–compulsive disorders (Rachman and Hodgson, 1979) and obesity (Hall, Hall, Hanson, and Borden, 1974; Hanson, Borden, Hall, and Hall, 1976), respiratory function in asthmatics (Alexander *et al.*, 1979), and no more effective than a placebo control with problem drinkers (Marlatt and Marques, 1977). This finding of differential efficacy of a particular treatment method across different disorders adds to the confidence that can be placed in those results showing treatment-specific effects of progressive relaxation training. Reliable differential outcome patterns of this nature are inconsistent with explanations that attribute treatment effects to the non-specific influences inherent in all forms of therapy. It is no accident that progressive relaxation training is effective with anxiety-related disorders in which there is a physiological arousal component (see Borkovec and Sides, 1979). Relaxation training was introduced in order to reduce physiologically based over-arousal (Wolpe, 1958). Progressive relaxation training appears to be more effective in the treatment of the more severely anxious patient compared to college students who do not have a specific anxiety problem (Borkovec and Sides, 1978; Lehrer, 1978). This is consistent with the notion that relaxation training is best suited for treating anxiety disorders with specific physiological components. It also indicates that some laboratory-based studies in which relatively non-anxious subjects were used are not adequate tests of progressive relaxation training.

In addition to specifying the nature of the problem under treatment, the procedure must be described adequately. Progressive relaxation can be administered in different ways with potentially different outcome results. For example, Goldfried and Trier (1974) investigated the effect that the training procedure had on speech-anxious subjects' eventual use of relaxation as a coping skill. Subjects were assigned to one of two relaxation treatments or to an attention-placebo control, each of which was carried out in five group sessions. The first relaxation condition utilized standard relaxation training. Subjects in this group were told that the training procedure would have the effect of automatically lowering their overall tension level, so that it would be easier for them to deal with a wide variety of anxiety-provoking situations, including those involving public speaking. Subjects in the second group, the self-control relaxation condition, were told that the purpose of the training procedure was to provide them with a coping skill which they could use in relaxing away tension in a variety of anxiety-provoking situations, including those involving public speaking. In both the standard and the self-control relaxation group, relaxation training was carried out during each session, as well as twice a week between sessions with the aid of taped instructions. From the second session on, however, subjects in the self-control group were also encouraged to apply the relaxation skills *in vivo*, whenever they felt themselves becoming tense. An attention–placebo condition completed the study. The results indicated a consistent superiority of the self-control relaxation procedure across behavioural and subjective measures. This superiority was particularly evident at a 6-week follow-up evaluation. The results of this and other studies summarized by Goldfried (1977) suggest that the way in which progressive relaxation training is presented to clients and then implemented in anxiety-related situations may be critical.

Systematic Desensitization

Systematic desensitization is one of the best known and most widely used technique in behaviour therapy. Developed by Wolpe for the treatment of neurotic disorders in which anxiety is the central element, it has been employed extensively in the treatment of anxiety and phobic disorders (Bandura, 1969; Franks and Wilson, 1973–1979; Paul and Bernstein, 1973; Rachman, 1968) and the procedure and its theoretical underpinnings have been the subject of intensive experimental inquiry that is unprecedented in the history of psychotherapy techniques (Davison and Wilson, 1973; Kazdin and Wilcoxon, 1976; Lang, 1969; Rachman, 1967). Some idea of the impressively large research literature on this technique can be gauged from the fact that Kazdin and Wilcoxon (1976) located seventy-four studies, in what they describe as a "cursory count" of *controlled group outcome studies* that were published in only five journals* during a short period (1970–1974). A comparable count of the many journals today that publish behaviour therapy research would reveal a much higher number.

The remarkable feature of this extensive clinical and research literature on systematic desensitization is that while there is lively debate over the theoretical mechanisms that are responsible for anxiety reduction, its therapeutic efficacy has been generally accepted (Bandura, 1977; Rachman, 1978; Wilkins, 1971). In a major review of the evidence on systematic desensitization in 1969, Paul was able to conclude that, "The findings were

---

*The journals reviewed were *Journal of Abnormal Psychology, Journal of Consulting and Clinical Psychology, Behavior Therapy, Behaviour Research and Therapy* and the *Journal of Behavior Therapy and Experimental Psychiatry*.

overwhelming positive, and for the first time in the history of psychological treatments, a specific treatment package reliably produced measurable benefits for clients across a broad range of distressing problems in which anxiety was of fundamental importance. 'Relapse' and 'symptom substitution' were notably lacking, although the majority of authors were attuned to these problems" (p. 159). In a detailed review 2 years later, Rachman (1971) summarized the experimental evidence on systematic desensitization as follows:

"Desensitization therapy effectively reduces phobic behaviour. It is unnecessary to ascertain the origin of the phobia in order to eliminate it and neither is it necessary to change the subject's basic attitudes or to modify his personality. The elimination of a phobia is rarely followed by symptom substitution. The response to treatment is not related to the trait of suggestibility. Relaxation alone, or accompanied by pseudo-therapeutic interviews, does not reduce phobias. The establishment of a therapeutic relationship with the patient does not of itself reduce the phobia. Interpretive therapy combined with relaxation does not reduce phobic behaviour. The induction of a state of subjective relaxation facilitates desensitization but is not a prerequisite. The technique can be used effectively even when the subject is not in a state of muscular relaxation" (p. 124).

Paul and Bernstein (1973) saw no reason to revise the previous Paul (1969) estimate of the efficacy of systematic desensitization, and 3 years later Leitenberg's (1976) review of the clinical and experimental evidence led him to comment that "it seems safe to conclude that systematic desensitization is demonstrably more effective than both no treatment and every psychotherapy variant with which it has so far been compared" (p. 131).

Despite the unusual amount of experimental support for systematic desensitization, several criticisms warrant careful consideration. These criticisms can be conveniently grouped into two broad categories: those that query the internal validity of studies of the efficacy of systematic desensitization, and those that concentrate on the external validity of these studies.

THE INTERNAL VALIDITY OF STUDIES OF SYSTEMATIC DESENSITIZATION

Objections to the internal validity of studies of systematic desensitization are best illustrated by reference to Kazdin and Wilcoxon's (1976) comprehensive review and methodological evaluation of systematic desensitization and non-specific treatment effects. Kazdin and Wilcoxon's conclusion is that there is no methodologically acceptable evidence to prove that the results obtained with systematic desensitization cannot be attributed to so-called non-specific treatment effects such as placebo influences and expectations of therapeutic improvement:

"The vast majority of studies have not determined empirically whether desensitization and nonspecific treatment control conditions are equal in credibility and expectancy for improvement generated in the clients. Recent research suggests that control conditions commonly employed in desensitization research are less credible than desensitization and generate less expectancy for improvement on the part of the clients, and that desensitization is not superior to control groups that unambiguously rule out as a rival hypothesis differential expectancies across treatment and control conditions. A review of the research that has controlled for expectancies for improvement does not support the proposition that desensitization has a specific therapeutic ingredient" (p. 729).

In their review, Kazdin and Wilcoxon emphasize that their stringent methodological analysis does "not impugn" the efficacy of systematic desensitization. None the less, their review and conclusions have been misinterpreted as support for the notion that there is little or no differential efficacy among alternative therapeutic approaches and that the common denominator in the assumed success of all treatment methods is one or other form of non-specific therapeutic influence.

In an effort to rule out an alternative explanation in terms of non-specific treatment influences, Kazdin and Wilcoxon required that the placebo conditions in controlled outcome studies had to have been empirically demonstrated to generate expectations of therapeutic improvement that were comparable to those elicited by systematic desensitization. They found that only five of the ninety-two studies they reviewed met these unusually stringent methodological requirements – the studies of D'Zurilla, Wilson and Nelson (1973); Gelder, *et al*. (1973); McReynolds, Barnes, Brooks, and Rehagen (1972); Steinmark and Borkovec (1974); and Wilson (1973). Kazdin and Wilcoxon's evaluation of these five controlled studies is that they "do not support the proposition that desensitization includes a specific therapy ingredient beyond expectancies for improvement" (p. 745).

Before examining the five studies selected by Kazdin and Wilcoxon, some general comments are needed. First, their introduction of a new criterion by which to judge desensitization leads to the dispatch – by a single blow – of no less than eighty-seven of the ninety-two studies collected for their review! This extraordinarily severe criterion of exclusion cannot be justified; the mayhem was, in our view, unduly influenced by some extremely poor research on nonspecific factors (e.g. Marcia *et al*. (1969)) and resulted in Kazdin and Wilcoxon unwisely excluding research work of the highest quality (e.g. Lang's research). Kazdin acknowledged the serious flaws of the Marcia experiment – but omitted to take account of Feist and Rosenthal's (1973) conclusive replication that, on its own, can discredit the Marcia findings. For example, they showed that Marcia *et al*.'s use of a stuffed specimen (rather than a live snake) in their snake-avoidance test was a serious mistake. We can now turn to the five surviving studies on which Kazdin and Wilcoxon concentrated their analysis.

The most ambitious study and the one that is clearly the most important and directly concerned with clinical phobias is the Gelder *et al*. study. Interestingly, this is the only one of the five studies that Kazdin and Wilcoxon view as an exception to the rule that systematic desensitization is no more effective than an equally credible placebo treatment. Gelder *et al*. compared systematic desensitization and flooding to an attention–placebo condition in the treatment of phobias. In the placebo condition the therapist presented phobic images to initiate the patient's free association but made no attempt to control the content of subsequent imagery or verbal responses. The clients were told that this exploration of their feelings would enhance self-understanding and decrease their anxiety. All treatment was carried out by experienced therapists explicitly trained in the administration of the different methods. An attempt was made to induce a high expectancy of success in half of the subjects by describing the treatment and therapist chosen in favourable terms and by showing them a video tape of a client who had benefited from the treatment they were to receive. Treatment effects were evaluated in terms of measures of behavioural avoidance, blind psychiatric ratings, client self-ratings, physiological responsiveness, and standardized psychological tests. The adequacy of the control group in eliciting expectancies of treatment success comparable to those evoked by the two behavioural methods was assessed directly.

Half of the clients were agoraphobics, the other half a mixed group of specific phobics.

Agoraphobia is regarded as more difficult to treat that simple phobias. They represent the sort of client Sloane *et al.* (1975) regarded as the appropriate focus of treatment outcome studies, and show the more generalized kind of anxiety disorder for which behaviour therapy is sometimes said to be unsuited. Clients were assigned to treatments and therapists in a factorial design that permitted an analysis of the possible interactions among treatment effects, therapist differences, type of phobia, and levels of expectancy. Treatment duration was fifteen weekly sessions, similar to the Sloane *et al.* study, with 3-month and 6-month follow-ups. In sum, the Gelder *et al.* (1973) study was sufficiently well designed and well executed to answer the question of what treatment method has what specific effect on what problem in whom. It provides one methodological model according to which specific treatment methods can be compared with each other and with an interpretable placebo control condition.

The results of this impressive study showed that systematic desensitization produced more improvement across multiple outcome measures that did this control condition, although some of these differences did not reach significance. Desensitization was not different from another treatment condition (flooding) included in the study. At 6-month follow-up, only a few of the treatment effects were still significant.

Kazdin and Wilcoxon did not interpret the Steinmark and Borkovec study as evidence that systematic desensitization is superior to an equally credible placebo treatment. However, as we have already mentioned, the results of this study, employing an innovative counter-demand strategy to rule out placebo influences and demand characteristics, clearly demonstrated that progressive relaxation and the single-item desensitization treatment were effective, independent of non-specific treatment factors. Our confidence in this conclusion is further strengthened by the replication of the significantly greater therapeutic effects of progressive relaxation, independent of placebo factors, by Borkovec and his colleagues (Borkovec, 1979). These findings cannot be explained away by appeal to non-specific treatment influences.

Wilson (1973) compared a modified version of systematic desensitization in which subjects with an intense fear of snakes were exposed to a standardized hierarchy of slides showing increasingly threatening scenes of harmless snakes, to an attention—placebo treatment fashioned after the pseudo-treatment method described by Marcia, Rubin, and Efran (1969). In this control procedure subjects were led to believe that they were witnessing slides of snakes presented at subliminal levels of awareness. In fact, they were exposed to tachistoscopic presentation of blank slides. Half of the subjects in both the actual treatment and the placebo conditions were given bogus feedback indicating that they were progressing successfully through the hierarchy of slides. Specifically, they were informed that each advance along the hierarchy of slides was contingent on their physiological measures showing that their anxiety to the previous slide had been reduced. A no-treatment control group completed this 2×2 factorial design with a single control group.

The results showed that the bogus feedback had no effect on subjects' avoidance behaviour following treatment. However, the modified systematic desensitization treatment produced significantly greater reduction in avoidance behaviour than the placebo treatment, despite the fact the placebo treatment was found to be as credible to the subjects as systematic desensitization and was as successful in creating expectations of therapeutic improvement as systematic desensitization. Wilson (1973) concluded that the results "strongly support the position that exposure to the feared situation, be it *in vivo,* pictorial, or imaginal, is a necessary precondition for the reduction of avoidance behaviour through systematic desensitization" (p. 120), and that "therapeutic instructions designed to engender positive expectations of successful outcome . . .

cannot . . . be considered to be the critical ingredient in systematic desensitization" (p. 121). The fact that non-reinforced exposure to anxiety-eliciting events is a critical component of effective treatment of phobic disorders has been repeatedly confirmed (Leitenberg, 1976; Marks, 1978).

Kazdin and Wilcoxon interpret this study to indicate the failure of systematic desensitization to improve significantly upon an equally credible placebo condition. As we have seen, however, the standardized form of systematic desensitization employed by Wilson was significantly superior to the placebo condition. The four treatment groups that made up the 2 X 2 factorial design were not significantly different from the no-treatment control group in terms of reduction of avoidance behaviour, although there was a trend ($p < 0.10$) in this direction. Some critics have chosen to emphasize this lack of statistical significant difference between the systematic desensitization and the no-treatment control group. The superiority of systematic desensitization over the equally credible placebo is inconsistent with Kazdin and Wilcoxon's conclusion that the efficacy of systematic desensitization can be attributed to favourable therapeutic expectations alone.

In contrast to Wilson's (1973) results, McReynolds, Barnes, Brooks, and Rehagen (1973) reported that systematic desensitization was no more effective than an equally credible placebo control treatment. Both the systematic desensitization and the equally credible placebo groups were significantly more successful in reducing avoidance behaviour than a less credible placebo group or a no-treatment control group. McReynolds et al. concluded that instilling positive expectations of therapeutic success is the critical factor that accounts for the efficacy of systematic desensitization. Addressing themselves to the apparent discrepancy between Wilson's (1973) and McReynolds et al.'s (1973) findings, Lick and Bootzin (1975) and Emmelkamp (1975) have suggested that the placebo treatment employed by McReynolds et al. may have been the more convincing of the two. Of course, this is an empirical question that remains to be tested. The literature on the role of expectations on treatment outcome in research on systematic desensitization has shown that making a priori assumptions about the impact of different instructional sets can be a hazardous undertaking (Rosen, 1975).

In trying to account for McReynolds et al.'s results, Franks and Wilson (1974) have suggested that the subjects in that study may have been only mildly fearful and hence most susceptible to placebo influences. Borkovec (1973) has shown that placebo effects are most likely to be marked when minimally fearful subjects are studied. Significant effects of a specific treatment technique such as desensitization are more likely to emerge with highly fearful subjects. However, a well-controlled study by Lick (1975) using highly fearful subjects lends support to Kazdin and Wilcoxon's general conclusion. In this study, systematic desensitization was compared to two pseudotherapy control treatments based on Marcia et al.'s (1969) procedure. Subjects in these control conditions were told that they would be exposed to subliminal presentations of their phobic stimuli and that their reactions would be monitored psychophysiologically. One group received fake GSR feedback after every session indicating that they were becoming less fearful, while the other group did not. Unlike the vast majority of analogue studies on fear reduction, genuinely fearful and well-motivated subjects were recruited from the community. Criteria for acceptance into the study included evidence of a specific behavioural inhibition regarding snakes or spiders, such as the inability to go camping or clean closets; failure to reach into an aquarium containing a snake or spider with a gloved hand; a willingness to participate in any one of three treatments after hearing brief descriptions thereof; and a $20 deposit to be refunded after completion of the study. Eight fortnightly treatment sessions were administered which means that the total time subjects spent in treatment compared favourably with Paul's (1966) landmark study. Even then not all desensitization subjects completed their hierarchies. This provides another index of the high intensity of the subjects' fear. Most analogue studies have typically used significantly fewer treatment sessions and still report completion of anxiety hierarchies, presumably because their subjects were not really phobic.

All three treatments were significantly superior to a no-treatment control condition in modifying behavioural, physiological, and self-report measures of fear but they did not differ from one another. The results for the three treatment groups in terms of self-report of fear were maintained at a 4-month follow-up. Assessment of subjects' expectancies at the end of the first session indicated that the desensitization and pseudotherapy plus fake feedback treatments induced marginally greater subject expectancies than pseudotherapy with feedback ($p < 0.1$). Subjects' expectancies were not significant correlated with treatment outcome.

The studies by Wilson (1973), McReynolds et al (1973), and Lick (1975) all used subjects with fears of snakes or spiders. More recently, Slutsky and Allen (1978) compared systematic desensitization to essentially the same placebo treatment used by Lick (1975) in the treatment of public-speaking anxiety in college students. This comparison was conducted in two contexts. The first was a laboratory/research context in which subjects were led to believe that the experimenters were studying visual imagery and its concomitant physiological reactions. The second was a clinical context in which subjects were informed that they were receiving a demonstrably effective form of treatment that would reduce their fear of public-speaking. There were no differences between the desensitization and placebo groups in terms of expectations of therapeutic improvement, although subjects in the clinical context reported significantly more positive expectations of treatment outcome than subjects in the research context. The results showed that whereas systematic desensitization was significantly effective in decreasing fear in both the research and clinical contexts, the placebo treatment produced significant fear reduction only in the clinical context. The superiority of desensitization was most marked on the physiological measures of public-speaking anxiety. The authors concluded that these data fail to support the view that desensitization works because it induces favourable therapeutic outcome expectations.

The D'Zurilla et al. study was the fifth investigation identified by Kazdin and Wilcoxon as a methodologically adequate test of the notion that the method's efficacy is due to the technique per se rather that favourable therapeutic expectations. As Kazdin and Wilcoxon point out, D'Zurilla et al. found that systematic desensitization was no more effective than a placebo or a no-treatment control group in alleviating fear or avoidance of dead, bloodied rats. In commenting upon this result, D'Zurilla et al. noted that the unusual nature of the fear in this study may have been responsible for the surprisingly poor showing of systematic desensitization.

"In contrast with the fears treated effectively by desensitization in past experimental studies (i.e., live animal phobias, test anxiety, speech anxiety), the fear of dead and bloody animals appears to be dominated more by the emotions of disgust and nausea. In this respect, it is more like the obsessive fear of contamination described by Marks (1969) and may often be part of a broader fear of contamination. On the basis of several clinical studies, Marks (1969) has reported that fears of this type do not seem to respond well to desensitization. He reports that anxiety reduction usually occurs very slowly and the treatment effects often fail to generalize outside the treatment situation. Considering Marks' report along with the results of the present study, it is suggested that systematic desensitization might be more limited in its effectiveness than originally believed, and that more controlled studies are needed which focus upon the more complex fears and aversions" (p. 683).

There is another point to be made in connection with the Kazdin and Wilcoxon analysis of outcome studies on systematic desensitization. In Paul's (1966, 1967) study desensitization was shown to be significantly more effective than an abbreviated form of psychotherapy, an attention-placebo, and a no-treatment control group at post-treatment and at a 2-year follow-up. This well-controlled study was not counted as evidence for the efficacy of desensitization *per se* by Kazdin and Wilcoxon because Paul did not report an assessment of how credible his attention-placebo control treatment was in developing positive expectations of therapeutic outcome. Indeed, Borkovec and Nau (1972) and McReynolds *et al.* (1973) have reported findings that suggest that the rationale of Paul's attention-placebo group is less convincing and credible than that of desensitization proper. However, it must not be forgotten that Paul demonstrated conclusively that systematic desensitization was greatly superior to the form of short-term psychotherapy he evaluated. Although it is clear that one cannot use this result to argue that psychotherapy is ineffective or that systematic desensitization would be more effective than alternative forms of psychotherapy (Kazdin and Wilson, 1978b), it seems to be straining credulity to dismiss Paul's psychotherapy treatment as less credible to the subjects in that study than systematic desensitization. The psychotherapy treatment was administered by well-qualified, practising psychotherapists who were using their preferred method of therapy; these psychotherapists reported that they were confident that the psychotherapy they conducted would be effective; and the subjects rated the therapists in the psychotherapy condition as no less competent nor less likeable than in the systematic desensitization treatment. In short, the psychotherapy condition in Paul's study can be regarded as a stringent and persuasive placebo treatment that was significantly less effective than desensitization. As such, Paul's findings offer strong evidence that systematic desensitization is more effective than a placebo treatment that satisfies even the demanding methodological criteria demanded by Borkovec and Nau (1972) and Kazdin and Wilcoxon (1976).

A similar argument can be made for other studies included in the Kazdin and Wilcoxon review but deemed deficient with respect to ensuring equal credibility between desensitization and placebo control conditions. An example is the Gillan and Rachman (1974) study in which desensitization was shown to be significantly superior both to a pseudo-therapy control treatment *and* a psychotherapy condition administered by psychiatrists with training in psychotherapy. The therapeutic expectations generated by these different treatments were not assessed, but whatever the fate of the pseudo-therapy condition, it is highly unlikely from everything that we know that the psychotherapy treatment was not perceived by the subjects in this investigation as comparable to desensitization in plausibility.

To sum up then, it is our view that the available evidence supports the claim that the well-established efficacy of systematic desensitization is attributable to the specific components of this technique itself, rather than to more general expectations of therapeutic improvement that are created by highly credible and persuasive treatment rationales. As we have indicated, three of the five studies identified by Kazdin and Wilcoxon as methodologically adequate for making this evaluation are consistent with this view, as are other well-controlled investigations such as Paul's (1966) comparative outcome study when desensitization is compared to alternative treatment methods as opposed to specific pseudo-therapy placebo control groups. Further support for the efficacy of desensitization as comes from studies demonstrating that the technique reduces fear when it is self-administered (Rosen, Glasgow, and Barrera, 1976, 1977) or when its administration is completely automatized (Lang, Melamed, and Hart, 1970). In neither of these studies was the therapist-administered version of the technique superior to the self-administered or automated (computer conducted) versions.

EXTERNAL VALIDITY OF RESEARCH ON SYSTEMATIC DESENSITIZATION

A major criticism of the evidence in favour of systematic desensitization is that most of it has been based on laboratory-based studies of relatively mild fears of "normal" college students (e.g. Barrios, 1977; Borkovec and O'Brien, 1976; Ciminero, Doleys and Williams, 1978; Kazdin and Wilcoxon, 1976). Indeed, much of the laboratory research has been cogently criticized (e.g. Bernstein and Paul, 1971). As Bernstein and Paul have pointed out, many researchers employing analogue designs have used *mildly* fearful subjects, largely untrained and inexperienced therapists, and have not always tested treatment procedures in a manner that is consistent with their clinical application. The fact that so many laboratory-based studies have used only mildly fearful subjects is unfortunate as these fears are amenable to a wide range of social influences that impede and obscure the demonstration of specific treatment effects (Borkovec, 1973; Borkovec and Rachman, 1979).

Many critics have responded to the inadequate studies of mildly fearful subjects by rejecting *all* laboratory studies of specific fears and phobias as irrelevant to the evaluation of behavioural methods in the treatment of neurotic disorders (e.g. Luborsky *et al.*, 1975). However, one does not want to throw the baby out with the bathwater. Properly done, as Bandura (1978), Bernstein and Paul (1971), Borkovec and O'Brien (1976), Kazdin and Wilson (1978b), Lang (1969) and others have been careful to point out, laboratory research on specific fears can make an important contribution to the development and demonstration of clinically effective treatment methods for anxiety and phobic disorders (see Borkovec and Rachman, 1979). Suffice it to say that we are in a position to conclude that well-controlled research has conclusively shown that systematic desensitization is effective in reducing even intense fears of snakes, small animals, and of social evaluative situations in selected subjects. Whether or not these successful results can be generalized to the often (but not always) more complex and debilitating anxiety and phobic disorders that usually come to the attention of clinical practitioners is an empirical question. Certainly there is a relative paucity of good outcome research on complex and severe anxiety and phobic disorders that would help to establish the limits of systematic desensitization. None the less, the available evidence is encouraging.

In an early study of systematic desensitization Gelder, Marks, Wolff, and Clarke (1967) compared systematic desensitization to both group and individual psychotherapy. Sixteen patients were assigned to the systematic desensitization and group psychotherapy treatments and ten patients were treated with individual psychotherapy. Among the phobias represented in these patients were simple phobias of heights, darkness, and birds; social phobias; and agoraphobia. Therapeutic outcome was evaluated by clinical ratings made by independent psychiatric assessors who were not "blind" to the therapy conditions. The exclusive reliance on psychiatric ratings is a shortcoming of this study and others like it. At the end of 9 months of treatment with systematic desensitization, patients had improved significantly more than those treated with either group or individual psychotherapy. At the end of group psychotherapy treatment, after 18 months, desensitization was no longer significantly superior. However, it must be remembered that at this stage the immediate post-treatment effects of psychotherapy were being compared to a 9-month follow-up of systematic desensitization treatment. Moreover, if we look at the proportion of patients who were rated as improved at the 18-month mark, systematic desensitization led the way with 9 of 16 (56%), followed by individual psychotherapy with 3 of 10 (33%), and group psychotherapy with an unimpressive 2 of 16 (12.5%).

In a continuation study by Gelder and Marks (1968), seven of the group psychotherapy patients who had failed to respond during either 18 months of group therapy of during a 6-month follow-up period were treated with systematic desensitization. Mean improvement in phobics may obscure interpretation of its efficacy. Thus Mathews points out that of the five outcome studies identified by Kazdin and Wilcoxon as methodologically adequate for comparing patients treated with systematic desensitization was maintained at a 4-year follow-up (Marks, 1971).

In a study of thirty-two multiphobic patients, eleven of whom were agoraphobics, Gillan and Rachman (1974) compared four matched therapy conditions: (a) standard systematic desensitization; (b) exposure only — desensitization conducted without training or instruction in muscle relaxation; (c) pseudo-therapy — relaxation training plus discussion of situations unrelated to the patient's phobias; and (d) psychotherapy — a combination of insight-orientated discussion and rational therapy. The first three groups constituted a replication of Rachman's (1965) attempt to ascertain the effective components of the systematic desensitization package. A maximum of thirty treatment sessions, each lasting 30 to 40 minutes, were administered, with other conditions matched accordingly. There was a treatment X therapist confound, in that Gillan treated the first three groups while six psychiatrists (with at least 6-months training in psychotherapy) conducted the psychotherapy sessions.

Ratings of patients' phobias by an independent and blind external assessor showed that the two desensitization groups did not differ significantly from each other, but that both were superior to either the pseudo-therapy or the psychotherapy conditions. Patients' ratings at both post-treatment and a 3-month follow-up indicated that those who had received desensitization were significantly less anxious than those who had received pseudo-therapy or psychotherapy. There was a marked discrepancy between the six psychotherapists' ratings of patient improvement and those provided by the external assessor or the patients themselves, the psychotherapists' ratings being consistently more favourable. Behavioural avoidance measures showed only one significant difference between desensitization and psychotherapy groups at post-treatment. The former stayed in their "most-feared" situation longer than did the psychotherapy patients. However, this difference was not significant at follow-up. Gillan and Rachman attributed the failure to show more differences on the behavioural measures to inadequacies in the nature of the behavioural tests themselves, i.e. the difficulties in trying to construct comparable tests for patients with different phobias. We have already described the Gelder *et al.* (1973) study that provides impressive evidence of the clinical value of systematic desensitization.

Mathews (1978) has argued that the failure to distinguish between the application of systematic desensitization to relatively mild fears in college students versus its use with clinical phobics may obscure interpretation of its efficacy. Thus Mathews points out that of the five outcome studies identified by Kazdin and Wilcoxon as methodologically adequate for comparing desensitization to placebo conditions, only the Gelder *et al.* (1973) investigation used clinically phobic patients. He suggests that Kazdin and Wilcoxon's conclusion might be qualified to refer primarily to fears that may differ from some clinical phobias. In a detailed analysis of the

Gelder *et al*. results, Mathews notes that on three measures of subjective anxiety, significant interactions were obtained between types of phobia and the effects of different treatments. In each case the interaction indicated that the placebo-control treatment was decidedly less effective with the agoraphobics than with the other patients. Similar trends were observed in all other measures of outcome, although they did not reach statistical significance. Mathews also points out that all patients, coming as they were to an established treatment facility, had uniformly high expectations of success, and that patients cannot be usefully distinguished on this dimension. This would suggest that the superior efficacy of systematic desensitization with highly fearful clinical patients cannot plausibly be ascribed to variations in such therapeutic expectations. With the Kazdin and Wilcoxon evaluation in mind, Mathews issues the following caveat:

> "Any conclusions that expectancy of improvement accounts for a large proportion of the change following desensitization must thus be qualified by noting two apparently discrepant findings: first that expectancy ratings may not relate to outcome in phobic patients, and second that unlike other fears, agoraphobia fails to respond to a plausible nonspecific treatment procedure that omits systematic exposure to fear-relevant scenes. Although such qualifications undoubtedly require support from further research before being accepted, they should at least be taken into consideration before any general conclusions are drawn about the role of nonspecific factors, such as expectancy of improvement, in accounting for changes in phobic behaviour" (p. 393).

CONCLUSION

Clinical lore usually has it that desensitization is most appropriate for specific, well-defined phobic reactions (Gelder *et al*., 1967; Wolpe, Brady, Serber, Agras and Liberman, 1973), but there is sound evidence that it can result in improvement even in more complex phobic reactions, such as agoraphobia (Gelder *et al*., 1973). It must be remembered that more complex and severe problems may well call for multifaceted treatment (see Wolpe, 1958). In addition to a technique such as desensitization, the behaviour therapist might need to employ assertion training to overcome interpersonal problems, resolve marital conflicts, and ensure that family members assist in maintaining treatment-produced success. Problems of concurrent depression might require behavioural treatment directed primarily at depression or the adjunctive use of drugs.

Finally, there is evidence that systematic desensitization is not necessarily the most efficient behavioural technique for treating neuroses. More recently developed techniques are capable of reducing fears and some neurotic disorders with which systematic desensitization has not been notably successful, e.g. obsessional–compulsive disorders.

Flooding

Unlike systematic desensitization which is based upon client-regulated, graduated exposure to anxiety eliciting stimuli while the client is deeply relaxed, flooding involves therapist-directed, prolonged exposure to high intensity anxiety-eliciting stimulation. It is important to distinguish between flooding and implosion therapy (Rachman, 1969). The latter is a form of treatment developed by Stampfl and Levis (1967) that relies upon exposure to intensely threatening imaginal material in an attempt to break down hypothetical neurotic defences by the elicitation of intense anxiety. The aversiveness of the phobic situation is deliberately exaggerated with an emphasis on horrifying scenes that include adverse consequences to the client. Another characteristic of implosion therapy is that much of the material the client is instructed to imagine is based on psychoanalytic concepts such as oedipal themes, repressed sexuality, hostility, sibling rivalry, fear of bodily harm and mutilation, and so on. Stampfl and Levis have called these stimuli "hypothesized-sequential" cues. By contrast, flooding usually is conducted *in vivo*, and psychoanalytically inspired stimulus material finds no place in the method. The deliberate evocation of anxiety is unnecessary, and fear-reduction occurs even in the absence of significant anxiety reactions. No attempt is made, as in implosion therapy, to introduce hyperbolic horrors as in the case of the obsessional—compulsive client who, fearing contamination and filth, was asked to imagine in less than exquisite detail the consequences of living in a septic tank.

There is no evidence that the inclusion of psychoanalytically based hypothesized-sequential cues in the flooding procedure has any beneficial effect, but the evidence does support the greater efficacy of *in vivo* as opposed to imaginal exposure to anxiety-eliciting situations. Marshall, Gauthier, Christie, Currie, and Gordon (1977) evaluated the effect of adding implosive material to flooding in the treatment of spider phobics. In the implosion scenes, subjects were asked to imagine being bitten and attacked by a spider, imagine a spider chewing their eyes, entering their mouth, and so on. In addition, the use of brief *in vivo* exposure to a spider at the end of each treatment session was compared with *in vivo* exposure that was delayed for 24 hours. The results showed that the inclusion of implosion-type material in the treatment procedure impaired outcome. Immediate *in vivo* exposure to the feared object proved to be most effective in reducing avoidance behaviour. These findings contradict the view, as expressed by advocates of implosion, that dynamic material is required. In a related study, Foa, Blau, Prout, and Latimer (1977) found that adding "horror" imagery to the flooding procedure had little effect on treatment outcome, It seems that, as originally suspected (Rachman, 1969), the inclusion of horrific or dynamic imagery, as in implosion therapy, is unnecessary for successful treatment.

Several reviews of flooding (Leitenberg, 1976; Marks, 1978; Mathews, 1978) and implosion (Levis and Hare, 1977) have been published. In evaluating the efficacy of flooding it is necessary to take account of the subject populations and problems with which it has been used (Mathews, 1978). In an early review of flooding and implosion therapy, Morganstern (1973) concluded that these methods, at best, were no more effective than systematic desensitization; that they entailed such disadvantages as high relapse rates or increased variability in outcome at follow-up (e.g. Barrett, 1969; De Moor, 1970); that they frequently produced negative side-effects such as nightmares and resistance to continued treatment (e.g. Barrett, 1969; Mealiea and Nawas, 1971; Willis and Edwards, 1969); and that their continued use was debatable. However, most of the early studies were carried out on subjects whose fears were mild and whose motivation for therapy was questionable (Levis and Hare, 1977). Mathews (1978) points out that the only study of clinically phobic patients in the Morganstern review was that by Marks, Boulougouris, and Marset (1971). In this study flooding was more effective than systematic desensitization, favourably low subject attrition rate was obtained, and adverse consequences such as patient "resistance" to treatment sessions were found to be generally non-existent. Participants in the laboratory studies of college students may have been less motivated and committed to treatment than the phobic patients treated by Marks *et al.* (1971).

Marks *et al*. compared flooding to systematic desensitization in a study of psychiatric patients using a crossover design in which the patients received six sessions of the one treatment followed shortly thereafter by six sessions of the other. The results showed that, although both treatments produced improvements on the combined ratings of the therapist and independent assessor of the main and total phobias, flooding produced significantly greater improvement. The physiological assessment reflected these findings in that flooding produced greater decrease in heart rate during periods when the patient imagined phobic material. For periods when the therapist was presenting the standard scenes, a greater reduction in the number of spontaneous fluctuations and maximum deflection was found for the group receiving flooding. Desensitization produced greater improvement with specific phobias, while flooding produced greater improvement in agoraphobias. A 1-year follow-up indicated that gains made during therapy had not disappeared. However, these results cannot be interpreted unambiguously since some of the patients received further treatment during this period. Also, the use of a cross-over design, in which all subjects received both treatments, precludes an interpretation of the follow-up findings.

Subsequent studies have documented the efficacy of flooding in the treatment of phobic disorders. Gelder *et al*. (1973), in the study already referred to, showed that flooding was significantly more effective than a stringent placebo control treatment and this allows one to attribute successful treatment of simple phobias and agoraphobia to flooding independent of placebo influences. However, this same study revealed no differences between flooding and systematic desensitization, nor were there any differences in the response of different types of phobias to flooding. Using subjects who were very fearful of either harmless snakes or spiders, Marshall *et al*. (1977) found that a combined flooding in imagination and *in vivo* method was more effective in reducing fear and avoidance behaviour than systematic desensitization or an attention-placebo group.

Research has revealed several factors that influence the outcome of flooding therapy:

(a) Flooding *in vivo* appears to be more effective than flooding in imagination. Indeed, one of the problems with the early studies reviewed by Morganstern (1973) was that they relied upon exposure in imagination to the anxiety-eliciting situations. It is noteworthy that in demonstrations of the efficacy of flooding in the treatment of phobic patients (e.g. Gelder *et al*., 1973; and Marks *et al*., 1971) imaginal exposure was followed in each session by *in vivo* exposure to the feared situation. In a controlled investigation of the relative value of imaginal versus *in vivo* exposure, Emmelkamp and Wessels (1975) compared imaginal, *in vivo*, and combined imaginal and *in vivo* flooding treatments in the treatment of agoraphobic clients. Clients' average age was 34 years (range 16–55 years), while the average duration of their disorder was 7 years (range 2–20 years). Following four 90-minute treatment sessions, *in vivo* flooding was found to be marginally more effective than imaginal flooding in terms of time clients were able to spend in the phobic situation ($p < 0.10$), and both therapist and client ratings of phobic anxiety and avoidance. Combined flooding was superior to imaginal flooding only on therapist ratings of anxiety and avoidance. These findings are consistent with those of Stern and Marks (1973) and Watson, Mullet, and Pillay (1973) with severely agoraphobic patients and with Marshall *et al*.'s (1977 – experiment 2) data on snake phobic subjects. The superior efficacy of flooding *in vivo* is consistent with other evidence showing that all fear-reduction techniques, including desensitization and modelling procedures, appear to be more successful when conduct *in vivo* rather than on a symbolic level((Bandura, 1977; Wilson, 1978).

In another major outcome study, flooding in imagination was compared to flooding *in vivo* in the treatment of agoraphobic patients by Mathews, Johnston, Lancashire, Munby, Shaw, and Gelder (1976). The three treatment groups were as follows: (a) eight sessions of imaginal flooding followed by eight sessions of flooding *in vivo*; (b) sixteen sessions of combined treatment; and (c) sixteen sessions of *in vivo* practice. The dependent measures were similar to those used by Gelder *et al.* (1973) including behavioural avoidance tests, clinical ratings of symptoms, psychometric tests, and psychophysiological recording. There was no significant difference among treatments at 8 weeks, 16 weeks, or at a 6-month follow-up. Although it had not been anticipated, there was evidence of a therapist effect on some outcome measures. As Mathews *et al.* (1976) note, this finding may have implications for clinical practice, even in highly standardized, effective methods such as flooding. At follow-up, patients' ranked eight components of their therapy in terms of their perceived therapeutic value. The therapists' encouragement and sympathy, followed closely by the *in vivo* practice component, were rated as the most helpful. Increased understanding, imaginal representation of anxiety-eliciting material, and diary-keeping were perceived to be of little value.

The failure to find differences among the three treatments could be due to the fact that they were all equally effective. Alternatively, this outcome could merely reflect the operation of non-specific treatment factors common to all methods. However, Mathews *et al.* reject the latter explanation on the grounds that the improvement observed in these agoraphobic patients was comparable to that obtained by Gelder *et al.* and significantly better than the minimal improvement shown by the highly credible placebo control condition in the Gelder *et al.* study. A more plausible interpretation of the results bears on the nature of the patients' activities between rather than during treatment sessions. Considerable emphasis was placed on the patients' self-directed practice attempts at *in vivo* exposure in their home settings. This is all the more likely since treatment spanned a relatively long time — 16 weeks — whereas previous studies demonstrating the superiority of *in vivo* over imaginal methods were much briefer in duration. This longer period allowed more time in which to practise. Mathews *et al.* conclude that "it is possible that the anxiety experienced while thinking about phobic situations eventually declines after any treatment involving exposure in reality of imagination, so that patients are less anxious before or during later practice at home. Alternatively, it may be that if a patient repeatedly thinks about phobic situations, regardless of anxiety, this is sufficient to increase the probability that the patients will eventually attempt to practice" (p. 371).

Johnston, Lancashire, Mathews, Munby, Shaw, and Gelder (1976) conducted an analysis of the weekly measures of change in the study just described and related these within-treatment measures to outcome at follow-up. Aside from confirming the presence of a therapist effect, Johnston *et al.*'s analyses show that the immediate effects of the treatment were different. Thus, *in vivo* exposure had immediate positive effects, whereas imaginal flooding had no obvious short-term effect. The authors suggest that both methods facilitate self-directed practice between sessions and that this is the effective agent of therapeutic change.

(b) Unduly brief exposures may be less effective. For instance, Stern and Marks (1973) found that 2 hours of continuous exposure *in vivo* was significantly more effective, at least in the short-term, than four separate half-hour sessions given in one afternoon, in the treatment of agoraphobics. Girodo and Henry's (1976) results suggest the value of continuous exposure to the feared situation. Too short a duration of exposure may, in certain circumstances, result in a temporary increase in phobic arousal (McCutcheon and Adams, 1973; Stone and Borkovec, 1975).

(c) Contrary to earlier beliefs, it is unnecessary to elicit anxiety during flooding. A specified requirement of implosion therapy is that *maximal anxiety must be evoked* in the patient if complete extinction of phobic responses is to ensue. To this end, as we have already mentioned, every effort is made to exaggerate the fearful nature of phobic stimuli. However, the evidence is consistent in showing that patients' anxiety level during flooding does not correlate with subsequent outcome (Hafner and Marks, 1976; Johnston *et al.*, 1976; Mathews, 1978; Mathews and Rezin, 1977; Mills, Barlow, Agras, and Mills, 1973; Stern and Marks, 1973).

(d) Consistent with the previous point, there is evidence that gradual *in vivo* exposure to the phobic situation* is as effective as rapid exposure to the maximally fear-producing situation (Boersma, Den Hengst, Dekker, and Emmelkamp, 1976).

(e) Flooding conducted by a live therapist produces better results than tape recordings of therapeutic instructions (e.g. Marks, 1978).

(f) Flooding conducted within a group setting can be as effective as individual treatment (e.g. Hafner and Marks, 1976; Hand, Lamontagne, and Marks, 1974).

(g) *In vivo* exposure treatment in which the exposure is client-controlled may be as effective as therapist-controlled exposure and is more cost-effective (e.g. Emmelkamp and Kraanen, 1977).

(h) Flooding conducted by trained nursing personnel is likely to be as effective as treatment carried out by clinical psychologists or psychiatrists. This increases the cost-benefit ratio for efficient delivery of treatment services (e.g. Marks, Hallam, Connolly, and Philpott, 1977).

CONCLUSION

To summarize, flooding has been shown to be an effective method for treating phobic disorders, including agoraphobia. Most effective when applied *in vivo* and for adequate periods of exposure, flooding can be carried out successfully by nurse-therapists and even self-administered under the guidance of a professional therapist.

In comparison with a demonstrably effective technique like systematic desensitization, flooding has proved to be either more effective (e.g. Boudewyns, 1975; Crowe *et al.*, 1972; Marks *et al.*, 1971; Marshall *et al.*, 1977) or at least equal in efficacy (e.g. Borkovec, 1972, 1974; Gelder *et al.*, 1973; Hussain, 1971). This is no mean feat.

The Treatment of Obsessional–Compulsive Disorders

One of the most common and serious criticisms of behaviour therapy is that, whatever its value in treating circumscribed disorders of a mild variety, it cannot deal with complex problems. Its value in overcoming these problems is discounted, sometimes out of hand. In so far as obsessional–compulsive disorders were concerned, this objection appeared to have some basis. Only limited successes were reported in the early days of behaviour therapy (see Rachman and Hodgson, 1980).

---

*Emmelkamp and Emmelkamp-Benner (1975) describe this gradual *in vivo* exposure treatment as self-observation. Others, including Wolpe (1958), would call it *in vivo* desensitization. A variation of this technique, in which the patient receives social reinforcement and feedback from the therapist about how much time they spend in the phobic situation, has been labelled successive approximation or reinforced practice (Leitenberg, 1976). Self-observation or *in vivo* desensitization has been shown to be as effective as successive approximation (Emmelkamp and Ultee, 1974) and flooding (Emmelkamp, 1974) in the treatment of agoraphobics. Everraerd, Eijken, and Emmelkamp (1973) found that flooding was as effective as reinforced practice in treating agoraphobic patients.

If it is agreed — and there will be few people to contest this view — that in the main obsessional—compulsive disorders are of considerable complexity, and are often chronic, severe, and disabling, then the success or failure of behaviour therapists' attempts to modify them provides a decisive test of this important criticism. If it can be shown that the methods of behaviour therapy are capable of producing significant modifications of obsessional—compulsive disorders, then the criticism can be discounted.

In our view the evidence on this question, despite its inevitable inadequacies and gaps, supports the view that behaviour therapy is indeed capable of producing significant modifications in these disorders. As we shall see, the evidence from three different sources points in the same direction. The pessimism conveyed by the early case histories has been superseded by a growing optimism, the non-controlled clinical series reported so far have a welcome consistency, and the controlled trials are both consistent within themselves and with the two sources of evidence already mentioned. Before embarking on an examination of the evidence, it is worth speculating on the reasons for our new optimism. In our opinion, the greatly improved capacity for modifying these powerful and resistant problems can be attributed mainly to two developments. In the first place there has been a switch from imaginal to *in vivo* treatments. These *in vivo* procedures appear to make a powerful contribution to the treatment of obsessional difficulties. The second development that facilitated therapeutic progress was the introduction of response-prevention methods in the late 1960s.

Prompted by the encouraging developments in research on flooding and modelling methods which are discussed more fully in the next section, and partly inspired by the success reported by Meyer (1966) in treating two severely disabled obsessional patients, a number of psychologists began experimenting with *in vivo* behavioural procedures. Meyer himself, in collaboration with Levy and Chesser, has continued to chalk up clinical successes and these are reported in his 1973 and 1974 series. According to his latest figures on fifteen severely disabled patients, the success rate is now in excess of 80%. The treatment procedure comprises *in vivo* exposure and response prevention, with the greatest emphasis placed on the latter element.

Using methods which share some common features, Rabavilas and Boulougouris (1976) in Athens have reported successes, as have Ramsay and Sikkel (1975) in Amsterdam, Wonnenberger *et al.* (1975) in Heidelberg, Boersma *et al.* (1975) in Groningen, Hackmann and McClean (1974) in Oxford, Emmelkamp and Kraanen (1977) in Holland, Foa and Goldstein (1978) in Philadelphia, and Catts and McConaghy (1975) in Australia. However, Heyse (1975) working in Munich has reported indifferent results. A brief guide to these findings is provided in Table 3.

At the Institute of Psychiatry in London and at the Maudsley and Bethlem Hospitals, Rachman, Hodgson, Marks, Sartory, Grey, Röper and their colleagues have carried out a series of investigations into the behavioural modification of obsessional—compulsive disorders. This work is described in detail by Rachman and Hodgson (1980), and summarized here.

In the first clinical study, the question addressed was whether or not *in vivo* methods of behavioural treatment are capable of bringing about clinically significant improvements in these handicapped patients. To this end Rachman, Hodgson, and Marks (1971a, 1973) compared the effects of therapeutic modelling and flooding, alone and then in combination. For purposes of the first and the successive studies, patients were selected whose disorders were sufficiently severe to merit admission to an in-patient unit. All of them had been affected for a minimum of 1 year and most of them for considerably longer than that period (mean 7.5 years). All of them had previously received other forms of treatment. During the first week of their admission to hospital a number of assessment procedures were carried out and then they entered two con-

TABLE 3

Summary Reference Table

Authors	Sample size	Exposure + R.P.	Control Group	Outcome	Follow-up
A. Series					
?yer et al. (1974)	15	Yes	No	10/15 asymptomatic or greatly improved	1–6 years
?nnenberger et al. (1975)	6	Yes	No	5 sig. improved	2 mths
?ls et al. (1973)	5	Yes	No	5 sig. improved	Unsystematic
?a and Goldstein (1978)	21	Yes	No	14 asymptomatic, 4 improved, 3 failures	± 6 mths
?rks, Hallam et al. (1976)	34	Plus supplements	No	Sig. group overall	Variable
?tts and McConaghy (1975)	6	Yes	No	All 6 improved	6 mths
?yse (1975)	24	Yes	No	7 failures, 10 much improved	1 mth
?msay and Sikkel (1971)	4	Yes	No	3 sig. improved	Variable
B. Control comparisons					
?chman et al. (1971)	10	Yes	Own control (relaxation)	6 much improved, 4 failures	2 years
?chman et al. (1973)	10	Yes	Ditto	7 much improved, 2 failures	2 years
?per et al. (1975)	10	Yes	Ditto	8 improved, 2 failures	6 mths
?chman et al. (1979)	40	± clomipramine	Ditto	Significant improvements behaviourally	1 year
?ersma et al. (1975)	13	Yes	Behavioural variants	Average 75% improvement	3 mths
?melkamp and ?raanen (1977)	14	Yes	Waiting list, and variants	Average 75% improvement	3 mths
?ckmann and ?cClean (1974)	10	Yes	Thought stopping	Sig. group changes	No
?bavilas et al. (1976)	12	Yes	Behavioural variants	6 much improved, 2 failures	No

secutive 3-week periods of treatment. The treatment consisted of fifteen sessions given every weekday during this 3-week period. The patients were reassessed at the completion of each phase of treatment, at the termination of treatment, and then again at three follow-up points. At the beginning of each treatment phase, patients were asked to resist the execution of rituals either during or between treatment sessions.

In the first study five patients received flooding treatment, while the other five received modelling treatment. In both conditions the active treatment period was preceded by a 3-week relaxation control treatment which was used as a basis for comparison. In flooding treatment the patient is asked to come into contact with most provoking situations (e.g. disease-contaminated specimens) as soon as possible — even in the early stages of the first session if he can tolerate it. Both during and after these sessions the patient is urged to refrain from carrying out his compulsive acts, i.e. response-prevention instructions are instituted. The response-prevention programme was monitored but not supervised directly. In modelling treatment the approach is graduated and moreover, each step is first demonstrated by the therapist model. By the second or third session the patient is encouraged to begin imitating the actions of the therapist. As with flooding treatment, response-prevention instructions are instituted at the start of the programme. This brief description of the methods used should not obscure the fact that in execution, the treatment may require a delicate hand.

Both the flooding and modelling forms of treatment produced large and significant improvements, but there were no differences between these two behavioural methods. In the second study, the modelling and flooding treatments were combined to see if their synergistic effect might exceed the effects of each method used separately. Once again it was found that the behavioural method was significantly superior to the control method but there was little reason to conclude that the combination of modelling and flooding conferred any advantage over each method used separately. This result was then checked with a new set of five patients and the outcome was no different. Substantial improvements were achieved on all the major measures and, what is most encouraging, within the space of a comparatively short period of treatment. It should be mentioned that, where necessary, some patients received additional treatment after the conclusion of the therapeutic trial. Hence the results given for the follow-up period are not a reflection simply of the therapeutic intervention provided during the experimental study period. It is also interesting to notice that the improvements in obsessional—compulsive problems were accompanied by improvements in other aspects of the patient's behaviour. A 2-year follow-up of these first twenty patients has been completed (Marks, Hodgson, and Rachman, 1975) and it is comforting to report that in the main the improvements have endured the 2-year period.

The effects of *in vivo* exposure plus modelling and response prevention, alone and in combination with pharmacotherapy (clomipramine), were assessed in the treatment of forty chronic obsessional—compulsive patients by Rachman, Cobb, Grey, MacDonald, Mawson, Sartory, and Stern (1979). The results were clearcut. The behavioural treatment produced significant improvements on behavioural measures of outcome, while the clomipramine was followed by significant improvements primarily on measures of mood, but also on some of the behavioural measures. Contrary to the authors' hypothesis, there were no interactions between the two treatments. The specificity of the treatment effects is inconsistent with alternative interpretations of these results in terms of so-called non-specific factors such as placebo or the therapeutic relationship.

ADDITIONAL EVIDENCE

The pattern of findings that has emerged from the sixteen reports published so far is encouraging despite one exception. At the outset it should be pointed out that only seven of the sixteen reports deal with studies that incorporated at least a modicum of experimental control, and in none of these seven was perfection achieved.

Meyer, Levy, and Schnurer (1974) presented the results obtained with their method of treatment (comprising exposure and response prevention) in fifteen moderate to severely ill obsessional–compulsive patients. The patients were treated sequentially and although few experimental controls (e.g. randomization, control treatment, etc.) were imposed, full clinical assessments were carried out by blind judges prior to and after treatment. Notwithstanding its shortcomings, this report is of considerable importance because of Meyer's contributions to the development of treatment procedures for obsessional and other neurotic disorders, and because of the excellent clinical results achieved. From the descriptions given there seems little doubt that the fifteen patients were moderately or severely disturbed, e.g. the mean duration of symptoms was no less than 15.6 years. Meyer *et al.* summarized their results this way: "With the exception of Case 9, every patient showed a marked diminution of compulsive behaviour, sometimes amounting to a total cessation of the rituals . . . it will be seen that at the end of treatment, out of 15 cases in the main group, 10 were either much improved or totally asymptomatic" (p. 251). The significance of this unusually good therapeutic outcome will not be lost on any one who has tried to help obsessional patients overcome their seemingly intractable problems. Although comprehensive follow-up information was not available to Meyer when the report was prepared, he has since informed us by personal communication that most of these patients have maintained their improvements.

In their non-controlled clinical study, Wonneberger *et al.* (1975) also achieved excellent if narrow therapeutic results, with inadequate generalization. Using a method of treatment that bears a close resemblance to the techniques used by Rachman and his colleagues (flooding, response prevention, and modelling), they obtain significant clinical improvement in six out of seven of their obsessional patients. "Six patients showed significant reductions in anxiety and obsessional–compulsive avoidance behaviour. Improvements were still present at follow-up eight weeks later and generalized to the daily life situation of five patients, but only to a limited extent. Striking was the patients' motivation and low anxiety level during treatment. As a further result the social behaviour of 5 patients was positively influenced. An increase of depressive mood was not observed" (p. 135). In their experimental analysis of the role of response-prevention, Mills *et al.* (1973) reported that each of their five cases showed a "dramatic reduction in the rate of ritualistic behaviour after a period of response prevention" (p. 524).

Important supporting evidence of the beneficial effects of exposure and response prevention was recently reported by Foa and Goldstein (1978), who treated twenty-one patients with excellent results. The patients were treated by prolonged exposure to stimuli that provoked discomfort, and strict prevention of rituals was ensured. Self-ratings and assessments by an independent clinical assessor were carried out prior to treatment, after 2 weeks of contact with the therapist but prior to formal treatment, again after 2 weeks of therapy, and at repeated follow-ups. There were no significant changes in the 2-week period prior to active treatment but significant improvements became evident at the end of the 2-week treatment period. These gains were maintained and even increased during the follow-up period, in the majority of cases. The therapeutic improvements spread beyond the targets symptoms to include occupational adjustment, social life, sexual adjustment, and family relations. The most striking feature of their results is that "two-thirds of the patients became asymptomatic after treatment". It is, of course, true that no control group was employed in this series, but the results are nevertheless a source of encouragement. The therapeutic changes were large, stable, and generalized.

Moreover, the major changes took place within the remarkably short time of 2 weeks of intensive treatment. The possible contribution of non-specific factors cannot be excluded but the fact that no changes were observed in the pre-treatment period, with or without therapist contact, rules out at least some of the commonly encountered non-specific therapeutic factors. A success rate in which two-thirds of the patients become asymptomatic within 2 weeks of intensive treatment conclusively rules out the possibility that the results can be attributed to spontaneous remission. Despite the impressive results, however, if we apply strict standards to this report, it has to be regarded as supportive but inconclusive.

Using comparable therapeutic procedures, admirable results were achieved under different conditions by trainee nurse-therapists working under the direction of psychologists and psychiatrists. Marks *et al.* (1977) supervised the treatment of thirty-four chronic obsessional—compulsive patients. In view of the fact that the treatment procedures were not standardized, and included a range of methods additional to exposure and response prevention, plus the fact that the necessary controls were absent, it is evident that this report cannot provide conclusive evidence about the effectiveness of the procedures. Nevertheless, as in the previous study by Foa, the results achieved in dealing with a chronic serious disorder were so large and impressive that they cannot be disregarded. On the contrary they can be taken as providing encouragement of a different type. They lead one to conclude that the *techniques* used to modify the problems of people with obsessional disorders can be transmitted and acquired with relative ease. The mean treatment time was 24 hours for out-patients and 34 hours for in-patients. The useful degree of improvement achieved during treatment was evident on all major measures. For example, the total amount of obsessional behaviour declined from 70% to a mere 20%, the discomfort experienced during rituals declined from 6 on an 8-point scale to less than 2, and so on. The authors' conclusions need no qualification: "The results are impressive as the obsessive compulsive patients as a group were severely incapacitated. The lack of standardized measures precluded formal comparison with obsessives treated by other professionals. However the results are of the same order as in obsessives treated by psychologists and psychiatrists" (p. 50).

Good results were reported by Catts and McConaghy (1975). Two of their six patients showed substantial reductions in ritualistic behaviour at discharge and these changes were maintained at follow-up. The remaining four patients were improved and made further important advances during the follow-up period. They concluded that their results are consistent with the claims of other workers in showing that "chronic compulsive behaviour can rapidly respond to relatively brief periods of ritual prevention with supervision" (p. 40). Catts and McConaghy commented on "the rapidity with which a marked reduction in symptoms occurred once ritual prevention was initiated, was considered impressive evidence of its efficacy". Because of the mixture of techniques they used and the absence of appropriate controls, their findings cannot be taken as confirming the claims made for the efficacy of behavioural treatment, but it is one more encouraging sign.

After studying Meyer's methods in London, Heyse (1975) returned to Munich and treated twenty-four in-patients, but with less success than his mentor. Seven remained unchanged, seven improved slightly, and ten showed moderate improvements. The comparison between modelling and response prevention methods yielded no differences. This report is the least encouraging so far and cannot be ignored, especially as the reasons for the seven failures are not known. It should be borne in mind, however, that the results, whatever discouragement they bear, are nevertheless superior to those claimed by rival techniques. It does recommend a sense of caution, however, and leaves unanswered the question of why Meyer's method, on this occasion, lost some of its effectiveness in transport.

Finally, the small series reported by Ramsay and Sikkel (1971) produced three out of four successes with a modelling exposure treatment combined with response prevention. So, with the possible exception of the work reported by Heyse, all of the non-controlled clinical studies have produced evidence to support the proposition that behavioural treatment is capable of producing significant improvements and these within a comparatively short period. It has been argued that the weight of this evidence, regardless of the inadequacies of each study examined separately, is too substantial to disregard. Allowing for the flaws in each of the studies, the magnitude and consistency of the changes are difficult to discount. The possibility that they were attributable to spontaneous remissions can be dismissed on the very good grounds that the changes occurred far too quickly for this explanation to hold water. The consistency from study to study appears also to discount the possibility that the results achieved in any one centre were a reflection of the special skills or enthusiasm of therapists involved. The results seem to be reproducible by independent workers.

Despite these persuasive arguments, we nevertheless retain the view that the evidence is significant but not conclusive. In the first place one requires reassurance that the findings are indeed accurate, uncontaminated, and reproducible: one also needs to know whether the changes were unduly inflated by the special enthusiasm of ambitious research workers, by the optimism generally associated with new methods, by the intensive attention provided for the patients, and so on. In order to rule out some of these possibilities, and to control for the considerable contribution that can be made by non-specific factors, it is essential to institute some form of controlled comparisons. And it is to studies which have incorporated such controls that we now turn attention.

We have already described the Maudsley studies by Rachman, Marks, and Hodgson, all of which incorporated a "placebo-relaxation control". Turning next to the controlled comparison between flooding and thought-stopping treatments carried out by Hackmann and McClean (1975), this report is remarkable for showing that even a comparatively small amount of treatment (4 + 4 sessions) was sufficient to produce a reasonable amount of clinical improvement − "a worthwhile clinical finding was that a fair amount of improvement occurred after only eight out-patient sessions" (p. 263). In a detailed analysis of this and the other controlled studies, Rachman and Hodgson (1980) raised the possibility that these patients were less disabled than those who participated in other trials. The changes achieved, and the brevity of the treatment, might have been unduly influenced by the comparative mildness of the disorder − and one hesitates to generalize from these findings.

In their controlled experimental trial, regrettably restricted by the small number of patients in each comparison group (n = 3 to 4), Boersma et al. (1975) reasonably concluded that "response prevention as carried out in this study is a very effective method of treatment for compulsions . . . the improvements of the clients was shown by the measurement in vivo, the anxiety and avoidance scales, and by all the scales of the Leyton Obsessional Inventory. In addition it was shown that at the end of treatment the client had become less depressed. . . . The extent of the improvements can be gauged from the fact that "the main compulsion, as measured in vivo, improved at the post-test on an average of 77.8%, and the other compulsions an average of 75.9%". In the clinical trial reported by Rabavilas et al. (1976) significant clinical improvements were obtained in a group of twelve obsessional patients. These improvements were obtained on all of the main clinical measures of obsesssional disorder, in anxiety and in avoidance behaviour. At the conclusion of the comparatively brief experimental treatment period, "six cases were improved . . . and they remain well . . . at six months follow-up. Four patients required further treatment with a mean of 9 sessions . . . they showed a moderate improvement by the end of additional treatment. Finally, 2 patients did not show any improvement."

Emmelkamp and Kraanen (1977) treated fourteen obsessional patients by gradual exposure *in vivo*. All patients had ten sessions of treatment, but for half of them the experiment was controlled by a therapist. The other seven controlled their own exposure experiences. Both versions of the treatment resulted in significant improvements on all of the major measures. The magnitude of the changes can be seen from the fact that on the behavioural test, the improvement in the main compulsion was no less than 74%. At the 3½-month follow-up, the stability of the improvements was confirmed. As before, although the therapeutic response was extremely encouraging, a minority of patients failed to improve.

CONCLUSIONS

It is reasonable to conclude that behavioural treatment is capable of producing significant changes in obsessional problems, and fairly rapidly at that. Clinically valuable reductions in the frequency and intensity of compulsive behaviour have been observed directly and indirectly. Significant reductions in distress and discomfort are usual, and the work of Boulougouris and his colleagues (1976) suggests that psychophysiological changes of a kind observed during the successful treatment of phobias take place. The admittedly insufficient evidence on the durability of the induced changes is not discouraging; allowing for the provision of booster treatments as needed (see, for example, Marks, Hodgson, and Rachman, 1975), the therapeutic improvements are stable. The successful modification of the main obsessional problems often is followed by improvements in social and vocational adjustment.

With the exception of symbolic modelling, which produced comparatively weak therapeutic effects (Röper, Rachman, and Marks, 1975), no significant differences between variants of behavioural treatment have emerged. Exposure to the relevant provoking conditions, followed by response prevention, appears to be a robust combination but we are not yet in a position to ascribe particular or essential effects to either element alone. Several explanations of the mechanisms involved in treatment have been offered but thus far none of them hold sway (Rachman and Hodgson, 1980).

In all the series and controlled studies reported so far, some clear failures occurred — the failure rate ranges between 10% and 30%. The reasons for such failures are not known but severe depression or the possession of over-valued ideas have been offered as possible villains (Foa, 1977). The influence of depression on obsessional disorders is acknowledged to be of importance (Rachman and Hodgson, 1980) but the presence of depression is not necessarily an obstacle to treatment.

Apart from the desirability of further, independent replications there is a need for more pertinent, precise, and prolonged assessments. Weaknesses in measuring techniques remain a major worry. As mentioned earlier, we also need clarification on the causes of failures, and on the mechanisms involved in successful treatment. Finally, as argued in Chapter 1, a major reappraisal of some of the underlying assumptions of this type of conventional outcome research is overdue.

The continued acceptance of these three assumptions in respect of obsessional disorders and their assessment is hard to justify: (i) obsessional disorders are unitary, they constitute a "lump"; (ii) they are psychiatric or psychological illnesses; and (iii) they can be assessed by general measuring procedures. Instead, it is argued (see Rachman and Hodgson, 1980) that (i) obsessional disorders comprise a set of loosely coupled components, (ii) they are best constructed as psychological problems but *not* illnesses (*people* with these problems rather than obsessional *patients*), and (iii) the components of obsessional disorders and their modification are best assessed by procedures designed to measure specific and situationally relevant behaviour, verbal reports, and psychophysiological reactions.

Modelling Procedures

Modelling processes and procedures have become increasingly important within behaviour therapy during the 1970s (Bandura, 1977b; Rachman, 1976). Major strides have been made in the scientific analysis of modelling during this period, both in terms of the underlying theoretical processes and applications to clinical and educational settings. These theoretical advances and practical developments are reviewed by Bandura (1977b), Rachman (1976), Rosenthal and Bandura (1978), and Rosenthal and Zimmerman (1978). Our focus here is on research evaluating the therapeutic success of modelling methods primarily with adult neurotic reactions.

Modelling refers to the process of observational or vicarious learning in which a person acquires new patterns of behaviour or displays formerly inhibited actions as a result of watching a model perform these activities. The latter process, or what Bandura (1977b) calls the disinhibitory effects of modelling, are especially important in the treatment of fears and phobias. The disinhibitory effects of modelling can be brought about in different ways, including having the person observe a live model in direct contact with phobic situation (often called live modelling), watch a filmed model engage in the feared activity (often called symbolic modelling), or even rehearse the model's actions in imagination (usually called covert modelling). Although we do not consider here the theoretical analyses of modelling effects (see Rachman, 1978), it should be noted that in terms of Bandura's (1977b) social learning theory of behaviour change, elimination of phobic reactions hinges on the modification of cognitive mediating processes that regulate such behaviour. As Rosenthal and Bandura (1978) put it:

"The nominal source of disinhibiting feedback counts far less than its impact on client's cognitive processes. New information may stem from direct contacts, observation of models' direct contacts, or purely imaginal rehearsal of contacts. But the locus of extinction is symbolic in each case. What changes is the predictive value of environmental events — their subjective meaning and judgements about their implications for action. When vicarious exposures lower avoidance enough that clients will attempt overt coping, direct experiences create further positive feedback until confident mastery is achieved" (p. 632).

Initial studies demonstrated that live and symbolic modelling successfully eliminated specific fears in phobic children (Bandura, Grusec, and Menlove, 1967; Bandura and Menlove, 1968). However, it has been Bandura's programme of research on the modification of phobic reactions in adults that has contributed most to our knowledge of the therapeutic efficacy of modelling. Before summarizing this line of research, a few comments on the subjects in these studies are in order. Unlike many laboratory investigations in which mildly fearful college students whose motivation change was questionable took part, the snake phobic subjects in Bandura's studies exhibited intense phobic reactions that they were strongly motivated to overcome. As a result of their phobias, these subjects were unable to participate in highly desired activities. Examples of this functional impairment of their daily life-styles included the inability to walk in the garden, go on camping trips, live in wooded areas, and so on. Aside from this behavioural avoidance, the majority of subjects reported recurrent nightmares and a variety of distressing thoughts and ruminations about snakes. Clearly the intensity of these fears is comparable to anything that might be treated in clinical practice and there is no cause for hesitation in viewing the results of these studies as direct evidence of therapeutic outcome. Earlier in this volume we indicated how drawing a dichotomous distinction between "analogue" studies of "normal" subjects versus "clinical" studies of psychiatric patients is misguided (see also Bandura, 1978; Borkovec and Rachman, 1979; Kazdin and Wilson, 1978b). When crucial dimensions of fears such as intensity and severity are equated, there are few, if any, differences in response to treatment between subjects recruited for a research investigation of psychiatric patients (e.g. Grey *et al.*, 1979).

In the first study in the series, Bandura, Blanchard, and Ritter (1969) compared systematic desensitization with symbolic modelling, participant modelling, and a no-treatment control group. Participant modelling is a multi-component method in which the person's feared activities are repeatedly modelled without the model experiencing any adverse consequences. The client is then encouraged and physically assisted by the therapist in jointly performing carefully graduated sub-tasks of increasing difficulty of previously threatening activities. The basic principle involves arranging the environment and supporting the client in such a way that the likelihood of the feared consequences is reduced sufficiently for the client to emit previously avoided behaviour, and to experience success in using his newly developed sense of emotional freedom and lack of behavioural restraint across a variety of everyday living situations. These experiences define the conditions which maximally facilitate the extinction of phobic reactions. Unlike Wolpe's systematic desensitization method, the extinction of anxiety responses is not regarded as a prerequisite for participation in the ultimately dreaded activities; rather, successful performance is considered to be the most effective means of modifying the associated anxiety (see Bandura, 1977). As the treatment progresses, the therapist gradually withdraws supportive aids until the client can fearlessly engage in the behaviour without assistance.

Following comprehensive pre-treatment assessment of the cognitive, affective, and behavioural components of their phobia about snakes, one group of subjects received orthodox desensitization treatment in which imaginal representation of increasingly aversive scenes involving snakes was paired with relaxation. A second self-administered symbolic modelling group relaxed themselves while observing a graduated film showing children and adults engaging in progressively more threatening interactions with a snake. The rate of presentation of the modelled stimuli was regulated by the subjects by means of a remote-controlled projector such that any anxiety-provoking scene was repeatedly viewed until completely neutralized before they moved on to the next scene in the hierarchial sequence. The third group received participant modelling.

Desensitization and symbolic modelling resulted in considerable improvement at post-testing, while the participant modelling method produced the greatest gains in eliminating phobic behaviour in 92% of subjects. Non-treated control subjects showed no change in any response measure. The control subjects subsequently received symbolic modelling without relaxation training. The results indicated no difference between symbolic modelling administered with or without relaxation. Several other findings from this well-designed study are noteworthy. First, not only did the treatment techniques effect substantial behavioural changes, but they also produced favourable changes in subjects' affective and attitudinal responses towards snakes, with participant modelling proving to be the most powerful form of treatment. Secondly, an analysis of a comprehensive fear inventory which was administered to the subjects before and after therapy revealed decrements in reported anxiety in situations other than the snake phobia specifically treated. Desensitization reduced the intensity of fears about animals in general, but only the modelling groups, particularly modelling with guided participation, produced an overall decrease in the number of fears about animals as well as a reduction in anxieties related to other areas of functioning, including both interpersonal and non-social situations. Non-treated controls showed no changes in either the intensity or number of fears. Finally, Bandura *et al.* administered the participant modelling procedure to all subjects who had shown only partial improvement at post-testing with the result that their phobic behaviour was completely eliminated in all cases. This demonstration indicates that specific technique variables were responsible for the therapeutic improvement rather than any characteristics of the subjects. All therapeutic gains were maintained at a 1-month follow-up. Subsequent studies by Blanchard (1970) and Bandura, Adams, and Beyer (1977) have replicated the greater efficacy of participant modelling compared to symbolic modelling.

It appears that *exposure* to the phobic situation is a valuable component of effective treatment. However, highly phobic individuals are, by definition, reluctant to confront the source of the fears. Bandura, Jeffery, and Wright (1974) demonstrated that participant modelling is successful because it provides a number of "performance aids" such as prior modelling of the feared activity by the therapist, joint performance of graduated sub-tasks and initial control of the feared situation by the therapist (e.g. holding the snake securely so as to afford the subject complete protection against imagined harm). The greater the degree of supportive performance aids in the participant modelling procedure, the more rapid and marked were the changes in avoidance behaviour and phobic attitudes. A later study by Bandura, Jeffery, and Gajdos (1975) indicated that following therapist-administered participant modelling with a period of self-directed practice by the subject, produced significantly greater fear reduction, more generalized behavioural changes, higher levels of self-efficacy, and less fear of threats beyond those specifically treated.

It is worth noting the clinical relevance as well as the statistical significance of the results achieved by Bandura and his colleagues in this series of studies on snake phobics. In addition to being able to touch and hold the snake during the post-treatment laboratory assessment, subjects usually displayed substantial and generalized decrements in fear and avoidance. Referring to the two most recent studies (Bandura and Adams, 1977; Bandura *et al.*, 1977), Bandura (1978) points out that 77% of all subjects treated with participant modelling showed marked improvement in being able to participate in preferred activities in the natural environment. The remaining 23% of subjects reported at least moderate improvement in this respect. Subjects also indicated marked (61%) or moderate (39%) reductions in frightening thoughts and recurrent nightmares about snakes. Typical of this generalized improvement is the subject who remarked that

> " 'I had nightmares about twice a month. I used to be afraid every time I walked into a dark room or got into a car alone at night, thinking that maybe there was a snake on the floor. I haven't had a nightmare since the treatment program. I also used to feel revulsion whenever I even heard the word "snake". My body tensed up, and I would often get a chill and feel sick in my stomach. That never happens anymore.' " (p. 264).

The efficacy of participant modelling is not confined to the elimination of snake phobias. Ritter (1969) found that participant modelling was superior to symbolic modelling in treating acrophobics successfully. Similarly, Peck (1977) reported that a treatment procedure that is best described as participant modelling was more effective than either symbolic modelling, systematic desensitization, an attention—placebo group or a no-treatment control group in the treatment of phobias of heights and rats respectively in retarded subjects. Owing to the small number of subjects per group, there were significant differences among the groups. However, there was an obvious trend clearly favouring the participant modelling group over other groups. All four of the subjects in the participant modelling group performed all of the approach behaviour, whereas only one subject in each of the other groups was able to meet this criterion. Participant modelling also proved to be more efficient than any of the other treatments, requiring fewer treatment sessions to effect greater behavioural and subjective changes.

Another study that bears on the efficacy of participant modelling is Crowe *et al.* (1972). Fourteen phobic subjects, including five agoraphobics, each received three forms of treatment in the context of a randomized block design. The treatments were systematic desensitization, implosion therapy, and reinforced practice or what they called shaping. As we have noted above, the latter technique consists of the following combined elements: graduated and repeated practice in approaching fear-producing situations; reinforcement for increasing approach; feedback of progress; and instructions designed to enhance expectations of success. Patients were instructed to withdraw temporarily if they experienced "undue anxiety" at any point. Crowe *et al.* comment that in some cases modelling was also employed thus making the treatment method difficult to distinguish from participant modelling. The implosion therapy condition was more akin to flooding in that the psychodynamic hypothesized sequential cues were omitted in favour of an emphasis on environmental anxiety-eliciting cues.

Evaluation of treatment outcome included both symptom rating scales and specifically constructed behavioural avoidance tasks, arbitrarily converted into 20-point scales. No difference was obtained on the rating scales, but shaping resulted in significant decreases on the avoidance tests. Flooding produced intermediate results not significantly different from either desensitization or shaping. The patients rated desensitization as the most preferred technique despite its lack of measured efficacy. The three therapies did not differ in efficacy in terms of the type of phobia treated (agoraphobia vs. specific phobic complaints), although the success order was consistent with the overall results, i.e. shaping, flooding, and lastly desensitization.

As Crowe *et al.* (1972) observed, the relative failure of desensitization is not too surprising given the brevity of treatment (three "preparatory" and four actual sessions of desensitization). The greater efficacy of shaping, and to a lesser degree flooding, suggests that both might be as, or more, efficient (if not more effective) than desensitization. The superior efficacy of shaping is attributed to its multifaceted nature and the fact that it is carried out in the fear-producing situation. Crowe *et al.* comment on the "generalization gap" from imaginal desensitization sessions, in which patients were able to imagine threatening events, to their subsequent inability to cope with *in vivo* situations.

Further evidence of the effects of modelling in the treatment of phobias comes from a study of phobic children of both anxious and non-anxious mothers by Windheuser (1977). He compared three treatment groups: a multifaceted *in vivo* exposure programme, *in vivo* exposure with self-instructional training and reinforcement for progress; the same programme with the added treatment of the mother's fear in the presence of the child; and a no-treatment control group. In the *in vivo* exposure plus modelling treatment, the mother was instructed to act as a coping model for her child. The mother's fear that was treated was in many but not all instances the same as the child's phobia. The interesting finding from this study is that the children of phobic mothers responded significantly more favourably to the *in vivo* exposure plus modelling treatment than the *in vivo* exposure treatment alone. The effect of a phobic mother was evident in the finding that children of phobic mothers did less well than children of non-phobic mothers within the same treatment condition. However, the results of this intriguing study should be interpreted cautiously because of the absence of direct behavioural measures of outcome.

Participant modelling has also chalked up significant success in the treatment of obsessional—compulsive disorders. In the Rachman *et al.* (1971) study described in the previous section, the treatment condition featuring gradual *in vivo* exposure with modelling can be described as participant modelling. Although significantly more effective than the control treatment, participant modelling in this study did not differ reliably from flooding alone. In summarizing the results of the 2-year follow-up of this and related studies, Marks *et al.* (1975) observed that modelling alone "conferred no advantage over exposure alone for the group as a whole, though it may help selected patients" (p. 349).

In another study Röper *et al.* (1975) assigned ten obsessional—compulsive patients to one of two treatment groups. The first received fifteen sessions of a control treatment in which patients modelled the therapist engaging in relaxation exercises, followed by fifteen sessions of participant modelling. The second received fifteen sessions of passive modelling in which patients observed the therapist engaging in behaviour the patient would normally avoid and/or be greatly distressed by, followed by fifteen sessions of participant modelling. Treatment was administered on an in-patient basis for a period of 5 to 7 weeks.

The results showed that modelling of exposure to the threatening activities produced significantly more improvement than modelled relaxation, which was ineffective in modifying compulsive rituals. Although both modelling treatments produced changes, Roper *et al.* concluded that "those observed after participant modelling treatment were more pronounced and were evident on a wider range of measures" (p. 274). A 6-month follow-up indicated that of the ten patients, four were much improved, four were improved, and two were unchanged – a clinical outcome similar to their earlier findings (Marks *et al.*, 1975).

Methodological problems preclude firm conclusions about the relative efficacy of passive and participant modelling. In the first place, as Roper *et al.* point out, both modelling procedures were confounded with instructions to the patients to refrain from carrying out their compulsive acts (i.e. response prevention instructions were in operation). In general, symbolic modelling has been found to be at least equal to systematic desensitization as a fear-reduction technique (Rachman, 1976; Rosenthal and Bandura, 1978), an impressive record given the demonstrable success of desensitization. Symbolic modelling is effective not only in eliminating snake phobias (Bandura *et al.*, 1969; Blanchard, 1970), but also in treating anxiety-related sexual dysfunctions. Nemetz, Craig, and Reith (1978) compared symbolic modelling procedures (conducted either on an individual or group basis) with a waiting-list control condition. The subjects were twenty-two inorgasmic women, fifteen of whom suffered from secondary orgasmic dysfunction and seven of whom reported primary orgasmic dysfunction. Treatment consisted of relaxation training followed by viewing forty-five videotaped vignettes depicting graduated sexual behaviour with instructions to practice the modelled activities at home. Multiple outcome measures were used, including the frequency of specific sexual behaviour as assessed by both the subject and her partner; global and specific measures of sexual attitudes; and subjective measures of anxiety about sexual behaviour.

The results indicated consistent improvement in treated subjects on all three categories of outcome measures. Women who did not receive treatment showed no improvement and even some evidence of deterioration. Successful treatment effects were maintained at a 1-year follow-up. The videotaped treatment procedure that Nemetz *et al*. described as symbolic modelling was similar to the method that Wincze and Caird (1976) called "video desensitization". In this study the videotaped treatment was shown to be significantly more effective than systematic desensitization and a waiting-list control condition in reducing sexual anxiety in non-orgasmic women. Similarly, McMullen and Rosen (1979) found that modelling was substantially more effective than no-treatment in developing orgasmic responsiveness in women with primary orgasmic dysfunction.

In terms of Bandura's social learning theory, the source or mode of the disinhibiting information that forms the basis of modelling is less important that the ultimate impact the information has on the cognitive mediating processes that are assumed to regulate behaviour. Thus in addition to live and symbolic modelling, the effects of covert modelling, in which the person imagines a model engaging in phobic behaviour, have been evaluated. In a series of well-controlled studies, Kazdin has not only demonstrated that covert modelling is more effective than control conditions in reducing avoidance behaviour and increasing assertive responses, but also has identified several procedural factors that critically influence treatment outcome.

In his first investigation with unassertive subjects, Kazdin (1974a) compared four treatment groups: (a) covert modelling plus reinforcement (subjects imagined scenes in which a model behaved assertively, and received reinforcement); (b) covert modelling (subjects imagined scenes in which a model behaved assertively); (c) no-model control (imagined scenes with neither an assertive model nor favourable consequences); and (d) a no-treatment control. Following four treatment sessions, both the model and the model-reinforcement groups improved significantly on self-report and behavioural measures of assertion. The model-reinforcement group was significantly more assertive on a behavioural role-playing test. These treatment gains were maintained at a 3-month follow-up. Although generalization of behaviour change was demonstrated within the laboratory setting, viz. from practised to novel role-playing tasks, no evidence of generalization of behavioural change to the natural environment was obtained. In a second study, using the same methodology, Kazdin (1975) showed that if subjects imagined multiple models rather than a single model behaving assertively, or the model(s) being reinforced for their actions, the treatment effects were enhanced.

In other studies with snake-fearful subjects, Kazdin (1975) found that if subjects imagined a coping model who gradually overcame initial fear as opposed to a "mastery" model who performed fearlessly from the outset, greater behavioural change was obtained. These findings are encouraging for two reasons. Firstly, they help to establish the efficacy of covert modelling, although its application to more severe problems remains to be investigated. Secondly, the finding that factors such as multiple and "coping" models whose actions carry favourable consequences are the most effective replicate similar findings with live and symbolic modelling (Bandura, 1977a; Meichenbaum, 1971; Sarason, 1975).

Covert and symbolic modelling methods seem to have comparable treatment effects (Rosenthal and Reese, 1976). However, covert modelling has been shown to be less effective than participant modelling. Thase and Moss (1976) compared two forms of covert modelling with participant modelling and a waiting-list control condition in the treatment of snake-fearful subjects. In the one covert modelling procedure, the subject imagined someone else engaging in coping behaviour towards the snake; in the second condition, subjects imagined themselves approaching the snake in a coping manner. Symbolic representation of a coping model was deliberately chosen since it has been shown to be the most effective form of covert and symbolic modelling.

Participant modelling was significantly more effective in reducing avoidance behaviour. Covert modelling was marginally more effective in reducing avoidance behaviour than was the control condition. Subjects who had failed to improve with covert modelling were then treated with participant modelling and showed significant improvement comparable to that of the original participant modelling group. These findings demonstrate that performance-based methods are more effective than techniques which rely entirely on symbolic induction processes. Thase and Moss argue that there is no clinical justification for using covert modelling unless participant modelling is impractical for one or another reason.

CONCLUSION

The evidence supports Bandura's original claims for the efficacy of modelling procedures in reducing fears. Although not reviewed in the present chapter, several studies have also shown the therapeutic value of modelling methods in developing novel behavioural repertoires and overcoming skill deficits (Bandura, 1977b; Rosenthal, 1976).

Modelling appears to be at least as effective as systematic desensitization in reducing phobias. In any comparative outcome study, care must be taken to ensure that treatments are discriminably different in implementation and are consistent with their theoretical and procedural specifications. Thus symbolic modelling and desensitization, for example, may yield comparable treatment effects because the differences between the two techniques may become so blurred during implementation that they involve essentially the same processes. On the one hand, as Rosenthal and Bandura (1978) point out, therapists frequently elaborate upon items in a desensitization hierarchy in a way which involves the patient's participation in the feared scene. On the other hand, patients themselves might alter the nature of the image they are instructed to conjure up. In a study comparing symbolic modelling and desensitization, Denney and Sullivan (1976) noted that subjects receiving desensitization spontaneously reported projecting themselves into the scenes even when instructed to imagine viewing only the spider. Careful questioning of subjects is necessary to ascertain the nature of the independent variable in studies that deal with covert processes.

Participant modelling, a procedure that relies upon treatment *in vivo,* appears to be more effective than its symbolic or covert counterparts. Yet this comparison needs to be conducted with a broader range of fears than has been the case to date. The practical advantages of covert modelling are obvious since imagery provides an efficient means of rehearsing phobic scenes (e.g. a fear of flying) or inhibited activities (e.g. being assertive with a superior) that would be difficult if not impossible *in vivo*. Indeed, this was one of the reasons that originally led Wolpe to use imagery in desensitization. The limits of covert modelling methods require definition through more research. In this connection it would be well to take seriously Rosenthal and Bandura's caveat that most of the research on covert modelling has been restricted to bright, cognitively sophisticated subjects. Clearly there will be patients for whom performance-based methods will be the preferred alternative simply because they do not have the imaginal prowess that may be required by these techniques.

Comparisons among *in vivo* treatment methods have yielded mixed results. The addition of modelling to graded *in vivo* exposure significantly enhanced therapeutic success in Windheuser's (1977) treatment of phobic children but not in Rachman *et al.*'s (1971) treatment of compulsive rituals. Conclusions that modelling adds little to *in vivo* exposure methods are premature. Whether or not modelling increases the efficacy of *in vivo* exposure will depend on the severity and type of problem under consideration. Rosenthal and Bandura make the sobering observation that "treatment planning is constrained by the specific activities the client will or will not undertake. Clients attempting or refusing to perform a given task sets the limits on the momentary content of treatment" (p. 640). Participant modelling includes a number of performance aids that are designed to prompt the recalcitrant client to make contact with the phobic situation. Among these aids, the verbal support of the therapist and prior modelling might prove to be decisive in cases of extreme fear.

CHAPTER 10

BEHAVIOUR THERAPY—II

In the brief time since Wolpe (1958) published his landmark text, behaviour therapy has developed from seemingly improbable foundations into a widely researched and routinely used form of treatment (e.g. American Psychiatric Association, 1973; Bergin and Lambert, 1978; Risley, 1977). Claims for the therapeutic success of some behavioural methods occasionally outstrip the available evidence, but it can be said that a reasonable scientific basis now exists for applying behavioural methods in clinical practice. Current debates over behaviour therapy centre not on the question of whether or not it is ever effective, but rather on problems of how and why it is effective in dealing with particular difficulties.

Not surprisingly, estimates of the efficacy of behaviour therapy and the adequacy of its empirical basis differ. Nor are these differences in the evaluation of the evidence on behaviour therapy confined to external critics of the approach; behaviour therapists themselves are far from unanimous in their appraisal of the outcome research (Franks and Wilson, 1973–1979). Yet whatever the nature of the disagreement over the overall efficacy of behaviour therapy, there are two issues on which there can be little dispute. The first is that the amount and quality of research on behavioural methods, although often uneven and unsatisfactory, far exceeds the empirical support that can be mustered for traditional psychotherapy, Much of this behavioural research has been facilitated by the unprecedented development of innovative and powerful research strategies for evaluating therapy outcome (Hersen and Barlow, 1976; Kazdin and Wilson, 1978b). The second is that behaviour therapy is applicable to a broader range of psychological, medical, and educational problems than traditional psychotherapy. The narrow view that behaviour therapy is appropriate mainly for the treatment of simple phobias or habit disorders, or that it is no more than a useful adjunct to psychotherapy, can be dismissed. As Sloane *et al.* (1975) emphasized, behaviour therapy "is clearly a generally useful treatment" (p. 224). This general applicability of behaviour therapy is all the more significant when it is remembered that traditional psychodynamic psychotherapy has been limited to neurotic and personality disorders (see, for example, Luborsky *et al.*, 1975; Candy *et al.*, 1972; Kernberg, 1973). Viewing the field from his vantage point as a psychiatrist, Chesser (1976) offered the following observation:

> "If one considers behaviour therapy as a broad approach which informs and influences the total management of the patient not only in hospital, then the range of applicability can be extended to crisis intervention in families . . . social work . . . group therapy . . . marital problems . . . family therapy . . . interpersonal problems, chronic neurotic depression, weight disorders, alcohol and drug abuse, some organic disorders, and the rehabilitation of patients with organic deficits or chronic schizophrenia" (p. 302).

In keeping with this view of the range of behaviour therapy, we now review the outcome data on the treatment of sexual dysfunction and deviance; the addictions; and institutionalized adult patients.

Sexual Dysfunction

From the start, the treatment of both male and female sexual disorders played a prominent part in behaviour therapy (Wolpe, 1958). The use of the Semans "stop–start" technique in the treatment of premature ejaculation, graded sexual contact and stimulation to ensure the dominance of positive sexual arousal over neurotic anxiety, non-demand procedures and imaginal and *in vivo* desensitization were all part of the early behaviour therapist's set of techniques. The notion that orgasm through intercourse is the only legitimate means of sexual gratification was not adopted, and the importance of partner participation in the treatment process was stressed. Years before Masters and Johnson, in the case of the single man without an available partner, behaviour therapists such as Wolpe recommended that a surrogate partner (a co-operative prostitute) be sought to assist the patient in overcoming his sexual inhibitions. However, it was the publication of Masters and Johnson's (1970) text that heralded the enthusiastic public and professional acceptance of what has come to be called "sex therapy".

Masters and Johnson do not identify their methods as "behaviour therapy", but their treatment programme can be categorized in this way. Many of the components of the Masters and Johnson programme are the behavioural methods described above. The nature of their programme is well known and need not be detailed here. Suffice it to say that it includes the behavioural assessment of variables which are currently maintaining sexual inadequacy; the psychodynamic notion that the client inevitably has some underlying psychopathology of which the sexual problem is but a surface manifestation is rejected; the pedagogical role of the therapist includes specific instructions; modes of social interaction are candidly modelled by the co-therapists in discussing emotionally charged sexual matters; there is the *in vivo* desensitization of performance-related fears about sex; and improved interpersonal communication and reciprocal reinforcement are emphasized (O'Leary and Wilson, 1975).

Interestingly, these rapid treatment behavioural techniques have been painlessly adopted by a variety of non-behavioural therapists, including many of a psychodynamic persuasion. The most notable example is Kaplan's (1974) attempt to rationalize the use of these behavioural techniques within the psychoanalytic framework. As we view it, contemporary sex therapy with its emphasis on brief, directive methods departs from essential psychoanalytic tenets. Whatever the fate of this unpromising attempt at theoretical integration (see Franks and Wilson, 1975), the fact is that nothing like these procedures was used by traditional psychotherapists until the advent of the Masters and Johnson book. As mentioned in Chapter 6, the treatment of sexual disorders by traditional psychotherapy has not been successful. Whatever the reasons for the adoption of behavioural methods by psychodynamically oriented therapists, they do not include the results of compelling experimental evidence demonstrating the superior efficacy of the approach. As is all too often the case in the psychological therapies, research follows adoption, rather than the correct way round. The research into the effects of sex therapy is only beginning to accumulate.

In contrast to the prior record of traditional psychotherapy,* the *uncontrolled* clinical findings on the behavioural treatment of sexual disorders have shown unprecedented success. The most persuasive results were those obtained by Masters and Johnson themselves. On the basis of 790 treated cases, they demonstrated a success rate of 81% at the end of their 2-to-3-week treatment programme, with 75% success at a 5-year follow-up. The latter figure was derived from 313 of the treated cases. As dramatic and encouraging as these results are, it is important to recognize their serious limitations. Masters and Johnson themselves point out that their clients were a highly select and selected sample uncharacteristic of the general population. The majority were upper–middle class, including a disproportionate number of doctors and behavioural scientists, who were very highly motivated. Without a long-term follow-up of all the clients who were treated, the overall outcome data, while strongly suggestive, are not conclusive. Yet our confidence in these findings is increased by the conservative manner in which Masters and Johnson evaluated treatment outcome and the fact that over 50% of their parents had received previous psychotherapy without success. This argues against attributing Masters and Johnson's success solely to placebo factors or expectations of treatment success. Noteworthy too is the fact that Wolpe and Lazarus (1966) reported comparable success rates using similar procedures with the same range of problems, while Laughren and Kass (1975), in a review of uncontrolled clinical findings on the use of *in vivo* desensitization, were led to remark that, "Considering some important differences in population and treatment methods, it is remarkable that the overall improvement rates tend to cluster around 80%" (p. 283).

Regrettably, Masters and Johnson's commendably careful reporting of treatment evaluation procedures and outcomes for specific sexual problems, has been followed less enthusiastically than their therapeutic techniques. Hartman and Fithian (1972), for example, substituted assurance for outcome data in advocating their somewhat modified version of the Masters and Johnson programme: "We can honestly assure candidates for therapy, that at the time of follow-up (two years), couples who have completed our two-week program describe the benefits achieved in approximately the same proportions as are reported by Masters and Johnson" (p. 205). Their excuse for not reporting outcome statistics is original, namely that it would breed "spurious competition" among different programmes and focus attention on the "numbers game of success rates". Similarly, Kaplan (1974) omits outcome data from her treatment programme save for an assurance that they are comparable to those reported by Masters and Johnson.

We can take some comfort from the fact that the relatively few *controlled* outcome studies on the treatment of sexual dysfunction do tend to support the highly favourable reports of uncontrolled clinical trials. Obler (1973) compared behavioural treatment to traditional group therapy and no-treatment. The behavioural treatment consisted of fifteen weekly sessions of

---

*Wright, Perreault, and Mathieu (1977) reviewed both psychodynamic and behavioural treatment approaches to the full spectrum of sexual dysfunctions. Echoing previous evaluations, they conclude that it is impossible to assess the efficacy of psychodynamic methods since nothing approaching a controlled study has been completed in this area. As Wright *et al.* point out, anecdotal case studies provide detailed descriptions of hypothesized underlying dynamics and the therapeutic process but fail to give details of treatment outcome. This eschewal of outcome information is illustrated in a recent study of the process of psychodynamic therapy in the case of a woman who sought treatment for what authors inappropriately labelled as "frigidity" (Horowitz, Sampson, Siegelman, Weiss, and Goodfriend, 1978). Details of the process mechanisms over the first 100 hours of therapy were provided, with no clarity about whether the client's sexual problem was treated successfully, save for a vague footnote to this effect.

systematic desensitization, supplemented by the use of sexual slides and films of sexual encounters, assertion training, and role-playing of situations related to sexual problems. Group psychotherapy, 1½ hours weekly over a 10-week period, was conducted by two trained therapists employing the typical procedures they used in their daily treatment of neurotic clients. The therapists described themselves as neo-Freudian in orientation. The therapy focused on reducing misconceptions, promoting greater insight, and interpreting underlying dynamics and repressions associated with sexual dysfunction. Subjects were shown the same slides and films that were used in the behavioural treatment. The subjects in this investigation were intelligent, highly motivated people who were referred from professional clinicians in community-based psychotherapeutic clinics and counselling services at universities in New York City. Multiple measures of outcome were assessed, including GSR and heart-rate responses to filmed material depicting sexual dysfunction, a variety of questionnaire measures, and records of all successful and unsuccessful sexual experiences as defined by a success-experience form provided for each subject.

Based on the subjects' success/experience ratios from pre- to post-treatment, the behavioural treatment produced significantly greater improvement than either group-psychotherapy or no-treatment. Forty-two per cent of the female and 61% of the male subjects' sexual encounters were successful as compared to only 3% of sexual attempts in the other two groups. Behaviourally treated subjects also showed greater reductions in physiological arousal to scenes of sexual failure and greater improvement on questionnaire indices of sexual stress. Eighty per cent (18 of 22) of the behaviourally treated subjects became "sexually functional" and Obler stated that these gains were maintained in an 18-months follow-up although the actual data were not reported.

A limitation of these findings is that Obler's report provides no information on treatment outcome on specific sexual problems. Indeed, it is unclear what the nature of the treated problems were. Similarly, outcome criteria such as "sexually functional" or "successful sexual experiences" are not defined, leaving open the questions about the specific nature of treatment changes. None the less, the results offer reasonably firm support for the efficacy of behaviour therapy, notwithstanding some misguided attempts to downgrade their value by emphasizing the so-called "volunteer student" nature of the subject population. Regardless of the separate question of the severity of the subjects' problems, which were of sufficient magnitude to warrant referral by other treatment facilities, the comparative superiority of behaviour therapy has not been challenged.

In a major comparative outcome study by Mathews, Bancroft, Whitehead, Hackmann, Julier, Bancroft, Gath, and Shaw (1976), thirty-six couples who reported sexual problems were treated with one of three methods: systematic desensitization plus counselling; directed practice, i.e. a modified version of the Masters and Johnson *in vivo* programme, plus counselling; and directed practice with minimal therapist contact. The counselling consisted of discussing sexual attitudes, reviewing treatment progress, and encouraging free comunication of sexual feelings between partners. In the minimal contact condition, therapeutic instructions were mailed to patients, with only two treatment sessions (at mid-treatment and at the end of therapy). The counselling component was absent from these sessions. All therapy was given in twelve weekly sessions. Of the thirty-six couples, eighteen had problems that arose primarily with the male partner (e.g. erectile failure or premature ejaculation). The most common complaint among the female patients was that of low interest in and arousal by sexual encounters. Thirteen reported failure in achieving orgasm. Both members of each couple were seen together, but half the couples in each therapy condition were treated by a single therapist and half by a dual-sex therapy team. Outcome measures included ratings of patients' sexual adjustment by an independent psychiatrist before and after therapy and at a 4-month follow-up; patient self-ratings and estimates of sexual activities; and therapist ratings of patients' sexual adjustment.

The results indicated that the directed practice plus counselling treatment produced slightly greater improvement ($p < 0.10$) than the other two treatments. Also, there was a marginally significant tendency ($p < 0.10$) for the dual-sex therapy team to be more effective than a single therapist in the directed practice plus counselling treatment. This finding is the first evidence to support Masters and Johnson's insistence on the necessity of a dual-sex therapy team. The modified Masters and Johnson treatment was approximately twice as effective as systematic desensitization plus counselling. The superiority of the *in vivo* over the imaginal treatment lends further empirical support to the consistent findings that performance-based methods are more effective than those based upon verbal or imaginal operations (cf. Bandura, 1977a). There was marked variability in the outcome for patients in the group who received directed practice with minimum therapist contact treatment. Mathews *et al.* suggest that some patients respond well to straightforward behavioural techniques whereas others, distinguished mainly by inter-personal and communication difficulties, will not respond to this treatment. Indeed, it appears that the latter's problems might even be aggravated.

A modified version of the Masters and Johnson programme was compared to chemotherapy (oxazepam) and a placebo control by Ansari (1976) in the treatment of erectile difficulties. The results of this study are inconsistent with the findings from other controlled investigations. At post-treatment, patients were classified as "recovered" ("patient completely satisfied with sexual functioning"), "improved" ("still occasional failures, less satisfied than recovered group"), or no change. Post-treatment, 15 of 21 (67%) of the Masters and Johnson group, 10 of 16 (63%) of the chemotherapy group, and 13 of 18 (72%) of the control group were considered to be either recovered or improved. An 8-month follow-up suggested that the two *treatment* groups had deteriorated, relative to the control group. Unfortunately, the results are difficult to interpret because of the methodological inadequacies that confound conventional com-parative outcome research. Ansari failed to specify the treatment procedures, the patient selection criteria, or the assessment procedures. The assumption that global labels such as "directive sex therapy" or a "Masters and Johnson-type program" subsume homogenous treat-ment components is probably untenable. Different treatment methods in different programmes that are labelled in the same way might explain differential success rates. Furthermore, evaluating treatment outcome in terms of the qualitative, global categories described above tends to obscure potential treatment differences. None the less, Ansari's results cannot be disregarded.

Other controlled studies have focused on the treatment of specific male or female‘ problems. Impotence was the target problem in a study by Kockott, Dittmar, and Nusselt (1975) that compared systematic desensitization to "routine therapy" and a waiting-list control group. "Routine therapy" was defined as the combination of advice and medication given by general practitioners and psychiatrists in Munich. Twenty-four patients, equally distributed across the three groups, were selected according to the following critera: inability to achieve intromission during the 6 months prior to therapy; a co-operative partner; and no organic disorder, sexual deviation (unspecified), or endogenous depression. Patients in the desensitization condition received fourteen treatment sessions, whereas those in the routine therapy were seen by psychiatrists for a total of four occasions at intervals of 3–5 weeks. A taped, semistructured interview, subsequently scored by the interviewer and two independent psychiatrists, served as a pre-post measure of therapeutic efficacy. No reliability figures were reported. In addition, penile plethysmographic measures were obtained from ten of the patients while they were asked to imagine two separate scenes involving sexual intercourse. All subjects provided subjective ratings of these two imagery scenes.

Although patients who received systematic desensitization reported less subjective aversion or anxiety to the thought of sexual intercourse at the end of treatment, behavioural improvements, as determined from the semistructured interviews, were minimal in both treatment groups. Only two patients in each group were judged to have been "cured" — defined as "erection maintained for at least 1 minute after intromission with intravaginal ejaculation before loss of erection" (p. 498). An increase in duration of erection up to 20% was observed in only four patients (at least one in each group) at post-treatment. However, there was no association between this increase in tumescence and the clinical ratings.

Kockott et al. attribute the ineffectiveness of systematic desensitization to the fact that it is a technique for "dealing with anxiety-related problems alone", whereas "during the behaviour analysis of the patients it became clear that there was a great number of other factors in addition to anxiety which seemed to maintain the behavioural disturbance" (p. 499). Unimproved patients were subsequently treated with a modified Masters and Johnson programme addressing some of the factors such as unrealistic standards and negative attitudes about sex. Of the twelve patients treated in this manner, eight were rated as cured, three showed no improvement, and one relapsed shortly after therapy. Marks (1978) reports an unpublished study by Schacht, van Vloten, Mol, and Edwards that similarly showed a Masters and Johnson-type programme to be more effective than systematic desensitization in the treatment of impotence and premature ejaculation.

Auerbach and Kilmann (1977) evaluated the effects of group systematic desensitization in the treatment of secondary impotence. Twenty-four subjects were matched in terms of age, severity of disorder, co-operativeness of partner, and marital status in being assigned either to a group desensitization treatment or an attention placebo-control treatment. The latter consisted of relaxation training unrelated to specific sexual functioning and developing rapport. Treatment lasted for fifteen sessions and was assessed in terms of a success/experience ratio that comprises the number of successful sexual experiences (i.e. achieves and maintains full intromission) divided by total number of attempts at intercourse. Both sexual and non-sexual relationship inventories were obtained before and after therapy. Four subjects in each treatment dropped out of therapy for reasons apparently unrelated to the specific methods employed.

The results showed that the group desensitization treatment was significantly more successful in improving erectile functioning. Subjects' self-reports of successful attempts at intercourse were corroborated by their partners. Specifically, the desensitization group showed an improvement of over 40% compared to less than 30% for the control group. This improvement was maintained over a 3-month follow-up period and control subjects who were subsequently treated showed considerable change. There are several commendable features about this study, and it provides added empirical support for the moderate efficacy of desensitization methods in the treatment of the form of sexual dysfunction with which Masters and Johnson obtained the least success. It is not clear why Auerbach and Kilmann obtained successful results in contrast to the ineffectiveness of systematic desensitization in the Kockott et al. (1975) study.

One of the most impressive findings of Masters and Johnson's own investigation was the successful modification of premature ejaculation in 182 of 186 cases! A study by Yulis (1976), while lacking a control group and thus not definitive, nevertheless furnishes clinical findings that lend support to Masters and Johnson's data. Yulis treated thirty-seven middle- or upper-class clients who were premature ejaculators. The average duration of their sexual problems was just over 8 years. Treatment was closely modelled on the Masters and Johnson programme, the client being treated together with his female partner by a dual-sex therapy team. The clients' assertive behaviour was assessed in role-playing sessions, and assertion training was administered at the therapist's discretion. Thirty-three of the men (89%) reported a "very satisfactory sexual relationship" at a 6-month follow-up on self-reports that were confirmed by their partners. Very satisfactory sexual adjustment was defined as between 80–100% "ejaculation-controlled sexual encounters" (p. 356).

An informative feature of Yulis' report is the data on generalization of improved ejaculatory control to sexual intercourse with partners other than those who participated in the therapy sessions. Of twenty-three clients who described sexual contact with at least one non-treatment partner, nine experienced persistent difficulties in ejaculatory control when attempting intercourse with the non-treatment partner. All nine clients (five of whom were married) reported episodes of premature ejaculation with their treatment partners following unsuccessful encounters with non-treatment partners. Yulis suggests that the success of the thirteen men who experienced no ejaculatory problems with non-treatment partners is attributable to the fact that eleven of these thirteen men received assertion training. Of the ten subjects who did not receive assertion training, seven experienced ejaculatory problems with non-treatment partners. Of course, these are *post hoc* analyses of the data, and are suggestive at best. However, they emphasize that treatment-induced improvement does not necessarily generalize. Specific steps must be taken to facilitate such generalization. Zeiss (1978) carried out a controlled study of the efficacy of a self-directed treatment programme for modifying premature ejaculation. Couples who reported difficulties with premature ejaculation received one of three treatments: a therapist-administered programme; a self-administered programme using a self-help treatment manual, with minimal contact with the therapist; or a totally self-administered programme in which the clients had no further contact with the therapist after two initial assessment and orientation sessions. The treatment manual consisted of a 12-week programme based on the techniques of Masters and Johnson. The results showed that the therapist-administered and the minimal contact treatments were significantly superior to the totally self-administered treatment programme but did not differ from each other. All six couples in the therapist-administered treatment and five of the six couples in the minimal contact treatment were classified as therapeutic successes according to the following critera: latency to ejaculation in intercourse more than 5 minutes with an improvement of at least 3 minutes from pre-treatment levels; and both partners expressed satisfaction about improvement in the male's ejaculatory control. None of the six couples in the totally self-administered treatment were classified as successes. A follow-up of eight of the eleven couples who had been classified as therapeutic successes, at 3 to 9 months after treatment, indicated that four couples had experienced some deterioration in ejaculatory performance or with their satisfaction with it.

As described in the preceding chapter, symbolic modelling has shown encouraging success in eliminating sexual anxiety and developing orgasmic responsiveness in women with primary or secondary orgasmic dysfunction (see McMullen and Rosen, 1979; Nemetz et al., 1978; Wincze and Caird, 1976). The behavioural treatment of orgasmic dysfunction was compared to a waiting-list control condition by Munjack, Cristol, Goldstein, Phillips, Goldberg, Whipple, Staples, and Kanno (1976). Twelve middle- to upper-class women with primary orgasmic dysfunction and ten with secondary orgasmic dysfunction, whose average age was 29 years, and who were currently living with their husbands, were assigned to either an immediate treatment or a delayed treatment group. The treatment programme consisted of heterogeneous techniques that were tailored to the individual case. Techniques included systematic desensitization, assertion training, modelling, cognitive restructuring, direct education using plastic models, *in vivo* homework assignments, and masturbation training using vaginal dilators and vibrators. Most patients were seen individually, without their husbands, about 75% of the time. All treatment was administered by two male therapists and one female therapist working alone. Outcome measures consisted of a number of personality questionnaires, an assessment interview with two blind assessors, and a "Sexual Adjustment Form" that sampled patients' reactions to specific aspects of sexual behaviour as well as frequencies of sexual behaviour.

Treatment was significantly more effective than no-treatment on several measures: (a) the percentage of patients experiencing orgasm during at least 50% of sexual relations; (b) the percentage of women reporting satisfactory sexual relations at least 50% of the time; (c) patients' ratings of positive reactions to various sexual activities; and (d) assessors' global clinical ratings of the women's sexual adjustment, as well as their feeling about sex. Only about one-third of the women were orgasmic in at least 50% of their sexual encounters at the end of the twenty sessions of treatment.

Somewhat predictably in terms of previous findings (McGovern, Stewart, and LoPiccolo, 1975), women with primary orgasmic dysfunction responded differently to those with secondary orgasmic dysfunction. At post-treatment, 22% of the primary and 40% of the secondary orgasmic dysfunctional patients were orgasmic in at least 50% of their sexual relations, whereas none was orgasmic before treatment. At follow-up, however, none of the primary orgasmic dysfunctional patients was orgasmic more than 50% of the time, whereas the percentage of secondary orgasmic dysfunctional patients had risen to 60%. In terms of global ratings at follow-up, the secondary dysfunctional women were judged to be significantly more improved than those with primary dysfunction.

Munjack *et al.* report that the therapists considered the husbands' presence to be highly beneficial to treatment outcome, and thought that greater participation by the husbands in more treatment sessions might have resulted in less "resistance" on their part of some of the husbands. Many of the women with primary orgasmic dysfunction appeared to have significant non-sexual problems. As a result, Munjack *et al.* suggest that twenty therapy sessions were too few to treat the marital discord before tackling the sexual dysfunction. They recommend that "couples must either be highly selected for marital harmony (if treatment for a sexual dysfunction is to be attempted directly and immediately) or first be treated for their interpersonal problems. Since marital and sexual problems are most often inextricable the combined problem should probably be treated by the same therapist or therapy team" (p. 502).

The behavioural treatment of primary orgasmic dysfunction, particularly the use of directed masturbation programmes within the context of a Masters and Johnson approach, has produced successes according to uncontrolled clinical reports (Kohlenberg, 1974; Lobitz and LoPiccolo, 1972; Reisinger, 1978; Schneidman and McGuire, 1976; Zeiss, Rosen and Zeiss, 1977). It is reassuring to see these promising results confirmed in a controlled outcome study by Riley and Riley (1978). A directed masturbation programme was compared to a control treatment consisting of the sensate focus component of the Masters and Johnson programme plus supportive psychotherapy. Patients were married, 26 years old on average, and were known to have no organic problem. All patients were seen weekly, together with their husbands, for 6 weeks and then every fortnight for another 6 weeks. Assessment of progress was based on both partners' report of sexual functioning.

Of the twenty women in the directed masturbation treatment, 90% were orgasmic at post-treatment. The comparable figure for the comparison treatment was 53%. Eighty-five per cent of the directed masturbation group as opposed to 43% of the comparison treatment group were orgasmic during intercourse at least 75% of the time. These results were maintained at a 1-year follow-up. Of eight failures in the comparison group who were subsequently offered directed masturbation treatment, seven became orgasmic, adding to the confidence we can place in these findings.

CONCLUSIONS

The consistency of uncontrolled clinical reports and findings of controlled outcome studies suggest that behaviour therapy is at least moderately effective and hence, is the preferred treatment method for sexual dysfunction. Extensive changes in sexual functioning have been produced and maintained over relatively lengthy follow-ups. The presence of marital conflict appears to complicate treatment and may result in less favourable outcomes. A multifaceted behavioural treatment approach is necessary in these instances (Brady, 1976). Most of the subjects in the investigations summarized here were intelligent, motivated, and committed to treatment. The success of behaviour therapy with populations that differ on these dimensions remains to be established. Finally, there is no conclusive evidence relating to the desirability of using a dual-sex therapist team rather than a single therapist.

Sexual Deviance

Aversion therapy has been the most widely used behavioural approach in the treatment of sexual deviation, and it is also the most controversial. As we shall show, the trend has been towards non-aversive treatment methods. There is now a sizeable literature on aversion therapy and comprehensive reviews of the theoretical niceties and experimental bases of these techniques are available (Bancroft, 1974; Hallam and Rachman, 1976; Rachman and Teasdale, 1969).

Despite unresolved theoretical difficulties and frequently expressed misgivings about the clinical wisdom of using aversive techniques, there is evidence that aversion methods are effective with some forms of sexual deviance. Transvestites, fetishists, and exhibitionists have been treated successfully through the informed application of aversion therapy. Using a multiple baseline design, Marks and Gelder (1967) showed that transvestites and fetishists who received a painful but tolerable electric shock to the forearm contingent upon engaging in deviant behaviour (both in imagination and *in vivo*) ceased their deviant behaviour at the end of therapy. Two of these subjects showed a reversal to their former deviance at a 1-year follow-up, however. The use of the single case experimental design enabled the investigators to demonstrate that the therapeutic improvement was attributable to the application of contingent shock rather than placebo factors or demand characteristics. Moreover, both subjective and objective measures of outcome were obtained, the latter being penile tumescence. The direct measurement of erectile responses by means of the penile plethysmograph has led to significant advances in the assessment and modification of male sexual problems (Barlow, 1977; Rosen and Keefe,1978). In a later report, Marks, Gelder, and Bancroft (1970) reported a 2-year follow-up of an increased sample of twenty-four sexual deviates who were treated in the manner described above. Transvestites, fetishists, and sadomasochists were all either "improved" (i.e. deviant behaviour infrequent and significantly less than before therapy), or "greatly improved" (deviant behaviour rare or absent). They also maintained their changed attitudes towards deviant stimuli. Although most patients occasionally experienced deviant thoughts, these were usually transient and accompanied by little sexual arousal. Seven transsexuals, however, all failed to show lasting improvement as a result of therapy, and returned to their previous modes of behaviour within 2 or 3 months following treatment. The differential response to treatment of transvestites and transsexuals can probably be ascribed to the fact that the former present a circumscribed pattern of behaviour which can be modified without necessarily involving or affecting other aspects of the individual's behavioural repertoire. In the latter, however, sexual desire is secondary to the overall gender-role reversal which characterizes the transsexual.

In a controlled study of the treatment of persistent exhibitionists, Rooth and Marks (1974) compared electrical aversion to both a self-regulation treatment and a placebo control method (relaxation training). Each patient received one form of treatment for a week over three consecutive weeks of therapy in an incomplete Latin square design. Treatment effects were assessed following each week of therapy. In the aversion treatment, electric shock to the forearm was associated with patients' reports of imaginal rehearsal of exposure as well as in vivo exposure in front of a mirror. In an effort to enhance generalization of treatment effects, patients were also asked to self-administer shocks contingent upon their fantasies of exposure in the privacy of their rooms and in the presence of realistic situations that carried the potential for exposure. The self-regulation treatment consisted of identifying the internal and environmental antecedents of exposure and developing alternative coping responses to these high-risk stimuli. In order to increase patients' awareness of the stimulus pattern that triggered acts of exposure, pre-recorded accounts of typical sequences of behaviour leading to exposure were repeatedly played back while patients exposed themselves in front of a mirror and tried to express the feelings they experienced. It should be noted that this self-regulation treatment also included an element of imaginal aversion treatment (covert sensitization).

A limitation of this study is that the results are based on patients' self-report. Both aversion therapy and self-regulation training were more successful than relaxation training, which produced no improvement at all. Aversion therapy appeared to be the most effective method, and potentiated the effects of self-regulation. Rooth and Marks attribute this latter synergistic effect to the possible weakening of deviant imagery or alteration in motivation by aversion treatment. A 1-year follow-up indicated that although some of the patients had again exposed themselves and four had been reconvicted, significant improvement was maintained. Treatment was continued during follow-up, but on a less intensive basis. As in other treatment studies of this kind in which patients receive more than one form of therapy, the follow-up findings cannot be attributed to a particular treatment. In view of the chronicity (mean duration of exposure history of 16 years) and severity of the problem (all but two patients had been convicted of indecent exposure, and all reported heterosexual difficulties), Rooth and Marks concluded that their results encourage the view that some persistent exposers can be helped by means of behaviour therapy.

The majority of controlled outcome studies on aversion conditioning have entailed the attempt to eliminate homosexual behaviour in male homosexuals. The greatest changes were reported by Feldman and McCulloch (1967) using their anticipatory avoidance (AA) learning technique. This technique consists of an ascending hierarchy of sexually arousing male slides which signal the onset of a painful electric shock, which the patient can avoid by pressing a switch and removing the slide from the screen within an 8-second interstimulus-interval. Progress up the hierarchy is contingent on the patient reporting negative emotions about the current slide, coupled with consistently short latency avoidance responses. Female slides, arranged in a descending order of attractiveness, are associated with shock avoidance on two-fifths of the trials. They remain on for 10 seconds and can only be removed by the therapist. The "anxiety relief" which is presumably engendered by this latter procedure is designed to promote heterosexual desensitization in combination with homosexual aversion. The average number of treatment sessions was twenty, with twenty-four trials per session. The results of this uncontrolled clinical trial indicated that at a 1-year follow-up, twenty-five patients (58%) were treatment successes, eleven were failures, and seven had defected from therapy. Success was defined as the reported cessation of overt homosexual behaviour. Therapeutic outcome was evaluated on the basis of structured interviews with Feldman and MacCulloch themselves, before, during, and after therapy, and on the Sexual Orientation Method (SOM) attitude scale. In a later controlled outcome study Feldman and MacCulloch (1971) compared the efficacy of a slightly modified version of their AA technique to a classical conditioning (CC) procedure in which the presentation of all stimuli were independent of the patient's behaviour, and a psychotherapy condition. Thirty homosexual patients were randomly assigned to the three groups and given twenty-four sessions of their respective treatment conditions. All patients who failed to achieve a specific criterion of change on the Sexual Orientation Scale were then re-assigned to one or other of the conditioning methods for an additional twenty-four sessions, depending on the nature of their initial treatment. All patients were followed up for at least 3 months with an average duration of 46 weeks. The dependent measures and evaluation procedures were similar to those used in the earlier study. The AA and CC methods proved to be equally effective in successfully modifying homosexual behaviour; approximately 57% of the patients receiving one or both conditioning techniques was a therapeutic success. Both these methods were significantly more effective than psychotherapy at follow-up.

Methodological problems complicate the interpretation of these results (Bancroft, 1974); they include the inadequacy of the outcome measures (Kazdin and Wilson, 1978b), the failure to match subjects on critical prognostic variables in assigning them to the different treatment conditions and the possibility of unintentional bias due to the fact that MacCulloch himself conducted the psychotherapy (Bancroft, 1974). A partial replication of the Feldman and MacCulloch investigation by James, Orwin, and Turner (1977) produced a significantly lower success rate (37%) than that reported by Feldman and MacCulloch. In a second study comparing the AA technique to systematic desensitization and a hypnotic procedure designed to increase heterosexual arousal, James (1978) found that only 22% of homosexual patients were "markedly improved" (an absence of homosexual behaviour and interests) at a 2-year follow-up. As with the original Feldman and MacCulloch studies, homosexual patients with previous heterosexual experience showed significantly greater change than those with exlusively homosexual backgrounds.

In their controlled study, Birk, Huddleston, Miller, and Cohler (1971) demonstrated that a modified version of the AA technique was significantly more effective in reducing male homosexual behaviour than a placebo control condition. Homosexual interest and behaviour appeared to be eliminated in five of the eight subjects in the aversion therapy group, but none of the placebo control group. Outcome measures included blind clinical ratings by an independent assessor and estimates of the frequencies of specific sexual activities. A 2-year follow-up indicated some relapse in the successfully treated subjects although two had achieved a sustained heterosexual adjustment. At the time this evaluation of aversion therapy was conducted, all subjects were undergoing long-term psychotherapy. None the less, the random assignment of patients to the aversion conditioning and placebo control groups permits us to attribute the findings to the specific AA technique. Tanner (1974) reported that the AA technique was superior to no treatment in "modifying some aspects of homosexual behaviour". These changes were principally in the direction of increased heterosexual interest, although little can be concluded about the effects of aversion therapy *per se* in this study.

In other comparative studies, Bancroft (1970) found no significant difference between electrical aversion therapy and systematic desensitization; McConaghy (1969) reported no difference between electrical and chemical aversion therapy, although both were more effective than no treatment; and McConaghy and Barr (1973) obtained little difference between electrical aversion therapy and a backward conditioning control procedure. The latter finding is damaging to conditioning explanations of the effects of aversion therapy (see Hallam and Rachman, 1976).

In sum, although moderately successful findings have been reported, methodological problems in most studies limit the confidence that can be placed in the results. Indeed, Bancroft (1974) has argued that the results of behaviour therapy in reducing homosexual behaviour are no better than the uncontrolled findings of traditional forms of psychotherapy. There appears to be broad consensus that multifaceted treatment programmes are required to alter sexual orientation and that in those cases where such a goal is appropriate, the emphasis should be on developing enhanced heterosexual functioning through the use of positive, self-regulation procedures rather than attempting to eliminate homosexual behaviour through aversion therapy (Adams and Sturgis, 1977; Barlow, 1973; Wilson and Davison, 1974). A fundamental principle of behavioural therapy is that it is the patient who has the primary say in setting the goals of therapy (Bandura, 1969; Stolz, 1977) and care must be taken to ensure that treatment objectives are not imposed by therapists or treatment agencies (Wilson and Evans, 1977). Consistent with this view is the fact that behaviour therapists have reported treatment programmes in which the goal is to help the homosexual achieve personal goals and adjustment as homosexuals (e.g. Kohlenberg, 1974; Russell and Winkler, 1977). There is not, and nor should there be, any assumptions made about the normality or desirability of striving for exclusively heterosexual goals.

Covert sensitization, or imaginal aversive conditioning, is a technique in which deviant sexual stimuli are repeatedly paired with aversive consequences in imagery (Cautela, 1967). An exhibitionist, for example, might be asked to imagine himself being apprehended by the police as a result of engaging in typically deviant sexual activities. Among the theoretical advantages of this technique are its emphasis on self-regulation of behaviour, the practical benefits of it being implemented in real-life situations without any cumbersome apparatus, and the fact that it spares therapist and patient the unpleasant experience of using electric shock. Regrettably, there are doubts about its therapeutic power.

Using single case experimental designs, Barlow, Leitenberg, and Agras (1969) and Barlow, Agras, Leitenberg, Callahan, and Moore (1972) showed that covert sensitization decreased unwanted sexual arousal in pedophiles and homosexuals. In the latter study, the authors assessed the separate and joint influence of therapeutic instructions and the actual procedure of pairing the aversive consequence with the unwanted behaviour. The results, as measured by subjects' penile tumescence responses to slides of the unwanted sexual activities, indicated that pairing the target behaviour with the aversive consequence was the critical factor in significantly reducing unwanted sexual arousal. These data argue against an explanation of treatment success with covert sensitization in terms of placebo factors or expectations of positive therapeutic, but provide too meagre a basis for firm conclusions. Additional evidence for the efficacy of covert sensitization comes from Brownell, Hayes, and Barlow's (1977) treatment of five patients each of whom displayed more than one form of sexual deviation. The use of a multiple baseline design, in which each deviant response pattern was treated sequentially while the effects of treatment on all deviant responses were assessed concurrently, showed that sexual deviance was eliminated only when paired with aversive consequences. Stable reductions in deviant sexual arousal were demonstrated in all five patients over a 6-month follow-up. Moreover, all five experienced satisfactory heterosexual interactions following treatment, as attested to by their wives' corroborative reports. Aside from demonstrating the efficacy of covert sensitization, the results of this small but well-controlled investigation indicate the specificity and functional independence among different patterns of sexual arousal that are often found.

An important finding of the Brownell *et al.* (1977) study was that the elimination of deviant arousal by means of covert sensitization did not result in an increase in arousal to heterosexual activities. As a consequence of this type of finding, which has often been reported in the clinical literature, increasing attempts have been made to develop desired heterosexual arousal and behaviour in the treatment of sexual deviants. There is the recognition that simply reducing or eliminating deviant arousal does not guarantee the development of a satisfactory alternative form of sexual expression. The various behavioural procedures that have been used to develop or to enhance heterosexual arousal and behaviour are discussed by Barlow (1973) and Brownell and Barlow (1979). Suffice it to point out here that the most popular and widely studied technique used so far is known by the clumsy term "orgasmic reconditioning". In this technique the patient is instructed to masturbate to his deviant fantasies in his customary fashion. However, just prior to the point of ejaculatory inevitability, he is instructed to switch to an erotic fantasy of desired heterosexual activity. This switch is then made progressively earlier in the sequence until the patients can initiate masturbation and achieve orgasm using heterosexual fantasies exclusively (Davison, 1968; Marquis, 1970).

Despite widespread clinical application and several uncontrolled reports of its efficacy, few controlled studies of this technique have been reported. In a review of the evidence for this technique, Conrad and Wincze (1976) pointed out that the only supportive data were flawed by one or more of several methodological problems, including confounded treatment design, lack of objective measurement, and exclusive reliance on self-reports of behavioural change. They described the treatment of four male homosexuals using orgasmic reconditioning with both psychophysiological and behavioural measures of outcome (the latter consisting of self-monitoring of daily sexual thoughts and behaviour). Although all four clients reported that their sexual adjustment had improved, their physiological and behavioural measures were unchanged. These findings are particularly troubling given that previous use has been dependent solely upon subjective reports of outcome. Painting a brighter picture, Brownell *et al.* (1977), in the investigation described above, found that orgasmic reconditioning was effective in increasing heterosexual arousal and behaviour. The use of the multiple baseline design and the inclusion of objective outcome measures of penile tumescence and specific sexual activities provide some support for the specific efficacy of this technique with selected forms of sexual deviance.

Marital Conflict

Until recently, the behavioural literature on the assessment and treatment of marital conflict was limited to uncontrolled clinical reports and inadequate outcome studies, an unhappy condition that could be said to have afflicted traditional non-behavioural approaches to marital therapy as well. The last few years, however, have witnessed an upsurge of interest in behavioural marital therapy and some ambitious research programmes have been initiated. Before reviewing the controlled outcome studies in this area a word or two about the nature of behavioural approaches to marital therapy is in order.

The behavioural approach to marital therapy is based upon the assumption that reciprocity of positive exchanges between partners forms the basis of a successful marriage. This view is an extension of Thibaut and Kelly's (1959) social exchange theory which holds that people are mutually striving to maximize rewards while minimizing costs. In time, the interaction of a particular couple comes to be governed by a set of norms reflecting a balance between rewards and costs. Briefly, marital conflict results from the presence of coercion (aversive control) rather than reciprocity (mutually agreeable positive control), with the eventual outcome of a low rate of positive reinforcers exchanged by the spouses so that each is less attracted to the other.

Contemporary behavioural treatment techniques for marital conflict have mixed heritage, deriving from operant and classical conditioning models, cognitive learning theory, and even communication analyses of interpersonal interactions (O'Leary and Turkewitz, 1978).

The central focus is on helping spouses learn more productive and positive means of achieving the desired behaviour changes in one another. Three categories of procedures have most commonly been used, separately or in combination, to reach this goal: (1) contingency contracting or marital agreements, (2) problem solving, and (3) communication skill training. The details of these treatment procedures are described by Jacobson (1978a), O'Leary and Turkewitz (1978), and Weiss (1978) among others.

A convincing demonstration of the efficacy of behavioural marital therapy is provided by Jacobson's research. In the first of two studies, Jacobson (1977) randomly assigned ten couples who reported dissatisfaction with their marriages to either a behavioural treatment or a minimal treatment waiting-list control group. The emphasis in the behavioural treatment group was on teaching the couples improved problem-solving strategies and the use of contingency contracts to increase reciprocity of positive exchange in the marital relationship. Multiple measures of outcome, including observational and self-report measures, were obtained. The observational measure was the Marital Interaction Coding System (MICS) developed by Weiss and his colleagues at the Oregon Research Institute, an assessment device that is widely used in behavioural studies of marital interactions. In this coding system interactions between partners are assessed on two dimensions: a "rewardingness" dimension, or the degree to which the spouses emit rewarding rather than punishing actions toward each other; and a problem-solving dimension in which the efficiency of marital communication in solving mutual problems is evaluated. Both verbal and non-verbal responses are videotaped and coded into a number of operationally defined categories. The MICS has been shown to differentiate distressed from non-distressed couples (Vincent, Weiss, and Birchler, 1975) and to be sufficiently sensitive to detect pre-post therapeutic changes (Weiss, 1978).

The behavioural treatment produced significantly greater improvement than the control group, on all measures. A noteworthy feature of Jacobson's study was the clever use of single-case experimental designs within a between-groups design. A multiple baseline design was used in which specific problems were treated sequentially. Only when they were explicitly treated were the problems resolved. These detailed experimental analyses strengthen the attribution of therapeutic improvement to the particular behavioural methods that were employed. Self-report measures at a 1-year follow-up indicated that these improvements had been maintained.

Subjects in this study were obtained from respondents to advertisements of the programme. Anticipating criticism that such subjects are not representative of "real patients" who voluntarily seek therapy in the clinical setting, Jacobson compared their pre-treatment scores on the Locke–Wallace (1959) Marital Adjustment Scale (MAS), a widely used assessment instrument in marital therapy, to couples treated in a clinical setting. There were no significant differences. Moreover, Jacobson reports that there "was every reason to believe that the sample resembled a clinical population in degree of disturbance. All participating couples were seriously contemplating separation, some had separated previously, and at least half of the couples had been in marital therapy previously in a clinical setting."

Limitations of Jacobson's first study included the small number of couples in each treatment, the absence of a credible placebo condition, and the administration of all treatment procedures by Jacobson himself. In the second study (Jacobson, 1978b), thirty-two couples who were experiencing marital problems were assigned to one of two behavioural treatments, a placebo control treatment, or a waiting-list control group. Three different therapists conducted the treatments. The two behavioural treatments differed with respect to the nature of the contingency contracts that were drawn up. The outcome measures were the same as those in the previous study. Both behavioural treatments produced significantly greater improvement than either the placebo treatment or the waiting-list control group. This superiority of behaviour therapy is all the more persuasive given that Jacobson demonstrated that the placebo treatment was perceived by subjects as highly credible and elicited comparable expectations of improvement, thereby satisfying the extremely rigorous methodological criteria set forth by Kazdin and Wilcoxon (1976).

O'Leary and Turkewitz (1978) compared a communication training procedure (including both behavioural and non-behavioural components), a condition that combined communication training with behavioural marital agreements (including written contracts), and a waiting-list control group. Couples were treated individually by one of five therapists. Both treatment groups improved significantly more than the control groups on self-report measures, but there was no significant difference between the two treatments. A behavioural problem-solving measure did not, however, demonstrate differences between the three groups (all couples changed in a positive direction on several of the categories). O'Leary and Turkewitz found an interesting interaction between age and treatment condition – younger couples found the addition of behavioural marital agreements to be helpful, while older couples improved more with the straight communications approach. They speculate that communications therapy is best for some problems and reinforcement-oriented programmes are more effective with others, and stress the need for research documenting the effects of various marital therapy procedures with various client populations and types of problems.

A study by Liberman, Levine, Wheeler, Sanders, and Wallace (1976) provides further support for the efficacy of a behavioural approach. They compared a behavioural *group* treatment (which included training in behavioural exchange, communication, and contingency contracting) to an "interaction-insight" group treatment (which stressed ventilation of feelings, problem-solving through discussion, and mutual support and feedback). Both treatments were carried out by the same three therapists. Both groups improved significantly on all of the self-report measures, and there were no differences between groups. Couples in the behavioural group improved significantly more on behavioural measures (MICS). These data showed that the members of the behavioural group displayed significantly more positive and mutually supportive verbal and non-verbal behaviour in their interactions as a function of treatment. These improvements were maintained at 6-month follow-up.

With multiple measures one would not be surprised to learn that specific methods may have different effects on different measures. Thus, Gurman and Kniskern (1977), in their analysis of the Liberman *et al.* study, assert that "deterioration effects" were noted for the behavioural treatment programme on two dependent measures (number of "pleases" and "marital activities"), and on one ("marital activities") for the interactional treatment. With respect to the marital activities, both treatment groups reported decreases in overall frequency from the month prior to treatment to the last month of treatment. However, this figure has to be interpreted in the context of both groups expressing less desire for change in the frequency of marital activities at the end of treatment. It appears arbitrary to categorize the decrease in frequency as a deterioration effect, and other interpretations are at least as plausible.

Despite its many methodological strengths, some caution in interpreting the findings of this study is warranted because of the relatively small number of couples treated and the fact that the same therapists (who may have been unintentionally biased in favour of behaviour therapy) conducted both treatments. If this were the case, however, it is awkward to account for the fact that the behavioural treatment was not superior to the comparison treatment on self-report as well as objective measures of outcome. Self-report measures are more susceptible to demand characteristics than objective performance. This pattern of results could be viewed as discriminant validity for the efficacy of specific behavioural techniques.

Reviews of the empirical status of behavioural marital therapy have included several analogue studies. An analogue study, in this connection, is one in which the couples are not necessarily distressed and in which the intervention is geared towards an isolated target behaviour rather than attempting to enhance the overall level of satisfaction in the relationship (Jacobson and Martin, 1976). Gurman and Kniskern (1978) have argued that of the seven studies that included appropriate control groups, only two yielded results demonstrating the superiority of behavioural treatment over no treatment. In a spirited reply, Jacobson and Weiss (1978) took Gurman and Kniskern to task for what they regard as errors of interpretation. According to Jacobson and Weiss, there are four controlled analogue studies that are directly relevant to the evaluation of behavioural marital therapy and three of these showed results that favoured behaviour therapy. A rejoinder by Gurman, Knudson, and Kniskern (1978) essentially restated their original view. Unfortunately, the value of this debate is limited by the fact that the majority of studies under discussion are unpublished.

Evaluating all the currently available evidence, Jacobson and Weiss (1978) conclude that "although behaviour therapy is not demonstrably more effective with couples than other approaches, behaviour therapy is the only approach that is demonstrably effective" (p. 159). A different perspective is offered by Gurman and Kniskern (1978) and Gurman *et al.* (1978) as part of their full review of the marital therapy literature. While acknowledging that there is suggestive evidence that behavioural marital therapy is effective, they also conclude that "the evidence of the efficacy of behavioural marriage therapy is no more persuasive than is the research on non-behavioural treatment" (p. 18). They are distinctly less enthusiastic about behavioural marital therapy studies than Jacobson and Weiss, faulting them on the grounds of inadequate follow-ups and the inclusion of marital couples who were only mildly distressed. (A detailed analysis of these issues is presented in Franks and Wilson, 1977–1979.)

At this point it is safe to conclude that behaviour therapy has shown clear promise as an effective and efficient method for dealing with marital problems, but comprehensive investigations of severely distressed couples, with lengthier follow-ups, are necessary before definitive conclusions can be reached.

Addictive Disorders

ALCOHOLISM

As in the case of sexual deviance, aversion therapy was the most widely used treatment procedure for alcoholism in the early days of behaviour therapy (Rachman and Teasdale, 1969). Three types of aversive therapy have been employed: electrical, chemical, and symbolic aversion methods. The outcome literature on these techniques is reviewed by Nathan and Briddell (1977) and Wilson (1978a). Briefly, the current evidence indicates that electrical aversion therapy is no more effective than placebo control conditions in decreasing alcohol consumption either in the laboratory or clinical setting (e.g. Hedberg and Campbell, 1974; Miller, Hersen, Eisler, and Hemphill, 1973; Wilson, Leaf, and Nathan, 1975) and there is scant empirical justification for its continued use as a treatment alternative (Wilson, 1978a).

In contrast to electrical aversion conditioning, uncontrolled clinical studies with nausea-inducing aversion conditioning have yielded promising results. Lemere and Voegtlin's (1950) findings are the most noteworthy in this respect, and were summarized by Bandura (1969) and Rachman and Teasdale (1969). More recently, Wiens, Montague, Manaugh, and English (1976) have reported detailed statistical analyses of patients treated at the Raleigh Hills Hospital in Portland, Oregon, a private facility devoted exclusively to the treatment of voluntarily admitted alcoholics with pharmacological aversion conditioning (emetine) modelled after Lemere and Voegtlin's original procedures. A 12-month follow-up of patients treated in one randomly chosen year (1970) showed an impressive abstinence rate of 63% (the correspondence with Lemere and Voegtlin's 60% success rate is striking). This figure represents data from 92% of the 261 patients treated that year; patients who could not be contacted were counted as failures. Approximately 60% of the patients who achieved abstinence availed themselves of an average of six booster sessions over the course of the follow-up year. The mean age of patients was 48.5 years; mean educational level was 13.8 years (a relatively well-educated sample). Only 7.7% reported being unemployed. In terms of hospital payment, 37.3% depended on personal financial resources, the remainder some form of insurance or employer reimbursement.

As with the Lemere and Voegtlin data (see Rachman and Teasdale, 1969), it is impossible to assess unequivocally the role of the emetine therapy, since patients received informal therapy sessions from counsellors, recovered alcoholics who themselves had been successfully treated by way of pharmacological conditioning. In addition, the value of the outcome data could be improved by independent assessments of more detailed measures of alcohol consumption during follow-up. Controlled studies designed to determine the efficacy of chemical aversion therapy are overdue.

Relatively few studies have evaluated the efficacy of symbolic aversion therapy (covert sensitization) in the treatment of alcoholism. The available data are not encouraging (e.g.

Hedberg and Campbell, 1974; Wilson and Tracey, 1976) and it is unlikely that this technique alone will be effective in the treatment of alcohol abuse.

As with other clinical disorders, the application of limited techniques (such as aversion therapy) to isolated aspects of the alcoholic's behaviour has given way to more sophisticated analyses of the nature of alcohol abuse and an emphasis on multi-component social learning treatment programmes. Among the several behaviour-therapy techniques that are now commonly used to treat alcoholics are social skills training; self-control procedures including self-monitoring, goal-setting and self-evaluation, self-reinforcement, and self-instruction; stress reduction techniques; modelling of non-abusive drinking; contingency management focused on reinforcing alternative behaviour; and social reinforcement of sobriety through group support (Marlatt, 1978; Miller and Mastria, 1978; Nathan and Briddell, 1977; Sobell, 1978). Each tactic is plausible, and in most instances the use of these varied behavioural procedures is based on laboratory and controlled clinical studies demonstrating that they are capable of decreasing excessive alcohol consumption. In the process, a number of traditional assumptions about the nature of alcoholism as a disease, and the explanatory value of such key concepts as craving and loss of control, have been challenged and new theoretical formulations advanced (Hodgson, Rankin, and Stockwell, 1978; Marlatt, 1978; Nathan, Marlatt, and Loberg, 1978; Pomerleau, Pertschuk, and Stinnett, 1976; Wilson, 1978b). For present purposes, it suffices to illustrate the successful use of these behavioural-treatment approaches with reference to some selected research programmes.

Few studies have been more widely quoted or have generated as much controversy as the Sobell and Sobell (1978) investigation of behaviour therapy in which one of the treatment goals was controlled drinking as opposed to the traditional outcome objective of total abstinence. Seventy male, chronic alcoholics who were in-patients at a state hospital, were assigned to four different experimental conditions: a controlled drinking group (CD–E), with N = 20, a controlled drinking control group, N = 20 (CD–C); a non-drinking experimental group (ND–E), with N = 15, and a non-drinking control group (ND–C) with N = 15. The two control groups received the conventional hospital treatment for alcoholics, such as large therapy groups, A.A. meetings, drug therapy. The experimental groups received seventeen sessions of a multi-faceted behavioural treatment programme in addition to the routine hospital programme.

The behaviour therapy sessions were devoted to making a detailed behavioural analysis of each alcoholic's drinking problem and to what the Sobells call "stimulus control" sessions. These consisted of identifying "subject-specific" setting events for each individual's drinking, training the subject to generate a series of alternative responses to those situations, evaluating each of the delineated alternatives for potential short- and long-term consequences, and then exercising the response which could be expected to incur the least self-destructive long-term consequences. In order to shape controlled drinking behaviour, subjects were permitted to drink during sessions 4 to 16 under specific contingencies. Taking a straight drink, gulping it, or consuming more than three total drinks within the session resulted in a 1-second electric shock on a variable ratio schedule. In addition, subjects were videotaped while drunk (sessions 1 and 2) and confronted with videotaped playback of their drunken behaviour in sessions 4 and 5 in order to provide feedback on their behavioural deficiencies.

A commendable feature of this study was that detailed comprehensive follow-up evaluations were obtained at each 6-month interval during the first 2 years and then 3 years after the end of therapy. Estimates of daily alcohol consumption were gathered, with every attempt made to corroborate subjects' reports by securing reports from significant others in the subjects' environment who could best substantiate their reports. For purposes of evaluating the results, abstinent and controlled drinking days (days during which 6 ounces or less of 86-proof liquor or its equivalent in alcohol content were consumed) or days during which subjects were incarcerated were summarized as "not functioning well". Both experimental groups were found to be significantly superior to their respective control groups in terms of number of days functioning well at both the 6-month and 1-year follow-up evaluations. At the 2-year mark the CD–E group was significantly different from the CD–C group. For the entire second year of follow-up, the CD–E subjects functioned well for an average of 89.61% of all days as compared to a mean of 45.10% of all days for the CD–C subjects. The differences between the ND–E and ND–C subjects approaches but did not reach significance at either the 18-month or 2-year follow-ups. Over the entire second year of follow-up ND–E subjects functioned well for a mean of 64.60% of all days, while ND–C subjects functioned well for a mean of 45.13% of all days. Differences between experimental and control group subjects were found not only on drinking behaviour but for adjunctive measures of functioning as well. An evaluation of adjustment to interpersonal relationships and problem situations revealed the same pattern of results as for drinking. Subjects in the CD–E group were classified as significantly more improved that CD–C group members at each follow-up over the 2-year period. Subjects in the ND–E groups were rated as significantly more improved than ND–C subjects during the first year, but not during the second year of follow-up.

Unlike the 1- and 2-year follow-ups which were conducted by the original investigators, the 3-year evaluation was an independently conducted, double-blind follow-up (Caddy, Addington, and Perkins, 1978). The results are strikingly consistent with those of the previous 2 years and are summarized by Caddy et al. as follows:

"Comparison of the controlled drinking experimental group with its control group showed the significantly better functioning of subjects in the experimental condition on a number of drinking and other life functioning measures. Comparison of the non-drinking groups indicated only one possible difference on the drinking related measures involving a trend for subjects in the experimental condition to abstain more than those in the non-drinker control group. On other life functioning measures, however, subjects in the non-drinking experimental condition showed consistent improvement over their respective control subjects. Both of the controlled drinking groups reported more controlled drinking days than the non-drinking groups throughout the third year follow-up period" (p. 345).

The Sobell and Sobell study is not without its limitations. It is unclear which of the treatment components were effective and it is puzzling why treatment produced such favourable long-term results but apparently had little impact on their subjects' alcohol consumption during probe sessions over the course of therapy (Nathan and Briddell, 1977). Subjects were selectively assigned to the controlled drinking groups because they had requested it, had significant social support in their natural environment, or had successfully practised controlled drinking in the past. Comparisons between controlled drinking and abstinent conditions were confounded. The many strengths of the Sobells' study include the detailed, multiple measures of outcome (both alcohol consumption in particular and broader indices of personal functioning); their astonishing determination in successfully contacting well over 90% of their subjects for detailed follow-up evaluations; and that relatively rare phenomenon in clinical outcome research, a comprehensive long-term follow-up over 3 years. Finally, the results of this study provide strong evidence that controlled drinking is possible, at least in some alcoholics. However unwelcome to some people, this important fact is now established (Armor, Polich, and Stambul, 1976, 1977; Miller and Caddy, 1977; Orford, Oppenheimer, and Edwards, 1976; Pomerleau *et al.*, 1976; Sobell, 1978).

Several laboratory studies have convincingly demonstrated that drinking, even in chronic alcoholics, is in large part under the control of response-contingent consequences (Cohen, Liebson, Faillace, and Allen, 1971; Wilson *et al.*, 1975). In a thorough and inventive extension of these operant conditioning principles to the treatment of alcoholics in the community, Hunt and Azrin (1973) designed a community-reinforcement programme in which vocational, recreational, social, and familial reinforcers for the alcoholic were developed and made contingent on continuing sobriety. Patients were given training in social skills and assisted in obtaining a satisfactory job, at which time they were discharged from the hospital. Inadequate and stressful marital and family relationships were modified by systematically increasing the mutual exchange of reinforcements between the patient and his wife and family. Special "foster" families were arranged for unmarried parents without a parental family. Since the patients' circle of friends had, as is typical of alcoholics, become restricted to other problem drinkers, a former tavern was converted into a self-supporting social club aimed at promoting more desirable forms of companionship and an expanded range of recreational opportunities which are incompatible with drinking.

Sixteen arbitrarily selected, hospitalized alcoholics were individually matched on the basis of employment history, family stability, and previous drinking history and then randomly assigned to either the community-reinforcement or the existing hospital-treatment programme. The latter consisted of twenty-five 1-hour didactic counselling sessions which described the workings of Alcoholics Anonymous, disseminated information relevant to drinking, and discussed typical problems of alcoholics.

A community maintenance programme was instituted following a patient's discharge from the hospital, during which a counsellor visited patients on a progressively less frequent basis to see that the procedures were continued, and to deal with any problems which arose. These visits also served as a means of continuously monitoring the progress of the ex-patients in terms of number of days on which drinking occurred, days unemployed, and time spent away from home. These observations were checked against independent evaluations conducted by a rater who was unaware that the patients had been treated differently, and shown to be highly reliable.

The results of this study showed the sustained superiority of the community-reinforcement programme over the 6 months follow-up in terms of percentage time spent drinking, unemployment, and reinstitutionalization.

These findings were replicated in a second study by Azrin (1976) that included a 2-year follow-up. The community-reinforcement treatment in this latter study was expanded to include, among other improvements, an innovative method for administering Antabuse, and once again proved to be significantly more effective than the control treatment. Azrin summarized the outcome: "The Community-Reinforcement clients drank only one-twenty-seventh as often as the control clients (2% of the time versus 55% of the time). The Community-Reinforcement clients were out of work less than half as much as the control treatment clients (20% of the time versus 56% of the time). The Community-Reinforcement clients were institutionalized less than one-hundredth as much as the control treatment clients (0.1% of the time versus 45% of the time)." Although questions can be raised about the adequacy of the control groups in both of these studies, methodological strengths such as the use of multiple measures of outcome, independent evaluation of success, and long-term follow-up, increases one's confidence in these results.

Several other studies demonstrate the greater efficacy of behavioural methods compared to alternative approaches or to control groups. Chaney, O'Leary, and Marlatt (1978) showed that social skills training for hospitalized alcoholics not only improved their level of interpersonal functioning but also resulted in significantly reduced drinking over a 1-year follow up. Pomerleau, Pertschuk, and Brady (1976) found that behaviour therapy was more effective than traditional group therapy in decreasing drinking and treatment drop-outs at a 6-month follow-up, and Vogler, Weissbach, and Compton (1977) have reported 18-month follow-up data indicating the efficacy of a broad behavioural treatment programme with both in-patient and out-patient alcoholics and less disturbed problem drinkers. Persuasive evidence of the success of behavioural self-control methods in the treatment of problem drinkers has been reported by Miller (in press) in a series of well-controlled studies. Parenthetically, the results of these studies, Vogler *et al.*'s research, and findings from the Addiction Research Unit at the Institute of Psychiatry (Hodgson *et al.*, 1978), suggest that controlled drinking may be more appropriate for the less chronic, less physically addicted alcohol abuser with a more stable social-vocational background.

As a whole, recent studies have consistently indicated the efficacy of behavioural methods in producing substantial changes in abusive drinking. A notable exception to this pattern is the study by Ewing and Rouse (1976) which has been criticized on a number of conceptual and methodological grounds (Franks and Wilson, 1977; Sobell, 1979).

CIGARETTE SMOKING

Summarizing behavioural treatment programmes aimed at eliminating or decreasing cigarette smoking, O'Leary and Wilson (1975) concluded that the results had been "uniformly unimpressive" (p. 342). Although a wide variety of techniques had been utilized in often well-designed studies, few treatment-specific effects had been demonstrated. Moreover, placebo treatments appeared to be as effective as explicit behavioural methods (Bernstein, 1969). For example, in an evaluation of eight different behavioural studies, McFall and Hammen (1971) showed that if drop-outs during the course of therapy were included, total abstinence rates "ranged between 7% and 40% with a mean of 26% at the end of treatment, and ranged between 9% and 17% with a mean of 13% at follow-up" (p. 80). McFall and Hammen suggested that "nonspecific" factors such as motivated subjects, structure, and self-monitoring that were common to all studies probably accounted for the similarity in outcome. Indeed, they demonstrated that a "nontreatment" programme based on these three "non-specific" elements produced results that paralleled those obtained in more formal treatment studies.

In two major reviews of the relevant literature, Bernstein and McAlister (1976) and Lichtenstein and Danaher (1976) showed that some progress has, at last, been made. One approach that has been shown to be an improvement on previous treatments is rapid smoking, a technique developed by Lichtenstein and his colleagues at the University of Oregon. In this technique the client is instructed to take a puff and inhale as (s)he normally would, every 6 seconds. Typically, each trial is terminated when the client is unable to tolerate another inhalation, and treatment sessions continue until clients state that they cannot tolerate another cigarette ("the point at which another drag or another cigarette would possibly cause physical illness, throwing up, dizziness, or choking" (Schmahl, Lichtenstein, and Harris, 1972). Strict instructions are given to abstain from smoking between sessions.

A series of studies by Lichtenstein and his associates has chalked up positive findings on the efficacy of rapid smoking. In the first study (Schmahl *et al.*, 1972), twenty-eight treated subjects were all abstinent after an average of eight treatment sessions. Of twenty-five subjects who were followed-up 6 months after treatment, sixteen were still abstinent. A second study by Lichtenstein, Harris, Birchler, Wahl, and Schmahl (1973) essentially replicated these results and demonstrated that rapid smoking was significantly more effective than an attention-placebo control treatment. Whereas 60% of subjects treated by rapid smoking were abstinent at a 6-month follow-up, only 30% had stopped smoking in the control group. Two additional studies by this group produced further evidence indicating that approximately 60% of subjects were abstinent at a 3-month follow-up.

Since most relapses occur during the first 3 months after an initially successful treatment programme (Hunt and Bespalec, 1974), the 6-months follow-ups reported by Lichtenstein provide useful support for this technique. These results are superior to those summarized by McFall and Hammen (1971), and to Hunt and Bespalec's (1974) summary of the data from eighty-nine outcome studies of a widely differing nature. Hunt and Bespalec concluded that less than one-third of all treated subjects who were abstinent at follow-up were able to avoid relapse over time. Recently, Lichtenstein and Rodrigues (1977) published long-term (2 to 6 years) follow-up data on the four studies mentioned above. Compared to an average abstinence rate of 54% at the 3 to 6 months follow-ups, 34% of treated subjects were still abstinent. Although only modestly successful, these findings, indicating odds of one in three of lasting abstinence, encourage the view that successful treatment methods can be developed for effectively modifying behaviour that has proved to be stubbornly resistant to treatment.

As we have repeatedly emphasized, evaluation of treatment outcome must be based on broader criteria than simple efficacy alone. In the case of rapid smoking, for example, questions have been raised about its safety. Its aversive effects may be due to a mild form of nicotine poisoning that is potentially hazardous (e.g. Horan, Linberg, and Hackett, 1977). Lichtenstein and Glasgow (1977) reviewed the evidence on the side-effects of rapid smoking and indicated what safeguards should be taken. They concluded that rapid smoking entails cardiovascular stress but that its effects are clinically insignificant, and not much greater than those of normal self-paced smoking. The procedure has been used with over 35,000 persons with few reported negative effects of consequence. Aside from the cardiac abnormalities in two subjects reported by Horan *et al.*, a few unpublished incidents are discussed by Lichtenstein and Glasgow. Based on their own incident-free use of the technique, they advocate a screening procedure in which subjects with a history of heart disease, high blood pressure, diabetes, bronchitis, or emphysema are automatically excluded from treatment. People who pass this preliminary screening are fully informed about the nature of the technique and its possible risks and benefits, and required to obtain their physician's approval.

The second treatment approach which Bernstein and McAlister (1976) found to be superior was a multifaceted intervention including self-control strategies and the development of non-smoking, alternative activities. Examples of this sort of treatment approach are studies by Flaxman (1976) and Lando (1977). In the Flaxman study, treatment procedures included developing a new hobby, playing with worry beads as a distractor, relaxation training, thought stopping, programming competing responses, self-reinforcement, the repetition of reasons for ceasing to smoke, and public statements of commitment to stop. Of subjects receiving this complicated package, those who used a target-date (2 weeks after starting treatment) procedure for stopping did significantly better than those who stopped immediately or those who tried to taper off. At a 6-month follow-up 50% of subjects who used the target-date quitting procedure were abstinent. A group that practised rapid-smoking in addition to all the above-mentioned methods showed an abstinence rate of 62%. Although these outcome figures are encouraging, the sort of omnibus treatment programme used by Flaxman makes it virtually impossible to uncover the effective agents of change.

Lando (1977) compared a multifaceted treatment programme consisting of aversive therapy (satiation), self-control training, contracting, and group support, with a minimal aversive conditioning treatment. The nature of the aversive treatment is unclear from the published report. However, booster sessions were provided for in the multifaceted treatment condition and involved a variation of rapid smoking. Both treatment groups received aversion therapy for 1 week. Thereafter the multifaceted treatment group received seven additional sessions over a 2-month period. At a 6-month follow-up, a remarkable 76% of subjects treated with the multifaceted programme were abstinent. Thirty-five per cent of subjects treated with aversive conditioning alone were abstinent. A second study by Lando (1978), in which he attempted to assess the effective elements of the overall programme, yielded significantly less successful results. Other less encouraging findings have been reported by Elliot and Denney (1978) and Glasgow (1978). In the former study, neither a multifaceted behavioural treatment programme consisting of rapid smoking, covert sensitization, relaxation training, self-reinforcement, cognitive restructuring, and behaviour rehearsal, nor a rapid smoking treatment alone was significantly superior to a non-specific control condition at a 6-month follow-up. In the latter study, too, rapid smoking alone or in combination with other behavioural procedures was not significantly more effective than a control treatment.

To sum up, there is a long way to go in developing a broadly effective, lasting method for helping people to stop smoking. The most pressing requirement in behavioural programmes is for effective maintenance strategies — an all too familiar problem in the treatment of addictive disorders.

OBESITY

In 1958 Stunkard, one of the foremost authorities in the subject, summarized the results of treatment of obesity in the following manner: "Most obese persons will not stay in treatment for obesity. Of those who stay in treatment most will not lose weight and of those who do lose weight most will regain it" (p. 79). Consistently discouraging findings from the medical and psychotherapeutic treatment of obesity did nothing to challenge this severely pessimistic appraisal of Stunkard's until Stuart's (1967) landmark publication of the results of his uncontrolled study of the behavioural treatment of eight obese clients. He reported astonishing successes — substantial weight losses ranging from 20 to 40 pounds or more that were sustained over a 1-year period. Stuart's paper triggered a burst of research on the behavioural treatment of obesity with the result that Stunkard and Mahoney (1976) were later to conclude that, "in an unprecedently short time . . . behavioural techniques have been shown to be superior to all other treatment modalities for managing mild to moderate obesity" (p. 54). Coming from Stunkard, whose earlier dismal conclusion was widely quoted, this re-evaluation is encouraging. However, Stunkard and Mahoney were careful to note that their relatively optimistic appraisal of behaviour therapy had to be qualified by the absence of long-term evaluations of therapeutic efficacy.

Behavioural research on obesity has continued to burgeon and several comprehensive reviews of the treatment outcome literature are available (e.g. Foreyt, 1977; Franks and Wilson, 1976–

1979; Jeffery, Wing, and Stunkard, 1978; Stunkard and Mahoney, 1976; Stunkard and Penick, 1979). Almost without exception, the behavioural treatment programmes that have been evaluated are variations of the basic programme used by Stuart (1967), and described more fully by Stuart and Davis (1972). As such, the principal techniques used are behavioural self-control methods that include some form of self-monitoring, stimulus control, self-reinforcement, contingency contracting, and procedures designed to control eating patterns directly. Treatment is almost always conducted on a group basis, the average duration of treatment ranging from approximately 4 to 12 weeks. The philosophy of the behavioural approach is to alter eating habits and patterns of physical activity rather than to place the person on a particular diet. A balanced, nutritious diet is generally recommended, but the person is allowed considerable flexibility in deciding which foods will be eaten. Simply stated, the aim is to teach people to lower the total number of calories they consume and to increase their energy expenditure through self-regulated behavioural strategies. Whatever the basic cause of obesity, weight is a function of this energy balance.

The current empirical status of outcome research on the behavioural treatment of obesity can be summarized in the following five points:

"(1) Behavioural treatment has proved more effective in producing weight loss than alternative treatment methods in the short-term; (2) studies comparing the long-term success of behavioural treatment of obesity have been conspicuous by their relative absence and where data on long-term efficacy exist they are often discouraging; (3) behavioural treatment programs have almost always produced weight losses that fall short of clinical significance even if they are statistically significant within individual studies; (4) behavioural treatment programs have been consistently characterized by massive inter-individual variability in outcome; and (5) reliable predictors of treatment outcome have yet to be identified" (Wilson, 1979).

After the initial, often dramatic successes of some behavioural programmes, therapeutic advances seem to have levelled off. Long-term maintenance of treatment effects has been no less a problem for behaviour therapy than for previous approaches. The data from a series of studies by the Halls and their associates illustrated what has become a relatively common pattern of outcome. In the first study, Hall, Hall, Hanson, and Borden (1974) found that a multifaceted and a more circumscribed, "simple" behavioural self-management treatment produced significantly greater weight loss than an attention-placebo treatment at post-treatment and at a 3-month follow-up. At a 6-month follow-up, however, these differences were no longer significant and both behavioural groups had regained significant amounts of weight. In the next study (Hanson, Borden, Hall, and Hall, 1976), three behavioural treatments differing in terms of the degree of direct contact with the therapist were collectively superior to a placebo and a no-treatment control group at post-treatment and at a 10-week follow-up. A 1-year follow-up showed that this difference had disappeared. As in the Hall et al. (1974) study, there was a marked subject attrition rate during treatment (21.8%), and an additional 11% of subjects dropped out during follow-up. Since programme drop-outs are usually failures, these results have particularly negative implications. A third study (Hall, Hall, DeBoer, and O'Kulitch, 1977) similarly showed that while behavioural treatments were significantly superior to a form of psychotherapy at the end of 10 weeks of therapy, this difference was no longer significant at 3 and 6 months follow-ups.

A 1-year follow-up of the Penick, Filion, Fox, and Stunkard (1971) study that compared a group behavioural programme with traditional group therapy showed that both treatments produced continued weight loss at 6- and 12-month follow-up evaluations (cf. Stunkard, 1972). While the behavioural treatment appeared to be more effective, statistical analyses of the follow-up findings were not described, making it impossible to draw any firm conclusion about long-term efficacy. Moreover, a 5-year follow-up of these patients indicated that the original treatment success had been largely eroded (Stunkard and Penick, 1979). Öst and Götestam (1976) conducted a 1-year follow-up of a comparative outcome study of a behavioural treatment versus a pharmacological (fenfluramine) treatment. Consistent with previous research, the behavioural treatment was significantly superior at post-treatment but not at the long-term follow-up. The 1-year results indicated that the majority of subjects in both treatment groups had regained substantial amounts of weight although the mean weight of the behavioural group was still significantly lower than the pre-treatment level. An important finding from this study is that the drug treatment produced negative side-effects of higher frequency and duration.

Troublesome, too, for the behavioural approach to obesity is the finding that weight losses have not been reliably related to estimates of change in specific eating habits (Brownell and Stunkard, 1978). (The Öst and Götestam study is an exception to this trend.) While this may simply reflect the difficulties inherent in measuring change in eating patterns accurately, it suggests caution in attributing treatment success to specific behavioural mechanisms.

For some critics, the empirical status of outcome research has been cause for disenchantment with behavioural methods. Thus Yates (1975) has referred to the treatment of obesity as an instance of "when behaviour therapy fails" (p. 133). However, it would be premature to dismiss the value of behavioural techniques for weight control. There are several reasons why behaviour therapy, despite its obvious limitations, is still the best available method in the treatment of at least mild to moderate obesity.

The first reason is that there are studies that report satisfactory long-term results of at least 1 year – see Wilson (in press a). Levitz and Stunkard (1974), for example, demonstrated that behavioural treatment produced significantly lower client attrition rates and greater weight reduction that either nutrition education or self-help (TOPS – Take Off Pounds Sensibly) control groups at post-treatment and at a 9-month follow-up. McReynolds and Paulsen (1976) compared a comprehensive behavioural self-control treatment to one emphasizing stimulus control procedures. There was no difference at post-treatment, but the stimulus control programme was significantly superior at 3- and 6-month follow-ups, but not at 9, 12, and 18-month follow-up. Although groups tended to regain weight increasingly after the 3-month follow-up, reasonably impressive rates of maintenance of treatment-produced weight loss of approximately 75% and 80%, respectively, were obtained at the 1-year follow-up. Similarly, a well-controlled study by Stalonas, Johnson, and Christ (1978) showed that 65% of subjects treated with behaviour therapy continued to lose weight or maintain weight losses at a 1-year follow-up. As another example, Kingsley and Wilson (1977) found that while individual behaviour therapy was followed by high relapse rate, a comparable *group* treatment produced satisfactory maintenance of weight loss over a 1-year follow-up. Stunkard, Craighead, and O'Brien (1978) found strong evidence of maintenance of weight loss at a 1-year follow-up of a standard behavioural self-control treatment programme. A mean weight loss of 23 lb at the end of 6 months of therapy improved to 26 lb at 6-month follow-up. Patients treated with fenfluramine lost an average of 14 lb during treatment but regained 10 lb over the course of the 6-month follow-up. A combined behaviour therapy and fenfluramine treatment showed the greatest weight loss at post-treatment (32 lb), but also was followed by a weight gain of 10 lb during the first 6-month follow-up. Lastly, Stuart and Guire (in press) reported a 15-month follow-up of 721 women who had reached their target weights in a behavioural treatment programme offered through Weight Watchers. The average member joined Weight Watchers classes weighing 162.1 lb and lost a mean of 19% of bodyweight. At a follow-up of roughly 15 months, 24.6% of the sample were at their goal weights, 28.9% were within 5% of their goal weights, 17.5% were from 6% to 10% above goal weights, and the remainder were more than 11% above goal weight. The fact that these data are based on a self-selected sample who did not drop out of the Weight Watchers programme, a common occurrence, limits their significance.

A second reason to believe that behaviour therapy might prove to be an effective treatment is that the majority of behavioural programmes that have been evaluated represent a restricted form of behaviour therapy that can and should be improved upon by the use of more multi-faceted, sophisticated treatments (Stuart, 1979; Wilson, in press b). Therapeutic components that promise to enhance previous treatment success include an emphasis on social skills training, the recognition of the role of cognitive influences, the inclusion of family members in the treatment process, and a systematic focus on energy expenditure through a carefully developed physical exercise programme. In addition, care has to be taken to ensure that well-trained qualified therapists conduct treatment programmes that are of sufficient duration to effect changes in what after all are well-established patterns of behaviour. A 4- to 6-week treatment programme conducted by inexperienced graduate students fails to test the potential of behaviour therapy.

The consistently promising short-term effects of behaviour therapy cannot be overlooked. As we have argued, evaluations of treatment outcome should distinguish between the initiation of therapeutic change, its transfer to the natural environment, and its maintenance (Bandura, 1969). These different phases of the overall treatment strategy may be governed by different processes, and maintenance can be ensured only to the extent that procedures designed to accomplish this goal are included in the treatment programme. Surprisingly few treatment studies have included explicit behavioural strategies to maintain treatment-produced weight loss. Systematic research on maintenance strategies is a recent and welcome development that may well result in improved behavioural treatment programmes for obesity and other addictive disorders which are characterized by disturbingly high rates of relapse. Among the maintenance strategies that have been investigated are booster sessions and the use of family members. The use of booster sessions has yielded disappointing results on the whole (Wilson, in press a). However, the inclusion of the obese person's spouse in the treatment programme appears to be a particularly promising means of producing stable treatment effects. Brownell, Heckerman, Westlake, Hayes, and Monti (1978) have demonstrated that the inclusion of spouses in a standard behavioural treatment programme produced significantly greater weight loss at 3- and 6-month follow-ups than treatments in which spouses did not participate. In Brownell et al.'s couples training programme, spouses learned to monitor their partners' behaviour, to model appropriate eating habits, and to assist their obese partners in coping with high-risk situations by engaging them in activities that were incompatabile with eating. Clients in the couples training treatment showed an average weight loss of nearly 30 lb 8½ months after the beginning of treatment. This clinically significant result ranks with the most impressive weight losses ever reported in a controlled outcome study. Impressive maintenance of weight loss at the 1-year mark has also been reported by Pearce, LeBow, and Orchard (1979) using a behavioural treatment programme that emphasized active participation by spouses in the entire therapeutic process. A mean weight loss of 14.34 lb at the end of a 10-week treatment programme improved to a mean weight loss of 18.19 lb at the 1-year follow-up. Greater attention to cognitive analyses of weight control and maintenance appears likely to facilitate lasting improvement (Rodin, 1978; Wilson, in press b).

Finally, bearing in mind the broader criteria for evaluating therapeutic outcome that were proposed by Kazdin and Wilson (1978a), behavioural procedures for the treatment of obesity have proven to be easily disseminable, efficient, and relatively cost-effective (Stuart, 1979). Treatment effects have been replicable across a broad range of different therapists, overweight populations, and situations. Behaviour therapy for obesity has been shown to be effective without appearing to produce adverse side-effects. "Symptom substitution" has been notably absent (Wollersheim, 1970) and weight loss in behavioural programmes appears to be correlated with generalized improvements in psychological well-being. Although depression has been associated with rapid weight loss (Stunkard and Rush, 1974), the evidence from behavioural programmes that stress gradual weight loss, point to a decrease (Stuart, 1979) or no overall change (Taylor, Ferguson, and Reading, 1978) in depression. This broadly beneficial effect of behavioural treatment is an important consideration in view of the frequently voiced concern that obesity might be a biologically normal state, the modification of which might cause negative physical and emotional impact (Nisbett, 1972).

We have suggested that its limitations notwithstanding, behaviour therapy is the preferred treatment for at least some forms of obesity. Of course, this should not be taken to indicate that the role of biological factors in the etiology and maintenance of obesity is discounted. The available evidence strongly indicates the importance of biological influences on weight control (e.g. Mahoney, Rogers, Straw, and Mahoney, in press; Wooley, Wooley, and Dyrenforth, 1979). Contrary to early behavioural assumptions, it is unclear whether or not the obese eat more than others or eat in a manner different from their normal weight counterparts. There are data to suggest that some people's metabolic systems come to respond in a way that encourages obesity rather than consistent weight loss. Recognition of these biological influences, as Wooley et al. point out, certainly does not contraindicate the application of behavioural principles and procedures in the treatment of obesity. It does, however, suggest more informed ways of using behavioural methods not only to facilitate weight loss but also to assist the obese person to develop sufficient self-confidence and interpersonal skills to cope with the social difficulties and discrimination that are frequently the unhappy consequences of obesity.

DRUG ABUSE

The systematic application of behavioural principles to the modification of addictions to narcotic, stimulant, and hallucinogenic drugs has been uncommon. Moreover, the clinical studies in this area of drug addiction have been rudimentary and the bulk of the behavioural literature is limited to uncontrolled individual case reports. In an evaluative review of the behavioural literature on drug abuse, Callner (1975) found that 74% of published studies consisted of individual case-reports. Of equally great concern is the sole use of self-report data as the measure of outcome in 52% of the studies. Only six of the twenty-two studies summarized by Callner included a discussion of follow-up measures.

A similar review of the behavioural treatment of drug abuse by Götestam, Melin, and Öst (1976) gives no cause for comfort. Of the thirty-eight studies they reviewed, Götestam et al.

concluded that only five used any type of experimental control. However, one was a single-group design, the other four single-subject designs that were very rudimentary. Not a single controlled group outcome study employing a control group was found, a telling comment on the lack of rigorous research in this area. Among the more fundamental problems with these studies have been inadequate assessment, lack of follow-up, and inadequate outcome measures.

In view of this less than auspicious picture, we cannot conclude that behaviour therapy currently offers any advantage over alternative approaches to drug abuse.

Psychotic Disorders

The application of behaviour therapy to psychotic disorders has been confined largely to the use of the principles and procedures of operant conditioning. Historically, Lindsley and Skinner were the first investigators to apply operant conditioning methods to psychotic patients in a systematic fashion (Lindsley, Skinner, and Solomon, 1953). Their purpose had not been to "cure" or treat psychotics, but to demonstrate the feasibility of modifying the behaviour of chronic psychotic patients by manipulating response-contingent reinforcements. Ever since those pioneering studies, reinforcement procedures have been the predominant means of the behavioural treatment of psychotic disorders, and have been applied to an ever-increasing range of behaviour in an increasingly complex and sophisticated fashion. This has culminated in the modification of entire social systems as in the token economy (Ayllon and Azrin, 1965; Kazdin, 1977), a far cry from the elementary lever-pulling responses that Lindsley and Skinner employed.

Other behavioural procedures have been used in the treatment of psychotic patients. Most notably, these have included social skills training and self-instructional training. Social skills training has consisted of the use of well-defined techniques like instructions, modelling, behaviour rehearsal, corrective feedback, and social reinforcement to develop specific inter-personal skills and problem-solving abilities to chronic psychiatric patients. The results of these relatively recent efforts have indicated that these behavioural interventions can significantly improve the functioning of chronic psychiatric patients and appear to be more effective than pseudotherapy control procedures (e.g. Eisler, Blanchard, Fitts, and Williams, 1978; Bellack, Hersen, and Turner, 1976; Hersen and Bellack, 1976 a and b). In the main, however, it has been the use of operant conditioning procedures, particularly the token economy, that has characterized behavioural interventions with psychotic and other institutionalized psychiatric populations, and the remainder of this chapter deals with this work.

Operant conditioning emphasizes the relationship between observable behaviour and its environmental consequences. Behaviour change is said to occur when certain consequences are *contingent* upon the occurrence of behaviour. Thus the cornerstone of operant conditioning approaches, the principle of positive reinforcement, refers to an increase in the frequency of behaviour that is followed, contingently, by a rewarding environmental event (i.e. a positive reinforcer). It is often the case that a new response cannot be established directly by reinforcing its occurrence because the response may never occur. The desired behaviour may be so complex that the elements which make up the response are not in the repertoire of the individual. Hence the critical importance in operant conditioning of shaping, a procedure in which the terminal behaviour is achieved by reinforcing small steps or approximations toward the final response rather than by reinforcing the final response itself. Armed with these and other basic learning principles such as negative reinforcement, schedules of reinforcement, prompting, and extinction, applied behaviour analysts have extended reinforcement procedures to an astonishingly diverse array of different problems across widely varying populations.*

A wealth of evidence has now accumulated demonstrating that specific responses of psychotic patients can be beneficially altered through the use of reinforcement methods. Among the many responses that have been modified have been apathy, disorganized thinking, social withdrawal, mutism or bizarre verbalizations, self-destructive behaviour, grooming and self-care activities (Ullmann and Krasner, 1973). Moreover, the use of single-subject methodology such as the ABAB reversal design has established the causal role of specific reinforcement procedures in changing behaviour of this sort. Of course, impressive as they are, these studies do not show that a psychotic disorder like schizophrenia can be "cured" by behaviour therapy. Overwhelmingly, these studies have been of the demonstration variety in which the purpose has been to show change and to relate that change to alterations in the reinforcement contingencies. The magnitude or clinical significance of the behavioural change has rarely been of primary concern, a limitation of this approach that we discuss below. For example, in the King, Armitage, and Tilton (1960) study, the operant interpersonal method was shown to be significantly more effective than verbal psychotherapy and occupational therapy in improving certain aspects of the patients' behaviour. However, enthusiasm for this comparative success must be tempered by the realization that only one of the subjects in the operant interpersonal treatment group was transferred from the closed hospital ward to an open ward, let alone successfully discharged. This is not a satisfactory clinical outcome. Furthermore, there is the question of whether or not similar improvements might not be produced more efficiently through the appropriate use of antipsychotic drugs such as the phenothiazines (Hersen, 1979).

The most ambitious and potentially important attempts to modify the behaviour of psychotic and other institutionalized psychiatric patients have involved the implementation of token economies. Briefly, the token economy consists of the following main elements: carefully specified and operationally defined target behaviour; back-up reinforcers, which are the "good things in life" or what people are willing to work for, the tokens which represent the back-up reinforcers; and the rules of exchange which specify the number of tokens required to obtain back-up reinforcers. Tokens are generalized conditioned reinforcers which have a number of advantages, such as bridging the gap between the target behaviour and the back-up reinforcers, permitting the reinforcement of any response at any time, and providing the same reinforcement for different patients who have diverse preferences in back-up reinforcers.

Beginning with the now classic token economy programme of Ayllon and Azrin (1965), a number of studies, predictably employing single-case experimental designs, have demonstrated that the token economy can effect widespread changes across different responses in institutionalized psychiatric patients (Hersen and Bellack, 1978; Kazdin, 1977). Unfortunately, even in those studies in which marked improvement was produced in the functioning of patients while they were hospitalized, the all too familiar pattern has been for a relatively rapid return to

*Our focus here is on the treatment of psychotic patients. However, it is important to note that reinforcement procedures have been applied with some success to the treatment of autistic, learning disabled, and retarded children; children with conduct disorders; academic and social problems in the classroom; delinquents, and adult offenders among others. The settings in which these reinforcement methods have been implemented include conventional psychiatric hospitals, schools, prisons, day-care centres, the home, and the community. The nature and results of these kaleidoscopic interventions are described in several excellent reviews of the relevant literature (e.g. Brigham and Catania, 1979; Kazdin, 1978; O'Leary and O'Leary, 1977).

hospital after discharge. Thus in one of the first major token economy studies, by Atthowe and Krasner (1968), approximately half of the patients who had improved sufficiently to warrant discharge from the hospital, required readmission within a year of their discharge. Even where the nature of the in-patient treatment has been extensive and concentrated on such real-life skills as problem-solving, decision-making, and self-management (Fairweather, 1964), the rates of rehospitalization have been discouragingly high. Indeed, it was estimated that roughly 70% of chronic patients who are discharged from mental hospitals return within 18 months regardless of the type of treatment they received while hospitalized (Fairweather and Simon, 1963).

Results such as these have led to the recognition that explicit programmes have to be developed in order to sustain the psychiatric patient in the community to which he or she returns following discharge from a mental hospital. Helping institutionalized patients to the point where they can be discharged from the hospital is just the first step; whether or not they make a successful return to the community and remain there hinges primarily on the extent to which deliberate actions are taken to facilitate and maintain this transition. An eminently sensible endeavour, implementing these maintenance programmes for previously hospitalized patients, is referred to by operant conditioners, with their penchant for mechanistic metaphors, as programming the natural environment.

Two examples of the extension of behavioural principles into the larger social environment may be cited by way of illustration of what can be achieved by a more comprehensive treatment programme. Atthowe (1973) reports on how patients from a token-economy programme, described by Atthowe and Krasner (1968), were shaped into spending more time working in a sheltered workshop in the grounds of the hospital. In this phase they earned money rather than tokens, and were reinforced on a delayed basis (e.g. at the end of the week) as they would be in the community setting. In the next step they were transferred to a self-help ward in the hospital where they assumed greater individual responsibility, such as taking their medication and holding progressively more demanding jobs outside of the hospital. Only one staff member, a social worker, was assigned to this ward. Ex-patients who graduated through the programme and were working outside the hospital served as important peer-group models and as co-therapists in motivating patients to leave the hospital.

The rehabilitation programme coordinates several employment opportunities for ex-patients in the community, including the operation of four gas stations, a house renovation crew, and a soft drinks and food concession. Of fifty-nine men discharged from the hospital, the readmission rate was less than 12% over a median follow-up period of 1 year — a remarkable improvement over the customary readmission figures. These patients lived outside the hospital and worked as foremen for the rehabilitation programme in projects on the hospital grounds. Fifteen per cent of the patients left the programme completely and were living and working in the community.

In another community-oriented treatment programme for psychotics, Fairweather, Sanders, Maynard, and Cressler (1969) assigned psychotic patients to two different treatment conditions. Both groups received the small-group training in problem-solving and decision-making skills as in the earlier Fairweather (1964) project. In this second study, however, as soon as the patients in one group were functioning adequately within the hospital, they were transferred to a semi-autonomous lodge located in the community. Under the initial supervision of a hospital staff member, and subsequently of a lay person, the patients assumed full responsibility for running the lodge, including the purchase of food and preparation of meals, regulating the administration of medication, managing their own financial affairs, and operating a money-making janitorial service. The necessity for specific training in job skills is underscored by the failure of these patients to perform even simple tasks such as gardening until they were deliberately trained. The operation of the lodge became fully autonomous after 33 months of functioning; all income was distributed among the lodge members according to each person's productivity and role within the system. The control group received the traditional assistance and out-patient therapy hospital patients get after being discharged. The results demonstrated the superiority of the group given a graduated transition into the community. This superiority was most evident in terms of the amount of time the patients maintained themselves in the community over a 40-month follow-up and the percentage of time that they were gainfully employed during this period.

As valuable as they are, and allowing for the greater flexibility that they provide the researcher, single-case experimental designs, or the methodological stuff of which most token economy evaluations are made, have their limitations (Bandura, 1976; Hersen and Barlow, 1976; Kazdin and Wilson, 1978b). These include the difficulties involved in studying behaviour which is to some extent irreversible, the statistical problems inherent in some of the Skinnerian techniques (including the partial or outright rejection of statistical techniques by some Skinnerian workers), and the difficulties involved in determining the relative contributions of different treatment variables. Single-subject methodology is particularly well-suited to demonstrating the value of new techniques initially. However, evaluation of the comparative merits of these techniques, once they are established, inevitably entails more conventional clinical studies with between-group comparisons and appropriate statistical analyses.

THE TOKEN ECONOMY COMPARED TO OTHER TREATMENT PROCEDURES

A number of studies have compared the token economy to other forms of treatment in the care of psychotic and other institutionalized psychiatric patients.* For convenience, these studies can be grouped according to whether the comparison treatment consisted of routine, general ward treatment, or a specific alternative form of therapy. Typically, routine ward treatment involves custodial care, although several unspecified activities and small amount of therapy of some sort may be included. Alternative treatments refer to active procedures that are better specified than custodial ward care and are associated with an explicit rationale from which the procedures are derived.

The results of eight studies comparing the token economy to routine hospital treatment have been summarized by Kazdin and Wilson (1978b) as follows:

"Comparisons of reinforcement programs with routine ward care indicate a relatively consistent pattern. Reinforcement programs have led to improvements on measures of cognitive, affective, and social aspects of psychotic behaviour, on specific behaviours in interviews and on the ward, and in global measures of adjustment or discharge from the hospital and subsequent readmission. Patient improvements in these areas are much

*For the most part, the studies reviewed in this section include in-patients diagnosed as schizophrenics, although diagnoses of other psychotic disorders or non-psychotic conditions such as organic disorders or mental retardation were occasionally reported.

greater for reinforcement than for routine care wards. Regrettably, comparisons of reinforcement and routine ward programs have been beset with methodological problems,
including bias in subject selection and assignment, confounds of treatment with changes
in the physical ward and in the hospital staff, and ancillary features of the hospital
environment" (p. 75).

Consequently, although strongly suggestive of the superiority of token economies, the
evidence falls short of unequivocal confirmation.

Kazdin and Wilson located seven studies comparing the token economy to alternative forms
of therapy in the treatment of psychotic patients. As a whole these studies were superior in
methodological quality to those in which the comparison condition was routine hospital
care. The specific treatments to which the token economy has been compared include role-
playing, verbal-psychotherapy, play therapy, recreational therapy, and milieu therapy. It should
be noted that the verbal psychotherapy comparison treatments in three of the seven studies
reviewed here were quite different from one another and, bearing in mind the folly of the
"therapy uniformity myth", should not be interpreted collectively as a test of something
called "psychotherapy". Commenting on these studies, Kazdin and Wilson concluded that in
"almost all of the available studies, reinforcement techniques have been more effective than the
comparative treatment" (p. 81). Here too, however, methodological problems preclude any
firm conclusion about the superiority of behaviour therapy, even though the present data are
encouraging. One of the difficulties that dictate caution in drawing firm conclusions concerns
the nature of the outcome measures in the above studies.

In his encyclopaedic review of the literature on the token economy, Kazdin (1977) pointed
out that most programmes have focused on a limited range of patient behaviour. Indeed, the
choice of what behaviour is selected for modification often appears to have owed more to the
methodological requirements and convenience of the researcher or the immediate management
interests of the hospital institution's staff than the clinical needs of the patients. Kazdin archly
offers the observation that,

> "If a naive observer were asked to infer the problems of select treatment populations
> based upon the focus on token programs, there might be considerable distortion of the
> population's defining characteristics. For example, a naive observer might infer that
> psychiatric patients consist of individuals whose main problems are the failure to bathe,
> dress, and groom themselves, get up on time, and attend activities punctually. The
> plethora of investigations that have focused on self-care would not make this inference
> unjust" (p. 198).

Although much of the research on token economies can be faulted on the grounds of clinical
relevance, it would be inaccurate to conclude that therapeutically significant activities have
been totally overlooked, as Kazdin hastens to point out. The Atthowe (1973) and Fairweather
et al. (1969) studies are illustrations of the sort of sophisticated, real-life coping skills that can
be developed throught the systematic use of behavioural procedures.

A second limitation of token economies has been the absence of appropriate follow-up
evaluations. With very few exceptions, studies in this area have been designed to demonstrate
behavioural change in hospitalized patients without due regard for ensuring generalization of
newly acquired response patterns to the real-life setting and their maintenance over time. A third
limitation of most studies on the token economy is that they over-emphasize the depth and
extent of environmental control of abnormal behaviour. There is a further implication,
erroneous of course, that if one is successful in modifying abnormal behaviour by a

conditioning procedure (for example) this demonstrates that the abnormal behaviour was originally produced by a similar conditioning procedure. This tendency to over-emphasize the importance of environmental contingencies in the regulation and maintenance of abnormal behaviour often has the unfortunate result of making the various types of disorder virtually indistinguishable. Carried to extremes, the operant view of abnormal behaviour would reduce one to expecting and, indeed, predicting that all abnormal behaviour, produced and maintained as it is largely by "social reinforcement", should be similar if not identical. The operant conditioning position, forcefully represented by Ullmann and Krasner's (1969) influential writings, is that there are no qualitative or inherent differences between the development, maintenance, and modification of psychotic and non-psychotic behaviour. Such a view minimizes the role of genetic factors and gives short shrift to the influence of biological processes in psychotic disorders. Although this view need not be shared in order to implement an effective token economy, there can be little doubt that the majority of investigators in this tradition are closely allied to the Ullmann and Krasner point of view.

It must be emphasized that not all behaviour therapists concur with this view of psychotic disorders. On the basis of factor analytic studies and other evidence, Eysenck and Rachman (1965) concluded that psychotic behaviour is qualitatively different from normal and neurotic behaviour in terms of etiology, treatment, and prognosis. In their view, psychosis is a form of biochemical and/or physiological malfunction with strong genetic determination. Psychotics might acquire neurotic habits, and these might be eliminated through the application of behavioural principles, but the psychosis is left largely unaffected by such measures. Wolpe's (1969) views on psychoses are similar (see also Rachman and Philips, 1978). Other critics such as Davison (1969) have contended that the operant conditioning formulation is simplistic and cannot account for the specific cognitive deficits usually observed in psychotic disorders. Among other lines of evidence, the relative insensitivity to change of a small but none the less significant number of patients in most token economy programmes calls into question the adequacy of reinforcement principles in explaining the modification let alone the etiology of different disorders (Davison, 1969).

In his evaluation of the efficacy of the token economy, Kazdin (1977) distinguishes between its relative and absolute success. With regard to relative efficacy, Kazdin suggests that "few if any methods begin to approach the demonstrated efficacy of the token economy" (p. 280). The difficulty in evaluating the token economy from the standpoint of absolute criteria, argues Kazdin, "is that the criteria themselves are unclear. It is not clear what the limits of therapeutic change are with many treatment populations. Thus, the goals that are attainable are unknown. These goals themselves depend upon developing effective treatments which extend the accomplishments of previous treatments" (p. 280). A better indication of the attainable goals of treatment with chronic, institutionalized psychotics is provided by the unparalleled study of Paul and Lentz (1978).

In terms of its methodological excellence, its attention to detail, the specification of the treatment methods, staff training and administration, the comprehensive nature of measurement of outcome, and the evaluation of cost-effectiveness, there has been nothing of this magnitude and quality. Its size and style, however, are likely to dismay all but the most persevering readers. A more serious problem is that the magnitude of the study ironically precludes any hope of independent replication.

The goals of this ambitious study, as stated by Paul and Lentz, were as follows:

"(1) To articulate and evaluate the comparative effectiveness of the two most promising therapeutic programs — milieu therapy and social-learning therapy — for returning the chronic mental patient to the community. Effectiveness in relationship to each other and to traditional hospital treatment, when all include systematic after-care services. (2) To identify the limits of change that can be accomplished with the overall programs within staffing restrictions characteristic of public mental hospitals. (3) To explore the systematic effects of both programs on differential areas of success. (4) To explore the prognostic value of patient characteristics and functioning for release and community stay, as well as postrelease environmental factors. (5) To demonstrate a feasible model for investigating institutional treatment outcome under actual clinical conditions, providing more rigorous design, controls and procedures than had been previously accomplished" (p. 15).

The subjects were chronic mental patients, all of whom had been diagnosed as process schizophrenics, were of low socio-economic status, had been confined to a mental hospital for an average of 17 years, and had been treated previously with drugs and other methods without success. Approximately 90% were maintained on drugs at the onset of the study. Their level of self-care was too low and the severity of their bizarre behaviour too great to permit community placement despite the efforts of the hospital administrators. According to Paul and Lentz, these subjects were "the most severely debilitated chronically institutionalized adults ever subjected to systematic study".

Twenty-eight of these subjects were assigned to each of three treatment groups so that the groups were "identical on level and nature of functioning and on every characteristic of potential importance to treatment responsiveness". Two identical, adjacent units were estab-lished at a mental health centre to house the psychosocial programmes — milieu therapy at one and social-learning therapy at the other — both staffed by the same personnel at a level equal to that existing in a comparison state hospital. The third group received typical hospital treatment at the comparison state hospital. As patients were released into the community, they were re-placed by similar subjects from the original pool of chronic patients in order to maintain equivalent groups.

The social learning treatment consisted of the direct application of principles of learning, including classical conditioning, a variety of reinforcement procedures such as shaping, prompting, and response cost or time-out, and the token economy. The milieu therapy con-sisted of a therapeutic community structure in the institution. Within this therapeutic com-munity the focus was on the communication of positive expectations, group cohesiveness and pressure directed towards normal functioning, and group problem-solving in which the "residents" (as the subjects in this study were called) were treated as responsible people rather than as custodial cases. The routine hospital therapy consisted of typical state hospital treat-ment of the chronic schizophrenic patient, emphasizing chemotherapy, custodial care with little psychological treatment, and little expectation of patient improvement. In contrast to the social learning and milieu treatments, both of which derived from a non-disease, re-educative model of treatment, the routine hospital therapy appears to have rested on a traditional model of treatment. The social learning and milieu treatments were

"equally high prestige programs in identical physical settings with exact equation in the degree of operationalization, clarity, specificity, explicitness, and order provided for both staff and residents. Both programs also provided identical activity structure and focus upon specific classes of behaviour, with the same staff not only conducting both programs, but equating time and focus within programs, with both running concurrently over the same time periods, subject to the same extraneous events" (Paul and Lentz, p. 423).

As a result of this unprecedented experimental control, conclusions about comparative efficacy of the different treatments can be drawn.

Continuous staff and patient assessments were obtained through objective behavioural observation and data sampling. Patients in all three groups were assessed through structured interviews and standardized rating scales before entering the project, at 6-month intervals, and prior to entering the community. Released patients were also reassessed at 6-month intervals. All relevant personal and social characteristics of staff and patients were evaluated. The relative efficacy of the two programmes was determined by a comparison of changes in specific components and overall lengths of functioning, release patterns, community stay rates, and number of patients served. The programmes were compared with each other and with a comparison group undergoing the usual hospital schedule. All patients successfully achieving release from the institution were systematically followed up for at least a year and a half after termination of the intramural stage of the project. Data were collected continuously for six years.

Paul and Lentz provide a mass of data and extensive analyses of outcome that we can only briefly summarize here. In short, the social learning treatment was followed by superior results. Continuous behavioural observation of patients' functioning in the hospital setting across the 4½ years during which the programmes were in effect, indicated that both the social learning and the milieu therapy programme were followed by major improvements at the end of treatment. However, the social learning treatment produced significantly greater reductions in bizarre behaviour and increases in adaptive behaviour such as self-care and interpersonal skills than did milieu therapy. Assessment of overall functioning on several standardized rating scales showed that the social learning treatment resulted in significantly greater improvement than the milieu therapy at each 6-month evaluation, and the routine hospital treatment at all but two of these different assessment periods. The effects of milieu therapy on these scales were less apparent than on the continuous behavioural observations. Patients in the routine hospital treatment failed to reflect a significant change in functioning over the 4½ years of the programme.

The data on comparative release rates are summarized in Table 4. The social learning treatment was followed by greater numbers of what Paul and Lentz call "significant releases" (i.e. a minimum continuous community stay of 90 days). In turn, milieu therapy was superior

TABLE 4

Comparative Rates of Significant Release at Termination of Intramural Programmes

Treatment programme	No.	% achieving significant release		
		Original equated groups	No.	All residents treated
Social-learning	28	96.4%	40	97.5%
Milieu therapy	28	67.9%	31	71.0%
Hospital comparison	28	46.4%	29	44.8%

Note: Significant release required a minimum continuous community stay of 90 days. Chi-square – 16.90, df = 2, $p < 0.01$ for original groups; Chi-square – 24.46, df – 2, $p < 0.01$ for ever-treated groups.

to the routine hospital programme. However, the overwhelming majority of *all discharges* were to private boarding and care homes (88.9%, 84.2%, and 100% respectively, for the social learning, milieu therapy, and hospital programmes) as opposed to independent functioning in the outside world. Of the original subjects, *only 10.7% of the social learning residents and 7.1% of the milieu therapy residents achieved release to independent functioning and self-support,* without rehospitalization. None of the patients from the routine hospital programme were successful in this respect. Paul and Lentz themselves note that the level of functioning required for remaining in extended-care facilities in the community was "marginal". However, given the severity of the subjects' problems and their chronically low level of functioning prior to treatment, successful release to community facilities such as boarding homes was a useful accomplishment. Improvement within the hospital setting and subsequent release were unrelated to differences in resident characteristics, prior treatment history, or initial level of functioning and in the relative absence of psychotropic drugs.

Given the consistently superior results of the treated groups during the hospital period, it has to be said that the discharge results are an anticlimax; indeed they threaten to deflate most of the early encouragements.

Surprisingly, drug administration was not a significant predictor of responsiveness to treatment. This trend is illustrated by reference to the administration of drugs during the last 6 months of the 4½ years of the treatment programmes. During this period, from the 91.7% of patients receiving psychotropic drugs at project entry, drug use in the routine hospital group increased to 100%. On the other hand, drug administration was reduced to 17.9% and 10.7%, respectively, for milieu and social-learning groups. Yet there was a significant improvement in functioning in both the social learning and milieu therapy groups at this time. Another finding of interest was the impact of an unscheduled "natural experiment" during the course of the treatment programme. During the 18-month period when the sixth, seventh, and eighth 6-month assessment intervals were made, a change in state policy governing the procedures employed in mental institutions forced the investigators to curtail the use of time-out in the social learning treatment and lengthy expulsion from the group in the milieu therapy as a means of curbing assaultive behaviour by residents. Marked increases in dangerous and aggressive acts were recorded during this period, notably in the milieu therapy programme. With the reinstitution of time-out and appropriately long exclusion from the group in the social learning and milieu programmes, the rate of aggressive or assaultive behaviour decreased once again during the final 6 months of treatment. This unscheduled "reversal design" indicates the effect of specific therapeutic components in the overall treatment programmes.

A follow-up evaluation of 1½ years was conducted after the termination of the three treatment programmes. Table 5 presents the data on the status at the final follow-up for all the residents treated in this study. The social-learning programme maintained its superiority over the other two groups, with over 90% of treated residents remaining continuously in the community at the time of the year and a half final follow-up, with some having maintained community stay for over 5 years. Although 70% of the residents treated by the milieu therapy programme were still in the community at the final follow-up, compared to fewer than 50% of the patients from the hospital group, these differences were not statistically significant with regard to the achieving significant release with continuing community stay. The social learning treatment was the most effective and the least expensive. Based on all these data from objective and standardized rating measures during the 4½ years that the treatment programmes were in use, and the release rates and community stays and cost-effectiveness figures, Paul and Lentz

TABLE 5

Status at Final Follow-up for all Residents ever Treated

Treatment programme	No.	Condition in institution of returnees and residents not achieving significant release			Residents achieving significant release with continuing community stay
		Worse	No change	Improved	
Social-learning	40	2.5%	2.5%	2.5%	92.5%
Milieu therapy	31	16.1%	9.7%	3.2%	71.0%
Hospital comparison	31	29.0%	9.7%	12.9%	48.4%

Note: Chi-square – 17.18, df = 2, $p < 0.01$ for an institution versus out of institution.

concluded that "social learning procedures clearly emerge as the treatment of choice for the severely debilitated chronically institutionalized mental patient" (p. 389). It is difficult to contest this view, at least in respect of in-hospital behaviour, but their claims are not borne out by the post-hospital results.

Nevertheless the findings encourage the view that effective and feasible procedures can be brought to bear in helping chronic mental patients. It can only be hoped that these findings will have the desired influence on the care of this the largest but most difficult and most wanting population of psychiatric patients. Aside from its implications for the care of the chronic mental patient, the Paul and Lentz study serves as a sound model for comparative outcome research with a severely disturbed population. Rigorous research and clinical objectives need not be incompatible. Indeed, clinical advances demand well-controlled, objective evaluations of promising treatment procedures.

Stoffelmayr, Faulkner, and Mitchell (cited by Paul and Lentz) systematically evaluated the relative efficacy of the token economy versus a milieu therapy programme. They assigned ten severely withdrawn, psychotic male patients to each of the following treatments: a token economy; two different milieu therapy programmes differing in degree of structure; and a routine hospital care group. Consistent with the findings from the Paul and Lentz study, Stoffelmayr *et al.* found that the token economy treatment produced significantly greater improvement in their patients' behaviour. The milieu therapy produced initial changes but these were not maintained. At the end of 1 year there was little difference between the milieu and routine hospital treatments. These results emphasize the importance of response-contingent consequences in the treatment and rehabilitation of the chronic mental patient.

CONCLUDING COMMENTS

Behaviour therapy is distinguished by its broad applicability to a diverse range of clinical, educational, and medical problems; the examples we have presented in this chapter do not exhaust the evidence on the therapeutic efficacy of behavioural methods as a whole. Looking ahead, one of the most active areas of behavioural research and therapy will increasingly be that of medical psychology, or what in the United States is now referred to as behavioural medicine (e.g. Doyle and Gentry, 1977; Rachman and Philips, 1980; Schwartz and Weiss, 1977). This promising extension of behaviour therapy techniques and methodology involves the treatment of a heterogeneous class of problems such as cardiovascular disease, pain, tension and migraine headaches, sleep disorders, gastrointestinal disorders, adherence to medical and psychological treatment regimens, and a number of other matters.

Reviewing the voluminous treatment outcome literature sampled in this chapter, it is clear that behaviour therapy has demonstrated its value in the treatment of several clinical disorders. Most of the available evidence indicates the short-term success of behavioural methods. Well-controlled studies of the long-term clinical efficacy of behaviour therapy are needed and have become a major priority for future research. A related concern is the need for more controlled clinical trials of procedures that have the backing of laboratory investigations but which nevertheless must still prove their worth in the clinical arena. We have tried to indicate the many positive achievements of behaviour therapy as well as noting existing gaps in our knowledge. It is not difficult to uncover inadequacies and limitations in behavioural approaches to clinical practice. However, when it is remembered that our current knowledge is based roughly on a mere two decades of systematic behavioural research and practice, the advances that have been made must be viewed as the single most significant development in the effective treatment of clinical disorders in recent times.

CHAPTER 11

COGNITIVE BEHAVIOUR THERAPY

Readers who contest the view that *thinking* is a comprehensible and useful psychological concept will be made impatient by this chapter, but are asked to refrain from engaging in passive, or indeed active, avoidance behaviour. If we take it as given that *thinking* is a valuable concept, and then move on to the premise that thinking can mediate emotions and actions (just as the reverse sequence can occur from actions to thoughts), it opens wide the door. The task of the cognitive therapist can be defined as the modification of behavioural and emotional disturbances by helping to modify the person's (or patient's) mediating thoughts. When the emphasis is placed on cognitive means of modifying these mediators then we have a *cognitive* therapy. Despite this significant shift in emphasis and numerous differences of theory, the methods used by cognitive therapists also incorporate behavioural procedures — as they themselves emphasize (e.g. Ellis, 1979). The emergence of cognitive behaviour therapy or cognitive behaviour modification (Beck, 1976; Ellis and Grieger, 1977; Goldfried, 1977; Mahoney, 1977b; Mahoney and Arnkoff, 1978; Meichenbaum, 1977a) is the most recent development within the broadly defined domain of behaviour therapy. This development is difficult to evaluate because it encompasses different conceptual views and diverse treatment techniques. The heterogeneous nature of this approach is illustrated by the disagreements among its leading proponents (cf. Ellis, 1977 a and b; Mahoney, 1977a; Meichenbaum, 1977b). None the less, the fundamental assumptions on which all cognitive behaviour therapy methods are based are that emotional disorders are a function of maladaptive thought patterns and that the major task of treatment is to restructure these faulty cognitions. Cognitive behaviour therapy embraces a broad range of treatment techniques, some of which evolved independently of behaviour therapy and others that are reconceptualizations or variations of procedures commonly employed by behaviour therapists. Mahoney and Arnkoff (1978) have identified the three major forms of cognitive behaviour therapy: cognitive restructuring methods; coping skills procedures; and problem-solving therapies. However, it is unquestionably the cognitive restructuring methods that make cognitive behaviour therapy a distinctive psychological treatment approach and by which it is widely known. The cognitive restructuring methods have been more extensively evaluated and it is to them that we now turn.

Cognitive Restructuring Methods

ELLIS' RATIONAL EMOTIVE THERAPY

The oldest of the cognitive restructuring methods is Ellis' (1962, 1977a) rational emotive therapy (RET). The details of RET are well known and require little elaboration here (see Ellis, 1970; Ellis and Grieger, 1977). Suffice it to say that it is not life events as such but the client's distorted perception of these events that purportedly induces emotional disturbance. Ellis lists twelve irrational core assumptions that are said to be at the root of this distorted perception or faulty thinking. Examples of this dirty dozen include the beliefs that "It is a dire necessity for an adult to be loved by everyone for everything he does", "It is easier to avoid than to face life difficulties and self-responsibilities", and "One has no control over one's emotions and one cannot help feeling certain things" (Ellis, 1970). Neurotics, it is said, do not always consciously or deliberately rehearse these irrational assumptions in everyday situations. These internal self-statements or beliefs appear to be automatic and pervasive in their influence because they have been repeated so often that they assume the status of an over-learned response.

Treatment consists of assisting the client to identify these irrational ideas and to replace them with more constructive, rational thoughts. The therapy usually includes (but is not limited to) the following procedural steps:

 (a) verbal persuasion aimed at convincing the client of the philosophical tenets of RET;
 (b) identification of irrational thoughts through client self-monitoring and the therapist's feedback;
 (c) the therapist directly challenges irrational ideas and models rational reinterpretations of disturbing events;
 (d) repeated cognitive rehearsal aimed at substituting rational self-statement for previously irrational interpretation;
 (e) behavioural tasks designed to develop rational reactions.

EMPIRICAL SUPPORT

In his review of the clinical and personality hypotheses that provide the basis for the RET system of therapy, Ellis (1977a) concluded that the research support for RET is "immense — indeed, almost awesome". It is important to distinguish between support for its theoretical assumptions, and outcome findings that bear on the therapeutic efficacy of RET. Our focus here is confirmed primarily to an evaluation of the latter rather than the former. However, some comments on the underlying assumptions of RET are in order.

Several studies provide support for the general notion that thoughts or self-statements can elicit emotional arousal (e.g. May, 1977; Rimm and Litvak, 1969). However, a recent study by Rogers and Craighead (1977) calls into question the pivotal assumption behind RET that specific negative self-statements mediate emotional states. In this study subjects cognitively rehearsed self-referent statements while physiological responses were monitored. The self-statements had been chosen to reflect identified problems and were either positively or negatively valenced. In addition, the self-statements varied in the extent of their discrepancy from the subjects' personal beliefs about themselves. The important finding from this investigation was that there were no differences between either positively or negatively valenced self-statements and neutral self-statements on any physiological response (heart rate, skin conductance, and finger pulse volume). The only significant finding was an interaction between valence and discrepancy of self-statements. Negative self-statements of moderate discrepancy generated greater arousal than moderately discrepant but positive self-statements. Rogers and

Craighead concluded that the relationship between cognitions and emotional arousal is more complex than that proposed by Ellis.

Further evidence indicating the greater complexity of the interaction between thoughts and feelings than that assumed by Ellis comes from LaPointe and Harrell's (1978) study of correlational relationships between specific cognitions and particular affective states. Contrary to RET, surprisingly few significant correlations were found. LaPointe and Harrel interpret their results to suggest that specific individual and situational variables mediate the relationship between thoughts and feelings.

Even if it is assumed that faulty thoughts contribute to emotional disorders, do the irrational assumptions listed by Ellis cause neurotic disorders? Goldfried and Sobocinski (1975) reported that the tendency to hold these irrational beliefs was indeed correlated with different forms of anxiety. Alden and Safran (1978) were able to differentiate among unassertive subjects who had sought treatment on the basis of their endorsement of the irrational assumptions identified by Ellis. Subjects who endorsed these assumptions described themselves as being more assertive and uncomfortable in situations requiring assertion — and in fact, were less assertive in a role playing task — than subjects who did not endorse the assumptions.* Of course, as Goldfried (1979) is careful to point out, the Goldfried and Sobocinski (1975) and Alden and Safran (1978) studies are correlational in nature, and one cannot argue from correlation to cause. It may be that increased emotional arousal and unassertive behaviour sensitize the person to certain irrational ideas.

In a well-controlled investigation of the assumption that one's images and self-statements mediate emotional and physiological arousal, Craighead, Kimball, and Rehak (1978) failed to replicate Goldfried and Sobocinski's (1975) findings. In the first of three experiments, Craighead and his colleagues compared students who scored extremely high on the social approval scale of the Irrational Beliefs Test (Jones, 1968) with students who obtained low scores on a number of measures while they were instructed to visualize scenes of social rejection. High-irrational subjects emitted significantly more negative self-referent statements than their low-irrational counterparts, but contrary to predictions from the RET model, no differences were obtained in terms of positive self-statement, self-report of emotional arousal, or physiological arousal. In the second and third experiments in this series, Craighead *et al*. similarly were unable to show differences in reported moods between high- and low-irrational subjects following visualization of social rejection scenes.

Finally there is no evidence that most neurotics share the irrational assumptions described by Ellis. Wilson and O'Leary (1980) have observed that Ellis's hypotheses about what is troubling the client may be irrelevant to a particular client's problems. Many clients assert that they do not hold such beliefs. In favour of Ellis's claims, Goldfried and Davison (1976) report that two of Ellis's notions are especially characteristic of neurotic clients — that "everybody must love me" and "I must be perfect in everything I do". However, these statements of belief are too global and imprecise. For example, few clients believe that literally "everybody must love me". Rather, this means that the client wishes that a few highly significant people love him or her. Similarly, the desire to be perfect in everything usually means that the client has

---

*Similarly, Schwartz and Gottsman (1976) found that the presence of negative self-statements was significantly associated with unassertive behaviour. Indeed, negative self-statements differentiated unassertive from assertive subjects, where subjects' knowledge of what to say and their ability to act assertively in hypothetical situations failed to distinguish between the two groups. It should be noted, however, that these negative self-statements were not based on Ellis' list of irrational ideas but were developed by Schwartz and Gottsman specifically for this study.

unduly high and strict standards of self-reinforcement with respect to specific areas of functioning.

TREATMENT OUTCOME STUDIES

One of the problems encountered in evaluating RET is the difficulty in deciding what defines the treatment. The lack of specificity and operational precision in Ellis's writings (1962, 1977a) prompted Goldfried (1977; Goldfried and Davison, 1976) to incorporate the basic concepts and procedures of RET within a closely defined and replicable treatment method called *systematic rational restructuring.* Goldfried's method differs procedurally from that of Ellis in that a Socratic approach is adopted in contrast to the direct challenging of clients' irrational cognitions that is the hallmark of Ellis' RET. However, the two methods are similar in purpose and will not be distinguished in this evaluation. Other treatment labels that are often assumed to be synonymous with RET include "cognitive restructuring" and "cognitive therapy". These labels often embrace a motley array of methods that differ on important dimensions. On the other hand, labelling a method as "RET" does not guarantee uniform or standardized procedures. Kiesler's (1966) notion of the "therapy uniformity myth" is apposite in these instances and outcome studies must be examined in detail in order to determine which procedures were employed.

Evaluation. Table 6 summarizes the controlled treatment outcome studies on RET.

It is clear that the twenty-one studies presented in Table 6 vary considerably in a number of different ways. In many studies the treatment procedures that were employed are described only in general terms and it is difficult to determine to what extent procedural differences may have contributed to some of the mixed results that are summarized in Table 6. Other studies show that the nature of the treatment designated as RET varies considerably. A critical dimension along which treatments vary concerns the degree to which they incorporated both verbal and behavioural components. For example, Emmelkamp, Kuipers, and Eggeraat (1978) restricted their cognitive restructuring treatment to cognitive relabelling, rational disputation of Ellis's list of irrational assumptions and self-instructional training. In a commentary on this study, Ellis (1979) stated that behavioural retraining is an indispensable component of RET and attributes the inferior showing of cognitive restructuring to this absence. Ellis (in DiLoreto, 1971) similarly attributed the limited efficacy of RET in the DiLoreto (1971) study to a watered-down version of RET that was too didactic in nature and failed to stress the importance of *in vivo* tasks. In like fashion, DiGiuseppe and Miller (1977) suggest that the relative ineffectiveness of RET in the Tiegerman (1975) investigation was due to the lack of "behavioural components such as behavioural rehearsal and outside assignments" (p. 86).

The study by Moleski and Tosi (1976) was the only one in which verbal and behavioural components of RET were systematically manipulated in a factorial design. Contrary to expectation, the inclusion of the behavioural component did not result in greater efficacy. However, these data are inconclusive as the authors themselves remark, since "The time limitations necessitated a less than ideal number of assignments (two) as well as duration of time devoted to each (two weeks). Had the assignments been of larger frequency and duration the results may have been more in the predicted direction" (Moleski and Tosi, 1976b). Another commendable feature of this study was the independent assessment of whether RET was procedurally distinct from systematic desensitization. As Kazdin and Wilson (1978b) have stressed, unequivocal

TABLE 6*

RET: Summary Tabulation of Controlled Outcome Studies

Authors	Population and problem	Type of control or comparison therapy	Measures	Outcome
Alden, Safran, and Weideman (1978)	Under-assertive clients	1. Cognitive behaviour modification (modified RET) 2. Social skills training 3. No-treatment control	Role-playing tasks and self-report measures of assertiveness	$1 \propto 2 > 3$
Brandsma, Maultsby, and Welsh (1978)	"Revolving-door" alcoholics	1. RET conducted by professional therapists 2. RET conducted by a lay therapist 3. Psychodynamic insight therapy conducted by professional therapists 4. Alcoholics Anonymous 5. No-treatment control group	Measures of alcohol consumption; measures of economic and social adjustment and legal status; MMPI and other self-report and questionnaire measures	$1 \propto 2 \propto 3 \propto 4 > 5$ on overall amount of alcohol consumed; $1 \propto 3 > 5$ in terms of number of "dry" days; $1 \propto 3 > 2, 4 \propto 5$ on economic index; 3 superior to 1, 2, 4, 5 in terms of legal problems
Casas (1975)	Public-speaking anxiety	1. Rational restructuring 2. Self-control desensitization 3. Waiting-list control	Behavioural observations, psychophysiological measures; self-report and questionnaire measures of anxiety	$1 = 2 = 3$
Carmody (1978)	Unassertive adults recruited through advertisement	1. RET plus behaviour rehearsal 2. Self-instructional training plus behaviour rehearsal 3. Behavioural rehearsal 4. Delayed-treatment control group	Behavioural observations and self-report measures of assertion and social anxiety	$1 = 2 = 3$ on all measures at post-treatment and 3-month follow-up. $1 > 2 \propto 4$ on in vivo test of generalization at post-treatment

*In these tables the major comparisons are presented in summary form. The direction and significance of the comparison is indicated by symbols showing that one technique was more effective ($>$), or less effective ($<$), not significantly different from ($=$) the other technique(s). The levels of statistical significance reported in the original article are used to reach conclusions about the cumulative efficacy of different techniques.

TABLE 6 (cont.)

Authors	Population and problem	Type of control or comparison therapy	Measures	Outcome
DiLoreto (1971)	Undergraduates with interpersonal anxiety	1. RET 2. Systematic desensitization 3. Client-centred therapy 4. Attention placebo 5. Waiting-list control	Behavioural observations, self-report and questionnaire measures of anxiety	$1 < 2 > 4 \propto 5$ On self-report of anxiety and behavioural observations at post-treatment and 3-month follow-up; $1 > 2 > 3, 4 \propto 5$ on increase in interpersonal activity beyond the treatment setting; $1 > 3, 4 \propto 5$ only with extroverts, $2 > 3, 4 \propto 5$ with both introverts and extroverts
Emmelkamp, Kuipers, and Eggeraat (1978)	Agoraphobic patients	1. Cognitive restructuring (consisting of modified RET and self-instructional training) 2. In vivo exposure	Behavioural measures, clinical ratings, and questionnaire measures of anxiety	$2 > 1$ on all measures
Goldfried, Linehan, and Smith (1978)	Test-anxious subjects recruited by advertisement	1. Rational restructuring 2. Prolonged exposure 3. Waiting-list control	Self-report and questionnaire measures of anxiety	$1 > 2 > 3$ at post-treatment; $1 > 2$ at 6-week follow-up
Jenni and Wollersheim (1979)	Coronary-prone men and women	1. RET 2. Stress management training 3. Waiting-list control	Self-rating scale of Type-A behaviour; anxiety questionnaire; blood pressure; and serum cholesterol	$1 > 3$ on self-report of Type-A behaviour; 1 and $2 > 3$ on anxiety measure; $1 = 2 = 3$ on blood pressure and serum cholesterol
Kanter and Goldfried (1978)	Subjects with interpersonal anxiety, recruited by newspaper advertisements	1. Rational restructuring 2. Self-control desensitization 3. Combined rational restructuring and desensitization 4. Waiting-list control	Behavioural observations; pulse-rate; self-report and questionnaire measures of anxiety	$1 = 2 = 3 = 4$ on behavioural observations and pulse rate; 1 and $3 > 4$ on most self-report measures; 1 and $3 > 2$ on some self-report measures. This pattern of results was maintained at a 2-month follow-up on self-report measures
Karst and Trexler (1970)	Speech anxiety	1. RET 2. Fixed role therapy 3. No-treatment control	Behavioural and self-report measures	$1 = 2 > 3$ on self-report; $1 = 2 = 3$ at 6-month follow-up

TABLE 6 (cont.)

Authors	Population and problem	Type of control or comparison therapy	Measures	Outcome
Lake, Rainey and Papsdorf (1979)	Men (n = 5) and women (n = 19) suffering from severe migraine headaches	1. Digit temperature biofeedback plus RET 2. Digit temperature biofeedback 3. Frontalis EMG biofeedback 4. Waiting-list controls	Daily headache self-ratings; medication	$1 \propto 2 = 3 \propto 4$ at post-treatment and 3 months follow-up
Linehan, Goldfried, and Goldfried, (1979)	Unassertive women subjects recruited by advertisement	1. Rational restructuring 2. Behaviour rehearsal 3. Rational restructuring plus behaviour rehearsal 4. Attention-placebo 5. Waiting-list control	Behavioural tests of assertion; self-report and questionnaire measures of anxiety	$3 = 2 = 1 > 4 \propto 5$ on most behavioural measures; $3 \propto 2 > 1$ on some behavioural measures; $3 = 2 = 1 > 4 \propto 5$ on self-report measures. Same pattern on self-report measures at 8–10 weeks follow-up, but statistically $3 = 2 = 1 = 4$. Groups 3 and 2 showed most generalization of improvement
Maes and Heimann (1972)	Test-anxious high-school students	1. RET 2. Systematic desensitization 3. Client-centred therapy 4. No-contact control	Physiological and questionnaire measures	$1 = 2 > 3 = 4$ on physiological measures; $1 = 2 = 3 = 4$ on questionnaire measures
Margolin and Weiss (1978)	Couples with marital conflict	1. Behavioural training plus cognitive restructuring 2. Behavioural training 3. Non-specific control treatment	Multiple subjective and observational measures of marital adjustment	$1 > 2 = 3$ on specific measures
Moleski and Tosi (1976)	Patients attending a clinic for treatment of stuttering	1. RET with in vivo tasks 2. RET without in vivo tasks 3. Systematic desensitization with in vivo tasks 4. Systematic desensitization without in vivo tasks 5. No-treatment control	Disfluency and speed of rating; questionnaire measure of anxiety	$1 \propto 2 > 3 \propto 4 > 5$ on speech disfluency at post-treatment; $1 \propto 2 > 3 \propto 4$ on speech disfluency and questionnaire measure at 1-month follow-up

TABLE 6 (*cont.*)

Authors	Population and problem	Type of control or comparison therapy	Measures	Outcome
Montgomery (1971)	Test-anxious subjects	1. RET 2. Systematic desensitization 3. Implosion therapy 4. No-treatment control	Questionnaire measures of anxiety	1 = 2 = 3 = 4
Osarchuk (1974)	Test-anxious subjects recruited by advertisement	1. Rational restructuring 2. Self-control desensitization 3. Rational restructuring plus desensitization 4. Prolonged exposure	Self-report and question-naire measures of anxiety	1 = 2 = 3 > 4 at post-treatment and 2-month follow-up
Straatmeyer and Watkins (1974)	Public-speaking anxiety	1. RET 2. RET minus active disputing component 3. Attention-placebo 4. No treatment control	Behavioural observations and self-report of anxiety	1 = 2 = 3 = 4 on all measures
Tiegerman (1975)	Interpersonal anxiety in college students	1. RET 2. Assertion training 3. RET plus assertion training 4. No-contact control	Self-report measures of assertion and anxiety	2 > 3 > 1 > 4
Trexler and Karst (1972)	Public-speaking anxiety	1. RET 2. Attention-placebo control (relaxation training) 3. No-contact control	Behaviour and self-report measures	1 > 2 = 3 at post-treatment and 6-month follow-up on two self-report measures; 1 = 2 = 3 on behavioural measures; 2 > 1 on one subjective anxiety rating
Wolfe and Foder (1977)	Unassertive women	1. Rational-behaviour therapy (behaviour rehearsal plus modelling plus RET) 2. Behaviour rehearsal plus modelling 3. A consciousness-raising group 4. Waiting-list control	Behavioural, self-report and questionnaire measures of anxiety	1 = 2 > 3 ∝ 4 on behavioural measure; 1 > 4 on one self-report measure

interpretation of comparative outcome studies requires that each treatment is implemented adequately in a manner consistent with its fundamental specifications and alternative treatments really are different in practice.

In contrast to many of the studies reviewed here, Brandsma, Maultsby, and Welsh (1978) provide detailed information on the nature of the RET method they employed in their ambitious evaluation of the treatment of chronic alcoholics. In addition to the usual cognitive procedures involving logical analysis and rational disputation, Brandsma et al. (1978) included "conditioning procedures" and other "self-administered behavioural change program(s) such as scheduling, stimulus control procedures, sipping (and) keeping a log of frequency and amount". The latter are well-established behavioural self-control techniques. It would be accurate to term Brandsma et al.'s (1978) treatment a multi-component cognitive-behavioural intervention that goes beyond what is commonly understood by the label "RET", despite the fact that independent assessors of each treatment identified the RET procedure as consistent with the basic specifications of that approach. In their useful series of outcome studies on rational restructuring, Goldfried and his associates provide operationally precise descriptions of this cognitive restructuring technique and specify exactly how it differs from the alternative behavioural techniques with which it is compared. As a result of this and other methodological strengths, the various studies by Goldfried's group permit relatively stronger conclusions to be drawn about the efficacy of cognitive restructuring than other studies listed in Table 6.

Procedural ambiguities and variations make it difficult if not impossible to make systematic comparisons among the different studies. Some examples may be cited. The duration of treatment varied considerably across studies, ranging from extremely brief (e.g. two or four sessions – Wolfe and Fodor, 1977; Trexler and Karst, 1972) to reasonably lengthy interventions (e.g. thirty sessions – Brandsma et al., 1978). Not surprisingly, Goldfried (1979) has suggested that failure to obtain therapeutic improvement in some studies may be directly attributable to treatments that were too short. Differences in treatment length may help explain apparent discrepancies in outcome between two studies.

In view of the often extreme brevity of treatment, it must be asked how it is possible to produce the profound change in philosophical outlook that Ellis sets as the goal of therapy in a handful of treatment sessions? One of the most important questions is whether or not a course of RET succeeds in modifying the irrational beliefs that are postulated to be the root cause of the client's problem. Successful outcomes that take place in the absence of the presumed changes in irrational thinking are open to varying interpretations. Furthermore, studies that show a significant change in irrational beliefs, do not necessarily produce a change in behaviour (e.g. Trexler and Karst, 1972). Results of this character are embarrassing for the RET rationale.

The methodological adequacy of the studies described in Table 6 is uneven. The therapists in these investigations differed in experience and training. In some cases the administration of alternative treatment by the same therapist (usually the investigator himself) introduced a therapist X treatment confound in the data. However, while appropriate experimental controls were lacking in some studies, others showed considerable methodological sophistication. For example, whereas DiLoreto (1971) did not independently determine the adequacy and credibility of the attention-placebo control condition in that study, Goldfried, Linehan, and Smith (1978), Kanfer and Goldfried (in press), Linehan, Goldfried, and Goldfried (1979), and Osarchuk (1974) all explicitly evaluated subjects' expectations of therapeutic success before and after the first treatment session and were able to show that their results could not be attributed to differential demand characteristics or to the credibility of the different treatment rationales (see Kazdin and Wilcoxon [1976] for a discussion of this issue). Another positive feature of many of the studies reviewed here was their inclusion of multiple objective and subjective measures of outcome. Predictably, different treatments produced different results on different measures, and interpretation of specific studies must take this into account.

A major limitation of the studies reviewed here, though it is hardly unique to them, is the conspicuous absence of long-term evaluation of treatment effects. With the sole exception of Brandsma et al.'s (1978) study that included a 1-year follow-up, the longest follow-up was only 6 months, and that in only two of the remaining eighteen studies (Karst and Trexler, 1970; Trexler and Karst, 1972) summarized in Table 6. Another limitation of the evidence on RET concerns the fact that the target problem in the majority of the studies was either test, speech, or mild to moderate interpersonal anxiety. It should be emphasized, however, that not all the studies used anxious college students, a practice that has (at times inappropriately) been criticized. The subjects in the Kanter and Goldfried (1979) and Linehan et al. (1979) studies, for example, were community residents who appeared to be more anxious than the college students in DiLoreto's (1971) study, which has been a target of the critics of analogue research.

Whether the outcome of RET is significantly affected by patients' initial level of anxiety is uncertain. It will be recalled that in the DiLoreto (1971) study, an early and widely cited evaluation of the efficacy of RET, systematic desensitization was significantly superior to control treatments with both introverted and extraverted subjects. RET, however, differed from control treatments only when the introverted subjects were considered. Trying to explain this inferior showing of RET, Goldfried (1979) has proposed that a reanalysis of the data indicates that the introverts were the more anxious subjects. Similarly, Goldfried (1979) notes a *post hoc* finding from the Casas (1975) study showing that within the rational restructuring treatment, subjects who scored highly on the Fear of Negative Evaluation Scale (Watson and Friend, 1969) improved significantly more than those whose scores were low. Could this mean that RET is especially effective with more anxious individuals?

Kanter and Goldfried (1979) tested this possibility in a study employing a 2 X 4 design in which anxiety level (high versus moderate) was crossed with treatment procedure (rational restructuring, self-control desensitization, rational restructuring plus self-control desensitization, or waiting-list control). Subjects were assigned to either the high or moderate anxiety condition on the basis of a median split of scores obtained on the Social Avoidance and Distress Scale (Watson and Friend, 1969). The results show no interaction between anxiety level and treatment procedure. This finding is inconsistent with Goldfried's (1979) explanation of the DiLoreto (1971) data. It would be premature, however, to conclude that anxiety level does not moderate the effects of cognitive restructuring procedures. For one thing, using scores from either the Social Avoidance and Distress Scale (Kanter and Goldfried, 1979) or the Fear of Negative Evaluation Scale (Casas, 1975) to discriminate between high and low socially anxious subjects is a questionable procedure. Goldfried (1979) himself points out that the Social Avoidance and Distress and the Fear of Negative Evaluation Scales might reflect the nature or pervasiveness of anxiety (i.e. general anxiety about social evaluation) rather than intensity of anxiety in relation to specific situations.

Given the disproportionate number of studies on test, speech, or mild to moderate interpersonal anxiety, studies with more varied populations with different and more severe problems are called for. Margolin and Weiss (1978) evaluated the efficacy of cognitive restructuring in the treatment of couples who were experiencing marital conflict. The specific cognitive restructuring procedure used in this study consisted of strategies "to interrupt the negative thoughts that can impede relationship improvement. The therapeutic procedures encouraged spouses to abandon blaming attributions, to accept greater personal responsibility for relationship failure, and to be more accepting of their partners' positive efforts. This approach ... is somewhat similar to Ellis's (1962) rational-emotive psychotherapy ..." (p. 1485). The results of Margolin and Weiss's investigation showed that a cognitive restructuring plus behavioural training produced significantly greater improvement across different measures than behavioural training alone or a non-specific control treatment. The limitations of this study include its brief duration (only four treatment sessions) and the use of unskilled therapists, some of whom were undergraduate students. Additionally, while this study bears on the efficacy of cognitive restructuring procedures in general, the specific method used by Margolin and Weiss cannot reasonably be viewed as a test of RET in particular.

RET has also been applied to samples of disturbed clients. Three such studies described in Table 6 are those by Brandsma et al. (1978), Emmelkamp et al. (1978), and Moleski and Tosi (1976). In a commendable attempt to evaluate the treatment of a complex and debilitating disorder in a controlled, long-term investigation, Brandsma et al. (1978) completed a comparative outcome study of RET with so-called "revolving-door" alcoholics, namely, clients who recurrently enter and then drop out of treatment. In this study, subjects were described as confirmed alcoholics of "lower middle class ... of low normal intelligence ... having legal troubles (e.g. arrested for drunkeness) but fairly socially and psychologically adept". There is wide consensus among professionals that this sort of alcoholic client is unusually difficult to treat successfully — hence the phenomenon of the "revolving-door" alcoholic. Subjects (262 were accepted into treatment) were randomly assigned to one of five different treatment conditions: (a) RET conducted by professional therapists who were skilled in the practice of RET; (b) Insight therapy conducted by experienced professional therapists of diverse backgrounds but who were instructed to adopt a psychodynamic approach; (c) RET conducted by a lay therapist who, as an ex-drug abuser, had been successfully treated by RET himself; (d) Alcoholics Anonymous (AA) started by two volunteers from a local AA group; and (e) a Control group whose members received no specific treatment and were provided with a list of different community agencies that offered services to alcoholics. The maximum duration of therapy was 30 hours, consisting by and large of weekly sessions on an individual basis. (The AA treatment condition, of course, was carried out in a group context.) Multiple measures of outcome were obtained, including numerous objective and subjective indices of improvement.

Of the 262 subjects who were initially accepted for treatment, 104 completed ten or more therapy sessions. There were significantly more drop outs in the AA condition than in the other treatment. At the end of treatment, measures of drinking behaviour consistently showed that all four treatment groups drank significantly less than the control group. The two treatments conducted by professional therapists (RET and Insight) produced the greatest number of "dry days", namely those days on which subjects consume no alcohol at all. All four treatment groups showed significant improvement compared to the control group in terms of arrests for drunkenness. Of these four treatment groups the Insight group showed the greatest reduction in legal problems such as being picked up by the police, being jailed, or making court appearances related to drinking. As an indicator of economic improvement, the professionally administered RET and Insight treatments were superior to the other groups with respect to owning a car. All groups, including the control group, showed improvement over time on general measures of adjustment.

Of the 104 subjects who completed ten or more sessions of therapy, eighty-one (77.9%) participated in follow-up sessions at 3, 6, 9, and 12 months after the end of therapy. The same general pattern of results observed at post-treatment was apparent, with the four treatment groups proving superior to the control group and with the professionally administered RET and Insight groups having the edge in efficacy. As the authors themselves caution, it is difficult to draw firm conclusions from these results. On the one hand, RET conducted by professional therapists tended to be superior to the no-treatment control group on several measures. On the other hand, RET was not superior to the Insight treatment. Treating severely addicted alcoholics successfully provides a searching test for any form of therapy and the failure of RET to improve upon the effects of the comparative Insight treatment must be evaluated with this in mind.

Emmelkamp *et al*. (1978) treated twenty-four agoraphobics with both cognitive restructuring and prolonged exposure *in vivo* using a cross-over design. Patients received five group sessions of each treatment, evaluations of outcome being made after each treatment and at a 1-month follow-up. Outcome was assessed in terms of multiple measures of *in vivo* behavioural performance, independent ratings of phobic anxiety and avoidance in different situations, and a variety of patient self-rating scales. Twenty patients completed the full treatment programme.

Prolonged *in vivo* exposure, irrespective of whether it was the first or second treatment produced significant improvement on the majority of outcome measures, including the behavioural measure of how long patients would persist in a planned walk away from the hospital, where the treatment was conducted, towards town. Cognitive restructuring did not result in significant improvement on the behavioural measure and produced relatively few significant changes on ratings of phobic anxiety or avoidance. These improvements were obtained mainly when cognitive restructuring was the first treatment to be administered. When cognitive restructuring followed prolonged exposure *in vivo* in the cross-over design, hardly any incremental change was noted. Comparatively, prolonged exposure *in vivo* was significantly more effective than cognitive restructuring on a variety of objective and subjective measures at post-treatment and follow-up.

The success of the prolonged exposure *in vivo* treatment was to be expected given that this form of treatment has been repeatedly demonstrated to produce significant improvement in agoraphobic patients (e.g. Emmelkamp and Wessels, 1975; Leitenberg, 1976; Marks, 1978). Several factors may explain the less than favourable showing by cognitive restructuring. Emmelkamp *et al*. (1978) suggest that this cognitive method might be less appropriate for a disorder such as agoraphobia than the less severe, social or evaluative anxiety problems that have been successfully treated by Goldfried (1979) and others. The reason, Emmelkamp *et al*. (1978) suggest, is that the degree of physiological arousal might be greater among agoraphobics and that this physiological arousal is less amenable to cognitive methods of modification. This issue of matching treatment techniques to particular types of problems is addressed later in this chapter.

Another reason for the relative ineffectiveness of cognitive restructuring in this study, as Ellis (1979) has pointed out, may have been the absence of specific behavioural homework assignments. The importance of such a behavioural component is underscored by Emmelkamp *et al*.'s (1978) observation that although the patients were able to think rationally while imagining phobic situations, they found it far more difficult to use rational self-statements in extra-clinic situations (e.g. on the way home from the hospital). Whether a combined cognitive-behavioural treatment would result in greater efficacy remains to be determined.

In contrast to the two previous studies, Moleski and Tosi (1976) found that RET was more effective than a no-treatment control condition or imaginal systematic desensitization in the treatment of stutterers who were patients at a Speech and Hearing Clinic. The superiority of RET was evident on multiple measures of the patients' attitudes towards stuttering, subjective anxiety, and actual speech disfluency. It is also worth recalling from our previous discussion of this study that the addition of two admittedly brief *in vivo* behavioural tasks in either the RET or systematic desensitization treatments did little to affect the results. Establishing that RET is a useful method for treating stuttering will require replication and extension of these findings, including a demonstration that improvement generalizes to different situations in the natural environment and that it is maintained over time. None the less, the results of this study provide support for RET as an effective form of treatment.

Conclusion. In sum, these studies do not provide adequate information on which to reach firm conclusions about the efficacy of RET as a treatment method. Evidence on the long-term efficacy of RET is lacking. Encouragingly, the evidence suggests that RET is more effective than no-treatment or placebo influences on some measures, in most studies. However, it is not possible to conclude that RET is superior to alternative treatment methods such as systematic desensitization, prolonged exposure, or behavioural rehearsal. DiGiuseppe and Miller's (1977) verdict that RET is more effective than systematic desensitization in reducing neurotic anxiety is difficult to sustain in the face of this sketchy and uneven evidence.

We have emphasized the critical importance of specifying the procedural components of RET in a clearly testable manner. In the past, a major problem arose from problems of definition, but recent developments threaten to make RET untestable. In response to criticism of the conceptual and empirical bases of RET made by Mahoney (1977a), Meichenbaum (1977b) and others, Ellis (1977a) argued that RET has been misinterpreted as a treatment approach that is restricted to cognitive restructuring by means of verbal persuasion and logical analysis. He asserts that RET, among other procedures, includes the use of all behaviour therapy techniques, encounter group exercises, Gestalt methods, psychodrama procedures, and unconditional acceptance of the client. In a major statement, Ellis (1977b) drew a distinction between a "general or inelegant RET" and "elegant RET". "Inelegant RET" is equated with cognitive behaviour therapy. Ellis illustrates this by referring to the treatment of an impotent client. Cognitively, the client would be shown that occasional failures need not mean inevitable failure, he would be taught the usual Masters and Johnson-type techniques, informed that there are other ways other than intercourse with which to satisfy his sexual partner, and encouraged to persist with the expectation that he will succeed sexually in the future provided he adheres to these therapeutic prescriptions. In "elegant RET", Ellis states that he would go beyond the cognitive behaviour therapy approach mentioned above.

"I . . . would also try to show this sexually malfunctioning male that even if he never became fully potent, that would be very inconvenient but not 'awful' or 'horrible'; that he could fully accept himself no matter what his sex partners or anyone else thought of him; and that there is no reason why he must or has to succeed sexually — or, for that matter, should succeed in any other goal that he wishes or prefers to succeed at. In the elegant version of RET, therefore, I would try to help him change his fundamental disturbance-creating philosophies, about sex or any other aspect of his life, and try to show him how to deal fairly comfortably, unneurotically, and nonself-downingly with any present or future difficulty that might arise. Although, therefore, elegant RET is invariably done in a general or inelegant RET framework, the reverse is not true: inelegant RET may well, particularly with certain types of clients, omit or treat lightly some of the goals and methods employed in elegant RET" (Ellis, 1977b, p. 74).

Acceptance of Ellis's definition would undermine the comparative research reviewed in Table 6. RET in this sense has yet to be tested, as Ellis (1977b) readily agrees. It is difficult to distinguish this expanded RET approach from Lazarus's (1977) multi-model therapy and it shares the same conceptual problems as the latter (cf. Franks and Wilson, 1976). The one distinctive feature that characterizes the "elegant" RET approach is Ellis's insistence on a basic shift in the client's thinking and philosophy about life as the critical mechanism of therapy and the ultimate criterion of treatment outcome. There is insufficient evidence that such a massive psychological change is feasible or necessary for successful treatment.

Meichenbaum's Self-instructional Training

A second form of cognitive restructuring is self-instructional training (SIT), a method developed by Meichenbaum (1977a). The rationale for this approach derives from two main sources: (1) Ellis's (1970) RET and its emphasis on irrational self-talk as the cause of emotional disturbance; and (2) the developmental sequence according to which children develop internal speech and verbal-symbolic control over their behaviour (Luria, 1961). According to this analysis children's behaviour is first regulated by the instructions of other people; subsequently they acquire control over their own behaviour through the use of overt self-instructions which they ultimately internalize as covert self-instructions.

SIT involves the following steps:

(a) training the client to identify and become aware of maladaptive thoughts (self-statements);

(b) the therapist models appropriate behaviour while verbalizing effective action strategies; these verbalizations include an appraisal of task requirements, self-instructions that guide graded performance, self-statements that stress personal adequacy and counteract worry over failure, and covert self-reinforcement for successful performance;

(c) the client then performs the target behaviour while verbalizing aloud the appropriate self-instructions and later by covertly rehearsing them. Therapist feedback during this phase assists in ensuring that constructive problem-solving self-talk replaces previously anxiety-inducing cognitions associated with that behaviour.

SIT was derived, in part, from Ellis's RET and there are important similarities between the two approaches, as well as some conceptual and procedural differences. Mahoney and Arnkoff (1978) have described these differences as follows:

"Both RET and SIT emphasize the importance of self-statements and thought patterns in adaptive and maladaptive behaviour. However, there are important differences in technique and focus. Where Ellis tends to focus on his set of 'core irrational ideas', Meichenbaum *et al*. have seemed to be more interested in idiosyncratic thought patterns. The latter have also devoted more attention to the role of graduated practice in their cognitive training package. In addition, self-instructional training presents a somewhat more heterogeneous package which contains elements of desensitization, modelling, and behaviour rehearsal. Of particular note is the fact that this approach emphasizes practical coping skills for dealing with problematic situations. While the major emphasis of RET is the *destruction* of maladaptive beliefs, self-instructional training supplants this with a *constructive* phase of skills development. Where RET highlights the *rationality* of a thought — believing that rationality is synonymous with adaptiveness — self-instructional training places more emphasis on its adaptiveness and its constructive alternatives. Thus, while RET posits differences in the thoughts of normal and distressed persons, a self-instructional therapist would place more emphasis on an individual's methods of coping with those thoughts (Meichenbaum, personal communication). In other words, it is not the content or incidence of irrational beliefs that differentiates normal and distressed persons — it is their learned means of coping with these beliefs" (p. 705).

Another procedural difference is that, contrary to Ellis's (1970) style of direct confrontation of clients' irrational ideas, but similar to Goldfried's (1979) approach, Meichenbaum (1977a) adopts a Socratic approach in which therapy is structured so that clients discover for themselves the inaccuracies and distortions in their thinking. The client is helped to identify and alter automatic thoughts through a more gentle and strategic progression of therapeutic intervention.

TREATMENT OUTCOME STUDIES

Unlike the case of RET, there are few difficulties in classifying evaluative studies of SIT since Meichenbaum (1977a) has specified the critical procedural components of this method. Stress inoculation is a variation of SIT and is included in the present review. In some cases treatment procedures that were described as "cognitive therapy", "cognitive training", "stress coping training", and "verbal controlling response" training in the original studies are included here because of their essential similarity to Meichenbaum's procedures. The two studies of "cognitive restructuring" by D'Zurilla, Wilson, and Nelson (1973) and Wein, Nelson, and Odom (1975) are included in Table 7 because these studies are considered to be similar to SIT and RET by proponents and opponents of the cognitive restructuring therapies alike (e.g. DiGiuseppe and Miller, 1977; Ledwidge, 1977; Mahoney, 1974). However, it should be noted that D'Zurilla *et al.* (1973) did not identify their cognitive restructuring procedure with either RET or SIT. Rather, their procedure was designed to provide subjects with a scientific explanation of the origin of their fears and to help them relabel fearful reactions. Although it has gone unnoticed in the literature, Thorpe's (1975) control group ("behavioural insight") was identical to the cognitive restructuring treatments described by D'Zurilla *et al.* (1973) and Wein *et al.* (1975). This underscores the need for operational definitions of treatment methods that all too often are loosely defined. Lastly, the Emmelkamp *et al.* (1978) study that was discussed in the previous section on RET is included here because SIT was one of the three components of the cognitive restructuring treatment programme.

Evaluation. Table 7 summarizes controlled outcome studies on the efficacy of SIT. The thirty-four studies reviewed in Table 7 cover a far wider range of problems than the preceding tabulation of studies on RET, including language and attentional behaviour in hospitalized schizophrenics, agoraphobia, impulsive obesity, impulsive disorders in children, pain responses, tension headache, anger, and social or evaluative anxieties. None the less, over 50% of these studies involved laboratory-based investigations of relatively mild problems of test, public-speaking, and interpersonal anxiety and fear of snakes or animals. In several other instances treatment effects were gauged in terms of improvement on laboratory analogue tasks of perceptual performance (e.g. Meichenbaum and Cameron, 1973; Meichenbaum and Goodman, 1971) or pain (e.g. Horan *et al.*, 1977). Horan *et al.*'s (1977) treatment of tension headache in

TABLE 7

Self-instructional Training: Summary Tabulation of Controlled Outcome Studies

Authors	Population and problem	Type of control or comparison therapy	Measures	Outcome
Arnold and Forehand (1978)	4- and 5-year-old impulsive children	1. Cognitive training 2. Response cost 3. Cognitive training plus response cost 4. Placebo control (instructions, practice, and feed-back)	Analogue measure of impulsivity; classroom matching task	1 = 2 = 3 = 4 on analogue measure of impulsivity, 1 and 3 > 4 on classroom measure
Bornstein and Quevillon (1976)	Overactive pre-school boys	1. SIT 2. Expectancy control (multiple baseline design across subjects)	On task behaviour during classroom activity	1 > 2; generalization of improvement from experimental task to the actual classroom: results maintained 22.5 weeks after baseline
Carmody (1978)	Unassertive adults recruited through advertisement	1. RET plus behaviour rehearsal 2. Self-instructional training plus behaviour rehearsal 3. Behavioural rehearsal 4. Delayed-treatment control group	Behavioural observations and self-report measures of assertion and social anxiety	1 = 2 = 3 on all measures at post-treatment and 3 month follow-up. $1 > 2 \propto 4$ on *in vivo* test of generalization at post-treatment
Douglas, Parry, Marton, and Garson (1976)	Hyperactivity in boys aged 6–12 years	1. SIT plus contingency management in some cases 2. No-treatment control	Psychometric measures of impulsivity and hyper-activity; teacher rating scale	1 > 2 at post-treatment and 3-month follow-up on psychometric measures. No generalization to classroom situation
Dunkel and Glaros (1978)	Obese women	1. SIT 2. Stimulus control 3. Combined SIT and stimulus control 4. Placebo control (relaxation training)	Weight-reduction quotient	1 > 4 and 3 > 2 at 7-week follow-up

TABLE 7 (cont.)

Authors	Population and problem	Type of control or comparison therapy	Measures	Outcome
D'Zurilla, Wilson, and Nelson (1973)	College students fearful of dead animals	1. Cognitive restructuring 2. Systematic desensitization 3. Graduated prolonged exposure 4. No-treatment control	Behavioural avoidance test; self-report and question-naire measures of anxiety	$1 = 2 = 3$; $3 > 4$ on behavioural test; $1 = 2 = 3$; $1 > 4$ on questionnaire measure
Emmelkamp, Kuipers, and Eggeraat (1978)	Agoraphobic patients	1. Cognitive restructuring (consisting of modified RET and self-instructional training) 2. In vivo exposure	Behavioural measures, clinical ratings, and questionnaire measures of anxiety	$2 > 1$ on all measures
Fremouw and Zitter (1978)	College students with speech anxiety	1. Self-instructional training plus relaxation training as a coping skill 2. Behavioural skills training 3. Attention-placebo control 4. Waiting-list control	Behavioural observations self-report and question-naire measures of anxiety	$2 \propto 1 > 4$ on behavioural observations; $2 \propto 1 > 3 \propto 4$ on one self-report measure; $1 = 2 = 3 = 4$ on questionnaire measures of generalization, this pattern of results main-tained at 2-month follow-up
Friedling and S. O'Leary (1979)	7- and 8-year-old hyperactive children	1. Self-instructional training 2. Attention-practice control	On-task behaviour; reading and arithmetic; teacher attention	$1 = 2$ on-task behaviour; $1 > 2$ on one arithmetic index (although interpretation is not unequivocal)
Girodo and Roehl (1978)	College students with a fear of flying	1. Self-instructional training 2. Preparatory information training 3. Combined self-instructional and preparatory training 4. Pseudo-treatment control	Questionnaire measure of somatic and cognitive components of anxiety during (a) routine flying and (b) on unexpected aborted landing approach (a stressor)	$1 = 2 = 3 = 4$ during routine flying; $1 \propto 3 > 4$ during unexpected stressor; $1 = 2 = 3 > 4$ at 4½-month follow-up on one measure; $1 = 2 > 3 \propto 4$ on another
Glass, Gottsman, and Shmurak (1976)	Heterosexual anxiety in male college students	1. SIT 2. Response acquisition (social skills training) 3. Combined SIT and response acquisition 4. Waiting-list control	Behavioural role-playing test; in vivo telephone calls; questionnaire measures	$1 \times 3 > 2 \propto 4$ on untreated role-play situations, number of telephone calls made, and impression made on females; $1 = 2$ on treated role-play situations; $1 = 2 = 3 > 4$ on role-play and phone call meas-ures at 6-month follow-up

TABLE 7 (cont.)

Authors	Population and problem	Type of control or comparison therapy	Measures	Outcome
Goren (1975)	Snake-fearful test-anxious college students	1. SIT 2. Systematic desensitization 3. Combined SIT and systematic desensitization 4. No-treatment control	Behavioural avoidance test; self-report and questionnaire measures of anxiety	1 = 2 = 3 > 4 with fear of snakes and test anxiety respectively
Glogower, Fremouw, and McCroskey (1978)	College students with communication anxiety	1. Knowledge and rehearsal of coping self-instructions 2. Insight into negative self-statements 3. Combination of 1 and 2 4. Discussion of feelings control group 5. Waiting-list control group	Behavioural observations; self-report and questionnaire measures of anxiety	$3 > 1 > 2 \propto 4 \propto 5$ on behavioural and self-report measures at post-treatment and at 6-week follow-up
Holroyd (1976)	Test-anxious subjects recruited by advertisement	1. Cognitive therapy 2. Group systematic desensitization 3. Combined cognitive therapy and desensitization 4. Pseudotherapy/group meditation 5. Waiting-list control	Analogue test performance; grade point average; self-report and questionnaire measures of anxiety	1 > 2 = 3 across all measures at post-treatment and 1-month follow-up
Holroyd, Andrasik, and Westbrook (1977)	Tension headache in community residents	1. Stress-coping training 2. EMG-biofeedback training 3. Waiting-list control	Daily recordings of headache; frontalis EMG readings; anxiety questionnaires	1 > 2 = 3 on headache recordings at post-treatment and 15-week follow-up
Holroyd and Andrasik (1978)	Tension headache in community residents	1. Cognitive self-control (adapted from therapies of Beck, Goldfried, and Meichenbaum) 2. Cognitive self-control plus training in relaxation as a coping skill 3. Headache discussion control group 4. Symptom-monitoring control group	Self-recording of headaches; psychosomatic checklist; EMG measures; assessment of medication usage	1 = 2 = 3 > 4 on patient ratings of headaches; 1 = 2 = 3 = 4 on EMG measures, medication usage; these results maintained at a 6-week follow-up

TABLE 7 (cont.)

Authors	Population and problem	Type of control or comparison therapy	Measures	Outcome
Horan, Hackett, Buchanan, Stone, and Demchik-Stone (1977)	Pain responses in college students	1. Coping skills training (SIT plus coping imagery) 2. Exposure 3. Coping skills plus exposure 4. Non-specific treatment (a "self-help" audiotape by Albert Ellis) 5. No-treatment control	Cold pressor and pressure algometer tasks	$1 = 3 > 2; 3 > 4; 2 = 4 = 5;$ no evidence of generalization of improvement
Hussain and Lawrence (1978)	Test-anxious college students	1. Test-specific stress inoculation training 2. Generalized stress inoculation training 3. Discussion control 4. Waiting-list control	A behavioural test and several self-report and questionnaire measures of anxiety	$1 = 2 = 3 = 4$ on behavioural test; $1 > 3 \propto 4, 2 > 4$ on subjective measures, results maintained at 8-month follow-up
Kanfer, Karoly, and Newman (1975)	5- and 6-year-old children fearful of the dark	1. Self-statements emphasizing competence 2. Self-statements aimed at reducing the aversiveness of the specific stimulus situation 3. Neutral self-statements	Behavioural measures of tolerance of the dark	$1 > 2 > 3$
Kendall and Finch (1978)	Impulsive children, average age of 10.5 years	1. SIT plus response cost contingency 2. Control group with non-contingent rewards	Performance task; self-report rating scales	$1 > 2$ on performance task; generalization to normal classroom according to teachers' ratings; improvement maintained at 2-month follow-up
Margolis and Shemberg (1976)	Process and reactive schizophrenics	1. SIT 2. Practice controls yoked to SIT subjects	Digit symbol and auditory distraction tasks	$1 = 2$
Meichenbaum (1971)	Snake-fearful subjects	1. Mastery modelling plus SIT 2. Mastery modelling alone 3. Coping modelling plus SIT 4. Coping modelling alone	Behavioural avoidance test; self-report measures	$3 \propto 4 > 1 \propto 2$ on all measures; $3 > 1 > 2$ on subjective measures

TABLE 7 (*cont.*)

Authors	Population and problem	Type of control or comparison therapy	Measures	Outcome
Meichenbaum (1972)	Test-anxious students	1. Cognitive modification (SIT plus relaxation training) 2. Systematic desensitization 3. No-treatment control group	Grade point averages, self-report and questionnaire measures of anxiety	$1 \propto 2 > 3$ on self-report of debilitating tests anxiety; $1 > 2 \propto 3$ on grade point average and other questionnaire measures of anxiety
Meichenbaum, Gilmore and Fedoravicius (1971)	Public-speaking anxiety	1. SIT 2. Systematic desensitization 3. Combined SIT and systematic desensitization 4. Attention-placebo 5. Waiting-list control	Behavioural observations, self-report and questionnaire measures of anxiety	$1 = 2 > 3 = 4 > 5$ on behavioural observations; $1 = 2 = 3 > 4 > 5$ on most subjective measures, results maintained at 3-month follow-up
Meichenbaum (1972)	Test anxious college students	1. SIT plus self-control desensitization (i.e. coping imagery and relaxation training) 2. Systematic desensitization 3. Waiting-list control	Analogue test performance; self-report and questionnaire measures, grade point average	$1 > 2 \propto 3$ on behavioural and subjective measures at post-treatment and 1-month follow-up
Meichenbaum and Cameron (1973): Exper. 1	Hospitalized Schizophrenics	1. SIT 2. Practice control 3. No-treatment control	Laboratory perceptual tasks	$1 > 2 > 3$
Exper. 2	Hospitalized schizophrenics	1. SIT 2. Yoked control group	Laboratory perceptual tasks	$1 > 2$; results generalized to an untreated task
Novaco (1976)	Adults with anger control problems	1. SIT 2. Relaxation training 3. Combined SIT and relaxation training 4. Attention placebo	Blood pressure and self-report during imaginal and role-playing tasks	$3 > 1 > 2 > 4$

TABLE 7 (*cont.*)

Authors	Population and problem	Type of control or comparison therapy	Measures	Outcome
Nelson and Birkimer (1978)	Impulsive 2nd and 3rd grade children	1. SIT 2. SIT plus self-reinforcement 3. Attention control 4. No treatment	Matching Familiar Figures (MFF) test	1 = 3 = 4; 2 improved significantly from pre- to post-testing
Robin, Armel and O'Leary (1975)	Kindergarten children with writing deficiencies	1. SIT 2. Direct training (feedback and social reinforcement contingent on performance) 3. No-treatment control	Handwriting performance	1 > 2 > 3; no evidence of generalization effects
Snyder and White (1979)	Adolescent delinquents	1. Self-instructional training 2. Contingency awareness 3. Assessment control	School attendance; impulsive behaviour performance in daily living requirements	1 > 2 and 3
Steele and Barling (1979)	Learning disabled children	1. Self-instructional training 2. Attention-placebo control 3. No-treatment control	Measures of direct treatment effects: the Developmental Test of Visual Perception; a Figure-Ground Visual Perception Test; Matching Familiar Figures Test. Measures of generalization: the WISC-R; the Devereaux Behavior rating scale	1 > 2 ∝ 3 on most measures of direct treatment effects at post-treatment and 5-month follow-up; 1 = 2 = 3 on generalization measures
Thorpe (1975)	Unassertive subjects	1. SIT 2. Systematic desensitization 3. Behaviour rehearsal 4. Behavioural insight therapy (actually the cognitive restructuring treatment of D'Zurilla *et al.* [1973])	Behavioural role-playing test; physiological measures; self-report and questionnaire measures of anxiety	1 = 3 > 2 ∝ on behavioural test; 1 ∝ 3 > 4, 2 > 4 on subjective measures, no evidence of generalization to untreated situations

TABLE 7 (cont.)

Authors	Population and problem	Type of control or comparison therapy	Measures	Outcome
Wein, Nelson, and Odom (1975)	Snake-fearful college students	1. Cognitive restructuring 2. Systematic desensitization 3. Verbal extinction 4. Attention-placebo 5. No-treatment	Behavioural, psychological and subjective measures	1 = 2, 4 = 5 on behavioural test; 1 = 5 on subjective measures
Weissberg (1977)	Public-speaking anxiety	1. SIT and self-control desensitization (coping imagery plus relaxation) 2. Systematic desensitization with coping imagery 3. Systematic desensitization (each group was divided in half so that three groups received direct treatment while the others received vicarious treatment, i.e., watching a video-tape)	Behavioural, self-report and questionnaire measures of anxiety	1 > 2 > 3 overall; direct treatments > vicarious treatment overall

the natural environment is an exception to this trend. As such the clinical efficacy of SIT with more severe problems across more heterogeneous patient populations remains to be demonstrated.

The methodological quality of these thirty-four studies ranges from excellent to inadequate. Several studies included exemplary control procedures. For example, Holroyd (1976) ensured the credibility of his pseudotherapy control group, and Holroyd *et al.* (1977) effectively employed a counter-demand design to rule out therapeutic expectations or placebo influences as alternative explanations of their data. Unfortunately Holroyd's research on headache has other shortcomings (Philips, 1977). In general, the research on SIT follows that of RET in omitting long-term follow-up evaluations, limiting the clinical significance of these findings. The longest follow-up that was reported was 6 months by Glass *et al.* (1976).

Conclusion. Within the limitations noted above, the overall pattern of results across the thirty-four studies in Table 7 is encouraging. SIT was compared with various control conditions and alternative forms of treatment including systematic desensitization, behaviour rehearsal, EMG biofeedback, and operant conditioning procedures. The findings suggest that SIT was significantly superior to control conditions in most studies and equalled or out-performed comparison treatments in others.

Generalization effects. The frequent failure to obtain generalization and maintenance of treatment-produced improvement in behaviour therapy has received increasing theoretical and empirical attention (cf. Bandura, 1977a; Franks and Wilson, 1978; Stokes and Baer, 1977). It is often assumed that the use of cognitive procedures such as RET or SIT will result in greater generalization of treatment effects than the modification of specific behavioural response patterns. The notion is that the alteration of cognitive mediating processes will result in change that is less stimulus-bound than that produced by behavioural techniques that modify behaviour directly. It is therefore of theoretical and practical importance to inquire whether cognitive treatment methods such as RET and SIT produce significant generalization effects.

Several of the studies in Tables 6 and 7 contain data on generalization. Consider the data on SIT first. On the positive side, Bornstein and Quevillon (1976), Glass, Gottsman, and Shmurak (1976), Kendall and Finch (1978). Meichenbaum (1972), Meichenbaum and Cameron (1973), and Meichenbaum and Goodman (1971) all reported evidence of generalization. However, these findings must be tempered by the following considerations. In neither the Kendall and Finch (1978) nor the Meichenbaum (1972) studies can generalized treatment effects be attributed to SIT *per se* since each cognitive therapy included other treatment techniques. Kendall and Finch (1978) combined a response cost procedure that involved tangible consequences with self-instructional training. In Meichenbaum's (1972) "cognitive modification" technique, test-anxious subjects were taught how to use relaxation as an active coping skill during guided rehearsal of specific responses in addition to SIT.

Meichenbaum and Goodman (1971) found generalized improvement in performance on the Picture Arrangement sub-test of the WISC but not the Block Design on the Coding sub-tests. Increased response latency was observed on the Matching Familiar Figures test, but the number of errors made did not change. SIT had no effect on classroom behaviour. The fact that children were trained on tasks almost identical to those which showed change permits only limited conclusions about generalization.

Uncontrolled factors might have contributed significantly to the generalization effects obtained by Bornstein and Quevillon (1976). Friedling and S. O'Leary (1979) point out that Bornstein and Quevillon did not assess the behaviour of the teachers in their study. As the authors themselves have acknowledged, increases in positive behaviour of the teacher may have been a key factor in the enhancement of generalization and maintenance effects. Of greater importance is the fact that the Bornstein and Quevillon (1976) findings have not been replicated. S. O'Leary (1977) has reported both her own and Bornstein's personal failure to replicate the original results showing generalization of improvement on laboratory analogue tasks to actual classroom behaviour.

In a study of the effects of SIT with 7- and 8-year-old hyperactive children, Friedling and S. O'Leary (1979) failed to find evidence of improvement in "on-task behaviour" in the classroom. Nor did the SIT group prove superior to the attention-practice control group on a measure of reading performance. The only positive effect of SIT was on an arithmetic task, although pre-treatment differences in performance complicate interpretation of this finding. Friedling and S. O'Leary observed that the training materials in their SIT group most closely resembled arithmetic problems and did not involve reading. They conclude that these data support the view that SIT has the greatest effect on skills that are already in the child's repertoire but which fell short of optimal performance. Additionally, they suggest that SIT generalizes to tasks that are most similar to the original training conditions. Finally, Friedling and S. O'Leary cite two unpublished doctoral dissertations (Combs, 1977; Jackson, 1977) that failed to show generalization of SIT to dissimilar tasks.

Several other studies demonstrating a treatment effect of SIT have failed to provide evidence of generalization of task- or situation-specific effects (Douglas, Parry, Marton, and Garson, 1976; Fremouw and Zitter, 1978; Horan, Hackett, Buchanan, Stone, and Demchik-Stone, 1977; Robin, Armel, and O'Leary, 1975; Steele and Barling, 1979; Thorpe, 1975). The study by Steele and Barling with learning disabled people is particularly noteworthy since it improves upon previous tests of SIT in several ways. In most studies of SIT relatively brief training sessions, typically ranging from 2 to 6 hours (e.g. Bornstein and Quevillon, 1976; Friedling and S. O'Leary, 1979), have been used. Steele and Barling investigated the effects of twenty training sessions over an 11-week period. Most importantly, Steele and Barling carried out an independent evaluation to check whether or not children were self-instructing as a result of treatment. Of the other studies of SIT reviewed here, only Robin, Armel, and O'Leary (1975) included a comparable assessment, even though it is critical to a theoretical analysis of SIT. Without a demonstration that subjects do self-instruct following treatment, behaviour change could not be attributed unequivocally to the effects of self-verbalization. Steele and Barling showed that subjects in their SIT group engaged in significantly more self-instruction than the controls. Direct effects of treatment, that focused specifically on perceptual skills, were reliably demonstrated. However, no generalization to academic tasks or classroom behaviour was found.

Nor do the generalization data from studies of RET in Table 6 provide much support for the notion that cognitive restructuring methods facilitate generalized treatment outcomes. One of the few studies reporting generalization effects is Carmody's (1978). He found that RET, SIT, and behaviour rehearsal were equally effective in increasing assertiveness in unassertive adults. However, on a contrived *in vivo* test of assertiveness in which subjects were presented with increasingly persuasive requests to help a confederate of the experimenter with some laboratory equipment, RET was significantly superior to both the waiting-list control condition and SIT. No such generalization effect was obtained on two other behavioural measures of assertiveness. One of these measures was performance during role-playing of specific situations that had not been part of the actual treatment process. There were no differences among the treatment or between the treatments and the control group. (These findings are consistent with Thorpe's [1975], and the treatment literature on assertion and social skills training as a whole.) The second unsuccessful measure was an unannounced phone-call at follow-up when a confederate of the experimenter tried to sell subjects a magazine subscription. As the author himself notes, these negative results limit the significance of the single finding on the contrived *in vivo* test. Moreover, it is unclear why RET should differ from SIT but not behaviour rehearsal on this measure. The logic of cognitive restructuring methods cannot easily accommodate such a finding.

Kanter and Goldfried (1979) have claimed that rational restructuring resulted in greater generalization of anxiety reduction to non-social situations in their comparative outcome study of rational restructuring versus self-control desensitization, and a waiting-list control condition in the treatment of social anxiety. A closer look at their data, however, indicates that this apparent generalization is a weak or tenuous one at best. First, it should be emphasized that there were no differences of any kind on either the behavioural or physiological measures of outcome. Secondly, Kanter and Goldfried (1979) used a trait anxiety inventory (Spielberger, Gorsuch, and Lushene, 1970) and the Irrational Beliefs Test (Jones, 1968) as their questionnaire measures of generalization. On these two measures, rational restructuring was significantly superior to self-control desensitization at post-test. In addition, rational restructuring resulted in a marginally significant superiority over the waiting-list control condition on the "Total Nonsocial" dimension of the S–R Inventory of Anxiousness (Endler, Hunt, and Rosenstein, 1962). Other items on this inventory failed to show any generalization effect. A similarly limited finding of generalized treatment effects produced by rational restructuring in the treatment of test anxiety that was confined to selected self-report measures, characterizes the Goldfried, Linehan, and Smith (1978) study.

More extensive data on the generalization produced by rational restructuring are reported by Linehan *et al.* (1979). The results of this study indicated that behaviour rehearsal, either alone or in combination with rational restructuring, showed the greatest improvement in assertion during role-playing outcome measures. One index of generalization was performance on novel role-playing situations at post-treatment. As a whole, behaviour rehearsal resulted in greater generalization than rational restructuring which in turn was superior to the waiting-list control condition. Another measure of generalization, similar to that employed by Carmody (1978), was a contrived situational test of assertiveness in the laboratory – the "nudge" test! In short, this test required the beleagured subject to respond assertively in the face of harassment by a confederate while completing a questionnaire and to refuse several unreasonable requests. Consistent with the previous results, behaviour rehearsal with or without rational restructuring produced the most generalization. Finally, interpreting changes on the Fear of Negative Evaluation and Social Avoidance and Distress Scales as evidence of treatment-produced generalization, Linehan *et al.* (1979) found that the only significant difference was the superiority of the combined behaviour rehearsal and rational restructuring procedure over the waiting-list control group.

In a comprehensive review of behavioural self-control methods in the treatment of test anxiety, Denney (in press) concludes that whereas behavioural techniques like systematic desensitization have typically produced decreases in self-report of debilitating anxiety, concomitant improvement in test performance and academic measures has been obtained infrequently. Denney also concludes that to the extent that treatment methods for test anxiety include some form of cognitive restructuring, significant changes on performance measures are more probable. Indeed, it appears that cognitive methods are well suited to the treatment of test anxiety, a point that we develop later in this chapter.

Related to the issue of generalization is Meichenbaum's (1973) contention that a cognitive restructuring method such as SIT is more effective in treating generalized or abstract anxiety disorders than a specific, more clearly defined anxiety-related problem. The basis for this proposal was a *post hoc* analysis of the Meichenbaum, Gilmore, and Fedoravicius (1971) data indicating that SIT was more effective with those subjects who scored high on the Social Avoidance and Distress Scale whereas the reverse was true for subjects with low scores on this scale. In a direct test of this hypothesis, Goren (1975) found that systematic desensitization and SIT were equally effective in producing significantly greater improvement than control groups in the treatment of both snake phobias (a highly focused specific fear) and test anxiety (a more abstract fear). Also inconsistent with this hypothesis is Kanter and Goldfried's (1979) finding that high versus moderate scores on the Social Avoidance and Distress Scale failed to interact with either rational restructuring or self-control desensitization. The hypothesis that cognitive restructuring methods would fare better than desensitization with a more generalized, abstract fear would have predicted an interaction between rational restructuring and subjects who scored high on the Social Avoidance and Distress Scale.

Beck's Cognitive Therapy

A third approach to cognitive restructuring is Beck's (1976) "cognitive therapy". Beck (1963) developed this cognitive approach to the understanding and treatment of clinical disorders, particularly depression, independently of Ellis's RET. There is considerable overlap among these cognitive restructuring procedures. As in RET and self-instructional training, the ultimate goal of cognitive therapy is the development of adaptive thought patterns. Cognitive therapy includes the following basic phases:

(a) clients become aware of their thoughts;

(b) they learn to identify inaccurate or distorted thoughts;

(c) these inaccurate thoughts are replaced by accurate, more objective cognitions; and

(d) the therapist provides feedback and reinforcement for cognitive and behavioural change.

The specific procedures used to accomplish these therapeutic objectives are described in a treatment manual (Beck, Rush, Shaw, and Emery, 1977). They are both behavioural and cognitive in nature. The former include the prescription of an explicit activity schedule, graded tasks aimed at providing mastery and success experiences, and various homework assignments. The latter include several techniques of which "distancing" and "decentering" are examples. Distancing is the ability to view one's thoughts more objectively, to draw a distinction between "I believe" (an opinion that is open to disconfirmation) and "I know" (an "irrefutable" fact). Teaching these clients to separate themselves from vicariously experiencing the adversities of others is known as decentering. For example, an agoraphobic women, hearing that a friend of her neighbour died of a heart attack, becomes anxious over the same thing happening to her family.

Evaluation. Controlled research on the efficacy of Beck's cognitive therapy is presently limited to a few studies. The most important of these is a major comparative outcome study that pitted cognitive therapy against pharmacotherapy in the treatment of depression at the out-patient Psychiatry Department at the University of Pennsylvania (Rush, Beck, Kovacs, and

Hollon, 1977). Subjects in this investigation were forty-one depressed out-patients (15 men and 26 women) between the ages of 18 and 65 years. On average, they had been chronically or intermittently depressed for about 9 years, 75% reported suicidal ideas and 12% had a history of previous suicide attempts. The majority had had previous psychotherapy without success and 22% had been hospitalized as a result of their depression. MMPI profiles indicated that these subjects were severely disturbed. Subjects were randomly assigned to either the cognitive therapy or the pharmacotherapy (imipramine) treatment. The therapists comprised eleven psychiatric residents, two post-doctoral and two pre-doctoral clinical psychologists, and three psychiatrists who had recently completed their training. Most therapists had minimal experience in the practice of psychotherapy although each had treated at least one depressed patient with cognitive therapy. All the psychiatrists had received substantial training and experience in the pharmacological treatment of depression. Treatment for both groups averaged 11 weeks.

Treatment outcome was assessed using self-rating and clinical rating scales of depression as well as standardized personality inventories. Patients completed the Beck Depression Inventory, the reliability and validity of which has been documented (Beck, 1967), and an independent clinician (who was not blind to the treatment procedures) completed the Hamilton Rating Scale for Depression (Hamilton, 1969) every fortnight. Complete evaluations were conducted at post-treatment and at monthly intervals during a 6-month follow-up.

Results showed that depression was substantially reduced by both treatments; however, cognitive therapy produced significantly greater improvement on self-ratings and clinical ratings of depression. Seventy-nine per cent of the clients in the cognitive therapy condition underwent marked improvement or complete remission as compared to 23% of the clients in the pharmacotherapy condition. These treatment differences were maintained at 3- and 6-month follow-ups. Aside from being more effective, cognitive therapy was associated with a significantly lower drop-out rate over the course of the study. This is an important finding since there is good evidence that many clients who drop out of treatment are treatment failures. If statistical analysis of outcome results are based only on those clients who complete treatment, a biased or artefactually favourable picture may emerge. In this study, cognitive therapy was superior to pharmacotherapy irrespective of whether the drop-outs were included in the analysis — an encouraging finding for the newer method.

Several features of this study require emphasis. The cognitive therapy was administered by eighteen different therapists. The majority of them were committed to the psychodynamic approach, had no expertise in cognitive behaviour therapy, and participated in the study as part of their psychiatric training. This minimizes the likelihood of an explanation of treatment differences based on therapist factors or demand characteristics as opposed to the cognitive therapy treatment *per se*. It also shows that cognitive therapy can be effectively provided by inexperienced therapists after relatively brief training. The independent clinicians ratings of subjects' depression were not blind, as a result of which bias may have been introduced. However, Rush *et al.* (1977) point out that these ratings paralleled self-ratings on the widely accepted Beck Depression Inventory.

The claimed superiority of Beck's cognitive therapy is particularly interesting since pharmacotherapy represented the most powerful comparative treatment method that could have been chosen. Tricyclic anti-depressant drugs have been shown to be more effective than other treatments, including traditional psychotherapy, and are widely viewed as the recommended therapy for depression. Moreover, the results obtained with pharmacotherapy in this study were said to be comparable to previous findings with anti-depressant drugs. From this, one may tentatively infer that it was the superiority of the cognitive therapy rather than the inadequacy of the drug treatment that accounted for difference in treatment outcome. However, in their commentary on the Rush *et al.* study, Becker and Schuckit (1978) argued that the pharmacotherapy condition was not an optimal test of drug treatment for depression. Specifically, Becker and Schuckit contend that imipramine may be less effective with the sort of chronically depressed population Rush *et al.* treated. They suggest that lithium carbonate is more appropriate for recurrent depressions. They also argued, and with success, that the drug dosages might have been inadequate. Most critical of all, the drugs were not administered for a satisfactory period. Rush *et al.* replied that their results were comparable to other findings obtained with drug treatments, but this is open to dispute. The queries about the adequacy of the drug treatment, combined with the possibility of rater bias, recommend caution in assessing the claims made by Rush *et al.* but the results undoubtedly encourage serious attention and replications.

The findings give initial support for the efficacy of cognitive therapy and its application to the treatment of depression in particular. An effective psychological method of managing depresssion would be of great value.

"Even if the efficacy of the Rush *et al.* cognitive approach only approximates the results of an optimally medicated chronic or recurrent comparison group, it would provide a substantial contribution. A fair number of patients have adverse side effects to routinely and sometimes inappropriately administered antidepressants (Kotin, Post, & Goodwin, 1973), and the effects of long-term usage of such drugs, while encouraging, has not been fully ascertained. Also it seems likely that diminished self-esteem, a central feature in many depressions, would be more durably enhanced by self-regulated than by drug-regulated measures. Patently, the job that remains is to determine who responds best to what" (Becker & Schukit, 1978, p. 196).

Beck's cognitive restructuring method has also been compared to a behavioural approach in the treatment of depression (Shaw, 1977). The behavioural treatment was based on Lewinsohn's (1974) analysis of depression, and included the use of directed activity schedules and behaviour rehearsal techniques designed to teach better communication and social reinforcement skills. An attention-placebo and a no-treatment control group completed the experimental design. The attention-placebo condition consisted of a non-directive group discussion of the subjects' feelings about their depression and why they were depressed. The subjects were college students aged between 18 and 26 years, a much younger population than Rush *et al.*'s. All treatment involved 16 hours of therapy over a 4-week period.

The results showed that the cognitive restructuring method produced significantly greater decreases in depression than either the behaviour modification or attention-placebo methods, as measured by self-ratings and clinical ratings. There was no difference between the behaviour modification and attention-placebo groups. An independent evaluation of subjects' perceptions of the value of the different treatment programmes revealed no significant group differences. This commendable methodological check strengthens the confidence that can be placed in the superiority of the cognitive restructuring method on this occasion. The degree of improvement was similar to that obtained by Rush *et al.* A 1-month follow-up indicated that the cognitive group was still superior to the behaviour modification group although the difference was no longer statistically significant. These findings provide further slight support for Beck's cognitive therapy, but they must be interpreted with equal caution. Firstly, 1 month is too short a follow-up period. The fact that the cognitive method was no longer significantly more effective at this point raises questions about its long-term value. Secondly, the investigator was the single therapist for all treatment groups. This treatment X therapist confound prevents one from discounting inadvertent therapist bias as an influence on the outcome of therapy.

In a similar comparative outcome study, Taylor and Marshall (1977) compared four treatment conditions: (a) a cognitive method based on Beck's approach; (b) a behaviour modification method based on Lewinsohn's approach; (c) a combined cognitive-behavioural group; and (d) a no-treatment control group. The subjects were undergraduate or graduate students who were less depressed than subjects in either the Rush *et al*. or Shaw (1977) studies. The combined method proved to be the most effective. However, the absence of follow-up measures and the fact that a single therapist administered all treatments diminishes the value of these results.

Although not an evaluation of Beck's cognitive therapy, a study by Zeiss, Lewinsohn, and Munoz (1979) is directly relevant to the appraisal of cognitive restructuring in the treatment of depression. Moderately to severely depressed out-patients were randomly assigned to one of three treatment groups focusing on either interpersonal skills; cognitive reappraisal; or an increase in pleasant events. The cognitive treatment was designed "to facilitate changes in the way patients thought about reality". Specifically, patients were asked to write "fixed-role" descriptions of how they would have to think to reduce their depression, a technique adapted from Kelly's (1955) fixed-role therapy. In addition, a number of other cognitive self-control techniques were employed "including thought stopping and Premacking of positive thoughts (Mahoney, 1974) and Meichenbaum's self-talk procedure. Rational-emotive concepts were covered, and a procedure for disputing irrational thoughts was presented . . ." (p. 433).

The results of this study are provocative. All three treatments showed significant improvement over time, across multiple measures of outcome. However, there were no significant differences among the treatments. Nor were treatment effects always significantly superior to the noticeable improvement shown by a waiting-list control group. None of the treatments had a specific effect on the dependent measure that was most closely related to the nature of the particular procedure in question. For example, behavioural measures of assertion and social skills were considered most relevant to the interpersonal skills training treatment while the cognitive treatment was predicted to affect measures such as ratings of cognitive style, self-report of specific thoughts, and the Subjective Probability Questionnaire. The latter was designed to tap Beck's (1976) conception of the cognitive triad — that depressed patients have a negative view of the self, the world, and the future. The absence of a differential affect on different measures is disappointing and we concur with Zeiss *et al*.'s caution that outcome studies should evaluate the extent to which treatment effects are directly related to changes in those variables that are assumed to mediate therapeutic improvement. Zeiss *et al*. speculate that the comparable effects of all three treatments — and the improvement shown by the waiting-list control group — might be attributable to increases in levels of self-efficacy, as suggested by Bandura (1977a). The problem with this analysis, however, is that we would expect the different treatments to produce different degrees of self-efficacy with corresponding differences in specific measures of outcome. These theoretical issues will have to be addressed in future studies on outcome research depression.

Conclusion. At the present stage of its development and evaluation, it is impossible to arrive at a conclusion about the efficacy of Beck's cognitive therapy. Clearly the positive findings on cognitive therapy require replication and extension. We also look forward to the application of cognitive therapy to disorders other than depression, such as phobias and other anxiety-related problems. None the less, the initial results are encouraging.

Discussion

The foregoing discussion provides a comprehensive although not exhaustive review of the present evidence on the efficacy of the different cognitive restructuring methods. Although we have referred to some studies that bear directly on the theoretical assumptions behind cognitive restructuring methods, particularly RET, our purpose has been to examine the available empirical evidence of therapeutic outcome. A full analysis of the theoretical basis of these treatment methods is beyond the scope of this chapter. However, whatever the theoretical limitations of cognitive restructuring techniques, they have been shown to hold considerable promise. Despite the limitations imposed by a heavy emphasis on the treatment of a relatively narrow number of problems, some unevenness in their degree of methodological adequacy, and the absence of the necessary long-term follow-ups of initial treatment success, cognitive restructuring methods have chalked up some encouraging results. In many instances these positive results have been obtained in well-controlled, methodologically sound studies that permit a safe interpretation of treatment efficacy. It is perhaps this feature of the developing literature on cognitive restructuring that is most reassuring — a welcome and refreshing commitment, in principle if not always in practice, to the rigorous experimental evaluation of techniques. Contrary to Bergin and Lambert's (1978) recent synopsis, cognitive restructuring methods do not rest on a lesser empirical base than traditional psychoanalytic, humanistic, or client-centred approaches. Rather, there is growing evidence of their efficacy, and a high rate of experimental successes.

As with any new development in the treatment of clinical disorders, cognitive restructuring methods have generated controversy. Whereas some have applauded the increasing prominence of this new cognitive connection, there are those who have been more critical (see Mahoney, 1974; Franks and Wilson, 1978, 1979; Rachlin, 1977). Much of the criticism of cognitive restructuring techniques has centred on the postulated theoretical mechanisms and the compatibility of these techniques with behaviour therapy (e.g. Wolpe, 1976). However, shifting the focus from *why* they might work, Ledwidge (1977) has also queried *whether* they work and whether their development should be encouraged. Comparing what he calls "cognitive behavior modification" (a major part of which is cognitive restructuring) with "behavior therapy", Ledwidge (1977) concluded that the former is a "step in the wrong direction". In view of the seriousness of this claim and the amount of controversy that Ledwidge's (1977) review has ignited (Franks and Wilson, 1979; Ledwidge, 1979; cf. Locke, 1979; Mahoney and Kazdin, 1979; Meichenbaum, 1979), it is worth taking a closer look at his argument. Without presenting a full critical analysis, the following points can be made.

In short, Ledwidge (1977) based his conclusion on three types of evidence: "(a) controlled studies comparing the effectiveness of the new cognitive behavior modification techniques with traditional behavior therapy procedures, (b) studies comparing the effectiveness of two traditional behavior therapy techniques in which one of the procedures relies less on cognitive operations than does the other, and (c) data from other areas of psychology (attitude change, perception) that bear on the relationship between cognition and behavior change." According to Ledwidge, the comparative outcome data indicate no difference between the two approaches. The latter two sources of evidence are said to favour behaviour therapy.

It can be objected, contrary to Ledwidge, that there is little to be gained by comparing arbitrarily defined categories of "cognitive" versus "behavioural" methods. In his analysis, behaviour therapy is distinguished from cognitive behaviour modification by the focus of the intervention. Behaviour therapy is defined as the treatment of maladaptive behaviour itself rather than some activity assumed to mediate the problematic behaviour. Cognitive behaviour modification is treatment aimed at altering thought patterns that mediate behaviour. Immediately a problem is encountered. The radical behaviouristic or operant conditioning approach is avowedly non-mediational and seeks to modify behaviour directly (e.g. Lacey and Rachlin, 1978) but the neobehaviouristic approach pioneered by Eysenck and Wolpe is an unequivocally mediational approach. One may prefer the mediational model of two-factor theory or some variation of that conditioning theory to a cognitive mediational model, but a mediational model remains a mediational model by any other name (Wilson and O'Leary, 1980). Ledwidge distinguishes between "behavior therapy" and "cognitive behavior modification" on debatable theoretical grounds.

For example, systematic desensitization is designated a behaviour therapy technique on the following grounds:

> "The technique qualifies as behavior therapy in that it concentrates on maladaptive behavior itself (autonomic reactions to phobic stimuli as reflected in subjective reports thereof) and is definitely not a CBM (cognitive behavior modification) technique in that no attempt is made to modify the client's patterns of thought (faulty premises, assumptions, attitudes, and the like) assumed to mediate the problematic behavior. Furthermore, the active ingredient in the reciprocal inhibition process is muscular relaxation, definitely a behavioral technique, and the rationale for the procedure (the learning of a response to a stimulus that is incompatible with the response to be eliminated) is derived from S–R learning theory" (p. 357).

This justification contains several logical and factual errors. First, asking the patient to imagine an event involves a cognitive process. Ledwidge acknowledges the obvious, namely, that patients are asked to "introspect". It simply will not do to try and escape the theoretical analysis that this fact requires by arbitrarily declaring that this is "trivial". Second, it is not the case that "the maladaptive behavior itself" is always an autonomic reaction to phobic stimuli. It is often the avoidance behaviour itself that causes phobics to seek therapy and that is the primary target of treatment (e.g. Leitenberg, 1976). Furthermore, it can be argued that the assessment and treatment of anxiety-related disorders requires a tripartite analysis in which the person's overt behaviour, autonomic arousal, and subjective distress all receive explicit attention (Hodgson and Rachman, 1974). Finally, contrary to Ledwidge's assertion about the "active ingredient" in systematic desensitization, the theoretical mechanisms of this technique are still a matter of debate (e.g. Bandura, 1977a; Borkovec, 1979; Davison and Wilson, 1973; Kazdin and Wilcoxon, 1976; Wilson and Davison, 1971). To take an example, Bandura (1977a) has proposed that systematic desensitization and other fear-reduction methods, such as flooding and modelling, work because they provide sources of information that alter self-efficacy expectations. If one accepted this interpretation then systematic desensitization would be classified as a "cognitive behavior modification" technique in terms of Ledwidge's scheme.

Modelling is another technique that Ledwidge classifies as "behavior therapy", despite Bandura's social learning theory which emphasizes the crucial role of cognitive mediating processes in observation learning. Although some operant theorists have struggled to fit vicarious learning into an operant conditioning framework, they have had little success. Rosenthal and Zimmerman (1978) provide an incisive analysis of the theoretical difficulties vicarious learning processes pose for the non-mediational operant approach. It is certainly the case that the various *in vivo*, symbolic, and covert modelling procedures that are currently employed by behaviour therapists and that enjoy considerable empirical support (Rachman, 1976;

Rosenthal and Bandura, 1978) have not *derived* from operant conditioning but from cognitive social learning theory. Classifying therapeutic techniques as "behavioural" or "cognitive" on the basis of theoretical mechanisms is to confuse process with procedure.

Another problem that a simplistic categorization of diverse therapeutic techniques encounters is that most treatment methods are multifaceted, consisting of behavioural, affective, and cognitive components. As such they defy sorting into simple categories. Beck's (1976) cognitive therapy is a case in point. Despite the name, it is a deliberate amalgam of explicit behavioural methods (e.g. graded *in vivo* behavioural assignments) and cognitive restructuring strategies (e.g. decentring and distancing). Then there is the previously emphasized point that behavioural *procedures* might be effective because they produce changes in cognitive *processes* that govern behaviour (Bandura, 1977a). For instance, in discussing the results of their study comparing prolonged *in vivo* exposure with a cognitive restructuring treatment, Emmelkamp *et al.* (1978) point out that:

> "Giving a form of treatment a name is not the same as elucidating the therapeutic process involved. Whether the treatment 'cognitive restructuring' does actually produce a modification of cognitive processes is a debatable point. On the other hand, the effects of prolonged exposure *in vivo* could at least partly be explained in terms of cognitive restructuring. During treatment with prolonged exposure *in vivo* clients notice, for example, that their anxiety diminishes after a time and that the events which they fear, such as fainting or having a heart attack, do not take place. This may lead them to transform their unproductive self-statements into more productive ones: 'There you are, nothing will go wrong with me'. A number of clients reported spontaneously that their 'thoughts' had undergone a much greater change during prolonged exposure *in vivo* than during cognitive restructuring. It is possible that a more effective cognitive modification takes place through prolonged exposure *in vivo* than through a procedure which is focused directly on such a change" (p. 40).

As a result of the problems involved in identifying the critical processes that are responsible for successful treatment procedures, a more useful approach to evaluation would entail a detailed analysis of methods in which the contribution of specific treatment components is assessed.

In terms of a social learning analysis (and indeed most other analyses), behaviourally based treatment methods would be predicted to be more effective than those that rely upon purely symbolic (imagery or verbal) operations (cf. Bandura, 1977a). The evidence tends to bear out this prediction. Participant modelling, a performance-based method, has been shown to be significantly more effective in eliminating phobic behaviour than either symbolic modelling or imaginal systematic desensitization (Bandura, Blanchard, and Ritter, 1969; Blanchard, 1970) or covert modelling (Thase and Moss, 1976). Similarly, Rachman and Hodgson (1979) have noted the superiority of performance-based treatment over imaginal and vicarious methods in the modification of obsessional—compulsive disorders. Other studies have shown the superiority of performance-based treatment over imaginal desensitization (Crowe, Marks, Agras, and Leitenberg, 1972; Sherman, 1972; Weissberg, 1977), imaginal flooding (Emmelkamp and Wessels, 1975; Stern and Marks, 1973), or cognitive restructuring (Emmelkamp *et al.*, 1978). Finally, Kockott, Dittmar, and Nusselt (1975) and Mathews, Bancroft, Whitehead, Hackmann, Julier, Bancroft, Gath, and Shaw (1976) reported that sexual dysfunction was most effectively treated by a Masters and Johnson-type programme that relied on directed practice *in vivo* as opposed to imaginal systematic desensitization. However, the early evidence suggesting that combined cognitive-behavioural therapy may be more effective than solely behavioural methods (e.g. Dunkel and Glaros, 1977; Shaw, 1977; Taylor and Marshall, 1977) or pharmacotherapy (Rush *et al.*, 1977) provides some support for the proponents of a combined cognitive-behavioural approach to the treatment of some disorders.

As Tables 6 and 7 show, it has been common practice to compare a technique such as systematic desensitization that has traditionally been dubbed as a behaviour therapy method (but incorporates imaginal stimuli), with techniques that emphasize covert verbal operations (e.g. RET or SIT) and are classified as cognitive methods. Once again, it is more constructive to analyse the contribution of specific treatment components than to engage in inferences about "behavioural" versus "cognitive" processes. From a social learning perspective such as Bandura's (1977b) there is little *a priori* reason to expect major differences in efficacy between those techniques that emphasize visual imagery and those that rely upon verbal operations. In the ultimate analysis, both sets of techniques involve symbolically based procedures. Difficult as it is to generalize from the findings in Tables 6 and 7, it can be argued that this appears to be the case. In general, there are few consistent, significant differences between systematic desensitization and either RET or SIT.

The efficacy of any technique cannot properly be assessed except in relation to specified problems. For example, cognitive restructuring methods appear to be particularly effective in the treatment of test anxiety (e.g. Denney, in press; Goldfried *et al.*, 1978; Holroyd, 1976; Osarchuk, 1974). The efficacy of cognitive restructuring methods with test anxiety should come as no surprise in view of recent analyses of this problem showing that cognitive and attentional processes are the critical factors in test anxiety as opposed to motivational and physiological processes (Sarason, in press). Holroyd, Westbrook, Wolf, and Badhorn (1978), for example, obtained behavioural, autonomic, and self-report measure of anxiety from test-anxious and non-test-anxious subjects respectively under different testing situations. As expected, test-anxious subjects performed more poorly and reported significantly greater levels of subjective distress in an analogue-testing situation. Of interest, however, is the finding that different measures of autonomic arousal did not differentiate between the high and low test-anxious subjects in response to the stress of the testing situation. The authors concluded that these results can be interpreted "as supporting cognitive formulations of test anxiety and indicating that deficits in information processing associated with test anxiety do not result from maladaptive levels of autonomic arousal" (p. 442).

Whereas test anxiety is amenable to cognitive treatment methods, other disorders seemingly require specific behavioural interventions. Goldfried (1979) is careful to caution that while there is evidence that "irrational self-statements may mediate anxiety, it should be noted that the research has focused exclusively on situations of a social-evaluative nature. It would be an overgeneralization to conclude that all forms of anxiety have their basis in irrational thinking." To take a specific example, Emmelkamp, *et al.* (1978) emphasize the greater levels of autonomic arousal in agoraphobics and suggest that the preferred treatment technique would be behaviourally based as in the case of prolonged *in vivo* exposure. It is improbable that all anxiety is cognitively based, and the specific relationship between thoughts and feelings will vary according to a range of person- and situation-specific variables (LaPointe and Harrell, 1978). Bandura (1969), Davidson and Schwartz (1976), and Lang (1971) have all described frameworks within which cognitive factors exercise varying degrees of influence on emotional resounding depending on the person, the problem, and the situation in question. They have also suggested how different treatment techniques might be required for different anxiety-related problems.

Lastly, in terms of the comprehensive framework of social learning theory that we have briefly described here, cognitive restructuring methods that systematically employ well-established induction procedures such as modelling, rehearsal, and corrective feedback for the modification of specifically targeted self-instructions would be expected to be superior to the unsystematic verbal methods of conventional psychotherapy. The growing evidence on the effects of SIT and rational restructuring therapy indicates that this expectation is well-founded.

In deciding that "cognitive behavior modification" is "a step in the wrong direction", Ledwidge relied heavily on a box score analysis of comparative outcome studies between "cognitive behavior modification" and "behavior therapy". He selected thirteen comparative studies for analysis and arrived at the following tally: "CBM (cognitive behavior modification) superior: 2; Behavior therapy superior: 3; Mixed results: 3; Neither technique superior on any measure: 5" (p. 368). On this basis he concluded that there are no differences between the two types of therapy.

The many inadequacies of the box score strategy in evaluating therapy outcome data will be discussed fully in the next chapter. Suffice it here to point out a few illustrations of the ways in which Ledwidge's use of this strategy obscures the task of evaluation. In the process of lumping together a diverse array of different techniques applied to different problems in different populations and evaluated by different outcome measures, Ledwidge falls prey to the therapist uniformity myth (Kiesler, 1966). Just as there is no uniform, homogeneous treatment called "psychotherapy" or "behavior therapy", so there is no internally consistent approach called "cognitive behavior modification". What this label refers to are a number of often distinctly different techniques, some of which include both cognitive and behavioural components as we have mentioned earlier. Yet as in all box score analyses, different techniques are weighted equally in the analysis, regardless of their respective levels of development, conceptual adequacy, or empirical backing.

Consider, for example, the comparison of the cognitive restructuring method employed by D'Zurilla, Wilson, and Nelson (1973) and Wein, Nelson, and Odom (1975) with either RET, SIT, or Beck's cognitive therapy. The former was originally devised as a control procedure for assessing the effects of systematic desensitization and does not begin to approximate the latter in terms of conceptual development, empirical support, or therapeutic sophistication. It was never intended to. Remember too that this "cognitive restructuring" technique of D'Zurilla *et al.* (1973) was employed by Thorpe (1975) as a control group in his comparative evaluation of the efficacy of SIT versus systematic desensitization and behaviour rehearsal in the treatment of unassertive subjects.* All three treatment groups were superior to the control group, indicating that SIT was more effective than this form of "cognitive restructuring". The problem here for the box score analyst is that two allegedly equal "cognitive behavior modification" methods differ in conceptualization and efficacy.

Similarly, it makes little sense to equate techniques such as misattribution therapy (Nisbett and Schachter, 1966) and idealized self-image training (Susskind, 1970) with the therapeutic approaches of Beck, Ellis, or Meichenbaum. So-called attribution therapy has been shown to be inappropriate and ineffective for clinical disorders (Bandura, 1977b; Davison and Wilson, 1973; Franks and Wilson, 1979) and no serious proponent of cognitive behaviour therapy would claim that it should be viewed as in any way equivalent to RET, SIT, or Beck's cognitive therapy. Idealized self-image training refers to a remote, and little if ever used technique that

*Ledwidge (1978) omitted the Thorpe (1975) study from his analysis.

cannot be taken seriously at this stage. To introduce such marginal methods into the evaluation of such widely used procedures as RET, SIT, and Beck's therapy is simply to muddy the already troubled waters.

In box-score analyses, widely differing patient populations, target problems, and outcome measures are collapsed into what often amounts to an indiscriminable mass. As we emphasize throughout this volume, the efficacy of a particular therapeutic technique is best evaluated in reference to a well-defined problem and in terms of clearly specified outcome measures. For example, our review of the evidence on cognitive restructuring methods suggests that they are treatment of choice in the case of a problem like test anxiety but probably are inadequate when it comes to the treatment of a disorder such as agoraphobia. Processing comparative outcome data through the box-score blender precludes the identification of such patterns. Similarly, judgements of therapeutic efficacy depend on the specific outcome measures in question. As we have shown in the foregoing analysis, different techniques have produced different effects on different outcome measures. One's evaluation of the efficacy of cognitive restructuring, or any other treatment methods for that matter, will vary depending on the measure that is chosen. These differences are not reflected in Ledwidge's summary tally of studies.

In concluding that cognitive behaviour modification is a step in the wrong direction, Ledwidge (1977) contrasted the "meager data supporting cognitive behavior modification to the enormous body of research validating the effectiveness of behavior therapy" (p. 370). Allowing for the difficulties inherent in his categorization of these two classes of therapy and the fact that the recent data on cognitive behaviour therapy were not available to him, Ledwidge's statement still misleads. As he acknowledges, cognitive behaviour therapy is a recent development within the broadly defined compass of behaviour therapy (cf. Mahoney and Arnkoff, 1978; Meichenbaum, 1977; Wilson and O'Leary, 1980). It is not surprising that the evidence collected so far is somewhat scanty. Nor is Ledwidge (1977) able to make a convincing case that the current interest in cognitive methods is a negative development that will impede progress. Arguments emphasizing the positive and heuristic nature of cognitive analyses within the broadly defined domain of behaviour therapy have been presented by Bandura (1977a), Mahoney and Arnkoff (1978), Meichenbaum (1977), and Wilson (1979) among others.

Rather than jump to premature conclusions about the cognitive connection being an unfortunate or misleading one, we prefer to reserve judgement until more evidence becomes available. There is a welcome willingness on the part of many proponents of cognitive methods to engage in the necessary research and to conduct rigorous evaluations of their procedures. In view of the fact that progress in clinical psychiatry and psychology has often been retarded by the reliance upon personal preference, unscientific practices and a neglect of appropriate evaluation, this commitment and receptivity to research represents a development of potentially far-reaching significance.

However, in addition to the general obstacles to evaluating any and all forms of psychological therapy, research into cognitive forms of therapy faces some formidable problems. Replication studies are essential but almost impossible to conduct. We already have three major and several minor variants, thereby giving rise to confusion which is compounded by the (understandable) reformulations proposed by contributors such as Ellis. Agreed definitions are required, precise technical specifications are essential, the therapists must adhere to these specifications and be seen to adhere to them. These are the prerequisites for carrying out the replication studies without which it will not be possible to advance beyond personal and possibly idiosyncratic successes.

CHAPTER 12

CONVENTIONAL COMPARATIVE
OUTCOME RESEARCH

Ever since Eysenck's (1952) classical paper in which he scrutinized the effects of psychotherapy, two main questions have dominated research on this subject. The first question is whether psychotherapy achieves any success at all. Is a person who is troubled by emotional problems likely to benefit from consulting a psychotherapist? Central to answering this question is the occurrence of spontaneous remissions of emotional disorders. Also pertinent is the question of whether or not psychotherapy produces improvements that exceed the effects of suggestion, demand characteristics, and placebo influences. Establishing that psychotherapy has "active ingredients" over and above the therapeutic potential of placebo factors and the like is a challenging task that demands conceptual clarity, methodological rigour, and inventiveness. Some of the promising advances that have been made in developing the necessary means of disentangling the active mechanisms of therapeutic change have been discussed briefly in Chapters 1 and 9–11.

Another major question prompted by Eysenck's influential analysis of treatment effects was whether one form of psychotherapy is more effective than another. For a variety of reasons, this question featured prominently in the debate over the relative merits of psychoanalytically oriented psychotherapy and behaviour therapy. However, other comparisons have been made, including studies of the effects of pharmacotherapy versus different psychotherapeutic methods. Comparative outcome research of this nature, pitting one major form of therapy against another, has been the primary focus of what we have called conventional psychotherapeutic outcome research.

In our view, the excessive reliance on comparative outcome research has been unfortunate. In the first place, most of the conventional comparative outcome research has been premature. A rational approach to studying the comparative effects of therapy (the second question) requires first demonstrating the efficacy and validity of specific treatment approaches (the first question). Once this is established, the *comparative* value of the methods can be investigated. In the second place, the majority of studies completed within the tradition of conventional comparative outcome research are conceptually flawed and lacking in methodological adequacy, so that it is difficult if not impossible to draw worthwhile conclusions from them. Premature and poorly designed, these conventional comparative outcome studies have fueled some fruitless controversies about what works better than what.

Greater progress in evaluating the effects of psychotherapy will be achieved by replacing the demonstrably inadequate research model of conventional comparative outcome research. Nevertheless there are several important reasons why one cannot ignore the traditional therapy outcome literature. In this chapter we set out these reasons, describe the nature of conventional comparative outcome research and how it is customarily interpreted by the leading proponents, and explain some of our criticisms of this line of thinking and research.

Comparative outcome research, as it has been traditionally conceived and executed, requires critical analysis if for no other reason than it usually is the primary basis on which investigators have tried to determine the efficacy of psychotherapy. Many people turn to this literature for supporting arguments about the relative merits of different approaches to mental health services. In this connection, comparative outcome literature takes on particular significance in the United States at present. The probable introduction of some form of national health insurance will demand difficult and controversial judgements about how to allocate mental health resources. Which forms of therapy should be covered and which should not? What is the best way of making these decisions? In assessing these issues professionals, politicians, and probably the public are bound to examine the existing evidence on comparative outcome effects. Accordingly, it is important to analyse the strengths and weaknesses of this body of literature and to evaluate the conclusions that have been and are likely to be drawn.

Another reason for examining conventional comparative outcome research is that there has been a resurgence of interest in this approach to assessing treatment efficacy. Particularly prominent is the Sloane et al. (1975) study to which we have already referred, the influential review of comparative outcome studies by Luborsky, Singer, and Luborsky (1975), and a statistically sophisticated analysis of the treatment outcome literature by Smith and Glass (1977). These widely discussed contributions arrive at two common conclusions: (a) psychotherapy is more effective than no treatment; and (b) it does not matter which form of psychotherapy is practised, since different methods appear to be equally effective. Needless to say, acceptance of these conclusions would have serious consequences for the funding and practice of psychotherapy. If taken seriously, and if acted upon, patients (regardless of their problem) would be advised to seek therapy — any therapy.

Finally, comparative outcome research warrants special evaluation in its own right. Whenever a comparative therapy investigation is published that contrasts techniques drawn from divergent conceptual positions, it tends to receive a great deal of attention. The attention is not always commensurate with the adequacy of the information, nor with its relation to the putative conceptual and methodological bases of the methods. Nevertheless, comparative research often is viewed as the bottom line for drawing conclusions about treatment efficacy. However, comparative research, at least as currently conducted in the majority of psychotherapy studies, presents thorny problems and has many limitations.

THE SLOANE et al. (1975) STUDY

Many of the conceptual and methodological difficulties inherent in the traditional model of comparative research, in which "behaviour therapy" is compared with "psychotherapy", can be illustrated by reference to the important outcome study reported by Sloane et al. (1975). There are three main reasons for focusing on this study. First, it epitomizes the traditional approach to comparative outcome research. Second, it probably is the best controlled study of its kind yet conducted. Third, it is credited with high methodological marks by a number of prominent and influential commentators (e.g. Bergin and Suinn, 1975; Bergin and Lambert, 1978; Garfield, 1976; Luborsky et al., 1975; Marmor, 1975; Wolpe, 1975).

In brief, ninety adult patients at an out-patient clinic were randomly assigned to one of three treatment conditions after being matched for sex and severity of disturbance. The patients were relatively well educated, young people with neurotic or personality problems. Severely disturbed patients were excluded. The three conditions were: psychoanalytically oriented psychotherapy conducted by three experienced therapists of this theoretical persuasion; behaviour therapy conducted by three equally experienced therapists; and a waiting-list control group. Patients in the control group received identical pre-treatment assessment interviews, were promised therapy after 4 months, and were contacted periodically to ascertain their status and to remind them of forthcoming treatment. Weekly therapy sessions lasted for 4 months, followed by a post-treatment evaluation and an 8-month follow-up. The dependent measures consisted of ratings of three primary "symptoms" (target behaviour); estimates of work, social and sexual adjustment derived from a structured interview; and an overall rating of improvement. These ratings were made by the therapist, by the patient, by an independent assessor, and by an "informant" who was a close friend or relative of the patient.

In terms of the target symptoms, roughly 50% of the control group and 80% of the behaviour therapy and psychotherapy groups were considered to be improved or recovered. Behaviour therapy was followed by significant improvement in both work and social adjustment, whereas psychotherapy resulted in only marginal improvement in work. Moreover, behaviour therapy was significantly superior to the other groups on the global rating of improvement. At the 1-year follow-up there were no overall differences among the three groups on any of the dependent measures. However, when differences between treatments were tested by individual t-tests, behaviour therapy patients showed significantly greater improvement on the "target behaviours" than the control group. Sloane et al. properly point out that differing amounts of treatment were given to the three groups after the 4-month treatment phase, and that this makes it unwise to attribute differences observed at 1 year solely to the respective treatments. However, a closer look at who received what treatment following the 4-month therapy period is of some slight interest.

Fifteen of the patients in the behaviour therapy group subsequently received more treatment. However, only three of these patients saw new therapists, who were psychoanalytically oriented, and hence complicated analysis of the outcome for these three patients at the 1-year follow-up. Nine patients in the psychotherapy group subsequently received additional treatment. These latter patients received substantially more treatment (a mean of 19.3 sessions) than the fifteen patients who had originally received behaviour therapy (a mean of 10.1 sessions). So that, except for three patients in the behaviour therapy condition, the extra treatment which patients in both the behaviour therapy and psychotherapy conditions received after the 4-months period was consistent with or a continuation of their original form of treatment. It is unlikely that the three patients whose type of treatment was changed at 4 months significantly affected the overall performance of the large behaviour therapy group.

More importantly, Sloane et al. failed to emphasize that the 1-year superiority of behaviour therapy over the original control group takes into account the fact that nineteen of the $former$ waiting-list control patients had meanwhile received psychotherapy between the 4- and 12-month evaluations. Moreover, the amount of treatment these patients received was substantial. Nine subjects had between 11–25 sessions, six more than 26 sessions of psychotherapy. In other words, the comparison between behaviour therapy and the original waiting-list control group at the 1-year follow-up can be interpreted as an additional, but much weaker, comparison between behaviour therapy and psychotherapy. (Of course, this comparison is confounded by the presumably different levels of experience between the therapists in the study and the psychiatric residents who conducted most of the therapy given after 4 months.)

Several commendable methodological features distinguish this study:

1. the use of experienced therapists in the experimental period;
2. the treatment of a large number of motivated clients;
3. successful random assignment of clients to groups;
4. the inclusion of a no-treatment control group;
5. a 1-year follow-up; and
6. virtually no subject attrition, which often impedes interpretation of outcome studies.

Furthermore, Sloane *et al.* are to be commended for the lucid and open-minded manner in which they reported the detailed findings of this ambitious study. Nevertheless, a number of problems attach to the study in particular and the approach to treatment evaluation in general.

Perhaps the most serious limitation of this study is the manner in which outcome was evaluated. Clinical ratings are unsatisfactory as the sole or main source of evaluation. Therapist and client ratings are useful, but vulnerable to a variety of influences that may, as Sloane *et al.* (1975) point out, distort or obscure outcome. For example, since both parties have invested time, effort, and money in a commitment to the treatment process, they might be reluctant to admit failure. Or they might have different ideas and expectancies about therapy and disagree about outcome.

The assessors' and informants' ratings appear to provide greater objectivity, but there are major problems here as well. An important limitation on the value of the assessors' ratings is the fact that these ratings were based on the clients' own descriptions during the assessment interview. Aside from the interview itself, the ratings were not based on observations of the clients' behaviour in "real-life" situations. Ideally, outcome measures should reflect the clients' functioning in the natural environment. These clinical ratings must be distinguished from systematic observations of actual behaviour. The therapist's, or by extension, an independent assessor's ratings of client functioning on the basis of a clinical interview has been uncritically accepted as an appropriate means of measurement. As such, it is consistent with the traditional psychotherapy model that is predicated on the assumption that the relationship between therapist and client is the primary vehicle through which change takes place and is to be evaluated. The behavioural approach, with its great emphasis on situational determinants of behaviour (Mischel, 1968; Kazdin and Wilson, 1978b), leads to the view that clients' behaviour in the clinical interview does not provide a satisfactory sample of their behaviour in the natural environment. Nor do changes that occur in the therapist—patient relationship necessarily generalize to other situations (Wilson and Evans, 1977). From a behavioural viewpoint, the assessor's ratings would have been more informative had they been based on samples of clinically relevant behaviour.

The correlations among the four types of raters indicate the problems involved in determining treatment outcome on the basis of the type of ratings gathered by Sloane *et al.* (1975). Correlations of therapists' ratings with those made by assessors, clients, and informants were .13, .21, and −.04, respectively. A significant correlation between the ratings made by assessors and clients (.65) is not surprising, given that assessors based their ratings on the information provided them by clients in interviews. Sloane *et al.* (1975) concluded that these "relatively low correlations support the hypothesis that different raters may have different goals for treatment or use different criteria for improvement" (p. 112).

The low intercorrelations among raters might not have been unexpected. As Bandura (1969) has commented:

> "Conflicting data of this sort are not at all surprising as long as they are not erroneously considered as measures of behaviour outcome but are understood instead as differences between therapists' judgmental responses (which rarely correlate perfectly with clients' actual behaviour functioning). Indeed, one would expect diminishing correspondence between actual behaviour and subjective ratings as one moves from objective measures of clients' behavior to their own self-assessments, from clients' verbal reports of performance changes to therapists' judgements of improvement, [to] therapists' inferences based on clients' self-reports to information that happens to get recorded in case notes, and from case notes of undetermined reliability to retrospective global ratings made by still another set of judges who never had any contact with the client" (p. 458).

Multiple measures of behaviour change, including both subjective and objective indices, are essential to treatment evaluation. Specifically, where anxiety is of central concern, explicit measures of three response systems — overt behaviour, physiological reactions, and self-report — are warranted. The necessity for this broader yet more specific evaluative framework is underlined by evidence showing that changes may occur in one of these systems but not the others; that changes may occur at different rates in these systems; that changes in one system are not necessarily correlated with changes in another; and that different systems may be differentially responsive to different treatment techniques (Borkovec, 1977; Lang, 1969; Rachman and Hodgson, 1974). From a behaviour therapy viewpoint, it is unfortunate that Sloane et al. did not attempt to obtain more behaviourally based outcome measures of psychological change. Ironically, in praising the Sloane et al. study, Bergin and Lambert (1978) asserted that one of its strengths is that the "outcome measures were varied and included those that would be expected to be especially appropriate for behavior therapy as well as the outcomes that could be considered target goals for psychoanalytically oriented psychotherapy" (p. 165). Bergin and Lambert's view is puzzling since no behavioural measures were taken.

In referring to measures that were appropriate targets for psychoanalytically oriented psychotherapy, Bergin and Lambert presumably mean the global rating of improvement and the measures of general social functioning. Curiously, it was on the global measure of overall improvement — what Sloane et al. call a "very subjective measure" — that behaviour therapy was significantly superior to psychoanalytically oriented psychotherapy. Similarly, behaviour therapy was marginally superior on the other measures of social functioning. Bergin and Lambert did not comment on this finding, and consistently cite the data from the target symptoms (presumably the measure made-to-measure for behaviour therapy) in concluding that behaviour therapy and psychotherapy were equally successful. There is nothing amiss with this. However, it becomes a case of their wishing to have their cake and eat it when, together with commentators such as Luborsky, Singer, and Luborsky (1975), they try to explain the lack of positive findings on psychotherapy by appealing to the emphasis on behavioural measures of outcome and the absence of measures appropriate to psychoanalytically oriented psychotherapy.* (This issue is discussed further in the next section.)

---

*"... we still face the problem of never having adequately measured the subtle intrapsychic changes that appear to occur in verbal psychotherapies. It is conceivable that sophisticated criteria of affective and cognitive changes would reveal differential consequences of different interventions; but, thus far, this has not been tested" (Bergin and Lambert, 1978, p. 170).

Even if objective measures of behaviour had been obtained, another problem with the Sloane *et al.* (1975) study stems from the use of an omnibus treatment package that makes it impossible to identify the critical change-producing variables. Sloane *et al.* drew up a list of stipulative definitions of both psychotherapy and behaviour therapy, and commendably gathered process data to show that the treatments, as implemented, adhered to these definitions. However, the "behaviour therapy" encompassed a wide range of procedures, including relaxation training, systematic desensitization, specific advice and direct intervention in problems, assertion training, role-playing, and aversion conditioning. Behaviour therapy is not a uniform, homogeneous treatment method. Rather it encompasses numerous techniques that are constantly being developed, tested, modified, and refined. For example, two of the techniques used in the Sloane *et al.* study — systematic desensitization and electrical aversion conditioning — were among the most important methods of behaviour therapy in its earlier stages. For various problems, more effective alternatives are now available (Bancroft, 1974; Rachman and Hodgson, 1979; Wilson, 1978). To this extent, the Sloane findings are out of date.

Interpretation of the Sloane *et al.* study is also limited by the nature of the patient population and problems that they treated. Bergin and Suinn (1975) predicted that the Sloane *et al.* (1975) study would be compared to Paul's (1966) study, and stated that it "is clearly superior in the sense of involving clinical cases representing a number of syndromes and treatment by experts in a natural setting" (p. 511). The claim that the treatment of diverse clinical cases confers any superiority is debatable. Rather, the inclusion of different types of problems treated by widely differing techniques compounds the difficulties involved in answering the outcome question, namely, determining the specific effect of a specific treatment on a specific problem.

Moreover, the nature of the clients' and their problems bears close analysis. Well educated, young, and not too severely disturbed, the clients typified the YAVIS type (Young, Attractive, Verbal, Intelligent, and Successful) that tend to have a favourable prognosis regardless of treatment (Goldstein, 1973). Selection criteria resulted in the exclusion of extremely disturbed clients (including sexual deviants and alcoholics); clients who did not request "talking therapy"; and clients whom the assessor — himself a psychotherapist — would not normally have considered suitable for psychotherapy. It can be argued that the clients selected for therapy were those likely to show greater responsiveness to virtually any form of social influence procedure (Bandura, 1969). This responsiveness to the social influence processes that are common denominator in virtually all forms of therapy may well have accounted for most of the observed improvement, creating a ceiling effect that minimized treatment differences. Consistent with this line of reasoning is the fact that 77% of both psychotherapy *and waiting-list clients* were rated as either improved or recovered on a scale of overall improvement at post-treatment! Further support for this analysis comes from the finding that psychotherapy was significantly less effective with clients who were severely disturbed, as reflected in target behaviour ratings and MMPI scores. Behaviour therapy was equally effective with clients showing low and high initial disturbance.

Finally, the adequacy of the Sloane *et al.*'s control group must be taken into account in drawing conclusions about the efficacy of either behaviour therapy or psychotherapy. One of the most striking features of the results is the improvement shown by the waiting-list control group. As compared to 93% of the behaviour therapy group, 77% of these control subjects were judged by the assessors to have improved on overall adjustment at the end of the 4-month treatment phase. The improvement rate on target symptoms of the control group was smaller (48%), but still substantial. Sloane *et al.* attribute this improvement in the control group to therapeutic processes involved in the active and public commitment to improvement, the diagnostic interview, and the intermittent telephone contacts with the clinic. However, their conclusion that the superiority of their two forms of treatment over the waiting-list control group demonstrates that success in therapy "is not entirely due ... to the placebo effect of the nonspecific aspects of therapy, such as arousal of hope, expectation of help, and an initial carthartic interview" (p. 224) is questionable.

Recent research has called into question the adequacy of various control groups in controlling for the placebo effects noted by Sloane *et al.*, and it has emphasized that the success with which control groups do equate for factors such as therapeutic expectancy should be documented in outcome studies (Borkovec and Nau, 1972; Kazdin and Wilcoxon, 1976). It could be argued that a more stringent control group, possibly equating amount of contact with a therapist, might have resulted in even greater improvement, perhaps even equal to that of the two forms of treatment. However, the inclusion of an attention-placebo control group that meets the exacting criteria spelled out by Borkovec (1977) and Kazdin and Wilcoxon (1976) for laboratory research may, as O'Leary and Borkovec (1977) point out, be impractical because of compelling ethical considerations and methodological complexities. The clinical setting is less the place for identifying specific mechanisms of therapeutic change than the place for demonstrating the efficacy of laboratory-tested techniques. This calls for alternative research strategies that depart from the conventional therapy outcome model.

To summarize, it is argued that insufficiently discriminating and inadequate methodology has characterized traditional outcome research and obscured possible differences between treatments. More conclusive evaluations of the relative efficacy of specific treatment methods over the social influence processes inherent in most forms of therapy will be possible to the extent that outcome studies focus on specific multiple measurements of the effects of well-defined treatment techniques applied to homogeneous groups of patients.

THE LUBORSKY et al. (1975) REVIEW

Perhaps the most influential review of comparative outcome studies currently available is that of Luborsky *et al.* (1975). From our perspective, the Luborsky *et al.* analysis exemplifies the limitations of the conventional approach to evaluating therapy outcome in general and is replete with conceptual and methodological problems.

Luborsky *et al.*'s thesis is that the issue of therapeutic efficacy must be decided on the basis of a consensus of "at least passably controlled studies". The best way to do this, they assert, is

"to consider [all studies] separately for each of the main types of comparisons that have been done; e.g. group vs individual psychotherapy, time-limited vs unlimited psychotherapy, client centered vs other traditional psychotherapies, and behavior therapy vs psychotherapy. For each type of comparison, a convenient 'box score' is given with the number of studies in which the treatments were significantly better or worse, or 'tie score' — our term for not significantly different statistically" (p. 995).

The box scores included 113 studies; only studies "in which some attention was paid to the main criteria of controlled comparative research were included" (p. 995). Luborsky *et al.* used twelve criteria for assessing the methodological adequacy of each study. Among these criteria were the random or matched assignment of subjects to groups, the use of "real patients", competent and experienced therapists, comparative treatments that were equally valued, outcome measures that "took into account the target goals of treatment", independent evaluation of treatment outcome, treatments of equal and sufficient duration, adequate sample sizes, and so on. Luborsky *et al.* note, however, that these criteria were "only to be considered as guidelines". The authors also emphasized that the studies they included "dealt with *young adults or adults,* and the majority of them were nonpsychotic patients. Since studies of patients seem more likely to have relevance to the problems of practitioners than studies of nonpatients, this review will consider only research in which bona fide *patients* were in *bona fide treatment* – excluded were role-playing studies and those using student volunteers" (p. 1000, original emphasis).

Luborsky *et al.* found support for the notion that "Everyone Has Won and All Must Have Prizes" – the verdict of the Dodo bird in Alice in Wonderland. "Most comparative studies of different forms of psychotherapy found insignificant differences in proportions of patients who improved by the end of psychotherapy" (p. 1003). This verdict and other conclusions, and the evidence on which they were based, require close inspection.

The first objection arises from the scope of the Luborsky *et al.* review. The exclusion of studies including "student volunteers" as opposed to "real patients" is a false dichotomy. So-called analogue research can play a useful role in the determination of the efficacy of treatment methods provided that the limits of generalizability to the clinical situation are assessed (Borkovec and Rachman, 1979). While we do not agree with Luborsky *et al.*'s arbitrary dismissal of a wealth of relevant and informative outcome research, their analysis nevertheless has to be evaluated on its own terms.

Even if Luborsky *et al.*'s boundaries for the inclusion of research studies are accepted, namely the treatment of "bona fide patients", problems are still encountered. For example, the authors claim that the studies they reviewed included "the general run of patient samples who seek psychotherapy" (p. 1006). This claim is difficult to support when one examines the bases for excluding certain studies. It turns out that Luborsky *et al.* restricted their analysis almost exclusively to neurotic clients of the YAVIS type, and thus it is thoroughly unrepresentative of the people with diverse problems whom community clinics, mental health centres, and other psychiatric services are supposed to help. Childhood disorders and a wide range of common adult problems (including addictive behaviour, sexual problems, psychotic disturbances) were excluded. (Parenthetically, the unusual classification of addictions as "simple habit disorders" is curious.) These omissions are puzzling coming from those who dismiss the relevance of so-called analogue research on grounds that it is not generalizable to the "real patient" population.

It is also difficult to understand why, given their own selection criteria, Luborsky *et al.* included certain studies in their box-score tables. A study by Pearl (1955), in which two forms of psychotherapy produced equivalent reductions on the California *ethnocentrism* scale, is included. Is this a dimension on which we should assess the relative merits of different forms of psychotherapy? Is this "disorder" representative of the problems for which the "general run of patients" seek psychotherapy? Luborsky *et al.* also included a study by Tucker (1956) who reported the effects of group therapy on soiling in chronic psychotic hospital patients. Aside from questions about the relevance of this problem to the "general run" of patients seeking psychotherapy, it must be remembered that Luborsky *et al.* specifically excluded behaviour therapy studies on the treatment of "habit disorders" such as "bed-wetting". It is not clear how the treatment of soiling in chronic hospital patients is more representative or relevant than the several well-controlled studies of enuresis (all excluded from the start). And if this study of psychotic patients is included, why are so many other ones excluded? As an example of the arbitrariness of categorizing one study as "analogue" and another as the "real" thing; we can look at Luborsky *et al.*'s (1975) exclusion of the studies by DiLoreto (1971) and Paul (1966), and their *inclusion* of Crighton and Jehu's (1969) brief report of twenty-three students who sought counselling for test anxiety. From Luborsky's point of interest, it surely would make greater sense to include highly controlled studies of specifiable, severe *problems* rather than base criterion for exclusion or inclusion of a study on what may prove to be the irrelevant *status of the subjects* concerned.

A second criticism of the conventional comparative outcome literature in general and the Luborsky *et al.* review in particular is the acceptance of the therapy uniformity myth. Kiesler (1966) identified several "uniformity assumption myths". One of these was the assumption that "psychotherapy" refers to a uniform, homogeneous treatment. In comparative research, special interest is taken in contrasting the techniques representative of different therapeutic schools. Thus, "psychotherapy" is contrasted with "behavior therapy", given that the traditions from which these methods are derived are in conflict. However, there is no "psychotherapy" to which other approaches can be compared in any general sense. There are only different methods of psychotherapy. The same point applies to behaviour therapy. There is no "behavior therapy" in the sense of a single specific technique that can be compared to other forms of psychotherapy. There are several different techniques subsumed under the rubric of behaviour therapy and many of them are based upon different assumptions and therapeutic procedures (Wilson, 1978c). A characterization of some of these techniques inevitably will misrepresent others, despite the fact that they are jointly referred to as "behavior therapy".

In their analysis, Luborsky *et al.* (1975) attempted to justify their comparative evaluation of "behavior therapy" by asserting that different behavioural treatment techniques do not differ from each other in relative efficacy (a poor basis for mixing them). However, there is evidence that some behavioural treatment methods are significantly more effective than others across different disorders. The same can be said of the newer cognitive-behavioural techniques evaluated in Chapter 11. Some of this evidence is described briefly in Chapters 9 and 10 (see also Bandura, 1977a; Frank and Wilson, 1973–79; Leitenberg, 1976; Rachman and Hodgson, 1980). Most of the studies on behaviour therapy included by Luborsky were confined to early tests of systematic desensitization, and hence their review, published in 1975, was out-dated from the start. Nowadays a broader range of effective techniques are employed by behaviour therapists.

A third objection to the Luborsky *et al.* review concerns their grading of the different studies.* All studies were graded according to the twelve criteria (rough guidelines) referred to earlier. Studies in which "the main criteria of research design were mainly satisfied" were given an "A". A mark of "B" was awarded to studies in which "one or two criteria were partially deficient", a "C" where "three or four were partially deficient"; a "D" where "three

---

*The grades which Luborsky *et al.* assign to different studies vary depending on which box score they appear in. For example, the Sloane *et al.* study receives a grade of B+ in the box score on psychotherapy versus behaviour therapy but is demoted to B in the box score on psychotherapy versus control treatments. The Gelder *et al* (1967) study ranks top with a grade of "A" when interpreted in terms of individual versus group psychotherapy but declines to a B+ in the context of a comparison between psychotherapy and behaviour therapy. King *et al.* (1960) go from a C+ to a C as the study moves from one box score to another. Luborsky *et al.* provide no explanation for the capricious qualities of these studies.

or four were partially deficient and one was seriously deficient". A reliability check between two of the authors on sixteen randomly selected studies yielded a correlation of 0.84.

Assigning grades of this nature to treatment outcome studies is an arbitrary and difficult procedure. Different investigators are likely to come up with different grades depending on the rules of evidence and methodological strictures they favour. From our perspective, virtually all of the studies chosen are more poorly designed than Luborsky et al. acknowledge.

Probably the most serious shortcoming of the vast majority of studies reviewed by Luborsky et al. is the unsatisfactory measurement of treatment outcome. Consider, for instance, some of the studies that received the highest methodological grades. A study by Gelder, Marks, Wolff, and Clarke (1967) received a grade of "A". Gelder et al. used clinical ratings to assess therapeutic improvement. The problems with relying upon clinical ratings as the sole determinant of outcome are illustrated in our discussion of the Sloane et al. study (see also Kazdin and Wilson, 1978b; Rachman, 1971). Although Gelder et al. employed an independent assessor to rate clinical outcome, they noted that it was impossible to keep the assessor "blind" because of repeated contacts with patients over the course of treatment. This contamination is common to many of the studies cited by Luborsky et al. A more serious measurement problem arises when therapy outcome is determined solely on the basis of psychological tests of dubious or undetermined reliability and validity. Witness the exclusive reliance (in studies graded no less highly than "B") upon such outcome measures as Q-sorts of self-ideal correlations (e.g. Schlien, Masik, and Dreikurs, 1962), the Rorschach (e.g. Peyman, 1956), the Thematic Apperception Test (e.g. Henry and Schlien, 1957), or the California Scale of Ethnocentrism (e.g. Pearl, 1955, which receives a B+ mark). Although it is empirically based, even the MMPI (e.g. Barron and Leary, 1955) is far from an adequate measure of outcome (e.g. Kazdin and Wilson, 1978b; Mischel, 1968). Worse still is the Endicott and Endicott (1964) study, which was given a rating of B. Outcome was assessed by the therapist on a subjective and unvalidated rating scale of therapeutic improvement. In addition, 16% of the patients in the psychoanalytically oriented treatment group completed fewer than four therapy sessions and were accordingly dropped from the data analysis. This is a dubious procedure (see Chapter 5).

The problems posed by an inadequate measure of treatment outcome cannot be overemphasized. To put it bluntly, if the outcome measure is unreliable, invalid, or simply insensitive or irrelevant to potential therapeutic effects, the study in question is uninterpretable and better ignored than included in a misleading compilation of investigations. There is now broad agreement that multiple objective and subjective measures of specific effects are necessary to evaluate any form of treatment.

Leaving aside specific differences in evaluations of methodological adequacy, major though these are likely to be, the general value of a grading system of the nature used by Luborsky et al. can be queried. Presumably the purpose of constructing the system was to see whether the different grades were related systematically to specific outcome results. Thus, in discounting the potential criticism that inadequate outcome measures explain the failure to find differences among different therapeutic approaches, Luborsky et al. (1975) appealed to their grading system. They asserted that "the best designed studies do not show a very different trend from those that are less well designed" (p. 1004), suggesting that this argues against any interpretation of their conclusions that is based on quality (of control, etc.).

Unconvincing as it is, Luborsky et al.'s argument about the utility of grades, contains a contradiction. On the one hand, they defend the inclusion of studies of inferior methodological quality on the grounds that there is *no difference* in trend between studies that were well designed and those that were poorly designed (if so, why bother with the poor studies?) However, they then adopt a different position in trying to account for the fact that their box-score analysis of studies on psychotherapy versus behaviour therapy produced thirteen tie scores and six in which behaviour therapy was significantly superior. Discounting this apparent superiority of behaviour therapy, the authors claimed that "five of the six comparisons were based on relatively poor research quality, i.e. ratings of C and D" (p. 1001). This places Luborsky *et al.* in an awkward position.

If they insist on attaching special emphasis to the better designed studies, they are able to discount the apparent superiority of behaviour therapy. However, once they allow such gradation of quality to enter into their assessment, the mainstay of their argument is undermined (as well as contradicting themselves). To be consistent, they should follow their discounting of the superiority of behaviour therapy by dismissing from consideration a majority of the studies contained in their report. Our own preference would be to take this strict course and dismiss all of the inadequate and flawed studies, and concentrate on the better-quality evidence.

The numerous problems in the majority of the studies reviewed by Luborsky *et al.* make it difficult to draw useful conclusions from between-treatment comparisons within the same study. The arbitrary and limited scope of the studies selected for review by Luborsky *et al.*, and the nature of the outcome measures on which the findings are based, combine to minimize the chances of showing significant differences between alternative treatments. The measures, such as global rating scales and questionable psychological tests, blur potential comparative effects by virtue of being too unreliable or insufficiently discriminating. The excessive reliance on studies of the treatment of mildly disturbed neurotic out-patients with heterogeneous problems obscures potential differential treatment effects because these are the patients who are most likely to respond favourably to any form of therapeutic influence, and who, if untreated, will show high levels of spontaneous remission. Advances in psychology are characterized by increasing specificity in the type of questions asked and the answers sought. As Kazdin and Wilson (1978b) have argued: "More definitive evaluation of the relative efficacy of specific treatment methods over the more general social influence process inherent in most forms of therapy will be possible to the extent that outcome studies focus on more specific multiple measurements of the effects of well-defined treatment techniques applied to homogeneous groups of clients" (p. 61).

In short, given the question they asked and the manner in which they went about trying to answer it, Luborsky *et al.*'s failure to find differences between alternative treatment methods is no surprise. On the contrary, it would have been remarkable had they uncovered reliable differences. The interpretive problems inherent in trying to make comparisons between different treatments used in the same study are compounded by Luborsky *et al.*'s attempt to make comparisons among different groups of flawed studies in the box-score approach. Using a dichotomous measurement criterion — statistically significant versus non-significant — the results of various treatment outcomes are indiscriminately summed across the different studies and represented as three distinct categories: "better than", "worse than", or "no different from" an alternative therapeutic approach.

The logic of this qualitative, global evaluative approach appears to be faulty. The box-score strategy is an attempt to answer the wrong question. To ask whether something called "psychotherapy" is more or less effective than something called "behaviour therapy" is, as we have argued above, unanswerable in any useful sense. The more appropriate outcome questions are what technique is most effective, for what problem, on which measures, and at what cost? The specificity of analysis that is demanded by these questions is incompatible with the global box score strategy of Luborsky *et al*. The practice of lumping together the results of different treatment techniques on different measures from studies that range widely in terms of methodological quality obscures more than it enlightens. Specific patterns of results are likely to be lost in this artificial mix produced by the box-score blender.

A major weakness of this box-score approach is that equal weight is ascribed to different studies despite the heterogeneity of treatment variables and the lack of standardized evaluation criteria. As Gardner (1966) observed, this results "in a kind of majority rule whereby two poor experiments are given twice as much weight as a single sound one" (p. 416). In the Luborsky *et al*. (1975) review, the extensive and ambitious Sloane *et al*. (1975) study of ninety patients with neurotic and personality disorders is regarded as roughly equivalent to Crighton and Jehu's (1969) brief report of twenty-three students treated for test anxiety. Or consider the hypothetical case in which one study (involving a particularly effective method) resulted in a massive, clinically significant treatment effect for therapy X as compared to therapy Y. Yet three other studies (involving somewhat different methods than those employed in the first study) found therapy Y marginally but statistically superior to therapy X. Does the numerical score of 3:1 reflect a substantive difference in clinical reality?

A fourth objection to the Luborsky *et al*. review is the implication that decisions about the effectiveness of different forms of treatment are based on information derived from *comparative* studies. Contrary to this view, treatment efficacy should be determined primarily on the basis of evidence accumulated in support of one or other method, regardless of its comparative value. The comparative effectiveness of either or both methods is of interest, but only secondary importance. It is possible for two methods of treatment to be indistinguishable in terms of their efficacy — even to the extent of being equally *ineffective*. The comparative effectiveness of a method would, by itself, be inconclusive; it is not beyond the bounds of possibility that two methods of treatment might be indistinguishable without either of them being superior to improvements which occur without therapeutic interventions.

Lest this argument be thought far-fetched, we can turn to the outcome study reported by Barron and Leary (1955). This study is included in Luborsky *et al*.'s comparative outcome table and is used to support the conclusion that there are few worthwhile differences in the effects of different types of therapy; in this instance, no difference between individual and group psychotherapy. One hundred and fifty neurotic patients were accepted for treatment, and of these twenty-three had to be placed on a waiting list until therapeutic facilities became available. They waited 6 months before beginning treatment, while those eighty-five patients who received group therapy and the forty-two who received individual therapy began with little delay. The results were as follows: "The . . . scores of patients undergoing both group and individual therapy showed significant improvement on symptom scales" (p. 245). So far, so good. However, it is the next part of the results that is noteworthy: "The therapy patients did not improve significantly more than did the waiting-list controls" (p. 245). Indeed, the authors go on to point out that "on the neurotic triad, the average decrease is slightly greater for the controls than for the group psychotherapy patients. The percentage of change for the better in those scales average 61% in the control group, which is slightly but not significantly, less than in the psychotherapy groups" (p. 244). Here we have a perfect example of two methods of psychotherapy which were equally effective (or ineffective!), but neither was more effective than a waiting-list control condition. Comparisons between treatments that are made in the absence of primary evidence of the effectiveness of at least one of the two methods concerned is inadequate and potentially misleading.

It is interesting that despite Luborsky *et al.*'s emphasis on *comparative* outcome studies as evidence of treatment efficacy, they included a box-score comparison between psychotherapy and "control" groups. It is this sort of analysis that is necessary in order to establish the efficacy of a particular therapeutic method, in its own right, before comparisons with alternative treatment methods are made. The studies reviewed by Luborsky *et al.* in their box-score analysis of psychotherapy versus control groups are important and call for a careful examination.

The first question is why they confined themselves to comparisons between psychotherapy and control groups? Why was this promising line of inquiry not extended to comparisons between behaviour therapy and control groups? As we point out in Chapters 9 and 10, research on behaviour therapy techniques has outstripped the rest of the field of psychotherapy in terms of the quality and quantity of controlled evaluations of the effects of specific treatment methods, relative to the influence of so-called non-specific factors like placebo and demand characteristics (Frank and Wilson, 1973–1978; Kazdin and Wilson, 1978b). Luborsky *et al.* do not explain this omission. Of course, it is the prerogative of all reviewers to delimit the scope of their review as they see fit. However, it is desirable to acknowledge the limitations of one's review and to provide some explanation for excluding a large body of research that appears to be relevant to their concerns.

This omission notwithstanding, Luborsky *et al.*'s analysis of studies on psychotherapy versus control groups is still of importance. On the basis of thirty-three comparisons derived from twenty-five studies, they concluded that "Twenty (or about 60%) of the comparisons significantly favored psychotherapy, but 13 showed a tie, meaning that the psychotherapy was not significantly better than the nonpsychotherapy in almost a third of the comparisons. None of the comparisons favored the control group" (p. 1003). A closer look at the studies on which this conclusion is based undermines Luborsky *et al.*'s position.

The first problem with this analysis concerns the nature of the control groups against which psychotherapy was compared. Almost without exception, the control condition was *the absence of treatment.* Several different types of experimental control are possible in conducting outcome research on psychotherapy (see Kazdin and Wilson, 1978b). Demonstrating that a particular form of treatment is superior to no treatment is useful, but does not rule out the possibility that non-specific effects such as placebo or contact with enthusiastic and committed treatment staff, and not the specific treatment technique(s), account for the therapeutic change. In essence, this is the thesis of Frank's (1961) classic analysis of commonly occurring therapeutic influences that are common to many forms of treatment. Even if the figures arrived at by Luborsky *et al.* on psychotherapy versus control groups could be substantiated, at best they would indicate that some formal intervention is more effective than the lack of treatment. Whether or not that improvement could be attributed to the specific psychotherapy method would still be an open question. The data from Luborsky's review provide no support for Bergin and Lambert's (1978) undocumented assertion that psychotherapy has been shown to be more effective than appropriate placebo treatments.

Limitations on space prohibit a detailed analysis of the remaining thirty-two studies which Luborsky *et al.* include in this box score. However, a full analysis is not necessary, and it is sufficient to point out some of the other problems by citing selected illustrations. Consider some of the studies rated as "B" in quality and recorded as evidence of psychotherapy being significantly more effective than control groups. One such study is that by Endicott and Endicott

(1964), referred to above. In this study the therapist who conducted all of the therapy also carried out all the assessment of outcome on subjective, global measures of unknown reliability or validity. Aside from this lethal flaw, the original authors did not state that the psycho-analytically oriented treatment produced statistically significant improvements, compared to the control group. Endicott and Endicott simply stated that 40% of the control (no treatment) group were rated as improved compared to 52% of the psychotherapy patients. Not surprisingly, in his compilation of psychotherapy outcome studies, Bergin (1971) classified (correctly, in our view) the Endicott and Endicott study as an instance of a *negative* outcome for psycho-therapy. Luborsky *et al.*'s use of this study to demonstrate the value of psychotherapy is as puzzling as their grading of the study as "B" (compare this to the C grade given in the King study described above).

Two additional studies cited by Luborsky *et al.* as evidence of the superiority of psycho-therapy over control groups are those of Karon and Vandenbos (1970) and Rogers and Dymond (1954). The former can be criticized severely, as we indicated earlier, and as the latter has been criticized effectively in other reviews of the outcome literature (e.g. Eysenck, 1960), there is little point in rehashing its shortcomings (such as the lack of an appropriate control group).

Peyman (1956) compared group psychotherapy to ECT and a routine hospital control group in the treatment of chronic schizophrenic patients. There were four treatment groups: group psychotherapy plus ECT; group psychotherapy; ECT alone; and routine hospital care. Treatment lasted for 6 months and therapeutic improvement was assessed by performance on the Wechsler—Bellevue, the Bender—Gestalt, and Rorschach tests. Luborsky *et al.* interpret the findings of this study to indicate the superiority of psychotherapy over the control group and enter two separate positive outcomes for psychotherapy in their box-score analysis. The data suggest otherwise.

Changes were obtained on the Bender-Gestalt and Rorschach but not on the Wechsler—Bellevue test. Although both the psychotherapy plus ECT and the psychotherapy-alone groups showed greater improvement than the control group, the level of statistical significance obtained was less than the commonly accepted 5% level.* Regardless of the degree of improvement of the two groups that received psychotherapy, the validity of using the Bender—Gestalt, the Wechsler, and the Rorschach as measures of therapeutic outcome can be questioned. Finally, it is difficult to understand how Luborsky *et al.* derived two positive outcomes for psychotherapy from this study. Aside from the psychotherapy-alone versus the control group comparison, which did show the superiority of psychotherapy, albeit at a less than conventional level of statistical significance, Luborsky *et al.* included the psychotherapy plus ECT versus control group comparison. The latter confounds two different treatments and is not relevant to the comparison of psychotherapy with no treatment. Besides, including both comparisons seems like a simple duplication of the same effect.

The well-known study by Rogers, Gendlin, Kiesler, and Truax (1967) on the effects of client-centred therapy with schizophrenics is included in Luborsky *et al.*'s box score as another example of the positive outcome of psychotherapy. Specifically, Luborsky *et al.* derive two outcomes from this study: a negative outcome (i.e. client-centred therapy not significantly different from the control group) at post-treatment, and a positive outcome (i.e. client-centred therapy significantly more effective at the 5% level than the control group)

---

*Luborsky *et al.* explicitly state that they recorded positive outcomes in their box score tables only if the treatment group in question was significantly better than the comparison group at the 5% level (p. 999).

at the 1-year follow-up. Rogers *et al.* compared client-centred therapy administered by therapists highly skilled in this approach to a routine hospital treatment programme that consisted of "occupational and recreational therapy, group meetings of an essentially therapeutic nature, in some instances group therapy" (p. 82). Subjects in this investigation received approximately 2 hours of therapy per week over a period ranging from 4 months to 2½ years. In some respects this was an ambitious and commendable study with clearly defined goals.

Multiple measures of outcome were collected, a welcome feature of the study. These measures included the MMPI, a Q-sort of self-ideal correlations, the Wittenborn Psychiatric Rating Scales, independent and blind assessments of the total psychological test battery by two clinical psychologists, therapist ratings, patients' ratings, and estimates of hospitalization status. The overall pattern of results was summarized by Kiesler, Klein, Mathieu, and Schoeninger (1967) as follows:

> "When the preceding complement of personality change and outcome measures is considered, support for [the hypothesis] which called for differential improvement in the therapy patients as a group in contrast to the controls, turns out to be quite limited. Only one criterion index revealed even a trend in support of the hypothesis – hospitalization rates one year after therapy termination showed that therapy patients as a group spent more time out of the hospital than did the controls, suggesting that their greater long-term success in maintaining release or parole from the hospital. *In all other respects the various outcome-change measures for the experimental and control groups were virtually identical*" (p. 277, italicization added).

One might go farther and note that the "trend" in favour of the therapy group spending more time out of hospital was just that. Examination of table 11.10 on page 275 of Kiesler *et al.*'s analysis of the results show that at no time during the 1-year follow-up was the therapy group significantly superior ($p = .05$) to the control group in terms of per cent time spent outside of the hospital. Indeed, at the 3- and 6-month follow-ups there was no difference whatsoever between the two groups. At the 12-month follow-up the therapy group enjoyed a slight statistical ($p < .10$) advantage over the control group. It is on this single "trend", unrepresentative of the results as a whole, that Luborsky *et al.*'s case for counting this study as an instance of a positive outcome for psychotherapy rests. Little wonder that other commentators have chosen to view the results from the Rogers *et al.* study as a negative outcome for psychotherapy (e.g. Bergin, 1971). Although it is not directly relevant to the analysis of the Rogers *et al.* (1967) study, the fact that subsequent research on client-centred therapy has failed to produce much evidence of therapeutic efficacy (e.g. Mitchell, Bozarth, and Krauft, 1977; Parloff, Waskos, and Wolfe, 1978) emphasizes the misleading nature of Luborsky *et al.*'s interpretation of the results of this study.

Luborsky *et al.*'s classification of the study by Schlien, Mosak, and Dreikurs (1962) is dubious. The problem here is that the same study is cited twice in the same table (page 999) with a slightly different description in each instance. Both versions are graded "B". The results of the study are straightforward. Four different treatment groups were compared: client-centred therapy of unlimited duration; time-limited client-centred therapy; time-limited Adlerian therapy; and a waiting-list control group. In addition a fifth group of normal subjects were assessed to provide another baseline against which to compare treatment effects. Time-limited therapy patients had a maximum number (twenty) of sessions. Unlimited client-centred therapy took an average of thirty-seven sessions. A Q-sort measure of self-ideal correlations was taken prior to treatment, after seven therapy sessions, at post-treatment, and at a 1-year follow-up. The results were that all three treatment groups showed a significant improvement at post-treatment, that was maintained at follow-up. These results reflect within-group improvement. No between-group statistical comparisons were reported although it appears that they would almost certainly have shown the three treatment groups to have improved more than the waiting-list control group. The problem with this study, of course, is that the exclusive reliance on this sort of Q-sort index as the measure of treatment outcome is unacceptable (see Chapter 7).

A better controlled study than those just discussed is that of Brill, Koegler, Epstein, and Forgy (1964), although this study only merited a "B" from Luborsky *et al*. Three different drug treatments (prochlorperazine, meprobamate, and phenobarbital) were compared with psychotherapy, a placebo control group, and no-treatment. The patients were non-psychotics, including those with personality disorders, neuroses, and psychosomatic disorders. The psychotherapy was psychoanalytically oriented, but mainly supportive. The average length of treatment was 5 months. One of the useful features of this study is that outcome was assessed at 5 and 10 weeks after therapy and at the termination of treatment, using multiple measures. These included a symptom checklist completed by the therapist, patient self-ratings, ratings by a relative (usually the husband) of the patient, the MMPI, and an independent evaluation by a social worker using the written reports on the patient's progress.

Brill *et al*. summarize their findings as follows:

". . . any differences between groups appear to be slight. Certain trends appear with moderate consistency, frequently approaching and occasionally reaching statistical significance. Since the treatment groups were equivalent, these consistent trends may be meaningful. It appears that the meprobamate and psychotherapy groups fairly consistently were rated slightly more improved that the placebo and the phenobarbital and prochlorperazine groups. The slight superiority of meprobamate is perhaps more significant than that of psychotherapy because it was evaluated blindly and because of the prejudice in favor of psychotherapy among patients and therapists. It should be emphasized that while these differences may approach statistical significance, the clinical significance of the small differences between groups is slight. The overall improvement shown by all groups, regardless of treatment, is in striking contrast to the minimal differences between groups and the lack of improvement in the no-treatment group" (p. 590).

In fact, psychotherapy was statistically superior to the control group only on the patient's self-rating of improvement and on the social worker's evaluation, and a couple of therapist ratings. It is worth noting Brill *et al*.'s emphatic conclusion that the "extent of bias in favor of psychotherapy . . . was quite startling" (p. 591).

Koegler and Brill (1967) later reported a 2-year follow-up of the Brill *et al*. (1964) findings which were based on the patients' status at post-treatment. After 2 years, "The most marked improvement is in the rated status of the waiting list (i.e. untreated) patients" (Koegler and Brill, 1967, p. 77). There were no significant differences among any of the groups. This suggests that at best, treatment (by drugs, psychotherapy or placebo) produced improvement more rapidly. The authors quote Frank's well-known position that ". . . the function of psychotherapy may be to accelerate a process that would occur in any case".

There is no point in continuing to belabour the inadequacies of the remaining studies included in Luborsky *et al*.'s box score of psychotherapy versus controls, or to add to the already lengthy list of Luborsky *et al*.'s selections and interpretations of studies. Nor is any useful purpose served by calculating revised estimates of Luborsky *et al*.'s box-score tally based on the various criticisms that we have presented. Our own preference is to abandon reanalyses of flawed research in favour of better designed studies that are based on an alternative model of treatment evaluation and that are likely to yield interpretable results. None the less, we cannot leave this critical appraisal of Luborsky *et al.*'s box-score analysis of comparative studies on psychotherapy without emphasizing that it provides inadequate support for the notion that psychotherapy is more effective than appropriate control groups.

Having affirmed the Dodo bird verdict that there are no differences between alternative forms of psychological therapies, Luborsky *et al.*'s second major conclusion is that "*a high percentage of patients who go through any . . . psychotherapies gain from them*" (p. 1003, original emphasis). As we have seen, however, all that can be concluded is that many patients appear to show some improvement whether or not they receive psychotherapy, or are in some form of control group.

Indeed, there is a sign that Luborsky *et al.* were obliged, belatedly, to take a defensive position. At the end of their review they anticipated a hypothetical "skeptic about the efficacy of any form of psychotherapy" who asks "See, you can't show that one kind of psychotherapy is any better than another, or at times, even better than minimal or nonpsychotherapy groups. This is consistent with the lack of evidence that psychotherapy does any good" (p. 1006). Their reply is that: "The nonsignificant differences between treatments do not relate to the question of their benefits — a high percentage of patients appear to benefit by any of the psychotherapies *or by the control procedures*" (p. 1006, original emphasis). This is a strangely ambiguous conclusion from some of the leading advocates of psychotherapy.

Consequences. Thus far we have discussed how Luborsky *et al.* arrived at their two major conclusions that (a) there are no significant differences between alternative forms of psychotherapy and that (b) a high percentage of patients seem to show improvement whether or not they receive formal psychotherapy. We can now consider the possible consequences of their conclusions apropos the continued support, investigation, and practice of psychotherapy.

To begin with, if the specific method used to treat someone does not seem to make much difference, why not assign patients to different methods on a random basis?

Luborsky *et al.* explicitly reject this option. One reason they offer is that a distinction should be drawn between the "amount" and the "quality" of therapeutic improvement. This appeal circumvents the central issue. There is nothing objectionable or untestable about demanding that "quality" of improvement be assessed. Detailed measures of multiple response systems, including various behavioural, physiological, and subjective indices, can provide the necessary information. Of course, this assumes that therapeutic goals are measurable according to established scientific criteria, an assumption not always well founded. Luborsky *et al.* lament the "failure to design outcome criteria that do justice to the complexity of the human personality", and refer to Malan's advocacy of "developing better measures that rely on clinical judgement to estimate the quality of the outcome" (p. 1005). Malan's bold attempts were described in Chapter 5.

A second reason Luborsky *et al.* advance for not following through the implications of their own findings is that "the studies we reviewed are almost entirely limited to relatively short-term treatment; that is, about 2 to 12 months. This is a glaring omission in the research literature. We do not know enough about what conclusions would be reached for long-term intensive treatment" (p. 1005). It is true that little is known about the efficacy of long-term therapy. The evidence, such as it is, is discussed in Chapter 6 and provides little comfort for Luborsky *et al.*'s implicitly hopeful view. At present there is no reason to suppose that long-term therapy is more successful than short-term therapy.

Instead of appealing to the absence of research on long-term psychotherpy, Luborsky *et al.* would have done better to concentrate on the evidence that they themselves reviewed. Assuming for the moment that different forms of psychotherapy are equally effective (a conclusion that we do not accept), why not rely upon broader outcome criteria than efficacy *per se* in deciding upon which therapies to support and refer patients to? Considerations of efficiency, cost-effectiveness, disseminability, and acceptability to the patients who receive treatment (consumer satisfaction) should all enter into a rational decision about which therapy is appropriate for whom, with what particular problem and with what objectives in mind. The way in which these broader outcome criteria might be used to complement the hitherto narrowly focused question of efficacy of outcome is discussed by Kazdin and Wilson (1978 a and b).

Clearly, if two equally effective treatments exist it is sensible to apply the shorter, less expensive alternative. Several examples of this potentially rewarding line of analysis could be drawn from the many studies included in their review. Indeed, in one of their box-score analyses Luborsky *et al.* compared "time-limited" to "time-unlimited" psychotherapy. Not surprisingly, in view of the criticisms mentioned, there appeared to be little difference between the two. Gelder *et al.* (1967), for example, found that systematic desensitization produced at least as much improvement in phobic patients after 9 months of treatment as psychotherapy after 18 months of treatment. In this instance, as in others, systematic desentization is the recommended treatment of choice on the grounds of efficiency if not efficacy. The greater applicability and efficiency of behaviour therapy methods are two of their most attractive features relative to traditional techniques. However, considerations of efficiency are relevant to other forms of treatment. Schlien *et al.* (1962) found that an average of eighteen sessions of either client-centred or Adlerian therapy produced at least as much if not more improvement than client-centred therapy of unlimited duration.

Luborsky *et al.*'s third reason is that "it is very likely that certain ingredients of the treatment that apply across treatment labels are the main influencers of outcome. The therapist, for example, can be supportive, warm, and emphatic in a variety of differently designated forms of treatment, and this may be a powerful influence on the outcome of treatment" (p. 1005). This is a familiar conclusion in the therapy outcome literature and was discussed in Chapter 7. Suffice it to state here that recent evidence has failed to support earlier notions of the relation between warmth, empathy, genuineness and positive therapeutic outcome. Moreover, even if this reasoning of Luborsky *et al.* is taken at face value, it still does not account for the comparable success of the control (often no-treatment) control groups in their box-score analyses.

Luborsky *et al.*'s fourth and final reason for rejecting the "random assignment" option is that they claim to have established an "especially promising" match between type of patient and type of treatment, on the basis of their review. Specifically, Luborsky *et al.* concluded that "behaviour therapy may be especially suited for treatment of circumscribed phobias" (p. 1004). A detailed review of the evidence by Kazdin and Wilson (1978b) contradicts this claim, for which Luborsky *et al.* provide no specific documentation. Both Kazdin and Wilson (1978b) and Agras, Kazdin, and Wilson (1979) concluded that behaviour therapy is applicable to a wider range of psychological disorders than traditional psychotherapy. Indeed, the notion that behaviour therapy is effective with simple habits and circumscribed phobias, while treatment of more complex forms of disorders should be reserved for traditional psychotherapy, is contradicted by the studies Luborsky *et al.* themselves cite — and by research evidence that finds no place in their review (e.g. Gelder, Bancroft, Gath, Johnston, Mathews, and Shaw, 1973).

Recall that in the Sloane *et al.* study, for example, behaviour therapy appeared to be more effective than psychotherapy in dealing with the severely disturbed patients. Sloane *et al.* emphasized that: "Behaviour therapy is clearly a *generally* useful treatment" (p. 226).

THE SMITH AND GLASS (1977) REVIEW

The verdict that psychotherapy is effective and that there are no significant differences between alternative treatment approaches has also been registered by Smith and Glass (1977). Two features of this review merit careful attention. Smith and Glass bring to bear on the problem of evaluating therapy outcome a novel statistical method which they term "meta-analysis". They report having reviewed close to 400 outcome studies on the effects of psychotherapy; on the face of it this is the most comprehensive analysis of the therapy outcome literature to date.

Smith and Glass do not disguise their views on the efficacy of psychotherapy. In the introduction to their statistical analyses they dismiss Eysenck's (1952) thesis as a "tendentious diatribe", refer the reader to "Bergin's (1971) astute dismantling of the Eysenck myth", and find Luborsky *et al.*'s (1975) review of the evidence for psychotherapy "reassuring" (p. 752). No attempt is made to defend these bold assertions. The only doubt that Smith and Glass express concerns the *number* of studies which Luborsky *et al.* included in their review. Instead of the approximately "40 controlled studies" Luborsky *et al.* are said to have reviewed, Smith and Glass maintain that the "number of studies in which the effects of psychotherapy and counselling have been tested in closer to 400 than 40" (p. 752). How representative the 40 are of the 400 is unknown. A second reservation Smith and Glass voice about the Luborsky *et al.* review is that "the 'voting method' was used; that is, the number of studies with statistically significant results in favor of one treatment or another was tallied. This method is too weak to answer many important questions and is biased in favor of large-class studies" (p. 752). Accordingly, Smith and Glass carried out their own review and analysis.

Encouragingly, the scope of this review is much broader than Luborsky *et al.*'s arbitrary limits. A study was included if it had "at least one therapy treatment group compared to an untreated group or to a different therapy group". Methodological quality was *not* a factor in the inclusion of studies. Smith and Glass adopted the following definition of what constitutes "psychotherapy" from Meltzoff and Kornreich.

> "Psychotherapy is taken to mean the informed and planful application of techniques derived from established psychological principles, by persons qualified through training and experience to understand these principles and to apply these techniques with the intention of assisting individuals to modify such personal characteristics as feelings, values, attitudes, and behaviors which are judged by the therapist to be maladaptive or maladjustive" (Meltzoff and Kornreich, 1970, p. 6).

In addition to psychotherapy studies, those labelled "counselling", but meeting the above definition were also included. "Drug therapies, hypnotherapy, bibliotherapy, occupational therapy, milieu therapy, and peer counselling were excluded. Sensitivity training, marathon encounter groups, consciousness-raising groups and psychodrama" (p. 753) were also excluded. In contrast to Luborsky *et al.*'s selection criteria, analogue studies were included. So too were "dissertations and fugitive documents".

Meta-analysis is the combination of the results of independent studies "for the purpose of integrating the findings" (Glass, 1976, p. 3). It is contrasted with primary analyses in which the data from a given study are analysed for the first time. The basic unit of meta-analysis is the "effect size", defined as the mean difference between the treated and control subjects, divided by the standard deviation of the control group. For example, an effect size of 1.0 indicates that "a person at the mean of the control group would be expected to rise to the 84th percentile of the control group after treatment" (p. 753). Smith and Glass calculated effect sizes for any type of outcome measure, even if this meant including more than one effect size from a single study. A total of 833 effect sizes were derived from 385 studies in this manner and they served as the "dependent variable" in the meta-analysis. The "independent variables" in the meta-analysis were the following sixteen variables in each study:

"1. The type of therapy employed, for example, psychodynamic, client-centred, rational-emotive, behaviour modification, etc.
2. The duration of therapy in hours.
3. Whether it was group or individual therapy.
4. The number of years' experience of the therapist.
5. Whether clients were neurotics or psychotics.
6. The age of the clients.
7. The IQ of the clients.
8. The source of the subjects — whether solicited for the study, committed to an institution, or sought treatment themselves.
9. Whether the therapists were trained in education, psychology or psychiatry.
10. The social and ethnic similarity of therapists and clients.
11. The type of outcome measure taken.
12. The number of months after therapy that the outcomes were measured.
13. The reactivity or 'fakeability' of the outcome measure.
14. The date of publication of the study.
15. The form of publication.
16. The internal validity of the research design" (p. 754).

Reliability of assessment of each study in terms of these different dimensions was checked by comparing the ratings of twenty studies by the two authors and four assistants, yielding a 90% or higher level of agreement.

Smith and Glass report several complex findings from their meta-analysis. The first finding is that the "average study showed a .68 standard deviation superiority of the treated group over the control group. Thus the average client receiving therapy was better off than 75% of the untreated controls." They interpret this statistic as demonstrating the efficacy of psychotherapy. A second finding of interest is the average effect sizes of the ten types of therapy Smith and Glass evaluated. The largest effect size for any therapy was .9 sigma for systematic desensitization. This was followed by rational-emotive therapy (.77), "behaviour modification" (.76), implosion therapy (.64), and so on. Client-centred therapy yielded an effect size of .63, psychodynamic therapy an effect size of .59, and Gestalt therapy a lowly .26.

These rankings are based on studies "not equated for duration, severity of problem, type of outcome, etc.". In order to equate for these factors, Smith and Glass moved to "a coarser level of analysis in which data could be grouped into more stable composites". Using multidimensional scaling techniques, Smith and Glass arrived at four broader classes of therapies. For reasons they do not make clear, Smith and Glass did not report the findings for this higher-order grouping of therapeutic approaches, but decided instead to study yet a "higher level of aggregation of the therapies, called 'superclasses' " (p. 757). The first superclass turned out to consist of Gestalt, implosion, systematic desensitization, and behaviour modification. It was then decided that there were not enough studies on Gestalt therapy so it was dropped from this superclass, which was then relabelled the behavioural superclass. The second superclass consisted of the remaining six therapies, i.e. "a composite of psychoanalytic psychotherapy, Adlerian, Rogerian, rational-emotive, eclectic therapy, and transactional analysis" (p. 757). The mean effect sizes of the two superclasses still showed the behavioural composite to be slightly superior to the non-behavioural composite.

Smith and Glass then report two additional findings. The outcome measures in the studies on behavioural therapies, they claim, were more subjective and susceptible to bias than those from non-behavioural studies. This led them to "suspect that the .2 difference between the behavioural and non-behavioural classes is somewhat exaggerated in favor of the behavioural superclass" (p. 758). Accordingly, Smith and Glass returned to their computer and examined "those studies, approximately 50 in number, in which a behavioural therapy and a non-behavioural therapy were compared simultaneously with an untreated control group". The results are "provocative", state Smith and Glass. "The .2 'uncontrolled' difference ... has shrunk to a .07 difference in average effect size" (p. 758). Finally, on the basis of this figure and additional regression analyses, Smith and Glass reached the end of their excursion through *post hoc* statistical analyses and abstract reclassifications of vaguely defined global treatment entities, and were able to declare that there are no differences among equally effective therapies.

A CRITIQUE OF THE SMITH AND GLASS REVIEW

Ideally, there should be a place for meta-analytic evaluations of groups of studies, but therapy outcome research is very far from the point where such a strategy is appropriate. Commenting on the value of meta-analysis, Cooper (1979) states that it is warranted when the studies in question "(a) share a common conceptual hypothesis or (b) they share operations for the realization of the independent or dependent variables, regardless of conceptual focus" (p. 133). Neither is currently true of the therapy outcome literature. The spread in quality of experimental design, in adequacy of measurement, and in conceptual focus is so great that attempts to integrate findings across such widely divergent research are doomed to muddy the troubled waters still further. Confusion, not clarification, is the result. Sacrificing quality for quantity is a misconceived exercise.

Advocating the increased use of meta-analytic methods over what he calls the "literary review" strategy of integrating findings from groups of studies, Cooper (1979) faults the latter for being "more susceptible to the idiosyncracies of a particular reviewer's perspective than are reviews using consensually validated statistical procedures" (p 132). Glass (1976) denigrates the usual research review: "A common method for integrating several studies with inconsistent findings is to carp on the design or analysis deficiencies of all but a few studies — those remaining frequently being one's own work or that of one's students or friends — and then advance the one or two 'acceptable' studies as the truth of the matter" (p. 4). What is described as a "literary review" is, of course, the mainstay of scientific debate (as well as of judicial and other assessments) and is not so easily replaced by statistical jiggery pokery. Critical judgements should not, indeed cannot, be dispensed with.

As the previous chapters in this volume and our discussion of the Luborsky *et al*. review make clear, therapy outcome research is at a rudimentary level of development. It is not a question of carping about nuances of experimental design — it often is a matter of whether or not a study had a control group. It is less a question of the selective citing of favoured studies than a matter of unearthing any well-controlled research on certain therapeutic methods. These methodological inadequacies amount to more than "picayune design requirements" (Glass and Smith, 1976). Smith and Glass are naive in prematurely applying a novel statistical method to dubious evidence that is too complex and certainly too uneven and underdeveloped for anything useful to emerge. The result is statistical mayhem.

Smith and Glass's disregard for the methodological *quality* of therapy outcome research is exemplified by their uncritical acceptance of Luborsky *et al*.'s review as evidence for the efficacy of psychotherapy. Even Luborsky *et al*. themselves, in answering their own self-styled sceptic, were not able to make an unambiguous claim for the efficacy of psychotherapy *per se* over that of control groups. Smith and Glass's easy acceptance of Bergin's (1971) case for the efficacy of psychotherapy ignores multiple criticisms of this appraisal (e.g. Rachman, 1971, 1973). This unwillingness to exercise critical judgement in the acceptance of therapy outcome studies is repeatedly documented throughout the list of over 400 studies used in their meta-analysis.*

There are several problems with the studies that Smith and Glass included in their meta-analysis. The first problem with their bibliography is what it omits. Aside from the use of an innovative statistical analysis, the distinctive contribution claimed by Smith and Glass is the comprehensiveness of their review. The authors emphasize that they have dug more deeply and unearthed more therapy outcome studies than previous reviewers of this literature. It comes as something of a surprise, therefore, to discover that their review is not comprehensive and inexplicably omits a number of major, well-controlled investigations. Consider their coverage of behaviour therapy. Of the seventy-five comparative outcome studies reviewed by Kazdin and Wilson (1978b), only twenty-six (35%) are included in the Smith and Glass bibliography! Some idea of the pattern of omissions can be gleaned by noting that Smith and Glass included twelve of the sixteen on neurotic disorders that were reviewed by Kazdin and Wilson, but included only one of twenty-four studies on the treatment of delinquency, enuresis, conduct problems, retardation, marital conflict, depression, and hypertension.

The massive omission of key behavioural studies is puzzling. Anyone familiar with the behavioural therapy literature over the past decade will not fail to notice the absence in Smith and Glass's meta-analysis of any studies by prolific and prominent researchers such as Azrin and O'Leary, to name only two. Only one of the several important studies on the treatment of fearful subjects carried out by Bandura and his colleagues is included, despite their importance (Bandura, 1977a). Similarly, only one of Lang's several key studies on systematic desensitization is included. There is scant trace of recent behavioural research on the treatment of obsessional—compulsive disorders. The clinical research studies of British investigators such as Gelder, Mathews, Bancroft, and Marks is largely overlooked; It is perhaps this selectivity that accounts for the dubious conclusion Smith and Glass drew concerning the superiority of systematic desensitization over flooding. Important and more recent studies on flooding are overlooked (see Chapter 9).

This omission of numerous studies of direct relevance to the question of therapy outcome is

*We are grateful to Dr. G. Glass for kindly supplying us with the bibliography used in their meta-analysis.

not confined to behaviour therapy. Many of the studies Luborsky *et al*. (1975) reviewed find no place in Smith and Glass's meta-analysis. For example, of the twenty-four studies Luborsky *et al*. reviewed in their box-score analysis of psychotherapy versus control groups, nine are omitted from the Smith and Glass bibliography.

A second major problem with the studies in the Smith and Glass meta-analysis is that a number of them are so flawed as to put them beyond the pale of acceptability. The report by Barendregt (1957), for example, is a comparison of two forms of therapy in which the outcome depends on three specially constructed Rorschach measures of unknown status. These measures cannot estimate the degree of therapeutic change, and it is doubtful if the author of this paper would forward it as evidence on which to base any conclusion, positive or negative, about the effects of psychotherapy. The report by Cooper (1963) is a retrospective comparison between the effects of various forms of behaviour therapy and conventional psychiatric care. The so-called control group was compiled retrospectively, precluding any form of random assignment, and the assessment of the effects of treatment was determined by inspection of the case-notes. So far from using random assignment, the patients in the one group were specially selected, largely on the grounds that they had failed to respond to any form of earlier treatment. Including this poorly designed study by Cooper while omitting the carefully planned and executed study of Gelder *et al*. (1973) on the same topic is unacceptable in a scholarly review. Zirkle (1961) discusses the effects of 5-minute sessions of psychotherapy and his paper should not be taken seriously. The paper by Bookhammer *et al*. (1966) assesses the effect of a particular form of analytically derived treatment by comparison with two unspecified forms of treatment. Six complex forms of assessment were used for each of the patients involved in the study, but all of this information was reduced to two gross-categories — improved or unimproved. These are the only data provided. The paper by Marcia, Rubin, and Efran (1969) is a poorly designed and executed study of desensitization (cf. Bandura, 1969; Davison and Wilson, 1973; Rimm, 1973), and the replication test carried out by Feist and Rosenthal (1973) — which is not included in the bibliography by Smith and Glass — discounted the result reported by Marcia *et al*.

Some of the items which are included in the bibliography are a puzzle. So, for example, the report by Sheldon (1964) describes the effects of community after-care services in dealing with former psychiatric patients. The word psychotherapy does not appear anywhere in the report, and nor does the term counselling. It is difficult to understand why they included an article on transactional analysis (Beckstrand, 1973) as a means of teaching writing to high-school pupils! Similarly, it is hard to see how one can justify the inclusion of the small and unsatisfactory report by Shore and Massimo (1966), discussed earlier, and deal with it in the same manner as the large and important Cambridge study involving several hundred subjects (Powers and Witmer, 1951).

The next weakness of the bibliography is the inclusion of studies that do not contain a control group. A mere comparison between two different forms of therapy, in the absence of any firm knowledge about the effectiveness of either form of treatment, is little short of useless. As we have stressed, it is possible for two methods of treatment to produce comparable results without placing us in a position to draw any conclusions about their value. The two treatments might be equally effective — or equally *ineffective*. The classic example of this type is illustrated in the report by Barron and Leary (1955) who found that two forms of psychotherapy produced roughly comparable changes, but neither of these changes exceeded the improvements observed to have occurred during the waiting control period (see above). An example of a study which failed to overcome this difficulty, and is included in the bibliography, is that of Ashby *et al.* (1957).

Another drawback to the bibliography is that no fewer than 144 of the items consist of unpublished dissertations. There is, of course, no fundamental objection to the use of dissertations (although some critics have objected that those parts of dissertations which are publishable are published), but a bibliography in which one-third of the entries comprises items which are virtually inaccessible presents difficulties and precludes the possibility of examining the details of the evidence. The composition of the bibliography is also weighted with studies of the effects of counselling, with no less than ninety-two items. Once again, there is no objection to the inclusion of counselling studies, but it is misleading to describe the article as a meta-analysis of "psychotherapy outcome studies". In view of the important theoretical and technical differences between psychotherapy and counselling, there are good grounds for evaluating these two procedures separately, rather than add to the confusion by lumping together demonstrably different procedures. No matter how sophisticated their statistical methods or ingenious their various ways of carving up the data, as Eysenck (1978) notes, Smith and Glass cannot escape that ultimately limiting condition faced by computer enthusiasts – *garbage in, garbage out*! Advanced analytic methods cannot transform poor data into good.

Smith and Glass subscribe to what Kiesler (1966) called the "uniformity assumption myths" of psychotherapy research and evaluation. Nowhere is this more damaging than with respect to measures of therapy outcome. The type of outcome measures incorporated in Smith and Glass' all-encompassing meta-analysis run the gamut, including disparate measures of anxiety, self-esteem, work or school achievement, physiological stress, projective tests, and the lot. Smith and Glass defend this strategy of mixing different outcome measures together by arguing that "all outcome measures are more or less related to 'well-being' and so at a general level are comparable" (p. 753). So much for the increasing mass of data demonstrating the importance of obtaining multiple measures of outcome due to the well-established fact that different treatments may have different effects on different measures, whether or not one is assessing anxiety (e.g. Rachman and Hodgson, 1974), sexual responsiveness (e.g. Wincze, Hoon, and Hoon, 1978), pain (e.g. Philips, 1978) or what have you (see also Ciminero, Calhoun, and Adams, 1977; Mischel, 1968, 1977).

Another uniformity assumption myth to which Smith and Glass subscribe is the therapy uniformity assumption, a weakness evident in the Luborsky review, discussed earlier. Smith and Glass's initial classification of ten types of therapy is problem enough. What does "behavior modification" include, and how does it compare with "eclectic therapy"? Implosion therapy is singled out for the top ten but why not modelling and its variations (for which extensive empirical documentaion exists – see Rachman, 1976; Rosenthal and Bandura, 1978) or behaviour rehearsal or assertion training? And why implosion therapy rather than flooding? Or does the term implosion include studies on flooding?

Bad turns to worse when Smith and Glass employ multidimensional scaling to create four broader classes of therapies. Extending Kiesler's point, we might call this the therapy uniformity myth squared. One of the four products of this statistical integration is the "ego therapies", i.e. transactional analysis and rational-emotive therapy. However, rational-emotive therapy has for some time been viewed by many psychologists as being related to or even as a part of behaviour therapy or, more recently, cognitive behaviour therapy. Combining it with transactional analysis and then constrasting it with behaviour therapy is misleading. However, matters get worse before they get better as Smith and Glass generate a third level of abstraction, the superclasses of therapies. This could be called the therapy uniformity myth cubed. Together with other commentators on therapy outcome research, including Bergin and Strupp (1970), Gottsman and Markman (1978), and others, we find it difficult to make useful comparisons between an entity called "psychotherapy" and another entity called "behaviour therapy". The prospect of comparing "the behavior therapies" to a conglomeration of "psychoanalytic psychotherapy, Adlerian, Rogerian, rational-emotive, eclectic therapy, and transactional analysis" (p. 757) is uniquely unpromising.

Other objections to the Smith and Glass meta-analysis involve the confusing mixture of patients and problems. No attempt is made to distinguish between the effect of this medley of treatments on schizophrenics, or alcoholics or adolescent offenders, or under-achieving college students, or phobic psychiatric patients, or subnormal patients, or patients suffering from migraine, or from asthma. Moreover, the effects of psychotherapy are assessed on the following problems among others – alienation, inadequate self-concept, asthma, insomnia, obesity, reading difficulties, mutism, homosexuality, under-achievement at school, delinquency, smoking, vocational problems, test anxiety, shyness, language delay, marital problems, excessive drinking, and so on. Evidently we have travelled a great distance from Paul's (1969) recommendation that we evaluate the effectiveness of the particular technique for the particular problem of the particular person, all the way to a spreading sludge of diverse problems.

Yet another uniformity myth that the meta-analysis forces Smith and Glass to embrace is that therapy effects evaluated at more than one time after treatment can be standardized and processed as equivalent bits of data within the same study and across different studies. Such an assumption conflicts with a concept of the behavioural and the social learning approaches to treatment. It can be argued* that outcome evaluation must distinguish between the initial induction of therapeutic change, its transfer to the natural environment, and its maintenance. It is important to distinguish among these different phases of treatment since they may be governed by different variables and require different intervention strategies at different times. Generalized behaviour change, for example, should not be expected unless specific steps are taken to produce generalization. Several different strategies have been demonstrated to facilitate generalization of treatment-produced improvement (e.g. Bandura *et al.*, 1975; Kazdin, 1977; Marholin, Siegel, and Phillips, 1976; Stokes and Baer, 1977).

In a similar fashion, a given treatment might produce highly significant improvement at post-treatment compared to appropriate comparative control groups, but show no superiority at a subsequent follow-up owing to the dissipation of the initial therapeutic effect over time. It would be premature to conclude that such a treatment method is ineffective; closer analysis may show that it is effective in inducing change, but fails to maintain change. It may be that by complementing the treatment method with different strategies designed to facilitate maintenance of change, long-term improvement may be effected. Within this expanded framework it may be that a specific treatment technique and a specific maintenance method are both necessary, although neither may be sufficient for durable therapeutic change.

The point is that it is inappropriate to use follow-up information as the sole criterion for a dichotomous all-or-nothing judgement about the success or failure of treatment. Even without

---

*We do not mean to suggest that it is only the social learning approach to treatment that draws a distinction between initial treatment effects and their maintenance over time. The distinction has been made explicit in the social learning approach but is equally relevant to other treatment approaches.

long-term follow-up data of treatment efficacy, a method that produces an initial effect may represent a useful starting-point for the design of a more enduring treatment.

There is a need for greater specificity of analysis in differentiating among initial treatment-produced change and its generalization and maintenance. For example, the relationship among these different phases of treatment will vary according to the specific behaviour that is the target of change. In the treatment of obesity, weight at post-treatment has been shown to bear no relation to weight at 1-year follow-up (Jeffery *et al.*, 1978). However, the initial treatment response of obsessional—compulsive patients appears to be a fair predictor of long-term outcome (Marks, Hodgson, and Rachman, 1975).

CONCLUSIONS AND CONFUSION – THROUGH THE LOOKING GLASS

A striking example of how the meta-analysis, with its disregard for the methodological quality of individual studies, can mislead is seen in Smith and Glass' conclusion that, "Implosive therapy is demonstrably inferior to systematic desensitization" (p. 757). It is difficult to know what Smith and Glass mean by implosive therapy (a term open to more than one interpretation), but if we assume that they included studies on flooding as part of implosive therapy, this conclusion is inaccurate. There is evidence that flooding, if taken to mean the use of prolonged exposure to the phobic situation, is at least as effective as systematic desensitization (e.g. Crowe, Marks, Agras, and Leitenberg, 1972; Gelder *et al.*, 1973; Leitenberg, 1976; Marks, Boulougouris, and Marset, 1971; Rachman and Hodgson, 1980).

Another dubious conclusion is their statement that "the reactivity or susceptibility to bias of the outcome measures was higher for the behavioural than the nonbehavioural studies" — and that "behavioural researchers showed a slightly greater tendency to rely upon more subjective outcome measures" (p. 758). This extraordinary claim is, to our knowledge, unique in evaluations of behaviour therapy. Behavioural researchers have repeatedly and strongly reiterated the value of objective measures of therapeutic change. Direct measures of avoidance behaviour, systematic behavioural observation, a variety of physiological measures of anxiety, sexual arousal and other functions were introduced by them, and are a major distinguishing characteristic of behaviour therapy (e.g. Bandura, 1969; Ciminero *et al.*, 1977; Franks and Wilson, 1973—1979). Ironically, the superior efficacy of behaviour therapy in comparative investigation has been attributed to the fact that "the criteria of change are often biased in the direction of being sensitive mainly to behavioural changes" (Bergin and Lambert, 1978, p. 180). In other words, Bergin and Lambert, whose conclusions resemble those of Smith and Glass, emphasize that behavioural researchers depend primarily on objective measures of outcome. Behaviour therapists have been taken to task for not including sufficient subjective measures of outcome, but never before criticized for exalting the value of subjective over objective measures.

Smith and Glass conclude that the differences among alternative approaches to therapy are "negligible". In emphasizing this finding from their meta-analysis they come close to compounding the conceptual and methodological failings of their review with selective citing from their own findings. Remember that a comparison of the effect sizes of all ten types of therapy, considered individually, revealed differences. Systematic desensitization, for example, was more successful than alternative methods. Smith and Glass decided that this was "an interesting and interpretable" finding. However, it is not mentioned again as they proceed through what we view as progressively questionable procedures, to combine the ten types of therapy into superclasses until they finally produce the conclusion that there is no difference between their two artificially created composites. It is this latter finding that they emphasize.

We are not attempting to invoke the findings from the comparison of the effect sizes of all ten therapies to proclaim the differential efficacy of systematic desensitization or any other form of treatment. The point at issue is that the superior precision and objectivity that a statistical analysis, such as meta-analysis, promises over a so-called "literary review" is more apparent than real. In commenting on their decision to include more than one type of outcome measure, or outcome measures recorded on more than one occasion after therapy, Smith and Glass acknowledge that the assumptions of inferential statistics are violated. However, they defend their decision by arguing that "the loss of information that would have resulted from averaging effects across types of outcome or at different follow-up points was too great a price to pay for statistical purity" (p. 754). This seems plausible, but it sits inconsistently with their attitude towards the conceptual and methodological assumptions discussed above. Smith and Glass were less fastidious in safeguarding statistical purity when constructing their methodological melange. How can we preserve the conceptual integrity of the subject matter on the one hand and salvage statistical purity on the other? The choice will vary as a function of who makes it, but the issue is more complex than Smith and Glass would have us believe.

ARE DIFFERENT FORMS OF PSYCHOTHERAPY EQUALLY EFFECTIVE?

The view that all forms of psychotherapy are winners and that there are no losers in the comparative outcome stakes has gained some support, and the Luborsky et al. (1975) and Smith and Glass (1977) reviews are cited as evidence for the absence of differential efficacy (see Bergin and Lambert, 1978; Orlinsky and Howard, 1978). Box score analyses like Luborsky et al.'s and Smith and Glass's meta-analysis, suggest that there is substantial empirical backing for their far-reaching conclusions, if only in terms of the number of studies and the quantity of data. However, a critical scrutiny of the proceedings shows that this claim is ill-founded.

We have examined three of the main sources of information that give rise to the view that there are no significant differences among equally effective psychotherapies – the Sloane et al. study, the Luborsky et al. review, and the Smith and Glass meta-analysis. In none of the three cases could we find satisfactory support for this view. A detailed critique of the Luborsky et al. and Smith and Glass reviews suggests that they are so flawed that they do more to confuse the therapy outcome research than to uncover useful relationships.

The literature contains other box-score analyses of comparative treatment outcome studies in addition to those selected for detailed consideration in this chapter. A prominent illustration of such an approach is Ledwidge's (1978) recent analysis of "behavior therapy" versus "cognitive behavior modification", the shortcomings of which are discussed in Chapter 13 below. Similarly, a box-score analysis that slices up the research literature pie in a different (but equally arbitrary) way from Luborsky et al. (1975), by Beutler (1977), is reviewed by Kazdin and Wilson (1978b). In one form or another, these and other box-score analyses of the comparative treatment outcome studies repeat the errors that have been identified in the Luborsky et al. and Smith and Glass reviews.

The claim is often made that poor data are better than no data at all. However, poor data from faulty studies can mislead and confuse. In accepting Smith and Glass' questionable conclusions, Orlinsky and Howard (1978) liken themselves to the doggedly optimistic boy in the old joke who cheerfully dug his way through horse manure reassured by his conviction that "there must be a horse in there somewhere". Orlinsky and Howard stated that "If study after flawed study seemed to point significantly in the same general direction, we could not help believing that somewhere in all that variance there must be a reliable real effect" (p. 288). Our search, including as it did the Luborsky *et al.* and Smith and Glass reviews, was unsuccessful.

The answer to the question of whether or not different therapeutic approaches have differential efficacy will come not from rehashes of flawed research, nor from attempts at statistical alchemy of existing inadequacies. Improved research that focuses on specific effects of well-defined treatments on multiple objective and subjective measures is what is called for. That such an endeavour will likely prove fruitful is suggested by recent developments in the field. In direct contradiction of the Luborsky *et al.* and Smith and Glass assertions, specific techniques have been shown to produce significantly greater improvement than others. Patients with phobic and obsessional—compulsive disorders appear more likely to derive benefit from treatment that is performance based than therapy that is strictly verbal or cognitive in nature (Bandura, 1977a; Emmelkamp, Kuipers, and Eggeraat, 1978; Leitenberg, 1976; Rachman *et al.*, 1979; Rachman and Hodgson, 1980). However, cognitive therapies seem to be the method of choice in the treatment of a problem such as test anxiety (Denney, in press). The treatment of sexual disorders has been enhanced by the introduction of behavioural methods that are superior to traditional psychotherapeutic methods (Franks and Wilson, 1976, 1978, 1979; Marks, 1978).

The tendency to accept the proposition that there are no significant differences among alternative forms of psychotherapy is premature and misguided. It is not difficult to imagine how the happy state of affairs, in which all psychotherapists "deserve prizes", could lead to a complacent view of the status quo. Were such an attitude to be fostered, it could reduce clinical inventiveness, to the serious disadvantage of patients. While the Dodo bird verdict has been accepted by many psychotherapists, there has been little attempt to follow through its implications. Acceptance of this verdict should highlight the importance of deciding on the funding of treatment programmes and the referral of patients to therapies on the basis of broader criteria of therapy outcome, such as efficiency and cost-effectiveness (Kazdin and Wilson, 1978b). Instead, little or no changes have been implemented or even advocated by proponents of this verdict. Whether or not differences between alternative therapies are definitively established, it is clear that considerations of efficiency and cost-effectiveness should play an important part in determining which therapies should be supported and to what extent. Similarly, stultifying consequences for psychotherapy research can be foreseen if scientific curiosity is blunted by acceptance of the Dodo view.

Finally, if the indiscriminate distribution-of-prizes argument carried true conviction, therapists and referral agencies would advise patients and clients that the particular form of therapy recommended — from a list of at least 10 possibilities — is a matter of indifference. Moreover, this advice should be offered *regardless* of the type of problem presented by the patient (see Smith and Glass). So, we end up with the same advice for everyone — "Regardless of the nature of your problem seek **any** form of psychotherapy". This is absurd. We doubt whether even the strongest advocates of the Dodo bird argument dispense this advice. If they begin to do so, they (and the profession as a whole) will quickly earn the deserved contempt of their prospective clients.

CHAPTER 13

SUMMARY AND CONCLUSIONS

Before reconsidering the advantages of adopting a fresh approach to the outcome problem in psychotherapy, we will review our assessments and arguments, and summarize the limitations of the conventional approach.

It is argued that conventional outcome research incorporates three assumptions of doubtful validity, and as a result the research is bound to be of limited value, leaves little room for development, and is at times misleading. The first assumption is that psychological difficulties and deficits can be accommodated within a medical model. We have argued that the over-extensive and undiscriminating construal of these difficulties as illnesses or signs of illnesses is mistaken. The second assumption is that key concepts in the theory of neuroses, such as fear and anxiety, are best conceived of in terms of the so-called lump theory. We argued to the contrary that fear and anxiety are better viewed as a set of at least three loosely coupled components. The third assumption is that many aspects of personality and disturbed personality, such as those included in the concept of neurosis, rest on a mistaken or exaggerated assumption about the generality of behaviour, traits, and psychological difficulties. Here we argue that the adoption of a theory (and allied measures) which assumes a greater degree of specificity of behaviour is preferable.

Once these three assumptions are set aside, we can proceed to a new attack on the question of therapeutic effectiveness. The definition of the person's problems and the means of assessing them would become more properly psychological and more specific. Unsuitable helping arrangements would have to be changed or replaced. The selection of closely specified measurements, preferably but not necessarily based on a three-systems analysis, would be advantageous and would enable one to study process and outcome questions simultaneously. A move towards greater directness, specificity, and multiplicity of measurements should be allied to the establishment of explicit treatment goals. In this way the effects of treatment can be determined in quantified degrees of success rather than in generalized reports of cure, relapse or improvement. This new emphasis on specificity also dictates that the evaluation of therapy outcome should distinguish between the initial induction of therapeutic change, its generalization across settings, and its maintenance. Different variables may govern each of these processes, and generalization and maintenance can be ensured only to the degree that procedures explicitly designed to accomplish these objectives are built into the overall treatment programme. The case for basing outcome research on clear and plausible hypotheses, and then testing them in experimental designs that incorporate specific measures of change that can be quantified, offers considerable advantages over the traditional approach, including comparative outcome studies of the conventional kind. At this stage of development it is preferable to assess the validity and effectiveness of specific methods of psychotherapy or of behaviour therapy, rather than to make gross comparisons between these broad categories.

The need for strict evaluations of the effects of various forms of therapy arises from several observations. In the first place, there is clear evidence of a substantial spontaneous remission; as a result any therapeutic procedure must be shown to be superior to "non-professional" processes of change. Closely allied to this point is the wide range of therapeutic procedures currently on offer and the competing and often exclusive claims for effectiveness. The lengthy business of separating the wheat from the chaff can only be accomplished by the introduction of strict and rational forms of evaluation. One important function of strict evaluation would be to root out those ineffective or even harmful methods that are being recommended. The availability of incisive methods of evaluation might have averted the sorry episode during which insulin coma treatment was given to a large number of hopeful but undiscriminating patients.

The occurrence of spontaneous remissions of neurotic disorders provided a foundation stone for Eysenck's (1952) sceptical evaluation of the case for psychotherapy. His analysis of the admittedly insufficient data at the time led Eysenck to accept as the best available estimate the figure that roughly two-thirds of all neurotic disorders will remit spontaneously within 2 years of onset. Our review of the evidence that has accumulated during the past 25 years does not put us in a position to revise Eysenck's original estimate, but there is a strong case for refining his estimate for each of a group of different neurotic disorders; the early assumption of uniformity of spontaneous remission rates among different disorders is increasingly difficult to defend.

Given the widespread occurrence of spontaneous remissions, and it is difficult to see how they can any longer be denied, the claims made for the specific value of particular forms of psychotherapy begin to look exaggerated. It comes as a surprise to find how meagre is the evidence to support the wide-ranging claims made or implied by psychoanalytic therapists. The lengthy descriptions of spectacular improvements achieved in particular cases are outnumbered by the descriptions of patients whose analysis appeared to be interminable. More important, however, is the rarity of any form of controlled evaluation of the effects of psychoanalysis. We are unaware of any methodical study of this kind which has taken adequate account of spontaneous changes or, more importantly of the contribution of non-specific therapeutic influences such as placebo effects, expectancy, and so on. In view of the ambitiousness, scope, and influence of the psychoanalysis, one might be inclined to recommend to one's scientific colleagues an attitude of continuing patience, but for the fact that insufficient progress has been made in either acknowledging the need for stringent scientific evaluations or in establishing criteria of outcome that are even half-way satisfactory. One suspects, however, that consumer groups will prove to be far less patient when they finally undertake an examination of the evidence on which the claims of psychoanalytic effectiveness now rest.

Since the First Edition was published, some slight progress has been made in the attempt to produce evidence to support the claims made on behalf of psychotherapy in general. Many people will complain that the evidence is modest and it has to be admitted that the scarcity of convincing findings is a continuing embarrassment. Nevertheless, it is our view that modest evidence now supports the claim that psychotherapy is capable of producing some beneficial changes — but the negative results still outnumber the positive findings, and both of these are exceeded by reports that are beyond interpretation.

The boldness and clarity of Rogerian psychotherapy were praised in the earlier edition and hope was expressed that further research would help to turn this approach into a viable and effective form of therapy. A review of the recent evidence is bound to give rise to widespread disappointment. It turns out that the specific claims made by and on behalf of Rogers can call on little empirical support, and as in the case of other forms of psychotherapy, the negative results outnumber the positive. Nevertheless this work served the useful function of preparing the ground for an improved understanding of the way in which therapists can facilitate the treatment process.

The dismal state of the evidence recruited to support the notion that psychotic patients might benefit from psychotherapy has not changed to any significant extent. During the past 25 years the flimsy case for the continued use of psychotherapy with psychotic patients has not been strengthened.

Modern behaviour therapy was less than 15 years of age when the First·Edition was published and the hope and expectation were that it would develop into a practical and effective way of helping people to overcome a wide range of psychological difficulties. At that stage the most important progress had been made in developing techniques for reducing anxiety and fears. The explosive growth of this subject makes a contemporary review a task of considerable magnitude. The early progress in combating anxiety has been consolidated and new methods have been added. In addition, and perhaps of greater importance in the long run, the scope of behaviour therapy has widened considerably and now encompasses a large number of psychological problems and deficits in the areas of clinical psychology and psychiatry, medicine, social work, and education.

One of the most challenging recent developments has been the growing application of the principles and procedures of behaviour therapy to an ever-wider range of medical problems, a development that has come to be known as "behavioural medicine" in the United States and "medical psychology" in Britain (see Rachman and Philips, 1978, 1980). After a long period of nearly exclusive association with psychiatry, clinical psychologists — behaviour therapists in particular — are widening their aims in the firm conviction that medical care could be improved if the ideas and methods of modern psychology were incorporated in the practice of medicine. We certainly endorse the view that the skilful and sensible application of psychology could enrich the theory and practice of medicine. It will come as no surprise to find that as psychologists made a wider contribution to medicine, it will, as in the case of psychiatry, inevitably lead to a re-examination of our definitions of illness and of health. Among the psychological contributions that can be made to medicine, Rachman and Philips (1978, 1980) list the following areas: "Problems of pain, sleep disorders, pill-taking, child development and care, intellectual retardation, hospital admissions, doctor—patient relationships, failure to adhere to medical advice, smoking, obesity, headaches, the management of cardiac disorders, psychiatric disturbances, sexual disorders, psychosomatic disorders, and so on" (Rachman and Philips, 1978, p. 25). Technical discussions of these matters are provided in the volumes edited by Rachman (1977, 1980).

For a variety of reasons the growth of behaviour therapy was accompanied and facilitated by the adoption of methods and standards used in experimental psychology. The improved methodology and strict standards march hand-in-hand, and are in turn closely linked to a number of theoretical developments of the kind discussed in this book. The increasing reliance on *psychological* (as contrasted with medical) theorizing and psychological methodology inevitably gave rise to a re-examination of the concepts which underlie the medical or psychiatric approach to abnormal behaviour. The application of medical theorizing to behavioural abnormalities was found to be over-extended and often inappropriate. The description of abnormalities, difficulties, and handicaps within a medical framework that employs concepts and terms such as diagnosis, prognosis, symptoms and cure, was found to be wanting and misleading. These criticisms were supported and in turn strengthened by the arguments of those psychologists who insisted that human behaviour shows a greater degree of specificity than is implied in most medical theorizing about normal behaviour and personality. For these complex and inter-related reasons, it has become evident that the conventional methods for evaluating the outcome of psychotherapy are too crude and often misleading.

To return to the specific achievements of behaviour therapy, it can safely be said that there are well-established methods for reducing anxieties and fears of various sorts, good progress has been made in establishing an equally powerful method for dealing with obsessions and compulsions, and significant advances have been made in dealing with some sexual dysfunctions. Some useful if slow progress has been made in improving the deficient social skills of people with interpersonal problems, at least a degree of progress has been made in shaping up rehabilitation programmes for people with chronic and disabling disorders, and even where progress has been rather disappointing (e.g. the treatment of smoking) there are a number of fresh and enlivening ideas under consideration.

The weaknesses of behaviour therapy are a narrowness of vision, an unacknowledged unwillingness finally to give up the underlying medical theories, and a slowness to develop alternative methods of providing new services. On the theoretical side, certainly as far as the fear-reduction methods are concerned, the critical question is different from that posed by psychotherapy: in the case of psychotherapy, one continues to ask *if* the method works; in the case of behaviour therapy, one asks *why* it works. There is no shortage of competing explanations for the effects of various forms of behaviour therapy; a unifying and widely accepted version is not available. It still is not clear whether each of the methods will require a separate explanation. An unsatisfactory resignation to the need for several explanations, with its lack of parsimony, is by no means inevitable, but neither is it so obviously avoidable.

Historians may well argue that the astonishingly rapid growth of cognitive behaviour therapy was a reaction to the narrowness that formed a part of early behavioural therapy. In undertaking this broadening of the theory and practice of behaviour therapy, the innovators were aware that the move was taking them away from what had for a long time been a fundamental tenet of the psychological theory which had provided so · useful a boost for the early development of behaviour therapy. As will be evident from our review of the evidence collected so far, cognitive behaviour therapy has scored some limited but significantly encouraging successes and is distinguished by the optimistic enthusiasm of the people who are carrying out the research. Our opinion of the present state of the evidence, combined with a historical perspective on the matter, is optimistic. We firmly expect cognitive behaviour therapy to develop into a valuable and interesting addition to the methods for assisting people in difficulty, but hope that vigorous attempts will be made to avoid making the same unnecessary assumptions that interfered with the progress of behaviour therapy itself. Our confidence in the value of this broadening of behaviour therapy will in time be open to quantification by measuring the size and number of chapters that will be required to review the evidence in the Third Edition of this book — if there is a Third Edition.

Apart from its theoretical attractions, which are complex but numerous, cognitive behaviour therapy, if it is successful, will considerably enrich the treatment strategies available to therapists and might make a useful contribution to overcoming the problems of inadequate generalization and maintenance of therapeutic change.

A significant contribution of behaviour therapy has been the development of innovative research strategies for the study of treatment outcome. These methodological strategies range from single-case experimental designs to a variety of different group designs, including highly controlled laboratory-based investigations, more applied evaluations of multifaceted therapy programmes, and improved comparative outcome studies (see Kazdin and Wilson, 1978b). These methodological innovations provide the means for conducting the detailed empirical analyses of specific outcome research questions that have been emphasized throughout this book. The research strategies are not confined to the evaluation of behavioural methods — they are applicable to any operationally defined and measurable treatment method. Related to this development of innovative methodological strategies in behaviour therapy are the significant advances in the measurement of treatment outcome. The increasingly refined use of multiple subjective and objective measures of outcome, particularly the triple response system analysis of anxiety-related disorders, has provided important new information.

Of course, not all outcome research in behaviour therapy has met the demanding standards of objective scientific analysis. Many studies have been trivial or of questionable relevance to therapeutic outcome, while others have suffered from the same methodological weaknesses that have plagued non-behavioural research studies. Long-term evaluations of treatment outcome have been notably lacking, although there is a welcome trend indicating that researchers are increasingly including appropriate follow-up evaluations in their investigations. None the less, it is fair to conclude that with the advent of behaviour therapy both the quantity and the quality of experimental research on therapy outcome have increased greatly. Never before have psychological treatment methods been subjected to such sophisticated and controlled methodological evaluation.

It is important to note that our criticism of conventional treatment outcome studies and our call for greater specificity in research is not entirely new. Bergin and Strupp (1970), for example, criticized some aspects of traditional group comparative outcome studies and advocated "the experimental case study and experimental analogue approaches" as alternative research strategies for elucidating the mechanisms of psychological change. Unfortunately, aside from excessive and inappropriate objections to group experimental designs and the use of inferential statistical procedures, they failed to specify the nature of their favoured alternative research strategies or how they would be used to facilitate the scientific analysis of treatment outcome. Agras *et al.* (1979) and Kazdin and Wilson (1978b), among other behavioural researchers, have described how the different single-case experimental designs and different group designs complement each other in a unified, overall perspective on the development, evaluation, and implementation of treatment methods.

Incidentally, the common criticism of much of the research on behaviour therapy, based on the claim that it is merely analogue research, is for the most part unconvincing and unlikely to affect progress. We consider analogue research to be not merely acceptable, but desirable (see Borkovec and Rachman, 1979). Analogue experiments have several strengths and can provide specific answers to specific questions, uncover new information, introduce flexibility, and lead to the construction of new methods and conceptions.

A major and repeated objection to analogue research is that the findings are not applicable to clinical, especially to psychiatric, problems and/or samples. The first reply to this objection is that a significant proportion of analogue research was indeed carried out for valid reasons that do not include clinical considerations. The conduct of non-clinical research on fear, and other problems, has its own justification. Nevertheless a good deal of the research has had an implied clinical application. In what sense and to what degree is this research not applicable to clinical problems? If it can be shown that clinical samples differ from others in the intensity or types of their fears (to take this as one example), then it is bound to follow that some or even most of the analogue findings will not be reproducible among clinical subjects. On the other hand, if the fears of analogue subjects are intense and similar in type to those of the clinical subjects, then generalizing from one group to the next is likely to be successful in most instances. The main objection to analogue research falls away.

Generalizing from a group of college students who are intensely fearful of snakes to a group of psychiatric patients who are equally fearful of snakes should produce few problems. The key determinants of generalized ability are the intensity and type of the problem, not the status of the subject sample. Hence, generalizing from results obtained with agoraphobic *patients* to animal phobic patients is far more risky than generalizing from animal phobic students to animal phobic patients. Guidance on how to help a psychiatric patient who has intense fears of speaking in public is more likely to come from the research of Paul (1966) and others, on students with similar fears, rather than on research carried out on agoraphobic patients. Even the very best research on agoraphobic patients may provide a poor guide to a clinician interested in helping his patient overcome a fear of public speaking. The wholesale dismissal of analogue research cannot be justified on empirical or on theoretical grounds. Calling a study an "analogue" is a description, not a criticism.

The transient popularity of conventional *comparative* outcome research may well have reflected a desire to reduce dissonance and/or the need to find justification for continuing with current practices. Whatever the explanation, the attempt to use comparative studies as a substitute for direct tests of the effects of particular forms of therapy was bound to be unsatisfactory. Nevertheless, it had the useful result of emphasizing once again the need for precise measurement, improved methodology, and the application of firm standards of judgement. The wide-scale comparison of mediocre evidence is no solution, and could never provide a substitute for refined research.

We feel confident that the adoption of improved strategies for evaluating the outcome of therapy will lead to fruitful research, significant findings, the development of effective treatment methods, and improved understanding of the theoretical mechanisms that are responsible for therapeutic change. Aside from the extended use of more sophisticated research methods and multiple subjective and objective measures of treatment effects, the most fundamental change which we would recommend is the adoption of a properly psychological approach to difficulties, problems, and handicaps. Abnormal behaviour and experiences should be approached and described in psychological terms, assessed as psychological phenomena, and measured accordingly. The concepts cure, relapse, prognosis, symptoms, and the rest will continue to have a limited use, but should be dismissed from discussions of what currently are regarded as behavioural difficulties or neurotic reactions. Instead, the people who have these sorts of problems would be assessed in psychological terms and the effects of the therapy or interventions designed to deal with these problems would be assessed by psychological methods. One would not determine the effectiveness of the action by obtaining clinical ratings of cure, or symptom improvement, or any of the other current practices. Instead, one might obtain measurements of the type and effectiveness of the person's social behaviour in a range of situations — is he able to initiate and continue the conversations with people of the opposite sex, is he able to make appropriate assertive responses when in danger of being exploited or unfairly treated? The shift from a medical to a psychological perspective will also require the development of alternative care systems – people who seek assistance in overcoming their problems, would be directed to psychological centres instead of clinics or hospitals. Once the problem has been identified and properly described, explicit goals should be established before the intervention programme is undertaken. This proviso is particularly important in outcome *research*. Unless the aims are made explicit and stated in quantified degrees of success, unsatisfactory aspects of conventional research will persist.

Finally, it is evident that health and psychological services will absorb an increasing amount of time, effort, and expense. On the one hand the need for human services is increasing rapidly while on the other hand the financial resources with which to meet this challenge seem to be diminishing. As the competitive pressures on the health and psychological services mount, the need for accountability becomes ever greater. We welcome this emphasis on accountability. Psychologists are bound to devote part of their time to analysing the cost-effectiveness of the methods that they develop. Improved new methods of overcoming psychological handicaps or problems will be of little value if they prove to be too time-consuming or expensive; we will have to broaden our criteria for evaluating treatment outcome. Efficacy alone is no longer sufficient, although fundamentally important. Efficiency and durability of change, ease of dissemination and implementation, accuracy of evaluation, and considerations of cost-effectiveness have to be taken into account (see Kazdin and Wilson, 1978a).

REFERENCES

Abramson, J., Terespolsky, L., Brook, J., and Kark, S. (1965) Cornell Medical Index as a health measure in epidemiological studies. *Br. J. Prev. Social Med.* **19**, 103–110.

Adams, H. E. and Sturgis, E. T. (1977) Status of behavioural reorientation techniques in the modification of homosexuality: A review. *Psychol. Bull.* **84**, 1171–1188.

Agras, S., Chapin, H., and Oliveau, P. (1972) The natural history of phobia. *Arch. Gen. Psychiat.* **26**, 315–317.

Agras, W. S., Kazdin, A. E., and Wilson, G. T. (1979) *Behavior therapy: Towards an applied clinical science.* San Francisco, CA: Freeman.

Alden, L. and Safran, J. (1978) Irrational beliefs and nonassertive behavior. *Cognit. Ther. Res.* **2**, 357–364.

Alden, L., Safran, J., and Weideman, R. (1978) A comparison of cognitive and skills training strategies in the treatment of unassertive clients. *Behav. Ther.* **9**, 843–846.

Alexander, A. B., Cropp, G. J. A., and Chai, H. (1979) Effects of relaxation training on pulmonary mechanics in children with asthma. *J. Appl. Behav. Anal.* **12**, 27–35.

Alexander, J. F. and Parsons, B. V. (1973) Short-term behavioral intervention with delinquent families: Impact on family process and recidivism. *J. Abnorm. Psychol.* **81**, 219–225.

American Psychiatric Association Task Force on Behavior Therapy. Report No 5: *Behavior therapy in psychiatry* (1973). Washington D.C.: American Psychiatric Association.

Anker, J. and Walsh, R. (1961) Group psychotherapy, activity program and group structure in the treatment of chronic schizophrenics. *J. Consult. Psychol.* **25**, 476–481.

Ansari, J. (1976) Impotence: A controlled study. *B. J. Psychiat.* **128**, 194–198.

Appelbaum, S. (1977) *The anatomy of change.* New York: Plenum Press.

Armor, D. J., Polich, J. M., and Stambul, H. B. (1976). *Alcoholism and treatment.* Santa Monica, CA: The Rand Corporation.

Armor, D. J., Polich, J. M., and Stambul, H. (1977) A reply to "The Rand Report: A brief critique". *Addictive Behav.* **2**, 147–150.

Arnold, S. C. and Forehand, R. (1978) A comparison of cognitive training and response cost procedures in modifying cognitive styles of impulsive children. *Cognitive Ther. Res.* **2**, 183–188.

Aronson, H. and Weintraub, W. (1968) Social background of the patient in classical psychoanalysis. *J. Nerv. Ment. Dis.* **146**, 91–97.

Aronson, H. and Weintraub, W. (1969) Predictor of change in classical psychoanalysis. *J. Abnorm. Psychol.* **74**, 490–497.

Ashby, J., Ford, D. H., Guerney, B., and Guerney, L. (1957) Effects on clients of a reflective and a leading type of psychotherapy. *Psychol. Monographs,* **71**, 1–32.

Ashcraft, C. and Fitts, W. (1964) Self-concept change in psychotherapy. *Psychother. Theor. Res. Pract.* **1**, 115–118.

Atthowe, J. M. (1973) Behavior innovation and persistence. *Am. Psychol.* **28**, 34–41.

Atthowe, J. and Krasner, L. (1968) A preliminary report on the application of contingent reinforcement procedures (token economy) on a "chronic" psychiatric ward. *J. Abnorm. Psychol.* **73**, 37–43.

Auerbach, A. (1961) A survey of selected literature on psychotherapy of schizophrenia. In A. Scheften (Ed.), *Psychotherapy of schizophrenia.* Thomas, Springfield.

Auerbach, R. and Kilmann, P. R. (1977) The effects of group systematic desensitization on secondary erectile failure. *Behav. Ther.* **8**, 330–339.

Ayllon, T. and Azrin, N. H. (1965) The measurement and reinforcement of behavior of psychotics. *J. Exp. Anal. Behav.* **8**, 357–383.

Azima, H. and Wittkower, E. (1956) Gratifications of basic needs in schizophrenia. *Psychiatry,* **19**, 121–129.

Azrin, N. H. (1976) Improvements in the community-reinforcement approach to alcoholism. *Behav. Res. Ther.* **14**, 339–348.

Azrin, N. H. (1977) Personal communication.

Baer, D. M., Wolf, M. M., and Risley, T. R. (1968) Some current dimensions of applied behaviour analysis. *J. Appl. Behav. Anal.* **1**, 91–97.

Baehr, G. (1956) The comparative effectiveness of individual psychotherapy and group psychotherapy. *J. Consult. Psychol.* **18**, 179–183.

Bancroft, J. (1970) A comparative study of aversion and desensitization in the treatment of homosexuality. In L. E. Burns and J. H. Worsley (Eds.), *Behaviour therapy in the 1970's.* Bristol, England: Wright.

Bancroft, J. H. (1974) *Deviant sexual behaviour.* Oxford: Oxford University Press.

Bandura, A. (1969) *Principles of behavior modification.* New York: Holt.

Bandura, A. (1976) Self-reinforcement: Theoretical and methodological considerations. *Behaviorism,* **4**, 135–155.

Bandura, A. (1977a) Self-efficacy: Toward a unifying theory of behavioral change. *Psychol. Rev.* **84**, 191–215.

Bandura, A. (1977b) *Social learning theory.* Englewood Cliffs, N.J.: Prentice-Hall.

Bandura, A. (1978a) On paradigms and recycled ideologies. *Cognitive Ther. Res.* **2**, 79–104.

Bandura, A. (1978b) Reflections on self-efficacy. In S. Rachman (Ed.), *Perceived self-efficacy: Analyses of Bandura's theory. Adv. Behav. Res. Ther.* **1**, 237–269.

Bandura, A. and Adams, N. E. (1977) Analysis of self-efficacy theory of behavioural change. *Cognitive Ther. Res.* **1**, 287–310.

Bandura, A., Adams, N. E., and Beyer, J. (1977) Cognitive processes mediating behavioural change. *J. Personality Soc. Psychol.* **35**, 125–139.

Bandura, A., Blanchard, E. B., and Ritter, B. (1969) The relative efficacy of desensitization and modeling approaches for inducing behavioral, affective, and cognitive changes. *J. Personality Soc. Psychol.* **13**, 173–199.

Bandura, A., Grusec, J., and Menlove, F. (1967) Vicarious extinction of avoidance behavior. *J. Personality Soc. Psychol.* **5**, 449–455.

Bandura, A., Jeffery, R. W., and Gajdos, E. (1975) Generalizing change through participant modeling with self-directed mastery. *Behav. Res. Ther.* **13**, 141–152.

Bandura, A., Jeffery, R. W., and Wright, C. L. (1974) Efficacy of participant modeling as a function of response induction aids. *J. Abnor. Psychol.* **83**, 56–64.

Bandura, A. and Menlove, F. (1968) Factors determining vicarious extinction of avoidance behavior through symbolic modeling. *J. Personality Soc. Psychol.* **8**, 99–108.

Barendregt, J. T. (1957) A psychological investigation of the effect of group psychotherapy in patients with bronchial asthma. *J. Psychosomatic Res.* **2**, 115–119.

Barendregt, J. T. (1961) *Research in psychodiagnostics.* Mouton, Paris.

Barlow, D. H. (1977) Assessment of sexual behavior. In A. R. Ciminero, K. S. Calhoun, and H. E. Adams (Eds.), *Handbook of behavioural assessment.* New York: Wiley.

Barlow, D., Agras, W. S., Leitenberg, H., Callahan, E., and Moore, R. (1972) The contribution of therapeutic instructions to covert sensitization. *Behav. Res. Ther.* **10**, 411–415.

Barlow, D., Leitenberg, H., and Agras, W. S. (1969) The experimental control of sexual deviation through manipulation of the noxious scene in covert sensitization. *J. Abnorm. Psychol.* **74**, 596–601.

Barrett, J. (1978) Prevalence of depression over a 12-month period in a non-patient population. *Archiv. Gen. Psychiat.* **35**, 741–744.

Barrios, B. A. (1977) Repeating the mistakes of the past: A note on subject recruitment and selection procedures in analogue research on small animal phobias. Association for Advancement of Behavior Therapy Newsletter, **4**, 19.

Barron, F. & Leary, T. F. (1955) Changes in psychoneurotic patients with and without psychotherapy. *J. Consult. Psychol.* **19**, 239–245.

Beck, A. T. (1963) Thinking and depression. *Arch. Gen. Psychiat.* **9**, 324–333.

Beck, A. T. (1967) *Depression: Clinical; experimental and theoretical aspects.* New York: Hoeber.

Beck, A. T. (1976) *Cognitive therapy and the emotional disorders.* New York: International Universities Press.

Beck, A. T., Rush, A. J., Shaw, B. F., and Emery, G. (1978) Cognitive therapy of depression: A treatment manual. Unpublished manuscript, University of Pennsylvania.

Becker, J. and Schuckit, M. A. (1978) The comparative efficacy of cognitive therapy and pharmacotherapy in the treatment of depressions. *Cognitive Ther. Res.* **2**, 193–198.

Beckstrand, P. E. (1973) TA as a means of teaching writing in high school. *Trans. Anal. J.* **3**, 161–163.

Beiman, I., Israel, E., and Johnson, S. A. (1978) During training and post-training effects of live and taped extended progressive relaxation, self-relaxation, and electromyogram biofeedback. *J. Consult. Clin. Psychol.* **46**, 314–321.

Beiser, M. (1971) A psychiatric follow-up study of normal adults. *Am. J. Psychiat.* **127**, 40–48.

Bellack, A. S., Hersen, M., and Turner, S. M. (1976) Generalization effects of social skills training in chronic schizophrenics: An experimental analysis. *Behav. Res. Ther.* **14**, 391–398.

Bellak, L. and Loeb, L. (1969) Psychoanalytic, psychotherapeutic, and generally psychodynamic studies. In Bellak and Loeb (Eds.), *The Schizophrenic Syndrome.* New York: Grune & Stratton.

Bendig, A. (1962) Pittsburgh scale of social introversion–extraversion and emotionality. *J. Psychol.* **53**, 199–210.

Bennet, I. (1966) Changing concepts in insulin coma treatment. In M. Rinkel (Ed.), *Biological Treatment of mental illness,* New York: Farrar.

Benson, H. (1975) *The relaxation response.* New York: William Morrow.

Bergin, A. E. (1963) The effects of psychotherapy: negative results revisited, *J. Counsel. Psychol.* **10**, 244–250.

Bergin, A. E. (1966) Some implications of psychotherapy research for therapeutic practice. *J. Abnorm. Psychol.* **71**, 235–246.

Bergin, A. E. (1967a) Further comments on psychotherapy research. *Int. J. Psychiat.* **3**, 317–323.

Bergin, A. E. (1967b) An empirical analysis of psychotherapeutic issues. In D. Arbuckle (Ed.), *Counseling and Psychotherapy.* New York: McGraw Hill.

Bergin, A. E. (1970) The deterioration effect. *J. Abnorm. Psychol.* **75**, 300–302.

Bergin, A. E. (1971) The evaluation of therapeutic outcomes. In A. E. Bergin and S. L. Garfield (Eds.), *Handbook of psychotherapy and behavior change.* New York: Wiley.

Bergin, A. E. (1975) Individual psychotherapy. In M. Rosenzweig and L. Porter (Eds.), *Annual review of psychology.* Palo Alto: Ann. Rev. Inc.

Bergin, A. E. (1979) Negative effects revisited: A reply. *Professional Psychology.*

Bergin, A. E. and Lambert, M. J. (1978) The evaluation of therapeutic outcomes. In S. L. Garfield and A. E. Bergin (Eds.), *Handbook of psychotherapy and behavior change,* 2nd ed., New York: Wiley.

Bergin, A. E. and Strupp, H. H. (1970) New directions in psychotherapy research. *J. Abnorm. Psychol.* **76**, 13–26.

Bergin, A. E. and Suinn, R. M. (1975) Individual psychotherapy and behavior therapy. In M. R. Rosenzweig and L. W. Porter (Eds.), *Ann. Rev. Psychol.* **26**, 509–556.

Bernstein, D. (1969) Modification of smoking behavior: An evaluative review. *Psychol. Bull.* **71**, 418–440.

Bernstein, D. A. and McAlister, A. (1976) The modification of smoking behavior: Progress and problems. *Addictive Behav.* **1**, 89–102.

Bernstein, D. A. and Paul, G. L. (1971) Some comments on therapy analogue research with small animal "phobias". *J. Behav. Ther. Exp. Psychiat.* **2**, 225–237.

Beutler, L. E. (1977) Cognitive vs. "other" psychotherapies: When is a cognitive therapy? Unpublished manuscript, Baylor College of Medicine.

Bieber, I. (1962) *Homosexuality: a psychoanalytic study,* Basic Books, New York.

Birk, L., Huddleston, W., Miller, E., and Cohler, B. (1971) Avoidance conditioning for homosexuality. *Arch. Gen. Psychiat.* **25**, 314–323.

Blanchard, E. B. (1970) The generalization of vicarious extinction effects. *Behav. Res. Ther.* **8**, 323–330.

Bockover, J. (1956) Moral treatment in American psychiatry. *J. Nerv. Ment. Dis.* **124**, 167–194.

Boersma, K., DenHengst, S., Dekker, J., and Emmelkamp, P. M. G. (1976) Exposure and response prevention in the natural environment: A comparison with obsessive–compulsive patients. *Behav. Res. Ther.* **14**, 19–24.

Boesky, D. (1976) Xerox: A new symbol. *Psychoanalytic Q.* **45**, 290–294.

Bookhammer, R. *et al.* (1966) A five-year clinical follow-up study of schizophrenics treated by Rosen's "Direct Analysis", compared with controls. *Am. J. Psychiat.* **123**, 602–604.

Bootzin, R. and Nicassio, P. (1977) Behavioural treatments for insomnia. In M. Hersen, R. Eisler, and P. M. Miller (Eds.), *Progress in behavior modification,* Vol. 4.

Borkovec, T. D. (1972) Effects of expectancy on the outcome of systematic desensitization and implosive treatments for analogue anxiety. *Behav. Ther.* **3**, 29–40.

Borkovec, T. D. (1973) The role of expectancy and physiological feedback in fear research: A review with special reference to subject characteristics. *Behav. Ther.* **4**, 491–505.

Borkovec, T. D. (1974) Heart-rate process during systematic desensitization and implosive therapy for analog anxiety. *Behav. Ther.* **5**, 636–641.

Borkovec, T. D. (1977) Investigations of fear and sleep disturbance: Methodological, measurement, and theoretical issues in therapy outcome research. In G. E. Schwartz and D. Shapiro (Eds.), *Consciousness and self-regulation: Advances in research.* New York: Plenum Press.

Borkovec, T. D., Grayson, J. B., and Cooper K. M. (1978) Treatment of general tension: Subjective and physiological effects of progressive relaxation. *J. Consult. Clin. Psychol.* **46**, 518–528.

Borkovec, T. D., Grayson, J. B., O'Brien, G. T., and Weerts, T. C. (1979) Relaxation treatment of pseudo-insomnia and idiopathic insomnia: An electroencephalographic evaluation. *J. Appl. Behav. Anal.* **12**, 37–54.

Borkovec, T. D. and Hennings, B. L. (1978) The role of physiological attention-focusing in the relaxation treatment of sleep disturbance general tension and specific stress reaction. *Behav. Res. Ther.* **16**, 7–20.

Borkovec, T. D. and Nau, S. D. (1972) Credibility of analogue therapy rationales. *J. Behav. Ther. Exp. Psychiat.* **3**, 257–260.

Borkovec, T. D. and O'Brien, G. T. (1976) Methodological and target behavior issues in analogue therapy research. In M. Hersen, R. M. Eisler, and P. M. Miller (Eds,), *Progress in behavior modification*, Vol. 3. New York: Academic Press.

Borkovec, T. and Rachman, S. (1979) The utility of analogue research. *Behav. Res. Ther.* **17**, 253–262.

Borkovec, T. D. and Sides, J. K. (1979) Critical procedural variables related to the physiological effects of progressive relaxation: A review. *Behav. Res. Ther.* **17**, 119–126.

Borkovec, T. D. and Weerts, T. (1976) Effects of progressive relaxation on sleep disturbance: An electro-encephalographic evaluation. *Psychosomatic Med.* **38**, 173–180.

Bornstein, P. H. and Quevillon, R. P. (1976) The effects of a self-instructional package on overactive preschool boys. *J. Appl. Behav. Anal.* **9**, 179–188.

Boudewyns, P. A. (1975) Implosive therapy and desensitization therapy with inpatients: A five-year follow-up. *J. Abnorm. Psychol.* **84**, 159–160.

Boudewyns, P. A. and Wilson, A. E. (1972) Implosive therapy and desensitization therapy using free association in the treatment of inpatients. *J. Abnorm. Psychol.* **79**, 259–268.

Boulougouris, J., Rabavilas, A., and Stefanis, C. (1977) Psychophysiological responses in obsessive–compulsive patients. *Behav. Res. Ther.* **15**, 221–230.

Boyer, L. and Giovacchini, P. (1967) *Psychoanalytic Treatment of Schizophrenic and Characterological Disorders.* New York: Science House Inc.

Brady, J. P. (1976) Behavior therapy and sex therapy. *Amer. J. Psychiat.* **133**, 896–899.

Brady, J. and Wienckowski, L. (1978) Update on the teaching of behavior therapy. *J. Behav. Ther. Exp. Psychiat.* **9**, 125–127.

Brandsma, J. M., Maultsby, M. C., and Welsh, R. (1978) Self-help techniques in the treatment of alcoholism. Unpublished manuscript, University of Kentucky.

Brauer, A. P., Horlock, L. F., Nelson, E., Farquhar, J. W., and Agras, W. S. (1979) Relaxation therapy for essential hypertension: A veterans administration outpatient study. *J. Behav. Med.*

Brigham, T. and Catania, A. C. (1979) *Handbook of applied behavior research: Social and instructional processes.* New York: Halstead Press.

Brill, A. A. (1944) *Freud's contribution to psychiatry.* New York: Norton.

Brill, N. and Beebe, G. (1955) *A follow-up study of war neuroses.* Washington VA, Medical Monogr.

Brill, N. Q., Koegler, R. R. Epstein, L. J., and Forgy, E. W. (1964) Controlled study of psychiatry outpatient treatment. *Arch. Gen. Psychiat.* **10**, 581–595.

Broadhurst, A. (1977) Psychological approaches to sexual problems. In S. Rachman (Ed.), *Contributions to medical psychology,* Vol. I. Oxford: Pergamon Press.

Brodman, K. *et al.* (1952a) The Cornell Medical Index Health Questionnaire III. *J. Clin. Psychol.* **8**, 119–124.

Brodman, K. *et al.* (1952b) The Cornell Medical Index Health Questionnaire IV. *J. Clin. Psychol,* **8**. 289–292.

Brodman, K. *et al.* (1954) The Cornell Medical Index Health Questionnaire. *Am. J. Psychiat.* **111**, 37–45.

Brody, M. (1962) Prognosis and results of psychotherapy. In J. Nodine and J. Moyer (Eds.), *Psychosomatic medicine.* Philadelphia: Lea & Febiger.

Brownell, K. D. and Barlow, D. H. (1980) The behavioural treatment of sexual deviation. In E. Foa and A. Goldstein (Eds.), *Handbook of behavioural interventions.* New York: Wiley.

Brownell, K. D., Hayes, S. C., and Barlow, D. H. (1977) Patterns of appropriate and deviant sexual arousal: The behavioural treatment of multiple sexual deviations. *J. Consult. Clin. Psychol.* **45**, 1144–1155.

Brownell, K. D., Heckerman, C. L., Westlake, R. J., Hayes, S. C., and Monti, P. M. (1978) The effect of couples training and partner co-operativeness in the behavioural treatment of obesity. *Behav. Res. Ther.* **16**, 323–334.

Bruch, H. (1974) Perils of behavior modification in the treatment of anorexia nervosa. *J. Am. Med. Ass.* **230**, 1419–1422.

Caddy, G. R., Addington, H. J., and Perkins, D. (1978) Individualized behavior therapy for alcoholics: a third year independent double-blind follow-up. *Behav. Res. Ther.* **16**, 345–362.

Callner, D. A. (1975) Behavioral treatment approaches to drug abuse: A critical review of the research. *Psychol. Bull.* **82**, 143–164.

Candy, J., Balfour, F. G. H., Cawley, R. H., Hildebrand, H. P., Malan, D. H., Marks, I., and Wilson, J. (1972) A feasibility study for a controlled trial of formal psychotherapy. *Psychol. Med.* **2**, 345–362.

Canter, F. (1969) The future of psychotherapy with alcoholics. In C. Frederick (Ed.), *The Future of Psychotherapy.* Boston: Little, Brown & Co.

Cappon, D. (1964) Results of psychotherapy. *Br. J. Psychiat.* **110**, 34–45.

Carkhuff, R. and Truax, C. (1965) Lay mental health counselling. *J. Consult. Psychol.* 29, 426–431.

Carmody, T. P. (1978) Rational–emotive, self-instructional, and behavior assertion training: Facilitating maintenance. *Cognitive Ther. Res.* 2, 241–254.

Cartwright, D. S. (1956) Note on "changes in psychoneurotic patients with and without psychotherapy". *J. Consult. Psychol.* 20, 403–404.

Cartwright, R. D. (1968) Psychotherapeutic processes. In P. Farnsworth (Ed.), *Annual Review of Psychology.* Palo Alto: Ann Rev. Inc.

Cartwright, R. D. and Vogel, J. (1960) A comparison of changes in psychoneurotic patients during matched periods of therapy and no-therapy. *J. Consult. Psychol.* 24, 121–127.

Casas, J. M. (1975) A comparison of two mediational self-control techniques for the treatment of speech anxiety. Unpublished doctoral dissertation, Stanford University, Stanford, California.

Catts, S. and McConaghy, N. (1975) Ritual prevention in the treatment of obsessive–compulsive neurosis. *Austral. N.Z. J. Psychiat.* 9, 37–41.

Cautela, J. (1967) Covert sensitization. *Psychol. Reports,* 20, 459–468.

Chaney, E. F., O'Leary, M. R., and Marlatt, G. A. (1978) Skill training with alcoholics. *J. Consult. Clin. Psychol.* 46, 1092–1104.

Chesser, E. S. (1976) Behaviour therapy: Recent trends and current practice. *Br. J. Psychiatry,* 129, 289–307.

Chinsky, J. and Rappaport, J. (1970) Brief critique of the meaning and reliability of accurate empathy ratings. *Psychol. Bull.* 73, 379–382.

Ciminero, A. R., Calhoun, K. S., and Adams, H. E. (1977) (Eds.) *Handbook of behavioral assessment.* New York: Wiley.

Ciminero, A. R., Doleys, D. M., and Williams, C. L. (1978) Journal literature on behavior therapy 1970–1976: Analysis of subject characteristics, target behaviors and treatment techniques. *J. Behav. Ther. Exp. Psychiat.* 9, 301–307.

Clein, E. (1959) A follow-up of non-attenders at the Maudsley Hospital. Dissert., London University.

Cohen, M., Liebson, I. A., Faillace, L. A., and Allen, R. P. (1971) Moderate drinking by chronic alcoholics. *J. Nerv. Ment. Dis.* 53, 434–444.

Collingwood, T., Hefele, T., Muehlberg, N., and Drasgow, J. L. (1970) Toward identification of the therapeutically facilitative factor. *J. Clin. Psychol.* 26, 119–120.

Conrad, S. R. and Wincze, J. P. (1976) Orgasmic reconditioning: A controlled study of its effects upon the sexual arousal and behavior of adult male homosexuals. *Behavior Ther.* 7, 155–166.

Cooper, H. M. (1979) Statistically combining independent studies: A meta-analysis of sex differences in conformity research. *J. Personal. Soc. Psychol.* 37, 131–146.

Costello, C. G. (1963) Behaviour therapy: Criticisms and confusions. *Behav. Res. Ther.* 1, 159–162.

Covi, L., Lipman, R., Derogatis, L., Smith, J., and Pattison, I. (1974) Drugs and group psychotherapy in neurotic depression. *Am. J. Psychiat.* 131, 191–198.

Cowden, R., Zax, M., and Sproles, J. (1956) Group psychotherapy in conjunction with a physical treatment. *J. Clin. Psychol.* 12, 53–56.

Cowen, E. and Coombs, A. (1950) Follow-up of 32 cases treated by non-directive psychotherapy. *J. Abnorm. Psychol.* 45, 232–258.

Cox, D. J., Freundlich, A., and Meyer, R. G. (1975) Differential effectiveness of electromyograph feedback, verbal relaxation instructions, and medication placebo with tension headaches. *J. Consult. Clin. Psychol.* 43, 892–898.

Craighead, W. E., Kimball, W. H., and Rehak, P. J. (1979) Mood changes, physiological responses, and self-statements during social rejection imagery. *J. Consult. Clin. Psychol.* 47, 385–396.

Cremerius, J. (1962) *Die Beurteilung des Behandlungserfolges in der Psychotherapie.* Berlin: Springer Verlag.

Cremerius, J. (1969) Spatschicksale unbehandelter Neurosen, *Berliner Arztekammer,* 12, 389–392.

Crighton, J. and Jehu, D. (1969) Treatment of examination anxiety of systematic desensitization or psychotherapy in groups. *Behav. Res. Ther.* 7, 245–248.

Cross, H. J. (1964) The outcome of psychotherapy. *J. Consult. Psycol.* 28, 413–417.

Crowe, M. J., Marks, I. M., Agras, W. S., and Leitenberg, H. (1972) Time-limited desensitization, implosion and shaping for phobic patients: A crossover study. *Behav. Res. Ther.* 10, 319–328.

Crowne, D. and Stephens, M. (1961) Self-acceptance and self-evaluative behaviour: a critique of methodology. *Psychol. Bull.* 58, 104–121.

Curran, D. and Partridge, M. (1955) *Psychological medicine* (4th edn.). London: Livingstone.

Curran, D. and Partridge, M. (1963) *Psychological medicine* (5th edn.). London: Livingstone.

Dallenbach, K. (1955) Phrenology versus psychoanalysis. *Am. J. Psychol.* 68, 511–520.

Davidson, R. J. and Schwartz, G. E. (1976) The psychobiology of relaxation and related states: A multiprocess theory. In D. I. Mostovsky (Ed.), *Behavior control and the modification of physiological activity.* Englewood Cliffs, N.J.: Prentice-Hall.

Davison, G. (1968a) Elimination of a sadistic fantasy by a client-controlled counter conditioning technique: A case study. *J. Abnorm. Psychol.* 73, 84–90.

Davison, G. C. (1968b) Systematic desensitization as a counterconditioning process. *J. Abnorm. Psychol.* 73, 91–99.

Davison, G. C. (1969) Appraisal of behavior modification techniques with adults in institutional settings. In C. M. Franks (Ed.), *Behavior therapy: appraisal and status.* New York: McGraw-Hill.

Davison, G. C. and Wilson, G. T. (1973) Processes of fear-reduction in systematic desensitization: Cognitive and social reinforcement factors in humans. *Behav. Ther.* 4, 1–21.

DeMoor, W. (1970) Systematic desensitization vs. prolonged high intensity stimulation (flooding). *J. Behav. Ther. Exp. Psychiat.* 1, 45–52.

Denker, P. (1946) Results of treatment of psychoneuroses by the G.P., *N.Y. State J. Med.* 46, 2164–2166.

Denney, D. R. (in press) Self-control approaches to the treatment of test anxiety. In I. G. Sarason (Ed.), *Test anxiety: Theory, research and applications.* Hillsdale, N.J.: Lawrence Erlbaum.

Dickenson, W. and Truax, C. (1966) Group counselling with college under-achievers. *Personnel Guid. J.* 4, 41–49.

DiGiuseppe, R. A. and Miller, N. J. (1977) A review of outcome studies on rational–emotive therapy. In A. Ellis and R. Grieger (Eds.), *Handbook of rational–emotive therapy.* New York: Springer.

DiLoreto, A. (1971) *Comparative psychotherapy.* New York: Aldine-Atherton.

Dittman, A. (1966) Psychotherapeutic processes. In Farnsworth, McNemar, and McNemar (Eds.), *Annual Review of Psychology.* Palo Alto: Ann Rev. Inc.

Douglas, V. I., Parry, P., Marton, P., and Garson, C. (1976) Assessment of a cognitive training program for hyperactive children. *J. Abnorm. Child Psychol.* 4, 389–410.

Dudek, S. (1970) Effects of different types of therapy on the personality as a whole. *J. Nerv. Ment. Dis.* 150, 329–345.

Duhrssen, A. and Jorswieck, E. (1969) Eine empirisch-statische Untersuchung zur Leistungsfahigkeit. Psychoanalytischer Behandlung, *Berliner Ärztekammer,* 12, 385–389.

Dunkel, L. D. and Glaros, A. (1978) Comparison of self-instructional and stimulus control treatments for obesity. *Cognitive Ther. Res.* 2, 75–78.

Dymond, R. (1955) Adjustment changes in the absence of psychotherapy. *J. Consult. Psychol.* 19, 103–107.

D'Zurilla, T., Wilson, G. T., and Nelson, R. (1973) A preliminary study of the effectiveness of graduated prolonged exposure in the treatment of irrational fear. *Behav. Ther.* 4, 672–685.

Eisler, R. M., Blanchard, E. B., Fitts, H., and Williams, J. B. (1978) Social skills training with and without modeling for schizophrenic and non-psychotic hospitalized patients. *Behav. Modification,* 2, 147–172.

Elliot, C. H. and Denney, D. R. (1978) A multiple-component treatment approach to smoking reduction. *J. Consult. Clin. Psychol.* 46, 1330–1339.

Ellis, A. (1957) Outcome of employing three techniques of psychotherapy. *J. Clin. Psychol.* 13, 344–350.

Ellis, A. (1962) *Reason and emotion in psychotherapy.* New York: Lyle Stuart.

Ellis, A. (1970) *The essence of rational psychotherapy: A comprehensive approach to treatment.* New York: Institute for Rational Living.

Ellis, A. (1977a) Rational–emotive therapy: Research data that supports the clinical and personality hypothesis of RET and other modes of cognitive-behavior therapy. *The Counseling Psychologist,* 7, 2–42.

Ellis, A. (1977b) Rejoinder: Elegant and inelegant RET. *The Counseling Psychologist,* 1, 73–82.

Ellis, A. (1979) A note on the treatment of agoraphobics with cognitive modification versus prolonged exposure in vivo. *Behav. Res. Ther.* 17, 162–163.

Ellis, A. and Grieger, R. (1977) *Handbook of rational psychotherapy.* New York: Springer.

Emmelkamp, P. M. G. (1975) Effects of expectancy on systematic desensitization and flooding. *Eur. J. Behav. Anal. Modification,* 1, 1–11.

Emmelkamp, P. M. G. and Emmelkamp-Benner, A. (1975) Effects of historically portrayed modeling and group treatment on self-observation: A comparison with agoraphobics. *Behav. Res. Ther.* 13, 135–139.

Emmelkamp, P. M. G. and Kraanen, J. (1977) Therapist-controlled exposure *in vivo* versus self-controlled exposure *in vivo*: a comparison with obsessive–compulsive patients. *Behav. Res. Ther.* 15, 491–495.

Emmelkamp, P. M. G., Kuipers, A. C. M., and Eggeraat, J. B. (1978) Cognitive modification versus prolonged exposure *in vivo*: A comparison with agoraphobics as subjects. *Behav. Res. Ther.* 16, 33–42.

Emmelkamp, P. M. G. and Ultee, K. A. (1975) A comparison of "successive approximation" and "self-observation" in the treatment of agoraphobia. *Behav. Ther.* 5, 606–613.

Emmelkamp, P. M. G. and Wessels, H. (1975) Flooding in imagination vs. flooding *in vivo*: A comparison with agoraphobics. *Behav. Res. Ther.* 13, 7–15.

Endicott, N. and Endicott, J. (1963) "Improvement" in untreated psychiatric patients. *Archs. Gen. Psychiat.* 9, 575–585.

Endicott, N. A. and Endicott, J. (1964) Prediction of improvement in treated and untreated patients using the Rorschach Prognostic Rating Scale. *J. Consult. Psychol.* 28, 342–348.

Endler, N. S., Hunt, J. McV., and Rosenstein, A. J. (1962) An S–R inventory of anxiousness. *Psychol. Monogr.* 76, No. 17, (Whole No. 536).

Ends, E. and Page, C. (1959) Group psychotherapy and concomitant psychological change. *Psychol. Monogr.* 73.

Ernst, K. (1959) *Die Prognose der Neurosen.* Berlin: Springer.

Esse, D. and Wilkins, W. (1978) Empathy and imagery in avoidance behavior reduction. *J. Con. Clin. Psychol.* 46, 202–203.

Everraerd, W., Rijken, H., and Emmelkamp, P. M. G. (1973) A comparison of flooding and successive approximation in the treatment of agoraphobia. *Behav. Res. Ther.* 11, 105–118.

Ewing, J. A. and Rouse, B. A. (1976) Failure of an experimental treatment program to inculcate controlled drinking in alcoholics. *Br. J. Addiction,* 71, 123–134.

Eysenck, H. J. (1952) The effects of psychotherapy: an evaluation. *J. Consult. Psychol.* 16, 319–324.

Eysenck, H. J. (Ed.) (1960) *Behaviour therapy and the neuroses,* Oxford: Pergamon Press.

Eysenck, H. J. (1963a) Psychoanalysis – Myth or science? In S. Rachman (Ed.), *Critical essays on psychoanalysis.* Oxford: Pergamon Press.

Eysenck, H. J. (1963b) Behaviour therapy, spontaneous remission and transference in neurotics. *Am. J. Psychiat.* 119, 867–871.

Eysenck, H. J. (Ed.) (1964) *Experiments in behaviour therapy,* Oxford: Pergamon Press.

Eysenck, H. J. (1969a) *The effects of psychotherapy.* New York: Science House, Inc.

Eysenck, H. J. (1969b) Relapse and symptom substitution after different types of psychotherapy. *Behav. Res. Ther.* 7, 283–287.

Eysenck, H. J. (1976) The learning theory model of neurosis – a new approach. *Behav. Res. Ther.* 14, 251–268.

Eysenck, H. J. (1978) An exercise in megasilliness. *Am. Psychologist,* 33, 517.

Eysenck, H. J. (1979) A unified theory of psychotherapy, behavior therapy and spontaneous remission. *Zeitsch. Psychol.* (in press).

Eysenck, H. J. and Rachman, S. (1965) *Causes and cures of neuroses.* London: Routledge & Kegan Paul.

Eysenck, H. J. and Wilson, G. (1973) *The experimental study of Freudian theories.* London: Methuen.

Fairweather, G. W. (1964) *Social psychology in treating mental illness: An experimental approach.* New York: Wiley.

Fairweather, G. W., Sanders, D. H., Cressler, D. L., and Maynard, H. (1969) *Community life for the mentally ill.* Chicago: Aldine.

Fairweather, G. W. and Simon, R. (1963) A further follow-up comparison of psychotherapeutic programs. *J. Consult. Psychol.* 27, 186.

Feifel, H. and Eells, J. (1963) Patients and therapists assess the same psychotherapy. *J. Consult. Psychol.* 27, 310–318.

Feifel, H. and Schwartz, A. (1953) Group psychotherapy with acutely disturbed psychotic patients. *J. Consult. Psychol.* 17, 113–121.

Feighner, J. P. *et al.* (1972) Diagnostic criteria for use in psychiatric research. *Archives of General Psychiatry,* 26, 57–63.

Feist, J. and Rosenthal, T. (1973) Serpent versus surrogate. *Behav. Res. Ther.* 11, 483–490.

Feldman, M. and Drasgan, J. (1951) A visual verbal test for schizophrenia. *Psychiatric Quart. Suppl.* 25, 55–64.

Feldman, M. P. (1977) *Criminal behaviour.* New York: Wiley.

Feldman, M. P. and MacCulloch, M. J. (1971) *Homosexual behaviour: Therapy and assessment.* Oxford: Pergamon Press.

Fisher, S. and Greenberg, R. (1977) *The scientific credibility of Freud's theories and therapy.* Sussex: Harvester Press.

Flaxman, J. (1976) Quitting smoking. In E. Craighead, A. E. Kazdin, and M. J. Mahoney (Eds.), *Behavior modification: Principles, issues, and applications.* Boston Mass.: Houghton Mifflin Company.

Foa, E. (1977) Lecture, Institute of Psychiatry, London.

Foa, E., Blau, J., Prout, M., and Latimer, P. (1977) Is horror a necessary component of flooding (implosion?) *Behav. Res. Ther.* 15, 397–402.

Foa, E. B. and Goldstein, A. (1978) Continuous exposure and complete response prevention in the treatment of obsessive–compulsive neurosis. *Behav. Ther.* 9, 821–829.

Foreyt, J. (1977) *Behavioural treatment of obesity.* New York: Pergamon Press.

Forsyth, R. and Fairweather, G. (1961) Psychotherapeutic and other hospital treatment criteria. *J. Abnorm. Soc. Psychol.* 62, 598–604.

Frank, J. D. (1961) *Persuasion and healing.* Baltimore: Johns Hopkins University Press.

Frank, J., Hoehn-Saric, R., Imber, S., Liberman, B. and Stone, A. (1978) *Effective ingredients of successful psychotherapy.* New York: Brunner/Mazel.

Franks, C. M. and Mays, D. T. (in press) Negative effects revisited: A rejoinder. *Professional Psychol.*

Franks, C. M. and Wilson, G. T. (1973) *Annual review of behaviour therapy: Theory and practice,* Vol. I. New York: Brunner/Mazel.

Franks, C. M. and Wilson, G. T. (1974) *Annual review of behavior therapy: Theory and practice*, Vol. II. New York: Brunner/Mazel.

Franks, C. M. and Wilson, G. T. (1975) *Annual review of behavior therapy: Theory and practice*, Vol. III. New York: Brunner/Mazel.

Franks, C. M. and Wilson, G. T. (1976) *Annual review of behavior therapy: Theory and practice*, Vol. IV. New York: Brunner/Mazel.

Franks, C. M. and Wilson, G. T. (1977) *Annual review of behavior therapy: Theory and practice*, Vol. V. New York: Brunner/Mazel.

Franks, C. M. and Wilson, G. T. (1978) *Annual review of behavior therapy: Theory and practice*, Vol. VI. New York: Brunner/Mazel.

Fremouw, W. J. and Zitter, R. E. (1978) A comparison of skills training and cognitive restructuring – relaxation for the treatment of speech anxiety. *Behav. Ther.* 9, 248–259.

Freud, S. (1922 Ed.) *Introductory lectures on psychoanalysis*. London: Allen & Unwin.

Freud, S. (1932) *New Introductory Lectures*. New York: Norton.

Freud, S. (1940) *An outline of psychoanalysis*. New York: Norton.

Friedling, C. and O'Leary, S. G. (1979) The effects of self-instructional training on second- and third-grade hyperactive children: A failure to replicate. *J. Appl. Behav. Anal.* 12.

Friess, C. and Nelson, M. J. (1942) Psychoneurotics five years later. *Am. J. Med. Sci.* 203, 539–558.

Gallagher, J. (1953a) Manifest anxiety changes concomitant with client centred therapy. *J. Consult. Psychol.* 17, 443–446.

Gallagher, J. (1953b) MMPI changes concomitant with client centred therapy. *J. Consult. Psychol.* 17, 334–338.

Gardner, R. A. (1966) On box score methodology as illustrated by three reviews of overtraining reversal effects. *Psychol. Bull.* 66, 416–418.

Garfield, S. L. (1976) Review of *Psychotherapy versus behavior therapy* by Sloane, R. B. *et al. Contemp. Psychol.* 21, 328–329.

Gelder, M. G., Bancroft, J. H. J., Gath, D., Johnston, D. W., Mathews, A. M., and Shaw, P. M. (1973) Specific and non-specific factors in behaviour therapy. *Br. J. Psychiat.* 123, 445–462.

Gelder, M. and Marks, I. (1968) A crossover study of desensitization in phobias. *Br. J. Psychiat.* 114, 323–328.

Gelder, M. G., Marks, I. M., and Wolff, H. H. (1967) Desensitization and psychotherapy in the treatment of phobic states: A controlled inquiry. *Br. J. Psychiat.* 113, 53–73.

Giel, R., Knox, R., and Carstairs, G. (1964) A 5-year follow-up of 100 neurotic outpatients. *Br. Med. J.* 2, 160–163.

Giel, R. *et al.* (1978) Mental illness, neuroticism and live events in a Dutch village sample. *Psychol. Med.* 8, 235–243.

Gillian, P. and Rachman, S. (1974) An experimental investigation of desensitization in phobic patients. *Br. J. Psychiat.* 124, 392–401.

Girodo, M. and Henry, D. R. (1976) Cognitive, physiological and behavioural components of anxiety in flooding. *Can. J. Behav. Sci. Rev.* 8, 224–231.

Girodo, M. and Roehl, J. (1978) Cognitive preparation and coping self-talk: Anxiety management during the stress of flying. *J. Consult. Clin. Psychol.* 46, 978–989.

Glasgow, R. E. (1978) Effects of a self-control manual, rapid smoking, and amount of therapist contact on smoking reduction. *J. Consult. Clin. Psychol.* 46, 1439–1447.

Glass, C. R., Gottman, J. M., and Shmurak, S. H. (1976) Response acquisition and cognitive self-statement modification approaches to dating skills training. *J. Counseling Psychol.* 23, 520–526.

Glass, G. V. (1976) Primary, secondary, and meta-analysis of research. *Educational Res.* 5, 3–8.

Glass, G. V. and Smith, M. L. (1976) Meta-analysis of psychotherapy outcome studies. Paper presented at the Society for Psychotherapy Research, San Diego, California.

Glogower, F. D., Fremouw, W. J., and McCroskey, J. C. (1978) A component analysis of cognitive restructuring. *Cognitive Ther. Res.* 2, 241–254.

Goldfried, M. R. (1977) The use of relaxation and cognitive relabeling as coping skills. In R. B. Stuart (Ed.), *Behavioral self management*. New York: Brunner/Mazel.

Goldfried, M. R. (1979) Anxiety reduction through cognitive-behavioral intervention. In P. Kendall and S. D. Hollon (Eds.), *Cognitive-behavioral interventions: Theory, research and procedures*. New York: Academic Press.

Goldfried, M. R. and Davison, G. C. (1976) *Clinical behavior therapy*. New York: Holt, Rinehart & Winston.

Goldfried, M. R., Linehan, M. M. and Smith, J. L. (1978) Reduction of test anxiety through cognitive restructuring. *J. Consult. Clin. Psychol.* 46, 32–39.

Goldfried, M. R. and Sobocinski, D. (1975) Effect of irrational beliefs on emotional arousal. *J. Consult. Clin. Psychol.* 43, 504–510.

Goldfried, M. and Trier, C. S. (1974) Effectiveness of relaxation as an active coping skill. *J. Abnorm. Psychol.* **83**, 348–355.

Goldstein, A. (1960) Patient's expectancies and non-specific therapy as a basis for (un)spontaneous remission. *J. Clin. Psychol.* **18**, 399–403.

Gomez-Schwartz, B., Hadley, S., and Strupp, H. (1978) Individual psychotherapy and behavior therapy. In M. Rosenzweig and L. Porter (Eds.), *Annual Review of Psychology*. Palo Alto: Ann. Rev. Inc.

Goren, E. (1975) A comparison of systematic desensitization and self-instruction in the treatment of phobias. Unpublished Masters Thesis, Rutgers University.

Götestam, K. G., Melin, L., and Öst, L. (1976) Behavioral techniques in the treatment of drug abuse: an evaluation review. *Addictive Behav.* **1**, 205–226.

Gottman, J. M. and Markman, H. J. (1978) Experimental designs in psychotherapy research. In S. L. Garfield and A. E. Bergin (Eds.), *Handbook of psychotherapy and behavior change* (2nd ed.). New York: Wiley.

Graham, S. R. (1960) The effects of psychoanalytically oriented psychotherapy on levels of frequency and satisfaction in sexual activity. *J. Clin. Psychol.* **16**, 94–95.

Greer, H. and Cawley, R. (1966) *Some observations on the natural history of neurotic illness*. Australian Medical Association.

Grey, S., Sartory, G., and Rachman, S. (1979) Synchronous and desynchronous changes during fear reduction. *Behav. Res. Ther.* **17**, 137–148.

Grinspoon, J., Wealt, J., and Shaker, R. (1968) Psychotherapy and pharmacotherapy in chronic schizophrenia. *Am J. Psychiat.* **124**, 1645–1652.

Grünbaum, A. (1976) Personal communication.

Grünbaum, A. (1977) How scientific is psychoanalysis? In R. Stern, L. Horowitz, and J. Lynes (Eds.), *Science and Psychotherapy*. New York: Haven Publ. Co.

Grünbaum, A. (1979) Epistemological liabilities of the clinical appraisal of psychoanalytic theory. *Psychoanalysis and Contemp. Thought*, **2**, No. 4.

Gurman, A. S. and Kniskern, D. P. (1978a) Behavioral marriage therapy: II. Empirical perspective. *Family Process*, **17**, 139–148.

Gurman, A. S. and Kniskern, D. P. (1978b) Deterioration in marital and family therapy: Empirical, clinical, and conceptual issues. *Family Process*, **17**, 3–20.

Gurman, S., Knudson, R. M., and Kniskern, D. P. (1978) Behavioral marriage therapy. IV. Take two aspirin and call us in the morning. *Family Process*, **17**, 165–180.

Hackmann, A. and McClean, C. (1975) A comparison of flooding and thought-stopping treatment. *Behav. Res. Ther.* **13**, 263–269.

Hafner, J. and Marks, I. (1976) Exposure *in vivo* of agoraphobics: Contributions of diazepam, group exposure and anxiety evocation. *Psychol. Med.* **6**, 71–88.

Hall, S. M., Hall, R. G., DeBoer, G., and O'Kulitch, P. (1977) Self and external management compared with psychotherapy in the control of obesity. *Behav. Res. Ther.* **15**, 89–96.

Hall, S. M., Hall, R. G., Hanson, R. W., and Borden, B. L. (1974) Permanence of two self-managed treatments of overweight. *J. Consult. Clin. Psychol.* **42**, 781–786.

Hallam, R. and Rachman, S. (1976) Current status of aversion therapy. In M. Hersen, R. M. Eisler, and P. M. Miller (Eds.), *Progress in behavior modification*, Vol. 2. New York: Academic Press.

Hamburg, D. A. (Ed.) (1967) *Report of an ad hoc Committee on Central Fact-gathering Data* (plus appendices). American Psychoanalytic Association, New York.

Hand, I., Lamontagne, Y., and Marks, I. M. (1974) Group exposure (flooding) *in vivo* for agoraphobics. *Br. J. Psychiat.* **124**, 588–602.

Hanson, R. W., Borden, B. L., Hall, S. M., and Hall, R. G. (1976) Use of programmed instruction in teaching self-management skills to overweight adults. *Behav. Therapy*, **7**, 366–373.

Hartman, W. and Fithian, M. A. (1972) *Treatment of sexual dysfunction*. California: Center for Marital and Sexual Studies.

Hastings, D. W. (1958) Follow-up results in psychiatric illness. *Am. J. Psychiat.* **114**, 1057–1066.

Haynes, S. N., Griffin, P., Mooney, D., and Parise, M. (1975) Electromyographic biofeedback and relaxation instruction in the treatment of muscle contraction headaches. *Behav. Therapy*, **6**, 672–678.

Hedberg, A. G. and Campbell, L. III. (1974) A comparison of four behavioral treatments of alcoholism. *J. Behav. Ther. Exp. Psychiat.* **5**, 251–256.

Heilbrunn, G. (1966) Results with psychoanalytic therapy and professional commitment. *Am J. Psychother.* **20**, 89–99.

Henderson, D. and Batchelor, I. (1962) *Henderson and Gillespie's textbook of psychiatry*, 9th edn., London: Oxford University Press.

Henderson, D. and Gillespie, R. (1947) *A textbook of psychiatry*, 6th edn. London: Oxford University Press.

Henry, W. and Schlien, J. (1958) Effective complexity and psychotherapy: Some comparisons of time-limited and unlimited treatment. *J. Projective Techniques*, **22**, 153–162.

Hersen, M. (1979) Limitations and problems in the clinical application of behavioural techniques in psychiatric settings. *Behav. Ther.* **10**, 65–80.

Hersen, M. and Barlow, D. H. (1976) *Single case experimental designs: Strategies for studying behavior change.* New York: Pergamon Press.

Hersen, M. and Bellack, A. (Eds.) (1978) *Behavior therapy in the psychiatric setting.* Baltimore, Md: Williams & Wilkins.

Heyse, H. (1975) Response prevention and modelling in the treatment of obsessive–compulsive neurosis. In H. Brengelmann (Ed.), *Progress in behaviour therapy.* Berlin: Springer Verlag.

Hodgson, R. and Rachman, S. (1974) Desynchrony in measures of fear. II. *Behav. Res. Ther.* **12**, 319–326.

Hodgson, R., Rankin, H. and Stockwell, T. (1978) Craving and loss of control. In P. E. Nathan, G. A. Marlatt and T. Loberg (Eds.), *Alcoholism: New directions in behavioral research and treatment.* New York: Plenum.

Hollingshead, A. and Redlich, F. (1958) *Social class and mental illness,* Wiley, New York.

Holmes, E. (1938) *An Experimental Study of Fear in Young Children.* Child Dev. Monogr. No. 20.

Holroyd, K. A. (1976) Cognition and desensitization in the group treatment of test anxiety. *J. Consult. Clin. Psychol.* **44**, 991–1001.

Holroyd, K. A. and Andrasik, F. (1978) Coping and self-control of chronic tension headache. *J. Consult. Clin. Psychol.* **46**, 1036–1045.

Holroyd, K., Andrasik, F. and Westbrook, T. (1977) Cognitive control of tension headache. *Cognitive Ther. Res,* **1**, 121–133.

Holroyd, K. A., Westbrook, T., Wolf, M. and Badhorn, E. (1978) Performance, cognition, and physiological responding in test anxiety. *J. Abnorm. Psychol.* **87**, 442–451.

Hoon, P. and Lindsley, O. (1974) A comparison of behavior and traditional therapy publication activity. *Am Psychologist,* **29**, 694–697.

Horan, J. J., Hackett, G., Buchanan, J. D., Stone, C. I., and Demchik-Stone, D. (1977) Coping with pain: A component analysis of stress inoculation. *Cognitive Ther. Res.* **1**, 211–222.

Horan, J. J., Linberg, S. E., and Hackett, G. (1977) Nicotine poisoning and rapid smoking. *J. Consult. Clin. Psychol.* **45**, 344–347.

Horowitz, L. M., Sampson, H., Siegelman, E. Y., Weiss, J., and Goodfriend, S. (1978) Cohesive and dispersal behaviors: Two classes of concomitant change in psychotherapy. *J. Consult. Clin. Psychol.* **46**, 556–564.

Horwitz, W., Polatin, P., Kolb, L., and Hoch, P. (1958) A study of cases of schizophrenia treated by "direct analysis". *Am J. Psychiat.* **114**, 870–873.

Hung, J. F. H. and Rosenthal, T. L. (1978) Therapeutic videotaped playback: A critical review. *Adv. Behav. Res. Ther.* **1**, 103–135.

Hunt, G. H. and Azrin, N. H. (1973) The community-reinforcement approach to alcoholism. *Behav. Res. Ther.* **11**, 91–104.

Hunt, W. A. and Bespalec, D. A. (1974) An evaluation of current methods of modifying smoking behavior. *J. Clin. Psychol.* **30**, 431–438.

Hussain, M. S. (1971) Desensitization and flooding (implosion) in treatment of phobias. *Am. J. Psychiat.* **127**, 1509–1514.

Hussain, R. A. and Lawrence, P. S. (1978) The reduction of test, state and trait anxiety by test-specific and generalized stress inoculation training. *Cognitive Ther. Res.* **2**, 25–38.

Imber, S., Frank, J., Nash, E., and Gleidman, L. (1957) Improvement and amount of therapeutic contact, *J. Consult. Psychol.* **77**, 283–393.

Imber, S., Nash, E., Hoehn-Saric, R., Stone, A., and Frank, J. L. (1968) A 10-year follow-up of treated psychiatric outpatients. In S. Lesse (Ed.). *An evaluation of the results of the psychotherapies.* Springfield: Thomas.

Jacob, R., Kraemer, H., and Agras, W. S. (1977) Relaxation therapy in the treatment of hypertension. *Arch. Gen. Psychiat.* **34**, 1417–1427.

Jacobson, E. (1938) *Progressive relaxation.* Chicago: University of Chicago Press.

Jacobson, N. S. (1977) Problem solving and contingency contracting in the treatment of marital discord. *J. Consult. Clin. Psychol.* **45**, 92–100.

Jacobson, N. S. (1978a) A review of the research on the effectiveness of marital therapy. In T. J. Paolino and B. S. McCrady (Eds.), *Marriage and marital therapy.* New York: Brunner/Mazel.

Jacobsen, N. S. (1978b) Specific and nonspecific factors in the effectiveness of a behavioural approach to the treatment of marital discord. *J. Consult. Clin. Psychol.* **46**, 442–452.

Jacobson, N. S. and Baucom, D. H. (1977) Design and assessment of nonspecific control groups in behaviour modification research. *Behav. Ther.* **8**, 709–719.

Jacobson, N. S. and Martin, B. (1976) Behavioral marriage therapy: Current status. *Psychol. Bull.* **83**, 540–556.

Jacobson, N. and Weiss, R. L. (1978) Behavioral marriage therapy. III. The contents of Gurman *et al.* may be hazardous to our health. *Family Process,* 17, 149–163.

James, S. (1978) Treatment of homosexuality. II. Superiority of desensitization/arousal as compared with anticipatory avoidance conditioning: Results of a controlled trial. *Behav. Ther.* 9, 28–36.

James, S., Orwin, A., and Turner, R. K. (1977) Treatment of homosexuality. I. Analysis of failure following a trial of anticipatory avoidance conditioning and the development of an alternative treatment system. *Behav. Ther.* 8, 840–848.

Jeffery, R. W., Wing, R. R., and Stunkard, A. J. (1978) Behavioral treatment of obesity: The state of the art. *Behav. Ther.* 9, 189–199.

Jenni, M. A. and Wollersheim, J. (1979) Cognitive therapy, stress management training, and the Type A behavior pattern. *Cognitive Ther. Res.* 3, 61–74.

Johnston, D. W., Lancashire, M., Mathews, A. M., Munby, M., Shaw, P. M., and Gelder, M. G. (1976) Imaginal flooding and exposure to real phobic situations: Changes during treatment. *Br. J. Psychiat.* 129, 372–377.

Jones, R. G. (1968) A factored measure of Ellis' irrational belief system, with personality and maladjustment correlates. Unpublished doctoral dissertation, Texas Technological College.

Jurjevich, R. M. (1968) Changes in psychiatric symptoms without psychotherapy. In D. Lesse (Ed.), *An evaluation of the results of the psychotherapies.* Thomas, Springfield.

Kalinowsky, L. (1967) Insulin coma treatment. In A. Freedman and H. Kaplan (Eds.), *Comprehensive textbook of psychiatry.* Baltimore: Williams, Wilkins.

Kalinowsky, L. and Hoch, P. (1952) *Shock treatments and psychosurgery in psychiatry,* 2nd edn. New York: Grune & Stratton.

Kanfer, F. H., Karoly, P., and Newman, A. (1975) Reduction of children's fear of the dark by competence-related and situational threat-related verbal cues. *J. Consult. Clin. Psychol.* 43, 251–258.

Kanter, N. J. and Goldfried, M. R. (1979) Relative effectiveness of rational restructuring and self-control desensitization in the reduction of interpersonal anxiety. *Behavior Therapy,* 10, 472–490.

Kaplan, H. A. (1974) *The new sex therapy.* New York: Brunner/Mazel.

Karon, B. P. and Vandenbos, G. R. (1970) Experience, medication, and the effectiveness of psychotherapy with schizophrenics. *Br. J. Psychiat.* 116, 427–428.

Karon, B. and Vandenbos, G. (1972) The consequences of psychotherapy for schizophrenic patients. *Psychotherapy: Theory, research & practice,* 9, 111–119.

Karst, S. and Trexler, L. (1970) An initial study using fixed role and rational-emotive therapies in treating public speaking anxiety. *J. Consult. Clin. Psychol.* 34, 360–366.

Karush, A., Daniels, G., O'Connor, J., and Stern, L. (1968) The response to psychotherapy in chronic ulcerative colitis. I. *Psychosomatic Med.* 30, 255–268.

Karush, A., Daniels, G., O'Connor, J., and Stern, L. (1969) The response to psychotherapy in chronic ulcerative colitis. *Psychosomatic Med.* 31, 201–226.

Kazdin, A. E. (1974) Effects of covert modeling and model reinforcement on assertive behavior. *J. Abnorm. Psychol.* 83, 240–252.

Kazdin, A. E. (1975) Covert modeling, imagery assessment, and assertive behavior. *J. Consult. Clin. Psychol.* 43, 716–724.

Kazdin, A. E. (1977) *The token economy.* New York: Plenum.

Kazdin, A. E. (1978a) Evaluating the generality of findings in analogue therapy research. *J. Consult. Clin. Psychol.* 46, 673–686.

Kazdin, A. E. (1978b) The application of operant techniques in treatment, rehabilitation, and education. In S. L. Garfield and A. E. Bergin (Eds.), *Handbook of psychotherapy and behavior change,* 2nd edn. New York: Wiley.

Kazdin, A. E. and Wilcoxon, L. A. (1976) Systematic desensitization and non-specific treatment effects: a methodological evaluation. *Psychol. Bull.* 83, 729–758.

Kazdin, A. E. and Wilson, G. T. (1978a) Criteria for evaluating psychotherapy. *Arch. Gen. Psychiat.* 35, 407–418.

Kazdin, A. E. and Wilson, G. T. (1978b) *Evaluation of behavior therapy: Issues, evidence and research strategies.* Cambridge, Mass: Ballinger.

Kedward, H. (1969) The outcome of neurotic illness in the community. *Social Psychiat.* 4, 1–4.

Kellner, R. (1967) The evidence in favour of psychotherapy. *Br. J. Med. Psychol.* 40, 341–58.

Kendall, P. and Finch, A. J. (1978) A cognitive-behavioural treatment for impulsivity: A group comparison study. *J. Consult. Clin. Psychol.* 46, 110–118.

Kendell, R. (1975) *The role of diagnosis in psychiatry.* Oxford: Blackwells.

Kernberg, O. and many others (1972) *Psychotherapy and psychoanalysis: Final report of the Menninger psychotherapy research project. Bull, Menninger Clinic,* 36, 1 and 2.

Kernberg, O. F. (1973) Summary and conclusions of 'Psychotherapy and psychoanalysis, final report of the Menninger Foundation's psychotherapy research project'. *Int. J. Psychiat.* 11, 62–77.

Kiesler, D. J. (1966) Some myths of psychotherapy research and the search for a paradigm. *Psychol. Bull.* 65, 110–136.

Kiesler, D. J., Klein, M. H., Mathieu, P. L., and Schoeninger, D. (1967) Constructive personality change for therapy and control patients. In C. Rogers, E. Gendlin, D. Kiesler, and Truax, C. (Eds.), *The therapeutic relationship and its impact: A study of psychotherapy with schizophrenics.* Madison: University of Wisconsin Press.

Kind, H. (1969) Prognosis. In L. Bellak and L. Loeb (Eds.), *The schizophrenic syndrome.* New York: Grune & Stratton.

King, G. F., Armitage, S. G., and Tilton, J. R. (1960) A therapeutic approach to schizophrenics of extreme pathology: An operant-interpersonal method. *J. Abnorm. Soc. Psychol.* 61, 276–286.

Kingsley, R. G. and Wilson, G. T. (1977) Behavior therapy for obesity: A comparative investigation of long-term efficacy. *J. Consult. Clin. Psychol.* 45, 288–298.

Kirsch, L., Wolpin, M., and Knutson, J. (1975) A comparison of in-vivo methods for rapid reduction of stage-fright in the college classroom: A field experiment. *Behavior Ther.* 6, 165–171.

Klein, H. (1960) A study of changes occurring in patients during and after psychoanalytic treatment. In P. Hoch, and J. Zubin (Eds.), *Current Approaches to Psychoanalysis.* New York: Grune & Stratton.

Klerman, G. L., Dimascio, A., Weissman, M. M., Prusoff, B., and Paykel, E. S. (1974) Treatment of depression by drugs and psychotherapy. *Am. J. Psychiat.* 131, 186–191.

Knapp, P., Levin, S., McCarter, R., Werner, H., and Zetzel, E. (1960) Suitability for psychoanalysis: A review of 100 supervised analytic cases. *Psychoanal. Q.* 29, 459–477.

Knapp, T. J. and Wells, L. A. (1978) Behavior therapy for asthma: A review. *Behav. Res. Ther.* 16, 103–116.

Knight, R. P. (1941) Evaluation of the results of psychoanalytic therapy. *Am. J. Psychiat.* 98, 434–446.

Kockott, G., Dittmar, F., and Nusselt, L. (1975) Systematic desensitization of erectile impotence: A controlled study. *Arch. Sexual Behav.* 4, 493–500.

Koegler, R. and Brill, N. (1967) *Treatment of psychiatric outpatients.* New York: Appleton–Century–Crofts.

Kohlenberg, R. J. (1974) Treatment of a homosexual pedophiliac using in-vivo desensitization: A case study. *J. Abnorm. Psychol.* 83, 192–195.

Kraus, A. R. (1959) Experimental study of the effect of group psychotherapy with chronic schizophrenic patients. *Int. J. Group Psychother.* 9, 293–302.

Kringlen, E. (1965) Obsessional neurosis: a long-term follow-up. *Br. J. Psychiat.* 111, 709–714.

Kurtz, R. and Gummon, D. (1972) Different approaches to the measurement of therapist empathy. *J. Consult. Clin. Psychol.* 39, 106–115.

Lacey, H. and Rachlin, H. (1978) Behavior, cognition and theories of choice. *Behaviorism,* 6, 177–202.

Lake, A., Rainey, J., and Papsdorf, J. D. (1979) Biofeedback and rational–emotive therapy in the management of migraine headache. *J. Appl. Behav. Anal.* 12, 127–140.

Lambert, M. (1976) Spontaneous remissions in adult neurotic disorders. *Psychol. Bulletin,* 83, 107–119.

Lambert, M., deJulio, S., and Stein, D. (1978) Therapist interpersonal skills. *Psychol. Bull.* 83, 467–489.

Landis, C. (1937) A statistical evaluation of psychotherapeutic methods. In L. E. Hinsie (Ed.). *Concepts and Problems in Psychotherapy.* New York: Columbia University Press.

Lando, H. A. (1977) Successful treatment of smokers with a broad-spectrum behavioral approach. *J. Consult. Clin. Psychol.* 45, 361–366.

Lando, H. A. (1978) Toward a clinically effective paradigm for the maintenance of nonsmoking. *Behav. Ther.* 9, 666–668.

Lang, P. E. (1969) The mechanics of desensitization and the laboratory study of fear. In C. M. Franks (Ed.), *Behavior therapy: Appraisal and status.* New York: McGraw-Hill.

Lang, P., Lazovik, A., and Reynolds, D. (1966) Desensitization, suggestibility, and pseudo-therapy. *J. Abnorm. Psychol.* 70, 395–402.

LaPointe, K. A. and Harrell, T. H. (1978) Thoughts and feelings: Correlational relationships and cross-situational consistency. *Cognitive Ther. Res.* 2, 311–322.

Laughren, T. P. and Kass, D. L. (1975) Desensitization of sexual dysfunction. In A. S. Gurman and D. G. Rice (Eds.), *Couples in conflict.* New York: Jason Aronson.

Lazar, N. (1973) Nature and significance of changes in patients in a psychoanalytic clinic. *Psychoanal. Q.* 42, 579, 591.

Lazarus, A. A. (1974) Women in behavior therapy. In V. Franks and V. Burtle (Eds.), *Women in therapy: New psychotherapies for a changing society.* New York: Brunner/Mazel.

Lazarus, A. A. (1977) Has behavior therapy outlived its usefulness? *Am. Psychol.* 32, 550–554.

Ledwidge, B. (1978) Cognitive behavior modification: A step in the wrong direction? *Psychol. Bull.* 85, 353–375.

Lehrer, P. M. (1978) Psychophysiological effects of progressive relaxation in anxiety neurotic patients and of progressive relaxation and alpha feedback in nonpatients. *J. Consult. Clin. Psychol.* 46, 389–404.

Leitenberg, H. (1976a) Behavioral approaches to treatment of neuroses. In H. Leitenberg (Ed.), *Handbook of behavior modification and behavior therapy.* Englewood Cliffs, N.J.: Prentice-Hall.

Leitenberg, H. (1976b) *Handbook of behavior modification and behavior therapy.* Englewood Cliffs, N.J.: Prentice-Hall.

Lemere, F. and Voegtlin, W. L. (1950) An evaluation of the aversion treatment of alcoholism. *Quart. J. Stud. Alcohol,* 11, 199–204.

Lesse, S. (Ed.) (1968) *An evaluation of the results of the psychotherapies,* Thomas, Springfield.

Levis, D. J. and Carrera, R. (1967) Effects of 10 hours of implosive therapy in the treatment of outpatients. *J. Abnorm. Psychol.* 72, 504–508.

Levis, D. J. and Hare, N. (1977) A review of the theoretical rationale and empirical support for the extinction approach of implosive (flooding) therapy. In M. Hersen, R. M. Eisler, and P. M. Miller (Eds.), *Progress in behavior modification,* Vol. IV, New York: Academic Press.

Levitt, E. (1963) Psychotherapy with children: A further evaluation, *Behav. Res. Ther.* 1, 45–51.

Levitz, L. S. and Stunkard, A. J. (1974) A therapeutic coalition for obesity: Behavior modification and patient self-help. *Am. J. Psychiat.* 131, 423–427.

Lewinsohn, P. M. (1974) A behavioural approach to depression. In R. J. Friedman and M. M. Katz (Eds.), *The psychology of depression: Contemporary theory and research.* New York: Wiley.

Liberman, B. (1978) The maintenance and persistence of change. In J. Frank *et al.* (Eds.), *Effective ingredients of successful psychotherapy.* New York: Brunner/Mazel.

Liberman, R. P., Levine, J., Wheeler, E., Sanders, N., and Wallace, C. J. (1976) Marital therapy in groups: A comparative evaluation of behavioral and interactional formats. *Acta Psychiat. Scand.,* Supplementum 266.

Lichtenstein, E. and Danaher, B. (1976) Modification of smoking behavior: A critical analysis of theory, research and practice. In M. Hersen, R. M. Eisler, and P. M. Miller (Eds.), *Progress in behavior modification,* Vol. 3, New York: Academic Press.

Lichtenstein, E. and Glasgow, R. E. (1977) Rapid smoking: Side effects and safeguards. *J. Consult. Clin. Psychol.* 45, 815–821.

Lichtenstein, E., Harris, D. E., Birchler, G. R., Wahl, J. H., and Schmahl, D. P. (1973) Comparison of rapid smoking, warm smoky air, and attention placebo in the modification of smoking behavior. *J. Consult. Clin. Psychol.* 40, 92–98.

Lichtenstein, E. and Rodrigues, M. P. (1977) Long-term effects of rapid smoking treatment for dependent cigarette smokers. *Addictive Behav.* 2, 109–112.

Lick, J. (1975) Expectancy, false galvanic skin response feedback, and systematic desensitization in the modification of phobic behavior. *J. Consult. Clin. Psychol.* 82, 917–931.

Lick, J. and Bootzin, R. (1975) Expectancy factors in the treatment of fear: Methodological and theoretical issues. *Psychol. Bull.* 82, 917–931.

Lindelius, R. (Ed.) (1970) A study of schizophrenia, *Acta Psychiat. Scand.,* Suppl. 216.

Lindsley, O. R., Skinner, B. F., and Solomon, H. C. (1953) *Studies in Behavior Therapy,* Status Report 1, Waltham, Mass.: Metropolitan State Hospital.

Linehan, M. M., Goldfried, M. R., and Goldfried, A. P. (1979) Assertion therapy: Skill training or cognitive restructuring? *Behav. Ther.* 10, 372–388.

Lobitz, W. C. and LoPiccolo, J. (1972) New Methods in the behavioral treatment of sexual dysfunction. *J. Behav. Ther. Exp. Psychiat.* 3, 265–271.

Locke, H. J. and Wallace, K. M. (1959) Short marital adjustment and prediction tests: Their reliability and validity. *Marriage and Family Living,* 21, 251–255.

Logan, C. (1972) Evaluation research in crime and delinquency. *J. Criminal Law.* 63, 378–398.

Lorr, M., McNair, D., Michaux, W., and Raskin, A. L. (1962) Frequency of treatment and change in psychotherapy, *J. Abnorm. Soc. Psychol.* 64, 281–292.

Lowe, C. (1961) The self-concept: Fact or artifact? *Psychol. Bull.* 58, 325–336.

Luborsky, L., Chandler, M., Auerbach, A., and Cohen, J. (1971) Factors influencing the outcome of psychotherapy. *Psychol. Bull.* 75, 145–195.

Luborsky, L., Singer, B., and Luborsky, L. (1975) Comparative studies of psychotherapies: Is it true that everyone has won and all must have prizes? *Arch. Gen. Psychiat.* 32, 995–1008.

Luria, H. (1961) *The role of speech in the regulation of normal and abnormal behavior.* New York, Liveright.

MacCulloch, M. J. and Feldman, P. (1967) Aversion therapy in the management of 43 homosexuals. *Br. Med. J.* 2, 549–597.

McConaghy, N. (1969) Subjective and penile plethysmograph responses following aversion-relief and apomorphine aversion therapy from homosexual impulses. *Br. J. Psychiat.* 115, 723–730.

McConaghy, N. and Barr, R. F. (1973) Classical, avoidance and backward conditioning treatments of homosexuality. *Br. J. Psychiat.* 122, 151–152.

McCord, J. (1978) A thirty year follow-up of treatment effects. *Am. Psychol.* 33, 284–289.

McCutcheon, B. and Adams, H. (1975) The physiological basis of implosive therapy. *Behav. Res. Ther.* 13, 93–100.

McFall, R. M. and Hammen, C. (1971) Motivation, structure, and self-monitoring: Role of nonspecific factors in smoking reduction. *J. Consult. Clin. Psychol.* **37**, 80–86.

McGovern, K. B., Stewart, R. C., and LoPiccolo, J. (1965) Secondary orgasmic dysfunction: 1. Analysis and strategies for treatment. *Arch. Sex. Behav.* **4**, 265–275.

McLean, P. D. (1966) Decision-making in the behavioral management of depression. In P. O. Davidson (Ed.), *Behavioral management of anxiety, depression, and pain.* New York: Brunner/Mazel.

McLean, P. D. and Hakstian, A. R. (1979) Clinical depression: Comparative efficacy of outpatient treatments. *J. Con. Clin. Psychol.* **47**, 818–836.

McMullen, S. and Rosen, R. C. (1979) Self-administered masturbation training in the treatment of primary orgasmic dysfunction. *J. Consult. Clin. Psychol.*

McReynolds, W. T., Barnes, A. R., Brooks, S., and Rehagen, N. J. (1973) The role of attention-placebo influences in the efficacy of systematic desensitization. *J. Consult. Clin. Psychol.* **41**, 86–92.

McReynolds, W. T. and Paulsen, B. K. (1976) Stimulus control as the behavioral basis of weight loss procedures. In G. J. Williams, S. Martin, and J. Foreyt (Eds.), *Obesity: Behavioral approaches to dietary management.* New York: Brunner/Mazel.

Maes, W. and Heimann, R. (1970) The comparison of three approaches to the reduction of test anxiety in high school students. Unpublished manuscript, Arizona State University.

Mahoney, M. J. (1974) *Cognition and behavior modification.* Cambridge, Mass.: Ballinger.

Mahoney, M. J. (1977a) A critical analysis of rational–emotive theory and therapy. *The Counseling Psychologist,* **7**, 44–45.

Mahoney, M. J. (1977b) Reflections on the cognitive-learning trend in psychotherapy. *Am. Psychol.* **32**, 5–13.

Mahoney, M. J. and Arnkoff, D. (1978) Cognitive and self-control therapies. In S. L. Garfield and A. E. Bergin (Eds.), *Handbook of psychotherapy and behavior change,* 2nd edn. New York: Wiley.

Malan, D. H. (1963) *A study of brief psychotherapy.* London, Tavistock Press.

Malan, D. H. (1976a) *Toward the validation of dynamic psychotherapy.* New York: Plenum Press.

Malan, D. H. (1976b) *The frontier of brief psychotherapy.* New York: Plenum Press.

Malan, D., Bacal, H., Heath, E., and Balfour, F. L. (1968) A study of psychodynamic changes in untreated neurotic patients. *Br. J. Psychiat.* **114**, 525–551.

Malan, D. H., Balfour, F., Hood, V., and Shooter, A. (1976) Group psychotherapy: a long term follow-up study. *Arch. Gen. Psychiat.* **33**, 1303–1313.

Marcia, J. E., Rubin, B. M., and Efran, J. S. (1969) Systematic desensitization: Expectancy change or counter-conditioning. *J. Abnorm. Psychol.* **74**, 382–387.

Margolin, G. and Weiss, R. L. (1978) Comparative evaluation of therapeutic components associated with behavioral marital treatments. *J. Consult. Clin. Psychol.* **46**, 1476–1486.

Margolis, R. B. and Shemberg, K. M. (1976) Cognitive self-instruction in process and reactive schizophrenics: A failure to replicate. *Behav. Ther.* **7**, 668–671.

Marholin, D., Siegel, L. J., and Phillips, D. (1976) Treatment and transfer: A search for empirical procedures. In M. Hersen, R. Eisler, and P. M. Miller (Eds.), *Progress in behavior modification,* Vol. 3, New York: Academic Press.

Marks, I. (1971) Phobic disorders four years after treatment: A prospective follow-up. *Br. J. Psychiat.* **118**, 683–688.

Marks, I. (1978) Behavioural psychotherapy of adult neuroses. In S. L. Garfield and A. E. Bergin (Eds.), *Handbook of psychotherapy and behavior change,* 2nd edn. New York: Wiley.

Marks, I. and Gelder, M. (1967) Transvestism and fetishism: Clinical and psychological changes during faradic aversion. *Br. J. Psychiat.* **113**, 711–739.

Marks, I., Gelder, M. G., and Bancroft, J. (1970) Sexual deviants two years after electrical aversion. *Br. J. Psychiat.* **117**, 73–85.

Marks, I., Hodgson, R., and Rachman, S. (1975) Treatment of chronic obsessive–compulsive neurosis by *in vivo* exposure. *Br. J. Psychiat.* **127**, 349–366.

Marks, I. M. (1969) *Fears and phobias.* London: Heinemann.

Marks, I. M. (1976) Management of sexual disorders. In H. Leitenberg (Ed.), *Handbook of behavior modification and behavior therapy.* Englewood Cliffs, N.J.: Prentice-Hall.

Marks, I. M., Boulougouris, J. C., and Marset, P. (1971) Flooding versus desensitization in the treatment of phobic patients: A crossover study. *Br. J. Psychiat.* **119**, 353–375.

Marks, I. M., Hallam, R. J., Connolly, J., and Philpott, R. (1977) *Nursing in behavioral therapy.* London: The Royal College of Nursing of the United Kingdom.

Marlatt, G. A. (1978) Craving for alcohol, loss of control, and relapse: A cognitive-behavioral analysis. In P. E. Nathan and G. A. Marlatt (Eds.), *Alcoholism: New directions in behavioral research and treatment.* New York: Plenum Press.

Marlatt, G. A. and Marques, J. K. (1977) Meditation, self-control, and alcohol use. In R. B. Stuart (Ed.), *Self-management: Strategies, techniques and results.* New York: Brunner/Mazel.

Marmor, J. (1975) The nature of the psychotherapeutic process revisited. *Can. Psychiat. Ass. J.* 20, 557–565.

Marmor, J. (1975) Foreword. In Sloane, R. B. *et al., Psychotherapy versus behavior therapy.* Cambridge, Mass.: Harvard University Press.

Marquis, J. N. (1970) Orgasmic reconditioning: Changing sexual object choice through controlling masturbation fantasies. *J. Behav. Ther. Exp. Psychiat.* 1, 263–271.

Marshall, W. L., Gauthier, J., Christie, M. M., Currie, D. W., and Gordon A. (1977) A flooding therapy: Effectiveness, stimulus characteristics and the value of brief *in vivo* exposure. *Behav. Res. Ther.* 15, 79–87.

Massimo, J. and Shore, M. (1963) The effectiveness of a comprehensive vocational oriented psychotherapeutic program for delinquent boys. *Am. J. Orthopsychiat.* 33, 634–642.

Masters, W. and Johnson, V. (1970) *Human sexual inadequacy.* Boston: Little Brown.

Masterson, J. (1967) The symptomatic adolescent 5 years later. *Am. J. Psychiat.* 123, 1338–1345.

Mathews, A. (1978) Fear-reduction research and clinical phobias. *Psychol. Bull.* 85, 390–406.

Mathews, A. and Rezin, V. (1977) Treatment of dental fears by imaginal flooding and rehearsal of coping behaviour. *Behav. Res. Ther.* 15, 321–328.

Mathews, A. M., Bancroft, J., Whitehead, A., Hackmann, A., Julier, D., Bancroft, J., Gath, D., and Shaw, P. (1976) The behavioural treatment of sexual inadequacy: a comparative study. *Behav. Res. Ther.* 14, 427–436.

Mathews, A. M., Johnston, D. W., Lancashire, M., Munby, M., Shaw, P. M., and Gelder, M. G. (1976) Imaginal flooding and exposure to real phobic situations: Treatment outcome with agoraphobic patients. *Br. J. Psychiat.* 129, 362–371.

May, J. R. (1977) Psychophysiology of self-regulated phobic thoughts. *Behav. Ther.* 8, 150–159.

May, P. (1971) For better or for worse. *J. Nerv. Ment. Dis.* 152, 184–192.

May, P. (1975) Schizophrenia – evaluation of treatment methods. In A. Freedman, H. Kaplan, and B. Sadock (Eds.), *Comprehensive Textbook of Psychiatry.* Baltimore: Williams & Wilkins.

May, P. and Tuma, A. H. (1965) Treatment of schizophrenia. *Br. J. Psychiat.* 111, 503–510.

May, P., Tuma, A., and Dixon, W. (1976) Schizophrenia – a follow-up study of results of treatment. I. *Arch. Gen. Psychiat.* 33, 474–478.

May, P., Tuma, H., and Dixon, W. (1977) For better or worse? *J. Nerv. Ment. Dis.* 165, 231–239.

May, P., Tuma, A., Potepan, P., and Dixon, W. (1976) Schizophrenia – a follow-up study of results of treatment. II. *Arch. Gen Psychiat.* 33, 481–486.

Mayer-Gross, W., Slater, E., and Roth, M. (1960) *Clinical psychiatry,* 2nd ed. London: Cassell.

Mays, D. T. and Franks, C. M. (1979) Getting worse: Psychotherapy or no treatment: the jury should still be out. *Professional Psychol.*

Mealiea, W. L. and Nawas, N. M. (1971) The comparative effectiveness of systematic desensitization and implosive therapy in the treatment of snake phobias. *J. Behav. Ther. Exp. Psychiat.* 2, 85–94.

Meichenbaum, D. (1971) Examination of model characteristics in reducing avoidance behavior. *J. Personality Soc. Psychol.* 17, 298–307.

Meichenbaum, D. (1972) Cognitive modification of test anxious college students. *J. Consul. Clin. Psychol.* 39, 370–380.

Meichenbaum, D. (1977a) *Cognitive behavior modification.* New York: Plenum Press.

Meichenbaum, D. (1977b) Dr. Ellis please stand up. *The Counseling Psychologist,* 7, 43–44.

Meichenbaum, D. and Cameron, R. (1973) Training schizophrenics to talk to themselves. *Behav. Ther.* 4, 515–535.

Meichenbaum, D., Gilmore, H., and Fedoravicius, A. (1971) A group insight verus group desensitization in treating speech anxiety. *J. Clin. Consult. Psychol.* 36, 410–421.

Meichenbaum, D. and Goodman, J. (1971) Training impulsive children to talk to themselves. *J. Abnorm. Psychol.* 77, 115–126.

Meichenbaum, D. H. (1973) Cognitive factors in behavior modification: Modifying what clients say to themselves. In C. M. Franks and G. T. Wilson (Eds.), *Annual review of behavior therapy: Theory and practice,* Vol. I. New York: Brunner/Mazel.

Meltzoff, J. and Kornreich, M. (1970) *Research in psychotherapy.* New York: Atherton.

Meyer, V. (1966) Modification of expectation in cases with obsessional rituals. *Behav. Res. Ther.* 4, 273–280.

Meyer, V., Levy, R., and Schnurer, A. (1974) The behavioral treatment of obsessive–compulsive disorder. In H. R. Beech (Ed.), *Obsessional states.* London: Methuen.

Miller, P. M., Hersen, M., Eisler, R., and Hemphill, D. (1973) Effects of faradic aversion therapy on drinking by alcoholics. *Behav. Res. Ther.* 11, 491–498.

Miller, P. M. and Mastria, M. A. (1977) *Alternatives to alcohol abuse.* Champaign, Illinois: Research Press.

Miller, W. R. (1979) Treating the problem drinker: Modern approaches. In W. R. Miller (Ed.), *The addictive behaviors: Treatment of alcoholism, drug abuse, smoking and obesity*. New York: Pergamon Press.

Mills, H. L., Agras, W. S., Barlow, D. H., and Mills, J. R. (1973) Compulsive rituals treated by response prevention. *Arch. Gen. Psychiat.* 28, 524–529.

Mintz, J. (1977) The role of the therapist in assessing psychotherapy outcome. In A. Gurman and A. Razin (Eds.), *Effective Psychotherapy*. Oxford: Pergamon Press.

Mischel, W. (1968) *Personality and assessment*. New York: Wiley.

Mischel, W. (1977) On the future of personality measurement. *Am. Psychologist*, 32, 246–254.

Mitchell, K., Bozarth, J., and Krauft, C. (1977) A reappraisal of the therapeutic effectiveness of accurate empathy, nonpossessive warmth and genuineness. In A. Gurman and A. Razin (Eds.), *Effective Psychotherapy*. Oxford: Pergamon Press.

Mitchell, K., Truax, C., Bozarth, J., and Krauft, C. (1973) *Antecedents to psychotherapeutic outcome*. NIMH Grant Report 12306.

Moleski, R. and Tosi, D. J. (1976) Comparative psychotherapy: rational–emotive therapy versus systematic desensitization in the treatment of stuttering. *J. Consult. Clin. Psychol.* 44, 300–311.

Monroe, J. and Hill, H. (1958) The Hill–Monroe inventory for predicting acceptability for psychotherapy in the institutionalized narcotic addict. *J. Clin. Psychol.* 14, 31–36.

Montgomery, A. (1971) Comparison of the effectiveness of systematic desensitization rational–emotive therapy, implosive therapy, and no therapy, in reducing test anxiety in college students. Unpublished doctoral dissertation, Washington University.

Moos, R. and Clemes, S. (1967) Multivariate study of the patient-therapist system. *J. Consult. Psychol.* 31, 119–130.

Morganstern, K. P. (1973) Implosive therapy and flooding procedures: A critical review. *Psychol. Bull.* 79, 318–334.

Most, E. (1964) Measuring change in marital satisfaction. *Social Work*, 9, 64–71.

Mowbray, R. and Timbury, G. (1966) Opinions on psychotherapy. *Br. J. Psychiat.* 112 351–361.

Muehlberg, N. Pierce, R., and Drasgow, J. (1969) A factor analysis of therapeutically facilitative conditions. *J. Clin. Psychol.* 25, 93–95.

Munjack, D., Cristol, A., Goldstein, A., Phillips, D., Goldberg, A., Whipple, K., Staples, F., and Kanno, P. (1976) Behavioural treatment of orgasmic dysfunction: A controlled study. *Br. J. Psychiat.* 129, 497–502.

Murray, E. J. (1962) Paper read at Am. Psychoanal. Ass. Conv., St. Louis, quoted by Costello, C. G. (1963).

Myerson, A. (1939) Theory and principles of the "total push" method in the treatment of chronic schizophrenia. *Am. J. Psychiat.* 95, 1197–1204.

Nathan, P. E. and Briddell, D. W. (1977) Behavioral assessment and treatment of alcoholism. In B. Kissin and H. Begleiter (Eds.), *The biology of alcoholism*, Vol. 5. New York: Plenum Press.

Nathan, P. E., Marlatt, G. A., and Loberg, Tor (Eds.) (1978) *Alcoholism: New directions in behavioral research and treatment*. New York: Plenum Press.

Nelson, W. J. and Birkimer, J. C. (1978) Role of self-instruction and self-reinforcement in the modification of impulsivity. *J. Consult. Clin. Pyschol.* 46, 183–184.

Nemetz, G. H., Craig, K. D., and Reith, G. (1978) Treatment of female sexual dysfunction through symbolic modeling. *J. Consult. Clin. Psychol.* 46, 62–73.

Newman, L. and Stoller R. (1969) Spider symbolism and bisexuality. *J. Am. Psychoanal. Ass.* 17, 862–872.

Nisbett, R. (1972) Hunger, obesity, and the ventromedial hypothalamus. *Psychol. Rev.* 79, 433–470.

Nisbett, R. and Schachter, S. (1966) Cognitive modification of pain. *J. Exp. Social Psychol.* 2, 227–236.

Novaco, R. W. (1976) Treatment of chronic anger through cognitive and relaxation controls. *J. Consult. Clin. Psychol.* 44, 681.

Noyes, R. and Clancy, J. (1976) Anxiety neurosis: A five-year follow-up. *J. Nerv. Ment. Dis.* 162, 200–205.

Obler, M. (1973) Systematic desensitization in sexual disorders. *J. Behav. Ther. Exp. Psychiat.* 4, 93–101.

O'Connor, J., Daniels, G., Karsh, A., Moses, L., Flood, C., and Stern, L. (1964) The effects of psychotherapy on the course of ulcerative colitis. *Am. J. Psychiat.* 120, 738–742.

O'Donnell, J. (1965) The relapse rate in narcotics addiction. In D. Wilner and R. Kassebaum (Eds.), *Narcotics*. New York: McGraw-Hill.

O'Leary, K. D. and Borkovec, T. D. (1978) Conceptual, methodological, and ethical problems of placebo groups in psychotherapy research. *Am. Psychologist*, 33, 821–830.

O'Leary, K. D. and O'Leary, S. G. (1977) *Classroom management* (2nd edn.). New York: Pergamon Press.

O'Leary, K. D. and Wilson, G. T. (1975) *Behavior therapy: Application and outcome*. Englewood Cliffs, N.J.: Prentice-Hall.

O'Leary, S. G. (1977) Behavioral treatment for hyperactive children. Paper presented at Association for Advancement of Behavior Therapy, Atlanta, Georgia, December.

O'Neal, P. and Robins, L. (1958) The relation of childhood disorders to adult psychiatric status. *Am. J. Psychiat.* 114, 961–969.

Orford, J. and Edwards, G. (1977) *Alcoholism*. Oxford: Oxford University Press.
Orford, J., Oppenheimer, E., and Edwards, G. (1976) Abstinence or control: The outcome for excessive drinkers two years after consultation. *Behav. Res. Ther.* 14, 409–418.
Orgel, S. (1958) Effects of psychoanalysis on the course of peptic ulcer, *Psychosomatic Med.* 20, 117–125.
Orlinsky, D. E. and Howard, K. E. (1978) The relation of process to outcome in psychotherapy. In S. L. Garfield and A. E. Bergin (Eds.), *Handbook of psychotherapy and behavior change* (2nd edn.). New York: Wiley.
Osarchuk, M. (1974) A comparison of a cognitive, a behavior therapy and a cognitive plus behavior therapy treatment of test anxious college students. Unpublished doctoral dissertation, Adelphi University.
Öst, L. and Götestam, J. (1976) Behavioral and pharmacological treatments for obesity: An experimental comparison. *Addictive Behav.* 1, 331–338.
Parloff, M. B., Waskow, I. E., and Wolfe, B. E. (1978) Research on therapist variables in relation to process and outcome. In S. L. Garfield and A. E. Bergin (Eds.), *Handbook of psychotherapy and behavior change* (2nd edn.). New York: Wiley.
Paul, G. L. (1966) *Insight versus desensitization in psychotherapy*. Stanford: Stanford University Press.
Paul, G. L. (1967) Insight versus desensitization in psychotherapy two years after termination. *J. Consult. Psychol.* 31, 333–345.
Paul, G. L. (1969a) Behavior modification research. In C. M. Franks (Ed.), *Behavior therapy: Appraisal and status*. New York: McGraw-Hill.
Paul, G. L. (1969b) Outcome of systematic desensitization. II: Controlled investigations of individual treatment, technique variations, and current status. In C. M. Franks (Ed.), *Behavior therapy: Appraisal and status*. New York: McGraw-Hill.
Paul, G. L. and Bernstein, D. (1973) *Anxiety and clinical problems: Systematic desensitization and related techniques*, Morristown, N.J.: General Learning Press.
Paul, G. L. and Lentz, R. J. (1977) *Psychological treatment of chronic mental patients*. Cambridge, Mass.: Harvard University Press.
Payne, R. (1970) The visual–verbal test: A review. In O. Buros (Ed.), *Personality tests and reviews*. New Jersey: Gryphon Press.
Pearce, J. W., LeBow, M. D. and Orchard, J. (1979). The role of spouse involvement in the behavioral treatment of obese women. Paper presented at the Canadian Psychological Association, Quebec City, Quebec, June 15.
Pearl, D. (1955) Psychotherapy and ethnocentrism. *J. Abnorm. Soc. Psychol.* 50, 227–229.
Peck, C. (1977) Desensitization for the treatment of fear in the high level retardate. *Behav. Res. Ther.* 15, 137–148.
Penick, S. B., Filion, R., Fox, S., and Stunkard, A. J. (1971) Behavior modification in the treatment of obesity, *Psychosomatic Med.* 33, 49–55.
Persons, R. (1967) Relationship between psychotherapy with institutionalized boys and subsequent community adjustment. *J. Consulting Psychol.* 31, 137–148.
Peterson, D. R. (1968) *The clinical study of social behavior*. New York: Appleton–Century–Crofts.
Peterson, D. R. (1970) The visual-verbal test: A review. In O. Buros (Ed.), *Personality Tests and Reviews*. New Jersey: Gryphon Press.
Peyman, D. A. R. (1956) An investigation of group psychotherapy on chronic schizophrenic patients. *Group Psychotherapy*, 9, 35–39.
Philips, C. (1978) Tension headache: theoretical problems. *Behav. Res. Ther.* 16, 249–262.
Phillips, E. L. (1957) *Psychotherapy: A modern theory and practice*. London: Staples.
Phillips, E. L., Railford, A., and El-Batrawi, S. (1965) The Q-sort re-evaluated. *J. Consult. Psychol.* 29, 425.
Piper, W., Debbane, E., and Garant, J. (1977) An outcome study of group therapy. *Arch. Gen. Psychiat.* 34, 1027–1032.
Pomerleau, O. F., Pertschuk, M., Adkins, D., and Brady, J. P. (1976a) Comparison of behavioral and traditional treatment for problem drinking. Paper presented at the Annual Meeting of the Association for the Advancement of Behavior Therapy, New York.
Pomerleau, O., Perschuk, M., and Stinnett, J. (1976b) A critical examination of some current assumptions in the treatment of alcoholism. *J. Stud. Alcohol*, 37, 849–867.
Popper, V. (1963) *Conjectures and Refutations*. London: Routledge & Kegan Paul.
Powdermaker, F. and Frank, J. (1953) *Group Psychotherapy*. Cambridge: Harvard University Press.
Powers, E. and Witmer, H. (1951) *An experiment in the prevention of delinquency: The Cambridge–Somerville youth study*. New York: Columbia University Press.
Psychrembel, W. (1964) *Klinisches Worterbuch*, Berlin: Gruyter.
Rabavilas, A. and Boulougouris, J. (1974) Physiological accompaniments of ruminations, flooding and thought-stopping in obsessive patients. *Behav. Res. Ther.* 12, 239–244.

Rachlin, H. (1977) A review of M. J. Mahoney's *Cognition and Behavior Modification. J. Appl. Behav. Anal.* 10, 369–374.

Rachman, S. (Ed.) (1963) *Critical essays on psychoanalysis.* Oxford: Pergamon Press.

Rachman, S. (1965) Studies in desensitization. *Behav. Res. Ther.* 3, 245–252.

Rachman, S. (1967) Systematic desensitization. *Psychol. Bull.* 67, 93–103.

Rachman, S. (1968) *Phobias -- Their nature and control.* Springfield, Illinois: Thomas.

Rachman, S. (1971) *The effects of psychotherapy.* Oxford: Pergamon Press.

Rachman, S. (1976) Observational learning and therapeutic modeling. In M. P. Feldman and A. Broadhurst (Eds.), *Theoretical and experimental bases of the behavior therapies.* New York: Wiley.

Rachman, S. (Ed.) (1977) *Contributions to medical psychology,* Vol. 1. Oxford: Pergamon Press.

Rachman, S. (Ed.) (1978) Perceived self-efficacy: Analyses of Bandura's theory of behavioral change. *Adv. Behav. Res. Ther.* 1, 139–269.

Rachman, S., Cobb, J., Grey, S., MacDonald, D., Mawson, D., Sartory, G., and Stern, R. (1979) The behavioral treatment of obsessional–compulsive disorders, with and without clomipramine, *Behav. Res. Ther.* 17, 467–478.

Rachman, S. and Hodgson, R. (1980) *Obsessions and compulsions.* Englewood Cliffs, N.J.: Prentice-Hall.

Rachman, S., Hodgson, R., and Marks, I. (1971) The treatment of chronic obsessional neurosis. *Behav. Res. Ther.* 9, 237–247.

Rachman, S., Marks, I., and Hodgson, R. (1973) The treatment of chronic obsessive–compulsive neurosis by modelling and flooding *in vivo. Behav. Res. Ther.* 11, 463–471.

Rachman, S. and Philips, C. (1975) *Psychology and medicine* (also, revised Ed., Penguin Books, 1978).

Rachman, S. and Philips, C. (1980) *Psychology and behavioral medicine.* New York: Cambridge University Press.

Rachman, S. and Teasdale, J. (1969) *Aversion therapy and behavior disorders: An analysis.* Coral Gables, Florida: University of Miami Press.

Ramsay, R. and Sikkel, R. (1971) Behaviour therapy and obsessive neurosis. European Conference on Behaviour Therapy, Munchen, 1971.

Riley, A. J. and Riley, E. J. (1978) A controlled study to evaluate directed masturbation in the management of primary orgasmic failure in women. *Br. J. Psychiat.* 133, 406–409.

Rimm, D. (1970) Comments on "Systematic desensitization: Expectancy change or counterconditioning?" *Behav. Res. Ther.* 8, 105–106.

Rimm, D. C. and Litvak, S. B. (1969) Self-verbalization and emotional arousal. *J. Abnorm. Psychol.* 32, 565–574.

Risley, T. (1978) *Winning.* New York: BMA Audio Cassette Publications.

Ritter, B. (1969) The use of contact desensitization demonstration-plus-participation, and demonstration alone in the treatment of acrophobia. *Behav. Res. Ther.* 7, 157–164.

Roback, H. (1972) Experimental comparison of outcomes in insight and non-insight oriented therapy groups. *J. Consult. Clin. Psychol.* 38, 411–417.

Robin, A. L., Armel, S., and O'Leary, K. D. (1975) The effects of self-instruction on writing deficiencies. *Behav. Ther.* 6, 178–187.

Robins, L. (1970) Follow-up studies investigating childhood disorders. In E. Hare and J. Wing (Eds.), *Psychiatric Epidemiology.* Oxford: Oxford University Press.

Rodin, J. (1978) Cognitive-behavioral strategies for the control of obesity. In D. Meichenbaum (Ed.), *Cognitive Behavior Therapy.* New York: BMA Audio Cassette Publications, 1978.

Rogers, C. R. (1957) The necessary and sufficient conditions of therapeutic personality change. *J. Consult. Psychol.* 21, 95–103.

Rogers, C. F. and Dymond, R. (1954) *Psychotherapy and personality change.* Chicago: Chicago University Press.

Rogers, C., Gendlin, E. T., Kiesler, D., and Truax, C. (1967) *The therapeutic relationship and its impact: A study of psychotherapy with schizophrenics.* Madison: University of Wisconsin Press.

Rogers, T. and Craighead, W. E. (1977) Physiological responses to self-statements: The effects of statement balance and discrepancy. *Cognitive Ther. Res.* 1, 99–120.

Rooth. F. G. and Marks, I. M. (1974) Persistent exhibitionism: short-term response to self-regulation and relaxation treatment. *Arch. Sexual Behav.* 3, 227–248.

Röper, G., Rachman, S., and Marks, I. (1975) Passive and participant modelling in exposure treatment of obsessive–compulsive neurotics. *Behav. Res. Ther.* 13, 271–279.

Rosen, G. M. (1975) Subjects' initial therapeutic expectancies towards systematic desensitization as a function of varied instructional sets. *Behav. Ther.* 6, 230–237.

Rosen, G. M., Glasgow, R. E., and Barrera, M., Jr. (1976) A controlled study to assess the clinical efficacy of totally self-administered systematic desensitization. *J. Consult. Clin. Psychol.* 44, 208–217.

Rosen, G. M., Glasgow, R. E., and Barrera, M., Jr. (1977) A two-year follow-up on systematic desensitization with data pertaining to the external validity of laboratory fear assessment. *J. Consult. Clin. Psychol.* 45, 1188–1189.

Rosen, J. (1953) *Direct analysis.* New York: Grune & Stratton.

Rosen, R. C. and Keefe, F. J. (1978) The measurement of human penile tumescence. *Psychophysiology,* 15, 366–376.

Rosenhan, D. (1973) On being sane in insane places. *Science,* 179, 250.

Rosenthal, D. (1962) Book review. *Psychiatry,* 25, 377–380.

Rosenthal, T. (1976) Modeling therapies. In M. Hersen, R. Eisler, and P. M. Miller (Eds.), *Progress in behavior modification,* Vol. 2. New York: Academic Press.

Rosenthal, T. L. and Bandura, A. (1978) Psychological modeling: Theory and practice. In S. L. Garfield and A. E. Bergin (Eds.), *Handbook of psychotherapy and behavior change* (2nd ed.). New York: Wiley.

Rosenthal, T. L. and Reese, S. (1976) The effects of covert and overt modeling on assertive behavior. *Behav. Res. Ther.* 14, 463–469.

Rosenthal, T. L. and Zimmerman, B. J. (1978) *Social learning and cognition,* New York: Academic Press.

Rosenzweig, S. (1954) A transvaluation of psychotherapy: a reply to Eysenck. *J. Abnorm. Soc. Psychol.* 49, 298–304.

Ross, A. O. (1978) Behavior therapy with children. In S. L. Garfield and A. E. Bergin (Eds.), *Handbook of psychotherapy and behavior change* (2nd ed.), New York: Wiley.

Rush, A. J., Hollon, S. D., Beck, A. T., and Kovacs, M. (1978) Depression: Must pharmacotherapy fail for cognitive therapy to succeed? *Cognitive Ther. Res.* 2, 199–206.

Russell, A. and Winkler, R. (1977) Effectiveness of assertive training and homosexual guidance service groups designed to improve homosexual functioning. *J. Consult. Clin. Psychol.* 45, 1–13.

Sacks, J. and Berger, S. (1954) Group therapy with hospitalized chronic schizophrenic patients. *J. Consult. Psychol.* 18, 297–302.

Saenger, G. (1970) Patterns of change among treated and untreated patients seen in psychiatric community metal health clinics. *J. Nerv. Ment. Dis.* 150, 37–50.

Sanford, N. (1953) Psychotherapy. *Ann. Rev. Psychol.* 4, 317–42.

Sarason, I. (Ed.) *Test anxiety: Theory, research and applications.* New York: Lawrence Erlbaum (in press).

Sarason, I. G. (1975) Test anxiety and the self-disclosing coping model. *J. Consult. Psychol.* 43, 148–153.

Sargant, W. (1959) Insulin treatment in England, in *Insulin Treatment in Psychiatry* (eds. M. Rinkel and H. Himwich). New York: Philos. Library, Inc.

Sashin, J., Eldred, S., and Van Amerongen, S. (1975) A search for predictive factors in Institute supervised cases: A retrospective study of 183 cases from 1959–1966 at the Boston Psychoanalytic Society and Institute. *Int. J. Psychoanalysis,* 56, 343–358.

Saslow, G. and Peters, A. (1956) Follow-up of "untreated" patients with behavior disorders. *Psychiatric Q.* 30, 283–302.

Satz, P. and Baraff, A. (1962) Changes in relations between self-concepts and ideal-concepts of psychotics consequent upon therapy. *J. Gen. Psychol.* 67, 291–298.

Scheflen, A. (1961) *A psychotherapy of schizophrenia.* Springfield: Thomas.

Schjelderup, H. (1955) Lasting effects of psychoanalytic treatment. *Psychiatry,* 18, 103–133.

Schmahl, D., Lichtenstein, E., and Harris, D. (1972) Successful treatment of habitual smokers with warm, smoky air and rapid smoking. *J. Consult. Clin. Psychol.* 38, 105–111.

Schneidman, B., and McGuire, L. (1976) Group therapy for nonorgasmic women: Two age levels. *Arch. Sexual Behav.* 5, 239–247.

Schorer, C., Lowinger, P., Sullivan, T., and Hartlaub, G. (1968) Improvement without treatment, *Dis. Nerv. System,* 29, 100–104.

Schwartz, G. E. and Weiss, S. M. (1977) What is behavioral medicine? *Psychosomatic Med.* 39, 377–381.

Schwartz, R. and Gottman, J. (1976) Toward a task analysis of assertive behavior. *J. Consult. Clin. Psychol.* 44, 910–920.

Seeman, J. and Edwards, B. (1954) A therapeutic approach to reading difficulties. *J. Consult. Psychol.* 18, 451–453.

Semon, R. and Goldstein, N. (1957) The effectiveness of group psychotherapy with chronic schizophrenic patients. *J. Consulting Psychol.* 21, 317–324.

Shapiro, A. K. (1976) The behavior therapies: Therapeutic breakthrough or latest fad? *Am. J. Psychiat.* 133: 2, 154–159.

Shapiro, D. (1969) Empathy, warmth, and genuineness in psychotherapy. *Br. J. Soc. Clinic. Psychol.* 8, 350–361.

Shapiro, D. (1971) The measurement and investigation of psychotherapeutic change. Unpublished Ph.D. Thesis, University of London.

Shaw, B. F. (1977) Comparison of cognitive therapy and behavior therapy in the treatment of depression. *J. Consult. Clin. Psychol.* 45, 543–551.

Sheldon, A. (1964) An evaluation of psychiatric after-care. *Br. J. Psychiat.* 110, 662–667.

Shepherd, M. and Gruenberg, E. (1957) The age for neuroses. *Millbank Memorial Bull.* 35, 258–265.

Shepherd, M., Oppenheim, A. and Mitchell, S. (1966) Childhood behaviour disorders and the child guidance clinic: an epidemiological study. *J. Child Psychol. Psychiatry.* 7, 39–52.

Sherman, A. R. (1972) Real-life exposure as a primary therapeutic factor in the desensitization treatment of fear. *J. Abnorm. Psychol.* 79, 19–28.

Shlien, J. M., Mosak, H. H., and Dreikurs, R. (1962) Effects of time limits: A comparison of two psychotherapies. *J. Conseling Psychol.* 9, 31–34.

Shore, M. and Massimo, J. (1966) Comprehensive, vocationally oriented psychotherapy for adolescent boys: A follow-up study. *Am. J. Psychiat.* 36, 609–615.

Siegel, S., Rootes, M., and Traub, A. (1977) Symptom change and prognosis in clinic psychotherapy. *Arch. Gen. Psychiat.* 34, 321–329.

Slater, E. (1970) Psychiatry: science and non-science, 3rd Mapother Lecture, Inst. of Psychiatry, London.

Slater, E. and Roth, M. (1969) *Clinical psychiatry* (3rd edn.), London: Bailliere.

Sloane, R. B., Staples, F. R., Cristol, A. H., Yorkston, N. J., and Whipple, K. (1975) *Psychotherapy versus behavior therapy.* Cambridge, Mass.: Harvard University Press.

Slutsky, J. M. and Allen, G. J. (1978) Influence of contextual cues on the efficacy of desensitization and a credible placebo in alleviating public speaking anxiety. *J. Consult. Clin. Psychol.* 46, 119–125.

Smith, M. L. and Glass, C. V. (1977) Meta-analysis of psychotherapy outcome studies. *Am. Psychol.* 32, 752–760.

Snyder, J. J. and White, M. J. (1979) The use of cognitive self-instruction in the treatment of behaviorally disturbed adolescents. *Behav. Ther.* 10, 227–235.

Sobell, M. B. (1978) Alternatives in abstinence: Evidence, issues and some proposals. In P. E. Nathan, G. A. Marlatt, C. T. Loberg (Eds.), *Alcoholism: New directions in behavioral research and treatment.* New York: Plenum Press.

Sobell, M. B. and Sobell, L. C. (1978) *Behavioral treatment of alcohol problems.* New York: Plenum Press.

Sotile, W. and Kilman, P. (1977) Treatments of psychogenic female sexual dysfunctions. *Psychol. Bull.* 54, 619–633.

Spielberger, C. D., Gorsuch, R. L., and Lushene, R. E. (1970) *The state-trait anxiety inventory (test manual).* Palo Alto, Ca: Consulting Psychologists Press.

Stalonas, P. M., Johnson, W. G., and Christ, M. (1978) Behavior modification for obesity: The evaluation of exercise, contingency management and program adherence. *J. Consult. Clin. Psychol.* 46, 463–469.

Stampfl, T. and Levis, D. (1967) Essentials of implosive therapy: A learning-theory-based psychodynamic behavioral therapy. *J. Abnorm. Psychol.* 72, 496–503.

Steele, K. and Barling, J. Self-instruction and learning disabilities: Maintenance, generalization and subject characteristics. Unpublished manuscript, University of Witwatersrand, Johannesburg, South Africa.

Steinmark, S. W. and Borkovec, T. D. (1974) Active and placebo treatment effects on moderate insomnia under counterdemand and positive demand instructions. *J. Abnorm. Psychol.* 83, 157–163.

Stern, R. and Marks, I. (1973) Brief and prolonged flooding. *Arch. Gen. Psychiat.* 28, 270–276.

Stevenson, I. (1961) Process of "spontaneous" recovery from the psychoneuroses. *Am. J. Psychiat.* 117, 1057–1064.

Stokes, T. F. and Baer, D. M. (1977) An implicit technology of generalization. *J. Appl. Behav. Anal.* 10, 349–368.

Stolz, S. B. and Associates (1978) *Ethical issues in behavior modification.* San Francisco: Jossey-Bass.

Stone, N. and Borkovec, T. D. (1975) The paradoxical effect of brief CS exposure on analogue phobic subjects. *Behav. Res. Ther.* 13, 51–56.

Stover, L. and Guerney, B. G. (1967) The efficacy of training procedures for mothers in filial therapy. *Psychotherapy: Theory, Research and Practice,* 4, 110–115.

Straatmeyer, A. M. and Watkins, J. T. (1974) Rational–emotive therapy and the reduction of speech anxiety. *Rational Living,* 9, 33–37.

Strupp, H. H. and Bergin, A. E. (1969) Some empirical and conceptual bases for coordinated research in psychotherapy. *Int. J. Psychiat.* 7, 18–90.

Strupp, H. H. and Hadley, S. W. (1977) A model of mental health and therapeutic outcomes: With special reference to negative effects in psychotherapy. *Am. Psychologist.* 32, 187–196.

Strupp, H. H., Hadley, S. W., and Gomes-Schwartz, B. (1977) *Psychotherapy for better or worse: The problem of negative effects.* New York: Jason Aronson.

Stuart, R. B. (1967) Behavioral control of overeating. *Behav. Res. Ther.* 5, 357–365.

Stuart, R. B. (1979) Weight loss and beyond: Are they taking it off and keeping it off? In P. O. Davidson (Ed.), *Behavioral medicine: Techniques for promoting life style change.* New York: Brunner/Mazel.

Stuart, R. B. and Davis, B. (1972) *Slim chance in a fat world.* Champaign, Ill.: Research Press.

Stuart, R. B. and Guire, K. (1978) Some correlates of the maintenance of weight loss through behavior modification. *Int. J. Obesity,* 2, 225–235.

Stunkard, A. J. (1958) The management of obesity. *New York J. Med.* 58, 79–87.

Stunkard, A. J. (1972) New therapies for the eating disorders. *Arch. Gen. Psychiat.* 26, 391–398.

Stunkard, A. J., Craighead, L., and O'Brien, C. (1978) New treatments for obesity. Paper presented at the American Psychiatric Association, Atlanta, May 11.

Stunkard, A. J. and Mahoney, M. J. (1976) Behavioral treatment of the eating disorders. In H. Leitenberg (Ed.), *Handbook of behavior modification and behavior therapy*. New York: Prentice Hall.

Stunkard, A. J. and Penick, S. (1979) Behavior modification in the treatment of obesity: The problem of maintaining weight loss. *Arch. Gen. Psychiat.* 36, 801–806.

Stunkard, A. J. and Rush, J. (1974) Dieting and depression re-examined: An initial review of reports of untoward responses during weight reduction for obesity. *Ann. Internal Med.* 81, 526–533.

Subotnik, L. (1975) Spontaneous remission of emotional disorder in a general medical practice. *J. Nerv. Ment. Dis.* 161, 239–244.

Sullivan, B. J. and Denney, D. R. (1977) Expectancy and phobic level: Effects on desensitization. *J. Consult. Clin. Psychol.* 45, 763–771.

Susskind, D. J. (1970) The idealized self-image (ISI): A new technique in confidence training. *Behav. Ther.* 1, 538–541.

Tanner, B. A. (1974) A comparison of automated aversive conditioning and a waiting list control in the modification of homosexual behavior in males. *Behav. Ther.* 5, 29–32.

Taylor, C. B., Farquhar, J. W., Nelson, E., and Agras, S. (1977) The effects of relaxation therapy upon high blood pressure. *Arch. Gen. Psychiat.* 34, 339–345.

Taylor, C. B., Ferguson, J. M., and Reading, J. C. (1978) Gradual weight loss and depression. *Behav. Ther.* 9, 622–625.

Taylor, D. (1955) Changes in the self-concept without psychotherapy, *J. Consult. Psychol.* 19, 205–209.

Taylor, F. G. and Marshall, W. L. (1977) Experimental analysis of a cognitive-behavioural therapy for depression. *Cognitive Ther. Res.* 1, 59–72.

Teuber, N. and Powers, E. (1953) Evaluating therapy in a delinquency prevention program. *Proc. Ass. Nerv. Ment. Dis.* 3, 138–147.

Thase, M. E. and Moss, M. K. (1976) The relative efficacy of covert modeling procedures and guided participant modeling on the reduction of avoidance behavior. *J. Behav. Ther. Exp. Psychiat.* 7, 7–12.

Thibaut, J. W. and Kelley, H. H. (1959) *The social psychology of groups*. New York: Wiley.

Thorpe, G. L. (1975) Desensitization, behavior rehearsal, self-instructional training and placebo effects on assertive–refusal behavior. *Eur. J. Behav. Anal. Modification*, 1, 30–44.

Thorpe, G. L., Amatu, H., Blakey, R., and Burns, L. (1976) Contributions of overt instructional rehearsal and "specific insight" to the effectiveness of self-instructional training: A preliminary study. *Behav. Ther.* 7, 504–511.

Tiegerman, S. (1975) Effects of assertive training, and cognitive components of rational therapy on the promotion of assertive behavior and the reduction of interpersonal anxiety. Unpublished doctoral dissertation, Hofstra University, New York.

Trexler, L. D. and Karst, T. O. (1972) Rational–emotive therapy, placebo and no-treatment effects on public speaking anxiety. *J. Abnorm. Psychol.* 79, 60–67.

Truax, C. (1963) Effective ingredients in psychotherapy. *J. Counseling Psychol.* 10, 256–263.

Truax, C. (1971) Effectiveness of counselor and counselor aides. *J. Counseling Psychol.* 18, 365–367.

Truax, C. and Carkhuff, R. (1967) *Toward effective counselling and psychotherapy*. Chicago: Aldine Press.

Truax, C., Fine, H., Moravec, J., and Millis, W. (1968) Effects of therapist persuasive potency in individual psychotherapy. *J. Clin. Psychol.* 24, 359–365.

Truax, C., Frank, I., and Imber, S. (1966) Therapist empathy, genuineness, and warmth and patient outcome. *J. Consult. Psychol.* 30, 395–401.

Truax, C. and Mitchell, K. (1971) Research on certain therapist interpersonal skills. In A. Bergin and S. Garfield (Eds.), *Handbook of psychotherapy and behavior change*. New York: Wiley.

Tucker, J. E. (1956) Group psychotherapy with chronic psychotic soiling patients. *J. Consult. Psychol.* 20, 430.

Ullmann, L. P. and Krasner, L. (1969) *A psychological approach to abnormal behavior*. Englewood Cliffs, N.J.: Prentice-Hall.

Ullmann, L. P. and Krasner, L. (1975) *A psychological approach to abnormal behavior* (2nd ed.). Englewood Cliffs, N.J.: Prentice-Hall.

Vincent, J. P., Weiss, R. L., and Birchler, G. R. (1975) Dyadic problem-solving behavior as a function of marital distress and spusal vs. stranger interactions. *Behav. Ther.* 6, 475–487.

Vogler, R. E., Weissbach, T. A., and Compton, J. V. (1977) Learning techniques for alcohol abuse. *Behav. Res. Ther.* 15, 31–58.

Vorster, D. (1966) Psychotherapy and the results of psychotherapy, *S. African Med. J.* 40, 934–936.

Walker, R. and Kelly F. (1963) Short-term psychotherapy with schizophrenic patients. *J. Nerv. Ment. Dis.* 137, 349–352.

Wallace, H. and Whyte, M. (1959) Natural history of the psychoneuroses. *Br. Med. J.* 1, 144–148.

Waters, W. F., McDonald, D. G., and Koresko, R. L. (1972) Psychophysiological responses during analogue systematic desensitization and non-relaxation control procedures. *Behav. Res. Ther.* 10, 381–393.

Watson, D. and Friend, R. (1969) Measurement of social-evaluative anxiety. *J. Consult. Clin. Psychol.* 33, 448–457.

Watson, J. P., Mullett, G., and Pillay, H. (1973) The effects of prolonged exposure to phobic situations upon agoraphobic patients treated in groups. *Behav. Res. Ther.* 11, 531–545.

Weber, J., Elinson, J., and Moss, L. (1967) Psychoanalysis and change. *Arch. Gen. Psychiat.* 17, 687–709.

Wein, K. S., Nelson, R. O. and Odom, J. V. (1975) The relative contributions of reattribution and verbal extinction to the effectiveness of cognitive restructuring. *Behav. Ther.* 6, 459–474.

Weinstock, H. (1961) Hospital psychotherapy in severe ulcerative colitis. *Arch. Gen. Psychiat.* 4, 509–512.

Weiss, R. L. (1978) The conceptualization of marriage from a behavioral perspective. In T. J. Paolino and B. S. McGrady (Eds.), *Marriage and marital therapy.* New York: Brunner/Mazel.

Weissberg, M. (1977) A comparison of direct and vicarious treatments of speech anxiety: Desensitization, desensitization and coping imagery, and cognitive modification. *Behav. Ther.* 8, 606–620.

Weissman, M., Kasl, S., and Klerman, G. (1976) Follow-up of depressed women after maintenance treatment. *Am. J. Psychiat.* 133, 757–760.

Whiteley, J. Burkhart, M., Harway-Herman, M., and Whiteley, R. (1975) Counseling and student development. In M. Rosenzweig and L. Porter (Eds.), *Annual review of psychology.* Palo Alto: Annual Rev. Inc.

Wiens, A. N., Montague, J. R., Manaugh, T. S., and English, C. J. (1976) Pharmacological aversive counter-conditioning to alcohol in a private hospital: One-year follow-up. *J. Studies on Alcohol,* 37, 1320–1324.

Wilkins, W. (1971) Desensitization: Social and cognitive factors underlying the effectiveness of Wolpe's procedure. *Psychol. Bull.* 76, 311–317.

Williams, R. B. and Gentry, W. D. (1977) *Behavioral approaches to medical treatment.* Cambridge, Mass.: Ballinger.

Willis, J. and Bannister, D. (1965) The diagnosis and treatment of schizophrenia. *Br. J. Psychiat.* III. 1165–1171.

Willis, R. W. and Edwards, J. A. (1969) A study of the comparative effectiveness of systematic desensitization and implosive therapy. *Behav. Res. Ther.* 7, 387–395.

Wilson, G. T. (1973) Effects of false feedback of avoidance behavior: "Cognitive" desensitization revisited. *J. Personality and Soc. Psychol.* 28, 115–123.

Wilson, G. T. (1978a) Aversion therapy for alcoholism: Issues, ethics, and evidence. In G. A. Marlatt and P. E. Nathan (Eds.), *Behavioral assessment and treatment of alcoholism.* New Brunswick, N.J.: Center for Alcohol Studies.

Wilson, G. T. (1978b) Booze, beliefs, and behavior: Cognitive processes in alcohol use and abuse. In P. E. Nathan, G. A. Marlatt and T. Loberg (Eds.), *Alcoholism: New directions in behavioral research and treatment.* New York: Plenum Press.

Wilson, G. T. (1978c) Cognitive behavior therapy: Paradigm shift or passing phase? In J. P. Foreyt and D. P. Rathjen (Eds.), *Cognitive behavior therapy.* New York: Plenum Press.

Wilson, G. T. (1978d) The importance of being theoretical: A commentary on Bandura's "Self-efficacy: Towards a unifying theory of behavioral change". *Adv. Behav. Res. Ther.* 1, 217–230.

Wilson, G. T. (1979) Behavioral treatment of obesity: Maintenance strategies and long-term efficacy. In P. O. Sjoden, S. Bates, *et al.* (Eds.), *Trends in behavior therapy.* New York: Academic Press.

Wilson, G. T. (1980) The current status of treatment approaches to obesity. In W. R. Miller (Ed.), *The addictive behaviors: Treatment of alcoholism, drug abuse, smoking and obesity.* New York: Pergamon Press.

Wilson, G. T. (1980) Behavior modification and the treatment of obesity. In A. J. Stunkard (Ed.), *Obesity for clinicians.* Philadelphia: W. B. Saunders.

Wilson, G. T. and Davison, G. C. (1971) Processes of fear reduction in systematic desensitization: Animal studies. *Psychol. Bull.* 76, 1–14.

Wilson, G. T. and Davison G. C. (1974) Behavior therapy and homosexuality: A critical perspective. *Behav. Ther.* 5, 16–28.

Wilson, G. T. and Evans, I. M. (1977) The therapist–client relationship in behavior therapy. In R. S. Gurman and A. M. Razin (Eds.). *The Therapist's contribution to effective psychotherapy: An empirical approach.* New York: Pergamon Press.

Wilson, G. T., Leaf, R. C., and Nathan, P. E. (1975) The aversive control of excessive alcohol consumption by chronic alcoholics in the laboratory setting. *J. Appl. Behav. Anal.* 8, 13–26.

Wilson, G. T. and O'Leary, K. D. (1980) *Principles of behavior therapy.* Englewood Cliffs, N.J.: Prentice-Hall.

Wilson, G. T. and Tracey, D. A. (1976) An experimental analysis of aversive imagery versus electrical aversive conditioning in the treatment of chronic alcoholics. *Behav. Res. Ther.* 14, 41–51.

Wincze, J. P. and Caird, W. K. (1976) The effects of systematic desensitization and video desensitization in the treatment of essential sexual dysfunction in women. *Behav. Ther.* 7, 335–342.

Wincze, J. P., Hoon, E. F., and Hoon, P. W. (1978) Multiple measure analysis of women experiencing low sexual arousal. *Behav. Res. Ther.* 16, 43–50.

Windheuser, H. J. (1977) Anxious mothers as models for coping with anxiety. *The Eur. J. Behav. Anal. Modification,* 2, 39–58.

Wing, J. K. (1966) Five-year outcome in early schizophrenia. *Proc. Roy. Soc. Med.* 59, 17–18.

Wing, J. K. (1968) Social treatments of mental illness. In M. Shepherd and D. Davies (Eds.). *Studies in psychiatry.* Oxford: Oxford Universtiy Press.

Wing, J. (1978) *Reasoning about madness.* Oxford: Oxford University Press.

Wing, J. and Freudenberg, R. (1961) The response of severely ill chronic schizophrenic patients to social stimulation. *Am. J. Psychiat.* 118, 311–322.

Wittenborn, J. (1961) Contribution and current state of Q-methodology. *Psychol. Bull.* 38, 132–142.

Wolberg, L. R. (1967) *Short-term psychotherapy.* New York: Grune & Stratton.

Wolfe, J. L. and Foder, I. G. (1977) Modifying assertive behavior in women: A comparison of three approaches. *Behav. Ther.* 8, 567–574.

Wollersheim, J. P. (1970) Effectiveness of group therapy based upon learning principles in the treatment of overweight women. *J. Abnorm. Psychol.* 76, 462–474.

Wolpe, J. (1958) *Psychotherapy by reciprocal inhibition.* Stanford: Stanford University Press.

Wolpe, J. (1964) The comparative status of conditioning therapy and psychoanalysis. In J. Wolpe (Ed.), *The Conditioning Therapies.* New York: Holt Rinehart & Winston.

Wolpe, J. (1969) *The practice of behavior therapy.* Oxford: Pergamon Press.

Wolpe, J. Foreword. In Sloane, R. B. *et al.* (1975), *Psychotherapy versus behavior therapy:* Cambridge Mass.: Harvard University Press.

Wolpe, J. (1976) Behavior therapy and its malcontents – II. Multimodal eclecticism, cognitive exclusivism and "exposure" empiricism. *J. of Behav. Ther. Exp. Psychiat.* 7, 109–116.

Wolpe, J., Brady, J. P., Serber, M., Agras, W. S., and Liberman, R. D. (1973) The current status of systematic desensitization. *Am. J. Psychiat.* 130, 961–965.

Wolpe, J. and Lazarus, A. A. (1966) *Behavior therapy techniques.* New York: Pergamon Press.

Wolpe, J. and Rachman, S. (1960) Psychoanalytic evidence: a critique based on Freud's case of Little Hans, *J. Nerv. Ment. Dis.* 131, 135–145.

Wonnenberger, M., Henkel, D., Arentewicz, G., and Hasse, A. (1975) Studie zu einem Selbsthife-program fur zwangneurotische Patienten. *Zeitschr. Klin. Psychologie,* 4, 124–136.

Wooley, S. C., Wooley, O. W., and Drenforth, S. R. (1979) Theoretical, practical and social issues in behavioral treatments of obesity. *J. Appl. Behav. Anal.* 12, 3–25.

Wright, J., Perreault, R., and Mathieu, M. (1977) The treatment of sexual dysfunction: A review. *Arch. Gen. Psychiat.* 36, 881–896.

Wylie, R. (1961) *The self concept.* Nebraska: University Nebraska Press.

Yates, A. (1975) *Theory and practice in behavior therapy.* New York: Wiley.

Yulis, S. (1976) Generalization of therapeutic gain in the treatment of premature ejaculation. *Behav. Ther.* 7, 355–358.

Zeiss, A. M., Lewinsohn, P., and Munoz, R. (1979) Nonspecific improvement effects in depression using interpersonal skills training, pleasant activity schedules, or cognitive training. *J. Consult. Clin. Psychol.* 47, 427–439.

Zeiss, A. M., Rosen, G. M., and Zeiss, R. A. (1977) Orgasm during intercourse: A treatment strategy for women. *J. Consult. Clin. Psychol.* 45, 891–895.

Zeiss, R. A. (1978) Self-directed treatment for premature ejaculation. *J. Consult. Clin. Psychol.* 46, 1234–1241.

Zirkle, G. (1961) Five-minute psychotherapy. *Am. J. Psychiat.* 118, 544–546.

Zubin, J. (1953) Evaluation of therapeutic outcome in mental disorders. *J. Nerv. Ment. Dis.* 117, 95–111.

NAME INDEX

Abramson, J. 37
Adams, H. 140, 168, 253
Adams, N. E. 151
Addington, H. J. 175
Agras, W. S. 3, 31, 38, 39, 118, 125, 137, 141,
  168, 226, 247, 255, 262
Alden, L. 197, 199
Alexander, A. B. 104, 127
Alkire 104
Allen, G. J. 133
Allen, R. P. 176
Andrasik, F. 212
Anker, J. 110, 111
Ansari, J. 161
Appelbaum, S. 4, 73, 74
Armel, S. 215, 218
Armitage, S. 185
Armor, D. J. 175
Arnkoff, D. 118, 195, 208, 229
Arnold, S. C. 210
Aronson, H. 55
Ashby, J. 253
Ashcraft, C. 80
Atthowe, J. M. 186, 188
Auerbach, A. 106
Auerbach, R. 162
Ayllon, T. 184, 185
Azima, H. 114
Azrin, N. 10, 176, 184, 185, 251

Badhorn, E. 227
Baehr, G. 102
Baer, D. 118, 217, 254
Balfour, F. 69
Bancroft, J. 160, 165–8, 226, 235, 247, 251
Bandura, A. 6, 10, 118, 128, 135, 139, 149–51,
  153–6, 161, 168, 173, 182, 187, 217, 223,
  225–9, 234, 235, 238, 251–5, 257
Bannister, D. 14, 106
Baraff, A. 109
Barendregt, J. 58, 59, 62, 252
Barling, J. 215, 218
Barlow, D. 3, 124, 141, 157, 166, 168, 169, 187
Barnes, A. R. 130, 132

Barr, R. 168
Barrera, M., Jr. 135
Barrett, B. 138
Barrios, B. A. 135
Barron, F. 20, 25, 38, 79, 83, 101, 239, 241,
  252
Batchelor, I. 14
Baucom, D. 125
Beck, A. 123, 195, 220–3, 226, 228, 229
Becker, J. 222
Beckstrand, P. E. 252
Beebe, G. 20
Beiman, I. 125
Beiser, M. 48
Bellack, A. S. 184, 185
Bellak, L. 106
Bendig, A. 45
Bennet, I. 13
Benson, H. 125
Berger, S. 111, 112
Bergin, A. 22, 23, 25, 28, 29, 40–8, 53, 55, 74,
  75, 77–9, 90, 97, 99–104, 119, 157, 224, 231,
  234, 235, 242–4, 248, 251, 254–6, 262
Bernstein, D. 128, 129, 135, 177, 178
Bespalec, D. 178
Beutler, L. E. 256
Beyer, J. 151
Bieber, I. 56
Bills, A. G. 82
Birchler, G. R. 170, 178
Birk, L. 167
Birkimer, J. C. 215
Blanchard, E. B. 150, 151, 153, 184, 226
Blau, J. 138
Boersma, K. 141–3, 147
Boesky, D. 50
Bookhammer, R. 115, 116, 252
Bootzin, R. 126, 132
Borden, B. L. 127, 180
Borkovec, T. D. 7, 53, 126, 127, 130–2, 134,
  135, 140, 141, 150, 225, 234, 236, 237, 262
Bornstein, P. H. 210, 217, 218
Boudewyns, P. A. 141
Boulougouris, J. 138, 142, 148, 255
Boyer, L. 106

289

SUBJECT INDEX